THE PUFFIN HISTORY OF THE WORLD
VOLUME 2

Roshen Dalal is the author of *Religions of India: A Concise Guide to Nine Major Faiths, Hinduism: An Alphabetical Guide, The Illustrated Timeline of History of the World*, the bestselling two-volume *The Puffin History of India, The Puffin History of the World, Volume 1* and *The Vedas, An Introduction to Hinduism's Sacred Texts*. She has an MA and PhD in Ancient Indian History from Jawaharlal Nehru University, New Delhi. She has worked on various research projects, taught at school and university level, and written numerous articles and book reviews. She lives in Dehradun.

The Puffin History

of the WORLD

VOL.2

Roshen Dalal

Illustrations by

Kallol Majumdar

PUFFIN BOOKS

PUFFIN BOOKS

USA | Canada | UK | Ireland | Australia
New Zealand | India | South Africa | China

Puffin Books is part of the Penguin Random House group of companies
whose addresses can be found at global.penguinrandomhouse.com

Published by Penguin Random House India Pvt. Ltd
7th Floor, Infinity Tower C, DLF Cyber City,
Gurgaon 122 002, Haryana, India

Penguin
Random House
India

First published in Puffin by Penguin Books India 2014

The views and opinions expressed in this book are the author's own and the facts
are as reported by her, which have been verified to the extent possible, and the
publishers are not in any way liable for the same.

ISBN 9780143331582

Typeset in Goudy Old Style by Eleven Arts, New Delhi
Printed at Repro India Ltd, Navi Mumbai

www.penguinbooksindia.com

For
Ardeshir and Kumkum

Contents

Contents

Contents

Contents

Introduction

This book begins in the year 1500, and is a continuation of *The Puffin History of the World: Volume 1*. In that book we saw that history is the story of the past, but that everything of the past cannot be included. We also saw that there are different approaches to history, that is, there are different ways of looking at the past, and that we know about the past both through material remains, and through various types of records.

After 1500, both material remains and records are far more numerous. There are buildings, monuments, art, sculptures, coins and records of all types. Records include letters, descriptions of events, accounts of expenditure, administrative records, travellers' descriptions, and much more. Based on all these sources, histories too were written. New historical studies continue to be written every year.

Yet it is interesting that no two countries write the history of the same events in the same way. After many rounds of discussion, historians of Germany and France published a history text together. But even in this, they included parallel versions of their analysis of the past.

Ways of looking at the past are constantly changing. In one example, the manner of writing the history of countries in Africa has changed considerably over the last fifty years. Earlier, the oral traditions of these countries were ignored, and Europeans wrote Africa's history based on their own sources. They could not believe that there had been any great achievements in the interiors of the African continent. It is only after African countries became independent that their histories were written in a more authentic way.

Sometimes, newly independent nations, or those undergoing political changes, deliberately rewrite their history, in order to put forward a glorified view of their past, or of their present. For instance, when Stalin was prominent in the USSR, histories written in that country praised him. Later, there were many critiques of him.

Such problems, along with new approaches to history, exist all over the world. In fact, even in the same country, no two people write history in the same way.

In this book we have tried to present a balanced view of the past, taking into account different viewpoints and approaches. So much has happened in the world, that everything cannot be included here. This book includes the main events and developments that have taken place, along with some interesting aspects of the past.

Though this volume can be read separately, it is best read along with the *Puffin History of the World: Volume 1*.

Both volumes are for young people, but can be read by people of any age.

BCE AND CE

BCE and CE are the abbreviations used in these two volumes for dates. BCE stands for 'Before Common Era' and CE for 'Common Era'. The Common Era is the calendar we generally use. These abbreviations are now increasingly used in all parts of the world instead of BC and AD. In this volume, the terms BCE and CE are used rarely, as the book begins in CE 1500, and all dates, unless otherwise mentioned are CE.

A NOTE ON DATES IN THIS BOOK

Even though we are dealing with a later time period than in Volume 1, some dates remain uncertain. In this book, different sources have been consulted to choose the most likely date.

SPELLINGS USED

There are many different languages in the world, and some of their sounds have no English equivalent. In this book, we have provided the English equivalents of names in European languages, and in general, have used the most accepted and authentic spellings.

1
The World in 1500

From the time of the Big Bang, when the universe first began, up to CE 1500, the world had been through many changes. At first nothing existed; then plants, birds, reptiles and animals emerged. After millions of years, finally human beings evolved. By 1500 almost all the regions of the world were occupied. There were contacts and connections across much of the known world; yet some regions remained isolated. The three continents of North America, South America and Australia were among these. The continent of Antarctica, as well as some islands, were yet to be occupied, or even visited.

In the 15th century and later this began to change.

Europe, Asia and Africa had trade and other connections since ancient times. The early Persian empires extended across Asia. Alexander the Great from Macedonia in Europe crossed through Asia on his expeditions of conquest, and reached northern Africa, which was then under Persian rule. His successors ruled parts of Asia and Africa. The Roman empire, too, ruled parts of Asia and Africa and traded with India. In the 8th and 9th centuries CE the Arab world provided a meeting point for the cultures of Asia, Europe and north Africa. Asian countries such as India and China had crossed the seas and occupied parts of

South East Asia. However, they had not attempted the conquest of regions in other continents. The Mongols connected much of Asia through their conquests and trade routes from the 13th century onwards and also invaded Europe. Merchants from Genoa and Venice had been involved in trade with Asia from the 11th century onwards. The Crusades, the great religious wars fought across Europe and Asia from the 11th century onwards, provided information about new routes and products available in different lands. In addition, there were travellers and merchants who moved across regions and continents. Among the better known was Marco Polo of Venice (1254–1324), who in the 13th century CE visited China, India and countries of South East Asia, as well as Persia. His accounts were read by others and added to Europe's knowledge of Asia. Other travellers included William of Rubrick (1220–93), the Italian Niccolo Dei Conti (1395–1469), Ibn Batuta (1304–69), the Russian Afanasy Nikitin (1413–72) and Abdur Razzaq (1413–82). There were many more, including Franciscan and Dominican monks, and ambassadors or envoys of various countries. Sir John Mandeville, who lived in the 14th century, put together a number of travellers' tales in a book titled *The Voyage and Travels of Sir John Mandeville, Knight*. It is not known who John Mandeville was, but the stories are interesting.

Among other travellers across the seas were Polynesians, the Vikings of northern Europe and the Mayas of Central America.

Arab traders visited all three continents, and Europeans too had begun to cross the world in their ships. Ships usually used the Black Sea or West Asian ports. In the region of Africa, ships from Europe and Arab regions usually did not go south of Morocco. There were overland routes by caravan across Central Asia.

Europe had benefitted from interaction with Asia and Africa. Despite all these contacts, however, European knowledge of many parts of Asia and Africa remained limited.

  The Puffin History of the World

CULTURAL AND OTHER DIFFERENCES

Though Europe and Asia were actually one continent with land connections, culturally there were many differences. Buddhism had spread across Asia, but remained unknown in Europe. Hinduism from India had influenced Buddhism, and in this way had a subtle influence on the regions where Buddhism spread. Hinduism, in a more direct form, had spread to parts of South East Asia. Judaism and Christianity originated in Asia, but though they were known in this continent, they were more prominent in Europe. Islam spread in Asia and Africa but apart from a temporary hold over Spain, could not displace Christianity in Europe. There were other religions such as Zoroastrianism, which were once widespread, but by 1500 they had declined. Though some Asian and European languages probably had a common origin, they had developed differently.

Europe had some other unique features when compared with Asia and Africa. Great technological innovations had taken place in India, China and the Arab regions, but by 1500 Europe had adopted these innovations and was progressing further. With the Renaissance, Europe had again become the centre of new ideas, as it had been at the time of the Greek states. Philosophical developments took place in other regions too, while in Europe science and political thought were developing.

A new era was beginning as Europe began to dominate the world.

EUROPEAN EXPLORATIONS AND EARLY CONQUESTS

From the second half of the 15th century, new routes began to be explored. Shipping technology and navigational techniques, too, improved. Earlier the sun and pole star had been used for navigation. The compass, originally from China, now began to be used. Latitudes had already been listed in tables by a 10th-century Irish astronomer. Navigational charts were known by the 13th century. Now both ships and methods of navigation became more advanced.

As described in Volume 1 of this series, Portugal and Spain had sponsored the early explorations. Crossing the Cape of Good Hope, Vasco da Gama of Portugal reached India in 1498. Pedro Alvares Cabral had landed in Brazil, and later in India in 1500. Christopher Columbus, supported by Spain, explored the Caribbean, and reached Central America and Venezuela. Among other early explorers were Giovanni Caboto (John Cabot, 1450-99), a Genoese who had a licence for exploration from Henry VII of England. Caboto left Bristol in 1497, and reached Cape Breton, an island near North America, which he thought was part of China.

What was the aim of these explorations? The initial objectives were mixed. It was hoped that the pioneering travellers would find new lands with gold and spices and would be able to achieve wealth and fame. But very soon these explorations were followed by conquest and then by exploitation of resources.

Soon thousands of ships sailed every year from ports across Europe and from those in the European colonies.

Even before 1500, Portugal and Spain had begun to compete for territories in their newly explored regions. In 1479, there was a trade treaty between Spain and Portugal in which trade in the Gulf of Guinea was given to the Portuguese.

In order to avoid war and conflict, the Pope regulated their spheres of influence. At first he worked out a temporary division. He divided the world between Portugal and Spain along a line 100 leagues west of the Azores. Later in 1494, the Treaty of Tordesillas was signed. It gave Portugal 'all the lands east of a line of longitude 370 leagues west of Cape Verde and to Spain all the lands west of it'. Vasco da Gama of Portugal therefore used the eastern route around Africa to reach India in 1498. Spain had to find a different, western route.

Ferdinand Magellan was an important early explorer. An account of the troubles he faced, given below, provides some idea of the difficulties of such explorations.

Ferdinand Magellan (1480–1521)

Ferdinand Magellan (known as Fernao Magelhaes in Portuguese) planned to find the Spice Islands by a western route. Though Magellan was Portuguese, his exploration was undertaken on behalf of Spain, where he lived from 1517. He obtained permission and most of the funds from Charles I of Spain, who was also later Charles V, the Holy Roman Emperor. Ferdinand and his companions were given a grand send-off at Seville on 10 August 1519. They then embarked from the port of Sanlúcar de Barrameda in September in five ships. The crew of the ships included 270 men from many different countries of Europe. Moving along the coast of Africa, they crossed the Atlantic and reached South America. Along the way there were many dangers and disasters, including a mutiny, after which one ship captain and some of the men were killed on Magellan's orders. There were storms at sea, and another ship captain refused to proceed further and returned to Spain. On 21 October 1520, Magellan sailed through the passage, later called the Straits of Magellan, and reached another ocean. Its waters were calm and peaceful, and he gave it the name Pacific Ocean. In March 1521, he and the remaining ships reached the Philippines from the west. Here Magellan made friends with two kings, but was killed in a battle with another.

Ferdinand Magellan, a portrait

After his death, the journey around the world was completed by Juan Sebastian Elcano. One ship and just a few men returned to Spain in September 1522. Altogether about 232 people died on this journey of exploration. But Magellan became famous. The Magellan Straits and the Megallinic Clouds (two close galaxies), among others, were named after him.

2
Europe: An Overview
1500–1800

B y the year 1500 great changes had taken place in Europe. More were to take place in the succeeding centuries.

THE LITTLE ICE AGE

Though between 1500 and 1800, the climate was not very different from today; it was somewhat colder. According to NASA sources, the period of colder weather existed from around 1550–1850. (Some scientists place the beginning of the cold period even earlier at 1250–1300.) This period has been called the Little Ice Age. At this time annual average temperatures in the northern hemisphere showed a slight decline and mountain glaciers expanded in the European Alps, as well as in areas outside Europe, including New Zealand, Alaska and the southern Andes. There were temperature variations in different regions. In north and central Europe, winters were more severe. Summers, too, were cooler, with more rain. Crops did not grow very well, and several famines took place.

NATURAL DISASTERS: THE MONSTER SWALLOWS YOU

Avalanches, storms, floods, fires, tsunamis, earthquakes and volcanoes were among the natural disasters that affected Europe. Over these 300 years there were many disasters in Europe and it is not possible to list them all. Avalanches were a risk in the snowy mountainous regions, specially in the Alps. Storm tides affected the North Sea coasts, particularly when a dike failed. Floods occurred along rivers and near seas. Rockslides were frequent. Among the greatest earthquakes was the one that took place in Portugal in 1755. Sixty thousand people died, and the impact was felt throughout Europe.

Volcanic eruptions and disasters in Asia, too, affected Europe.

In many areas where there were disasters, people prayed for protection and erected new churches or chapels. In Portugal, St Alexius was considered the protector against earthquakes.

GRENOBLE

In September 1733, the river Drac in Grenoble (France) flooded. This was one of several floods, but this particular event was described in a long poem by a grocer named Andre Blanc dit la Goutte. After descriptions of the rising river, he wrote, 'Grenoble, you are lost. The monster swallows you.' Natural disasters were truly like monsters, difficult to combat or to guard against.

PLANTS, ANIMALS AND BIRDS

In the high mountains and Arctic regions of north Europe, trees do not grow, but mosses, lichens, shrubs and flowers can be found. Much of Europe is covered with mixed deciduous and coniferous forests. Conifers include pines and firs, while among other trees are birch, elm, oak, hawthorn and maple. In the southern regions, olives, grapes, oranges and other fruit trees grow. As more and more land was cleared for agriculture, the nature of the natural vegetation began to alter. In addition, new types of plants and trees were imported, and some were deliberately planted. Cities and towns expanded, and this, too, affected the natural vegetation.

Wild animals that inhabited this region included deer, bear, elk, bison, wolf and boar. In the north, there were reindeer. Chamois and ibex roamed in the Alps and Pyrennes. There were numerous other smaller animals such as foxes, hares and hedgehogs. There were also various birds, including swans, storks and nightingales. By 1500, some animals such as the elk, auroch and the European bison had become greatly reduced in number. New animals and birds, however, reached Europe from different countries and exotic animals from other regions, such as llamas, elephants and rhinoceros, soon came to be known.

Historiae Animalium (The History of Animals)

Bestiaries were books written in Europe describing animals (beasts), birds, and some aspects of nature. They were compiled from the 2nd century CE onwards. There were also separate volucraries depicting birds. They were illustrated and accompanied by descriptive passages, which included moral lessons. The animals and birds also represented aspects of God or of people.

Conrad Gesner (1516–65), a Swiss doctor and professor, used earlier bestiaries as well as later knowledge to compile a five-volume work called *Historiae Animalium*. It contains 4500 pages, with both written text and illustrations. Volume 1 studies four-footed animals, which give birth to live infants. Among these are bull, goat, camel, dog, cat, deer, rabbit, porcupine, elephant, horse, lion and mouse, as well as unicorn and rhinoceros (the story of this rhinoceros is given later in Chapter 5). A drawing of each animal was accompanied by a corresponding text in Latin. Volume 2 deals with those four-

footed animals that reproduce through eggs; Volume 3 is on birds; Volume 4 is about fish and aquatic animals; Volume 5 describes scorpions and reptiles. Some illustrations were done by Conrad Gesner, others by various artists. Gesner is considered the father of zoology.

There were also books written describing trees, plants and herbs.

POPULATION

It is difficult to get exact estimates of population in Europe, but rough estimates are available. According to these, by 1500 the population was around 70–80 million. Over the next 200 years, it grew to almost 150 million, and by 1800 approximately 180–200 million. This

Illustrations from a page from Historiae Animalium *by Conrad Gesner*

was about one-sixth of what it is today. Few people lived beyond their forties. There were many temporary and regional variations because of famine, poor harvests, warfare and various diseases, including plague.

LANGUAGES

Different languages were spoken across Europe. The main language groups were Slavic, Germanic, Italic, Greek, Albanian, Celtic, Finno-Ugrian, and Basque. Each language group had a number of sub-languages or branches. By 1500, regional languages were well developed and being used increasingly. Turkish languages, too, were spoken.

KINGS AND NOBLES

The kings were supreme, but nobles were also important. Nobles were of different categories. They could be hereditary or created by kings. The three main occupations for nobles were managing their own estates, serving as warriors or joining the Church.

KNIGHTS

Knights, foot soldiers and archers were three categories of warriors before 1500 CE. By 1500, knights as fighting warriors had declined. Several knights became part of the nobility and were not vassals of any lord. Knights had once worn armour, and fought with lances and swords. They had to be specially trained to fight like this. But in the 16th century guns, gunpowder and cannon were increasingly used. Steel crossbows were another type of weapon. Armour did not protect against these weapons and the old type of knightly training and skills were no longer required.

ARMIES

Kings began to maintain standing armies. Officials, who were paid in money rather than through land grants, were employed. Much of the taxation in various countries was used to pay for the standing armies now maintained by kings.

SOME TRENDS IN GOVERNMENT

By 1500, only England, France and to a limited extent Spain and Portugal had some kind of a national identity. The concept of a sovereign state was still not clear in the 16th and 17th centuries. At this time states were more like private property that the king obtained through marriage, inheritance or conquest. Boundaries constantly changed and land was transferred along with the inhabitants. Religion, trade, wealth and overseas possessions were causes of war. New lands were settled. Up to about 1750, governments of Europe underwent very few changes. They were mainly monarchies except for Great Britain, the United Provinces, the cantons of Switzerland and some republics of Italy.

After 1750, some governments began to carry out reforms. They may have been influenced by the new ideas emerging. (See Chapter 6.) Among the countries that initiated economic reforms were Naples, Spain, Portugal and some Italian states. The practice of having resident diplomats began to develop from the 15th–16th centuries, and gradually there were permanent resident ambassadors who were granted a special status. Earlier too heralds or messengers had been employed who enjoyed special protection. But even in 1800 ambassadors of Europe were mainly unpaid noblemen and not salaried civil servants.

Overall between 1500 and 1800, political reforms did take place, some initiated by the king or government, others by the people. The year 1800 was still very different from modern times. Communication was poor. A telegraph system that was invented in the 1790s operated through pulling ropes. Weapons had somewhat improved and troops could move slightly faster than in 1500 but not at great speed. There was no standing police force of a modern kind and no system of income tax. European governments had to protect themselves from revolts by their own people, as well as against foreign powers.

3

Europe: Economy and Society—Some General Aspects 1500–1800

Economically and socially, Europe was divided between west and east along the river Elbe. East Europe was relatively backward with little social or economic change until the 19th century. Various explanations have been given for this:

(i) The East had a shorter period of cultivation.
(ii) It had less fertile soil.
(iii) These two factors limited agricultural growth.
(iv) There were often raids by Central Asian nomads.
(v) To the south were the Balkans and the frontier with Turkey where numerous wars took place.

FEUDALISM

Feudalism, a system of landholding, had existed in Europe from around CE 800. In Western Europe in the 16th century, there were still large landholdings known as fiefs. These were now owned by nobles of different kinds, by some categories of knights, and by other people.

In Eastern Europe and Russia, the feudal system continued.

In Spain there were new feudal aspects, as previous Arab estates were still given as grants to soldiers. In France and England, its economic aspects disappeared by 1800.

AGRICULTURE

Agriculture gradually changed through use of new technology and by production for the market. The iron plough was used and there were better yokes for oxen and harnesses for horses. There were specialized types of cultivation and more peasants were paid wages instead of remaining tied to the land like serfs. But peasants still remained poor. The manor (landlord's estate) produced crops for sale instead of for its own use. Monasteries also grew crops and exploited forest products. The main crops in Western Europe were wheat, barley, oats and hay. Millets, sorghum, buckwheat and rye were grown in some areas. Clover and turnips began to be cultivated after 1600. Grapes, olives and sugar cane were among the crops in Italy and Spain. New crops were introduced in Europe from Asia and the Americas. Though rice was grown in parts of Europe even in the first century CE, its cultivation was widespread from 15th century onwards. Spices, too, were brought from Asia. In the 16th century, tobacco, cacao, maize, potatoes, sweet potatoes and manioc reached Europe from the Americas. Maize began to be grown in southern and eastern Europe, in Romania, Serbia and Hungary. Tobacco was grown in Spain by 1556 and reached England by 1585.

Cattle and dairy farming, as well as sheep rearing, expanded.

The potato

Of all these new foods, perhaps the most important was the potato. Today the potato is the fifth most important crop in the world, after wheat, corn (maize), rice and sugar cane. Before the arrival of the Europeans, the Incas and other cultures of South America greatly valued the potato.

Initially the potato was not popular in Europe, and considerable efforts were made to get people to eat it. To persuade people to grow and eat the potato, Louis XVI of France began to wear a potato flower in his button hole. It became a style statement, and others at court wore it too. But once the potato gained acceptance, it provided subsistence even in times of famine. According to some historians, the potato contributed to the European domination of the world after 1750, because it led to economic prosperity and self-sufficiency in food in Europe.

That its value was recognized and appreciated in Europe is indicated by a statue of Sir Francis Drake, made in 1853 by the sculptor Andreas Friederich and erected in Offenburg, in south-west Germany. It showed his right hand resting on a sword, and the left holding a potato plant. On the base was an inscription stating: 'Sir Francis Drake, disseminator of the potato in Europe in the Year of Our Lord 1586. Millions of people who cultivate the earth bless his immortal memory.'

The statue was destroyed later in 1939. The inscription was not correct, as Francis Drake did not have much to do with the spread of this plant, but it does indicate the importance of the potato.

FERTILIZERS

The potato also had other effects. It led to the intensive use of fertilizers, first Peruvian guano, and after this was infected by the Colorado beetle, arsenic. This paved the way for the development of chemical fertilizers that contained arsenic.

CRAFTS, INDUSTRIES AND TRADE

By 1500, a number of skilled craftsmen thrived in Europe. Earlier Asian craftsmen were very advanced, particularly in the production of ceramics and textiles. In the 14th and 15th centuries, European craftsmen progressed in these fields as well as in mechanical and engineering skills. Wool and cotton textiles were produced. Mining and metalworking were other important industries. By 1800, France and England were most advanced in trade and manufacture, but agriculture predominated even here. In the 18th century, Russia, too, became more industrialized. Most industries were connected with agriculture. A few among them were brewing, weaving and dyeing.

Within Europe there was trade in agricultural and other products. Trade extended beyond Europe to the former Byzantine empire and to Arab lands up to Africa. Wars took place over trade and commerce. Asian rulers bought mechanical toys from European fairs and looked for European help in making firearms.

THE MECHANICAL SWAN

Europe specialized in making mechanical toys. Among those that still survive is a beautiful swan. This life-size swan sits in a stream made of glass and works with a clockwork device. When wound up a music box plays, and the glass rods rotate, so that the stream looks as if it is flowing. There are fish in the water. The swan turns its head and then bends down to catch a fish, before returning to its position. This silver swan is now on display at the Bowes Museum, England. It was designed by John Joseph Merlin (1735–1803).

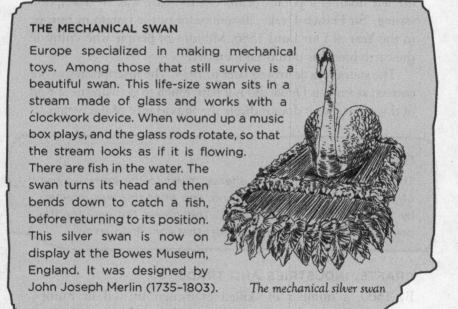

The mechanical silver swan

TOWNS

New towns sprang up, though most of the population was still rural. In 1500, there were nine European cities with a

AMSTERDAM

Amsterdam, today the capital of the Netherlands, is located on the river Amstel. In the 12th century it was just a small village, where villagers were involved in fishing, but by 1700 it had become an important port and city, with a population of 2,00,000. It was a city where intellectuals, artists, and people of different religions lived together. It was called the Venice of the North, because like Venice of Italy, it has a number of islands connected by bridges, and canals crossing the city between the islands. Trade through Amsterdam went to North and South America, Africa and Asia. Amsterdam merchants were part of the Dutch East India Company and the Dutch West India Company.

Even today there are many old buildings in Amsterdam. The Royal Palace is 350 years old. It was once the city hall, but was converted into a palace in 1808. It has marble floors and beautiful chandeliers, and is decorated with paintings and sculptures. The Oude Kerk (Old Church) is Amsterdam's oldest building, dating to 1300. It began as a small chapel dedicated to St Nicholas, the patron saint of sailors. A hundred years later, another Church called Niewe Kerk was founded.

The drowning pump room: According to stories of 17th-century travellers, there was a strange room in Amsterdam in which people who did not like hard work were placed. This room kept filling with water. To stay alive the person there had to continuously use a hand pump to keep the water from rising over his head. After they came out of there, perhaps no work seemed too hard!

population of 1,00,000 or more. By 1700, there were around 24. Among the main cities were Amsterdam, Paris and London. In Europe, several cities and towns practised a system of self-government. Towns were surrounded by walls and kings granted them charters and privileges. Amsterdam was one of the largest cities.

MONEY

Money in the form of coins existed in Europe from ancient times, but it was not always used. Barter was another system of exchange. This consisted of exchanging items of similar value. After CE 1000, money was increasingly used. Paper money and the cheque were first used in Europe in the 18th century.

Money was acquired through taxes and through trade.

Wealth increase also took place by bringing forested land under cultivation or establishing new towns in uninhabited areas.

BANKS

The Bank of England was founded in 1694. This institution and the Bank of Amsterdam, founded in 1609, grew to have international influence. There were other banks and merchant establishments dealing with credit and finance. There were joint-stock companies which had their own shares. In the 17th century, these were quoted in London coffee houses, and then in the London Stock Exchange. Other countries also had banks. The idea of using money to make more money had begun (see capitalism in Chapter 25). Life insurance and actuarial science were introduced.

PRICES

After 1500, prices rose two to four times in some areas. This meant that the increase in salaries did not really help. Both peasants and landowners suffered. Towards the end of the 16th century, there were revolts and disorder.

Some believed that new sources of gold and silver from America was the cause of the price rise. This may have contributed to it but the problem had started even before a large amount of American gold reached Europe. The price rise continued till the beginning of the 17th century and then slowed down.

DOLLAR

The dollar that is America's currency today was once used in Europe. It originated in the 16th century in Jachimov, a Bohemian town in the Joachimsthal. There was a silver mine there and a mint was established in 1518 where silver coins were produced. The coins were first known as Joachimsthaler, and later as thaler. It was part of the currency of Central Europe, and was even copied in Spain. Spanish taleros or 'pieces of eight' was part of the coinage of the Americas. In English the thaler was known as the dollar. Money from Sweden was used in the 18th century, known as the daler, a term also derived from 'thaler'. The Maria Theresa dollar of 1751 was minted in millions. It continued to be minted posthumously, even later by Mussolini to finance his Abyssinian War, and by the British in Bombay. The dollar was adopted from Europe by the USA in 1787, and by Canada in 1871, but it lost status in Europe.

WOMEN

Women had an inferior position, but had progressed in many ways. Between 1500 and 1800, several queens and empresses ruled over Europe, including in England, Austria, Russia, Sweden and other countries.

By the end of the 18th century, unmarried women and female artists and novelists were known in Europe. Some women who joined the church were very learned and spiritual. They were also good administrators. Though there were other learned women too, formal education was on the whole denied to them. Their rights of inheritance were limited.

RELIGION

In 1500, the Church still controlled or influenced most aspects of life in Europe. It was the Church which recorded births, deaths, baptisms, and provided moral and social guidelines. The Church also administered justice and controlled large tracts of land.

Monasteries existed all over Europe, which provided an alternate way of life to resident monks and nuns. Monasteries were also centres of education.

Apart from the official practices of the Church, popular, devotional and regional forms of religion were widespread. These were based on earlier religious practices. The Catholic Church had already faced a lot of opposition before 1500, but remained prominent in western Europe, though the Orthodox Church was well established in eastern Europe.

THE REFORMATION

In the 16th century, the Reformation ended the religious unity of western Europe.

Martin Luther

Martin Luther was an Augustinian monk from 1505 to 1520 when he was excommunicated, that is, banned from the Church. Augustinians were a Catholic religious order, named after St Augustine of Hippo (CE 354–430).

Luther and many others of that time were against indulgences and other malpractices. Indulgences were certificates issued by the Pope. These could be bought. They promised a reduction of penalties in the next world, for any sins committed in this one. In 1517, Luther wrote a protest consisting of 95 points (known as the Ninety-five Theses) against these and other practices. He nailed these outside a church in Wittenberg. Many people agreed with what he wrote and his points were translated, printed and circulated everywhere in Germany. It became part of German politics and developed into a German national movement. Luther also questioned some Catholic beliefs, including confession, absolution and the celibacy of priests. Luther was not only excommunicated but also declared an outlaw in 1521 by Charles V.

His views, however, continued to spread. One of his important ideas was that everyone should read and understand the Bible for himself, and not depend on priests. To make this easier, Luther translated the New Testament into German. Soon Germany was divided between Protestants and Catholics. Luther's ideas spread to other countries in Europe as well.

THE MORNING STAR OF WITTENBERG—MARTIN LUTHER AND THE GREAT ESCAPE

In 1525, Martin Luther renounced his religious vows to marry Katharina von Bora. She was a great help to him. But how and why did he get married?

Katharina was a nun who had been sent to a monastery at the age of five. She, along with eleven other nuns, appealed to Luther to be rescued. He arranged for their dramatic escape in 1523 through a councilman and merchant who

Katharina von Bora, a portrait by Lucas Cranach the Elder, 1526

delivered herring to the monastery. The nuns escaped by hiding inside the herring truck.

But the young women could not be left by themselves. Their families would not take them back, and homes, marriages or jobs had to be found for them. Luther made arrangements for them all, but finally married Katharina himself. They had a very happy union. Luther called her his 'Morning Star of Wittenberg'.

Calvinism

New forms of Protestantism emerged in Europe and America including those based on Bible study. Ulrich Zwingli (1484–1531) began to protest against some Catholic practices in Switzerland.

Later Calvinism was one type of Protestantism that had a large following particularly in Switzerland. Jean Calvin (1509–64), called John Calvin in English, was a Frenchman. He believed that only the Elect, the chosen few of God, could attain salvation. Following the commandments of God and the sacraments indicated one was part of the Elect. Calvin drew up a constitution for Geneva (Switzerland) with very strict rules. People were executed for blasphemy, witchcraft and adultery. Adulterous women were drowned and men beheaded. Calvin was against dancing, singing, gambling, drinking, playing games and wearing bright clothes. He declared that the Bible should be read every day. No form of God nor any religious symbol should be depicted. From Geneva Calvinism spread to France, where by 1561 there were 2000 congregations (religious groups). It also spread to the Netherlands, England, Scotland and even to some parts of Germany.

COUNTER REFORMATION

The Counter Reformation brought in reforms in Catholicism. The Council of Trent, which first met in 1543, was an important aspect of it. This formulated principles for Catholicism that lasted till the 19th century. Some of the aspects that had been criticized by Luther and others were changed.

JESUITS

Ignatius Loyala formulated a new religious order that was recognized in 1540 by the Pope as the Society of Jesus. They became important missionaries in Europe and the world.

ORTHODOX CHURCHES

Orthodox Churches also began to form separate sects. The first schism (spilt) had taken place between the Western and Eastern Churches in 1054. The Eastern was known as the Eastern Orthodox Church and was prominent in the Byzantine empire and in Russia. The Moscow Patriarchate was created in 1589. This provided the Russian Orthodox Church with a separate status. There were other churches in eastern Europe which practised Orthodox rites but acknowledged the Pope as the supreme head of the church.

4

Europe: The Holy Roman Empire 1500–1806

cross Europe, there were numerous small and large
kingdoms. As feudalism declined kings became more
powerful and began to increase direct control over
their territories. Now governments started getting involved
in matters that had earlier been left to feudatories. The
kingdoms were ruled by a number of administrators appointed
by the king.

After 1500, new countries and states began to emerge
in Europe. All over the continent there were struggles for
independence. These struggles were mainly a protest against
difficult economic conditions. Groups of people who had
some kind of unity based on language, culture and location got
together, but there was no strong sense of nationalism.

Numerous wars, too, were fought over these 300 years.

Among the European kingdoms, the Holy Roman Empire
was still important.

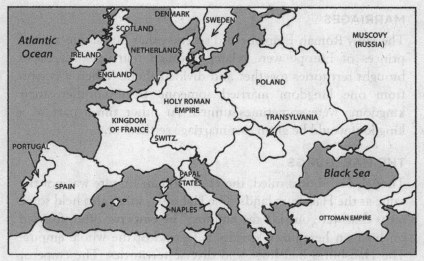

Europe in 1600

THE HOLY ROMAN EMPIRE

By 1500, the Holy Roman Empire consisted of a large area mainly in the present region of Germany in Central Europe. The emperors used to be elected, but the Habsburgs were the main rulers of the empire from 1438, when Albert, a Habsburg ruling over Austria, became the emperor with the title Albert II.

The territory of the empire and the extent of its powers varied at different times. Within it there were some kingdoms as well as smaller units such as duchies and estates. Most of it was ruled in name by the emperor and the Imperial Diet, but many of the territories were virtually independent. In the 16th century new administrative measures were introduced, but the region remained disunited. By the 17th century, the empire was in decline. Minor German princes still wanted to retain its structure, but the more powerful wanted independence.

MARRIAGES

The Holy Roman Emperor and several other kings, queens and princes of Europe were related through marriage. Marriages brought territories together and divided them. When a person from one kingdom married someone from another, their kingdoms were sometimes united. At other times part of a kingdom would be given as a marriage settlement.

THE HABSBURGS

Though Habsburgs ruled, the Holy Roman Empire was not the same as the Habsburg lands. The Habsburg kings also held some areas that were outside the empire. The emperor often focused on his own hereditary kingdoms instead of the whole empire. The Habsburgs had huge and diverse territories. The emperor was at times also King of Hungary, Duke of Milan, Archduke of Austria, along with other titles.

THE EMPERORS: 1500–1806

Maximilian I (1493–1519)	Joseph I (1705–11)
Charles V (1519–58)	Charles VI (1711–40)
Ferdinand I (1558–64)	Interregnum (1740–42)
Maximilian II (1564–76)	Charles VII of Bavaria (1742–45)
Rudolf II (1576–1612)	Habsburg-Lorraine
Matthias (1612–19)	Francis I of Lorraine (1745–65)
Ferdinand II (1619–37)	Joseph II (1765–90)
Ferdinand III (1637–57)	Leopold II (1790–92)
Leopold I (1658–1705)	Francis II (1792–1806)

Details of some of the emperors and the main events are given below:

Maximilian I

Maximilian, the eldest son of Frederick III, was ruling as Holy Roman Emperor in 1500. Maximilian, who was also a writer and a poet, had to fight several wars to defend his domains.

Maximilian, a portrait by Albrecht Durer (1471–1528)

Maximilian's son, known as Philip the Handsome, married Joanna of Castile, the future queen of Castile and Aragon (the two parts of Spain) in 1498. This alliance later led to an increase in the Habsburg territories, when Charles V became the king.

Charles V

Charles was the son of Philip and Joanna. As Philip passed away before his father, Charles succeeded his grandfather Maximilian and became Charles V, Holy Roman Emperor. Charles inherited other territories. From his father, Philip, he had received the Netherlands, which had been part of Burgundy. From his grandfather he inherited Austria, the Tyrol, Franch-Comte, Alsace and several areas of Italy. From his mother he acquired the Spanish kingdoms, including Sicily from Aragon and the Americas from Castile. In 1516, Charles began to rule the joint territories of Castile and Aragon as Carlos I. Castile and Aragon later formed the territory of Spain. Charles was at first well liked in Spain but then lost his popularity as he focused mostly on Habsburg interests.

Charles tried to take care of and rule the whole territory of the empire but the lands under his control were too diverse and vast.

The Peace of Augsburg

After the Reformation, the Empire became divided between Protestants (Lutherans) and Catholics. The Emperor remained Catholic but some of the dukes and princes became Protestants primarily to oppose him. Some of these Protestant rulers formed the Schmalkaldic League in 1531. It was named after Schmalkalden in Thuringia where they met. This League wanted both political and religious freedom for Protestants. Emperor Charles V ignored it for some time, but finally fought a war in 1546–47, and defeated the League. Despite this, the Peace of Augsburg was signed in 1555. This treaty allowed the princes to choose between Lutheranism and Catholicism in their own territories. The ruler's religion became the religion of the people. If any people had different beliefs and wanted to move out, they were allowed to do so. However, only Lutheranism was allowed, not other Protestant groups. After this there was 50 years of religious peace in Germany. The Emperor remained Catholic but without this agreement he could not retain the loyalty of the German princes.

Abdication of Charles V

Charles V abdicated in 1556. Spain went to his son Philip II, the Austrian lands to his brother Ferdinand. Thus the Habsburg territories were divided. Charles was the last emperor to be crowned by the Pope. After him the emperors had less power, but there was peace for some time within the Empire.

Charles V, a portrait painted in 1548

THE THIRTY YEARS' WAR (1618–48)

This war happened in four main phases and included several different battles.

The first phase, lasting from 1618 to 1623, can be called the Bohemian phase. Ferdinand II became king of Bohemia in 1617 and of Hungary in 1618. He was aiming to become the Holy Roman Emperor. Ferdinand II was a Catholic, but the population was mainly Protestant. They asked Ferdinand to protect their rights, but he did not help them. The Bohemian Protestants in Prague, their capital, then attacked the king's palace and threw two of the ministers out of a window. This took place in 1618 and marked the beginning of what has been called the Thirty Years' War. After this, Bohemia elected its own king, Ferdinand V. However, Ferdinand II became Holy Roman Emperor in 1619.

In this phase the Bohemians (Czechs) were defeated, and Calvinist Protestants expelled.

In the second phase, 1625–29, Christian IV, king of Denmark and Norway, came to the help of the Protestant princes. But once again, by 1629, the Catholic forces won. By the Treaty of Lubeck, the Danish forces withdrew and their provinces, which had been captured in the war, were returned.

By now, other kings of Europe began to feel the Habsburgs were becoming too powerful, and feared for their own territories. The war was no longer based only on religious differences.

The Swedish phase took place from 1630 to 1635. Gustav II Adolf of Sweden joined the war on the Protestant side in 1630. Both groups had successes, but again the Catholics were the main winners. The Peace of Prague 1635 ended this phase, with some clauses in favour of the Lutherans of Saxony. But Gustav was killed in one of the battles.

The last phase of the war, known as the French phase, began in 1635, with France declaring war on Spain. Sweden and some German states supported France. France and Sweden won victories, even while diplomatic talks were going on to end the war.

The Peace of Westphalia (1648)

Peace was finally signed on 24 October 1648. It had many aspects and was quite elaborate. It regulated both religious issues and boundaries. Among the main provisions, the Calvinists in Germany received the same rights as Lutherans and Catholics. The independence of Switzerland and the United Provinces was officially recognized. Each state in the Holy Roman Empire gained independence, and the Empire, as well as the Emperor, thus lost control. Along with this the power of the Austrian Habsburgs declined. France received a number of territories, while Sweden, Saxony, Brandenburg and Bavaria too gained. However, some amount of fighting continued until 1654. The German states suffered the most in the war, and the population declined by almost half. France became the major European power. The boundaries created by this treaty remained for about a hundred years, though local conflicts continued. After this, wars were fought mainly for political gain and not for religion. And Catholics and Protestants were separated forever.

The Peace of Westphalia of 1648 was a turning point. Religious wars were no longer waged. Spain's military supremacy came to an end.

About this war, the historian Cicely Veronica Wedgewood wrote: 'They wanted peace and they fought for thirty years to be sure of it. They did not learn then, and have not learned since, that war only breeds war.'

A PATCHWORK CARPET (FLICKENTEPPICH)

At the time of the Peace of Westphalia in 1648, the Empire consisted of about 350 territories. The rulers were known as princes but actually included kings, dukes, counts, abbots, bishops and others. Because of this, the empire was called 'a patchwork carpet'.

OTHER WARS

There were numerous other wars across Europe. Through these wars boundaries of kingdoms changed, and they rose and fell in power. Many of these were wars of succession. These wars were struggles for power, but at the same time they reflected how the kings of Europe were closely related. The Holy Roman Emperors, too, were involved in these conflicts. These Emperors still had a title, but enjoyed very little authority, except in their own Habsburg lands.

War of the Spanish Succession

Charles II of Spain died in 1700 without an heir. In his will Charles II left the Spanish territories to Louis's grandson, Philip of Anjou. Louis had accepted this. The kings of Austria, the United Provinces (Netherlands) and England, wanted Charles of Austria, an archduke and younger son of the Holy Roman Emperor, Leopold I, as the next king of Spain. Joseph Ferdinand of Bavaria, Leopold's grandson, was another candidate. As they did not want war, England and the United Provinces at first accepted Philip of Anjou as Philip V of Spain. But when Louis XIV tried to control Spanish territories, the European powers feared that France would become dominant. They formed the Grand Alliance consisting of the Emperor, the United Provinces, Austria and England. Louis XIV added to the problems by recognizing James III in exile as the king of England, while the Protestant William III was the ruling king. Brandenburg and most of the states of the Holy Roman Empire supported the Grand Alliance. Later Portugal joined them. On the other side France and Philip V of Spain were supported by Bavaria, Cologne, Mantua, Savoy and a few other states. The War of the Spanish Succession began in 1702. The Grand Alliance won a number of victories. The war was fought not only in Europe but in North America, where it was known as Queen Anne's War.

The Peace of Utrecht ended the war, and was signed in 1713. Philip was allowed to be king of Spain, but a union between Spain and France was banned. England acquired some territories such as Nova Scotia and Newfoundland from France, and Gibraltar and Minorca from Spain, as well as some trading rights. The Treaty of Rastatt and Baden was signed in 1714. This gave the Spanish Netherlands (present Belgium) to Austria.

The War of Austrian Succession (1740–48)
In 1740, the Holy Roman Emperor Charles VI died, leaving behind no male heirs. His daughter, Maria Theresa, inherited his Austrian lands. Other kings of Europe had earlier agreed to this, but now rulers of Europe tried to acquire these lands.

Frederick II, the king of Prussia, started the war when he invaded and occupied Silesia, a province within Austria. Spain, France, Poland, Bavaria and Saxony supported him. Hungary, Britain and the Netherlands helped Maria Theresa. Maria allowed Prussia to occupy most of Silesia, and Prussia withdrew from the war. The French were defeated by the British and Hanoverians at Dettingen. Charles Albert of Bavaria became the emperor, Charles VII, in 1742. Maria was married to Francis Stephen of Lorraine, and in 1745 with the death of Charles VII, he became the emperor as Francis I. Maria Theresa was now in a better position. The war ended with the Treaty of Aix-la-Chapelle in 1748. All lands except Silesia were returned to her.

Seven Years' War (1756–63)
The Seven Years' War was fought both within and outside Europe in an attempt to gain territory and trading rights. The war was fought mainly in Europe, India and North America, but also in Central America, part of west Africa, and the Philippines.

In 1756, Frederick the Great of Prussia attacked Saxony and Bohemia. Austria, who was allied with France, Russia and

Sweden, attacked Prussia. Britain and Hanover joined the war on the side of Prussia. In 1762, Russia agreed to a peace, and Austria in 1763. Britain and France continued the war in North America and India. (See Chapter 20 for the war in North America, which began in 1754.)

The Peace of Paris was signed in 1763 between Britain and France, who was allied with Spain. Britain gained territories in America and India. Spain too gained in the war. (See Chapter 19.) Prussia and Austria signed the Treaty of Hubertsburg in 1763. By this, Prussia retained its hold on Silesia.

THE LAST DAYS OF THE EMPIRE

The Habsburg emperors remained concerned with the rising power of Prussia. Meanwhile, the French Revolution (1789) took place and there was the threat of an invasion by France. From 1792 to 1802 Austria, Prussia and other states of the Empire came together in an attempt to defeat France. However, they were not able to do so, and France continued to expand its territories. By 1806, seventeen states of the Holy Roman Empire, which had been conquered by France, were reorganized by Napoleon, emperor of France, and named the Confederation of the Rhine. Then on 6 August 1806, the Holy Roman Empire was formally dissolved.

After the Congress of Vienna in 1815, a new confederation was created.

GREGORIAN CALENDAR

Various countries and regions used different calendars. Up to 1582 most countries of Europe used the Julian calendar. This was a solar calendar which began to be used in 45 BCE and was named after Julius Caesar, who introduced this calendar in 46 BCE. Though a solar calendar, it was not that accurate, and a new calendar was introduced by Pope Gregory in 1582. Roman Catholic countries began to use the new calendar straightaway, but others took some time. Britain adopted it in 1782 and Russia in 1918. This is the calendar that most countries use for official purposes today.

In the Gregorian calendar, the year begins on 1 January, and there are 12 months and 365 days, with an extra day in a leap year.

5

Europe: Scandinavia, Spain and Some Other Countries 1500–1800

Here we look at some of the countries of Europe that went through numerous changes during these 300 years.

SCANDINAVIAN COUNTRIES

Norway, Sweden and Denmark had a closely related history. Denmark was the dominant country. Norway was united with Denmark in 1380, and remained under its rule till 1814. Along with Norway, Iceland and the Faroe Islands came under Denmark. Later Greenland, too, became part of Denmark.

Sweden was united with Denmark and Norway in 1397 but later resented Denmark's dominance. After rebellions against Denmark, in 1523 most of Sweden became independent, under King Gustav I Vasa. A number of other kings ruled, as well as some queens. Queen Christina ruled from 1644 to 1654. At her court there were poets, musicians and scholars. In the 17th century, Sweden conquered part of Poland and some territories of Russia, but its power declined in the 18th century.

THE GREAT NORTHERN WAR

Sweden had become powerful, and controlled the Baltic Sea. To check her power, Denmark, Poland and Russia combined their forces to attack her. Charles XII, king of Sweden, only eighteen years old, put forward a great defence and came to be known as 'the Swedish meteor'. Soon Denmark made peace. Russia was defeated in some battles. The war with Poland continued, till the Polish king abdicated in 1706. Stanislaus Leszczynski, who was an ally of Charles, became the Polish king. But when Charles invaded Russia, he was defeated at Poltava in the Ukraine.

Charles died in a battle in 1718. After Charles's death his sister Ulrika Eleanora came to the throne. In 1721, the Peace of Nystadt ended the war. Some territories were returned to Sweden, but it was Russia who emerged as a strong power. Sweden lost territory in Finland to Russia.

Another war with Russia took place from 1741 to 1743 and more territory was lost. Finland now hoped to gain independence. The Russian empress Elizabeth Petrovna promised to make

Finland a separate territory under Russia. By 1809, Finland came under Russia and became an autonomous grand duchy.

ICELAND

Iceland has several hot springs and geysers. It also has more than 200 volcanoes and experiences frequent earthquakes. The only naturally growing fruit are bilberries and crowberries. Birch and fir trees once covered part of the region but now trees are few. The Arctic fox was once the only land animal. Reindeer were introduced in the late 18th century. Rodents reached here in ships but Iceland has no reptiles, nor frogs or toads. There are birds including puffins, swans and ducks, whales and seals on the coasts, and fish in the rivers. In 1380, Iceland entered a union with Denmark. In 1661, King Frederick III became the absolute monarch of Denmark and Norway, and by 1662 his absolute rule was enforced in Iceland. The power of the Althing, Iceland's traditional Parliament, was soon taken away.

Around CE 930 Iceland had a population of 60,000–90,000. In the first national census of the early 18th century, the population was estimated at 50,000. Soon there was a further decline. Between 1707 and 1709 there was a smallpox epidemic. Later there were famines, followed by the Mount Hekla eruption in 1766 and the Laki volcano eruption in 1783. In the latter, more than 9000 people died. Many faced poverty and the population was reduced to about 35,000. But from 1750 local people began to set up small-scale industries. In 1787, positive changes began when trade restrictions were reduced.

The term geyser is named after Geysir, a geyser (hot spring) in south-west Iceland. Boiling water from this can reach a height of 60m or more.

SPAIN

In 1469, Isabella of Castile married Ferdinand of Aragon. This marked the beginning of the unification of Spain. In the year 1474 they became the joint rulers of Castile and then in 1479, of Aragon. After the conquest of Granada in 1492, Spain was almost unified. Castile and Aragon were ruled jointly from 1516, and were referred to as Espana (Spain) but were legally united only under Philip V (1707–15).

After the voyages of Christopher Columbus (see Chapter 22) Spain soon began conquests and settlements in the Americas. Spain was powerful even within Europe and reached its height at the time of Philip II (ruled 1556–98). Philip had received his father, Charles's Spanish territories, including Spain, the Spanish Netherlands and Sicily. In 1580, he also took over the Portuguese territories belonging to his mother. Portugal, as well as its overseas territories, came under Spain from 1581 to 1640. Philip was married to Mary Tudor, and was for some time the king of England.

MUDEJARS AND MORISCOS

Mudejars: a term for Muslims who lived in Spain after the conquest of Granada. In the 16th century they were forced to convert to Christianity and were known as Moriscos. Unconverted Muslims were expelled in 1610. Mudejar is also a term for a style of architecture which combined Islamic elements with Romanesque, Gothic and Renaissance styles.

The Inquisition

The Spanish Inquisition was set up by a papal bull (order) in 1478 and began to function in Castile in 1480. The authority of the Inquisition extended across Castile, Aragon, Sicily, Sardinia

  The Puffin History of the World

and Spanish territories in the Americas. Jews were expelled and Moriscos had strict rules. Mainly Lutherans (Protestants) were persecuted by the inquisition.

THE NETHERLANDS

In the 16th century, the Spanish Netherlands consisted of the present countries of the Netherlands to the north, and Belgium to the south. Netherlands means the 'low-lying lands' and these countries are also called 'the Low countries'. The western region is below sea level. Dykes, canals and dams were made from medieval times to drain water from the low-lying areas, giving the Netherlands a unique landscape. Without this the land would be flooded by the sea and by rivers. 'Polder' is the term for the reclaimed land.

The Dutch revolt

From 1568 to 1648, the Netherlands was involved in a struggle against Spain. One of the reasons was religion. Spain was a Catholic country, but in the northern Netherlands, Protestantism (Calvinism) was prominent. William of Orange, known as William the Silent, was an important leader of the revolt. After much fighting, seven Dutch republics joined together by the Union of Utrecht in 1579, forming the United Provinces. These provinces were Gelderland, Friesland, Holland, Groningen, Overijssel, Utrecht and Zeeland. They declared their independence in

William of Orange, a portrait

1581. However, William of Orange was assassinated in 1584. The Spanish then recovered most of the territories. The Union continued to fight for its independence and was helped both by France and England.

In 1588, the English attacked and defeated the Spanish Armada, a strong fleet of Spanish ships. There was a truce between the Spanish and the Dutch from 1609 to 1621, but the war continued till 1648. By the Treaty of Munster, the Dutch republic of the United Provinces became a legal reality.

Growth in prosperity

Even while this revolt continued for 80 long years, the Dutch provinces were growing in strength. They had a strong navy, good engineers, a system of banking and a democratic government. People with different religious views, scientists, writers, philosophers and artists lived there. New universities were founded.

Agriculture, fishing and trade prospered. Flowers, particularly tulips, were exported to France.

Wind power was important and there were 9000 windmills by 1800. Rivers and canals were used for transport.

This period was known as its golden age.

Dutch colonies

Soon the Netherlands became a great colonial power. Two trading companies were founded, the Dutch East India Company in 1602 and the Dutch West India Company in 1621. These two together covered much of the world and later came in conflict with England in several areas.

The government

The United Provinces was governed by an assembly with representatives of each of the seven provinces, along with the

Stadtholder, which became hereditary. William III of Orange was Stadtholder from 1672 to 1702 and also king of England from 1689. After 1715, following the war of Spanish succession, the Dutch power weakened. William III had no heirs, and after his death, John William Friso, a relative, took over. His son became Stadtholder and took the title William IV in 1747. Because of internal problems and conflicts, French troops supported by Dutch citizens in exile invaded and replaced the United Provinces with the Batavian Republic (1795–1806), which had a different type of government, based on that in France. In 1806, the Kingdom of Holland was formed, under Louis Bonaparte, the brother of Napoleon.

The historic region of Frisia (now Friesland) maintained its own language and culture even after joining with the Netherlands in 1579. It has its own traditional music and dance.

BELGIUM

Belgium was also part of the Spanish Netherlands. In 1581, when seven provinces formed the United Provinces, the region of Belgium remained under Spain. Even in 1648 Belgium and Luxembourg remained under Spain. But soon both France and Austria attempted to gain control over the region.

France gained some territories in 1659 by the Peace of Pyrennes. Following this, France received part of Flanders by the Peace of Utrecht (1713–15), but most of the territory came under Austria. In the War of Austrian Succession the region came under the French, but then returned to Austria by the Treaty of Aix-la-Chapelle in 1748. Belgium enjoyed a brief period of independence in 1790, after Austrian control was restored. In 1797, Belgium came under France by the

Treaty of Campo Formo. In 1814, the area was occupied by the opponents of Napoleon. The final Battle of Waterloo took place in Belgium.

The kingdom of Netherlands was formed in 1815 and united with Belgium.

Belgium seceded in 1830.

PORTUGAL

Portugal had started explorations and overseas settlements from the 15th century. However, its growth was checked from 1580 to 1640 when she came under the Habsburgs of Spain. Portugal regained its independence in 1640, with the help of France. King John IV (ruled 1640–56) was the first king of the House of Braganza. Portuguese prosperity revived to some extent in the 17th and 18th centuries.

SWITZERLAND

In Switzerland there were several small city states or cantons. In 1291, the Swiss Confederation was founded comprising three cantons. More states gradually joined and by 1499 the Swiss Federation was virtually independent.

In 1515, Switzerland became politically neutral. It was recognized as an independent state by the Peace of Westphalia, 1648. Swiss neutrality was maintained even through the world wars.

HUNGARY

In the second half of the 15th century, Hungary, under king Matthias Corvinus (ruled 1458–90), became one of the most powerful kingdoms in Europe. Matthias obtained control of Austria, Lusatia, Moravia and Silesia, and had a centralized administration and a strong army. Serbia and Transylvania (part of present Romania) were also under Hungary. But after the defeat of Matthias, feudal lords became influential and there was struggle and conflict both within Hungary, and from outside. The Habsburgs, Turks and groups within Hungary fought for control. By the Treaty of Karlowitz of 1699, most of Hungarian territories, including Transylvania, came under the Habsburgs.

POLAND

Poland's territories were constantly changing.

Zygmunt II, also called Sigismund II (ruled 1548–72) was the last king of the Jagiellon dynasty. After him nobles gained control and kings were elected by the Sejm, a bicameral legislature. Poland and Lithuania were formally united in 1569, by the Union of Lublin, and were known as the Polish-Lithuanian Commonwealth.

Poland-Lithuania's power and territories gradually began to decline because of numerous wars.

The last days of Poland-Lithuania

Augustus II, king of Poland and elector of Saxony, died in 1733. Stanislaus Leszczynski, who had been king of Poland from 1704 to 1709, was chosen as the next king. Louis XV of France was married to Stanislaus's daughter and supported him. Spain and Sardinia also backed Stanislaus, but Austria and Russia wanted Augustus II's son, Augustus III to be the king. Austria and Russia won after a year-long war. Augustus III became the king.

In 1764, Stanislaus II Augustus came to the throne after the intervention of Russia. He ruled up to 1795. By this time Austria, Prussia and Russia had encroached on and finally taken over Poland-Lithuania, by three 'partitions'—of 1772, 1793 and 1795. Stanislaus lived in St Petersburg after this, and wrote his memoirs. Polish nationalists and intellectuals migrated to other parts of Europe.

AN ELEPHANT AND A RHINOCEROS

Europe did not have any elephants or rhinoceroses. But a few of these reached here from South Asia.

Hanno, a white elephant, was born in 1510 in India. He was transported to Portugal. In 1514, King Emmanuel I of Portugal gifted him to Pope Leo X in Rome. He was escorted to Rome from Lisbon in a ship by the Portuguese ambassador Tristao da Cunha. When Hanno reached Rome, Pope Leo constructed a place for him to stay and became very fond of him.

Hanno took part in festivals and processions. But perhaps the climate did not suit him, and three years later he fell ill. He did not recover and died soon after. Pope Leo was sad, and composed a poem on him. A memorial was erected for Hanno, and the artist Raffaello Santi drew a special portrait of him.

Other elephants as well as a rhinoceros soon reached Europe. The rhinoceros was gifted to the Portuguese in India, and sent in a ship to Lisbon. The animal had with him its caretaker, named Osem, and plenty of rice to eat. Starting out in January 1515, the ship stopped at Mozambique, St Helena and the Azores, and reached Lisbon, the capital of Portugal, in May.

No one there had seen a rhinoceros before, and everyone came to look at him.

The Pope seemed to like exotic animals. The king of Portugal sent the rhinoceros to the Pope. But unfortunately there was a great storm, and along the way, the ship sank. However, the rhinoceros became famous.

Many people made sketches of it from memory or imagination, and among them was the great artist Albrecht Durer. He did not get it quite right, but his woodcut is still famous. Prints were made from the woodcut, and millions of copies have been sold.

6

Europe: Art, Culture and Science 1500–1800

I n Europe there were new trends in art, culture and science. The period from the 14th to the 17th centuries has been called the Renaissance, meaning 'rebirth' or new birth. Within this time period, more changes took place after 1500. These new ideas were linked with the Reformation (see Chapter 2), and with new developments in science.

NEW IDEAS

New ideas spread across Europe. People began to believe they could gain control over the world in which they lived, instead of entirely depending on divine power. These ideas were also influenced by developments in science and technology.

Here we take a look at a few of the influential thinkers of Europe.

René Descartes (1596–1650) was a French philosopher and mathematician who lived in the Dutch republic. He is called the 'father of modern Western philosophy' and his most important book, *Meditations on First Philosophy*, is still studied today. This emphasizes the importance of reason and was originally written in Latin. Blaise Pascal (1623–62) of France, a philosopher, mathematician and physicist, also believed in reason. He put forward the theory of mathematical probability and made other contributions to mathematics and science. He made a mechanical adding machine that has been called the world's first computer.

Descartes's ideas were further developed by rationalists such as Baruch Spinoza and Gottfried Leibniz.

Baruch Spinoza (1632–77), a great Dutch philosopher, had a mathematical and logical view of the universe. Among his works are *Ethica Ordine Geometrico Demonstrata* (Ethics Demonstrated with Geometrical Order).

Gottfried Leibniz (1646–1716) was a German philosopher and mathematician. He discovered the principles of calculus and invented an advanced calculating machine. In philosophy, *Monadology* is his best-known work. In this he put forward the idea that there were innumerable monads or centres of spiritual energy in the world.

In England, John Wilkins and Robert Boyle (1627–91) formed the Royal Society for the Improvement of Natural Knowledge in 1660.

THE AGE OF ENLIGHTENMENT

These new ideas led to even more radical thinking, and the term the Age of Enlightenment or Age of Reason is used for the period approximately between 1650 and 1789, particularly the 18th century, before the French Revolution. The enlightenment did not reject God, but believed truth could be discovered through observation and deduction, not by blind belief.

Voltaire, whose real name was Francois Marie Arouet (1694–1778), was among the great thinkers of this time. More than a hundred published books of his are known. He wrote plays, stories, poems and works on philosophy.

Charles Louis Montesquieu (1689–1755) was another French writer who wrote about existing conditions. His book *Spirit of the Laws* (1748) deals with political theory. In this he suggested that government power be divided among the king, the legislature or parliament, and the judiciary.

Denis Diderot (1734–84), a French philosopher and writer, compiled a 35-volume encyclopedia, which promoted rational thinking. Voltaire and Rousseau were among the contributors.

Jean-Jacques Rousseau (1712–78), a French Huguenot born in Geneva, wrote a number of books. *Contrat Sociale* (The Social Contract) was one of the most influential. He was one of the greatest writers of the enlightenment. (See below for his views on education.)

David Hume (1711–76), a Scottish philosopher, contributed to empirical and sceptical thinking and explained ethics and morality.

Thomas Hobbes in his book *Leviathan* argued in favour of the absolute power of the state (not king), which could not be limited by customary or divine laws or anything else. There were only practical limits to law.

The Rights of Man

Thomas Paine (1737–1809) was born in Norfolk, England. Paine went to the American colonies and wrote in support of their independence. He even fought in their army in the War of Independence (see Chapter 3). He returned to Britain in 1787 and wrote his classic, *The Rights of Man*, in 1791–92. This supported the French Revolution but was not liked in England, and Paine had to escape to France. There he was welcome, but when he began to criticize the violence of the revolutionaries, he was put behind bars. In prison he wrote another great book, *The Age of Reason*. In this he wrote that though God had designed the universe, it then functioned like a machine. Paine was released in 1794 and returned to the US in 1802. He died there in poverty and neglect.

Dare to know

Immanuel Kant (1724–1804), a German philosopher, summed up the spirit of the enlightenment in one of his sayings: 'Dare to know.' *The Critique of Pure Reason* is his most important book. In another work, *Foundations of the Metaphysics of Morals*, he stated that reason was the basis for moral action. Kant influenced numerous other philosophers in the 19th and 20th centuries, including Johann Gottlieb Fichte, Hegel and Schelling.

THE INDIVIDUAL AND SOCIETY

The concept of individualism goes back to the days of Plato but became more prominent during and after the Renaissance. The main idea is that individual needs and concerns were as important as the needs of society, if not more so. Thus concepts of individual liberty and human rights emerged. This was further explored by Kant and other philosophers.

EDUCATION

By 1400, there were more than 50 universities in Europe. New officials were required in administration, law and justice, and economic affairs. These officials required new types of training and education. More universities and institutes of learning were founded after 1500.

With the Reformation, there were new thoughts on the nature of children and methods of education. The concept of original sin had influenced ideas on education. This concept in Christianity, and particularly in Roman Catholicism, indicated that everyone was born with the tendency to do wrong. They inherited this from Adam, the first man, when he disobeyed God in the Garden of Eden. (This is a story in the Bible.) Those who believed in this felt education should be used to remove and control these wrong tendencies that existed in each child. Such education could be quite harsh.

But different views too were expressed.

John Locke of England, in 1693, wrote *Some Thoughts Concerning Education*, making an attempt to understand children. He believed that first physical health should be ensured, through washing in cold water, being in the open air, and wearing loose clothing. He advised a limit on non-vegetarian food, and the use of less sugar and salt. He then went on to describe how to get children to behave well. The child should learn to use reason instead of emotion. He explained how this could be achieved without any harsh methods. He also put forward an integrated framework for academic learning. In addition to academics, the child must also have a manual skill. Locke's ideas were quite influential.

Jean-Jacques Rousseau wrote *Emile* in 1762, one of the pioneering books on education. At first *Emile* was banned, but during the French Revolution it gained prominence. Rousseau followed some of Locke's ideas, but emphasized that children should be allowed to be themselves. Children should be allowed to grow and develop, before they were taught from books or learnt a trade. Around the age of fifteen, the child could learn to be a loving and feeling individual, capable of responding to the needs of others. The book also explored women's education. Though Rousseau began by saying, 'In what they have in common they are equal,' he on the whole regarded women as inferior. Rousseau totally rejected the idea of original sin and said children had an 'innocent' nature. He criticized the custom of sending children to work in factories. Using his ideas, J.B. Basedow (1724-90) wrote *Elementarwerk*, an educational manual. A school based on Rousseau's ideas was opened at Dessau. In Poland a national education mission was set up in 1772-73, one of the first in Europe. Polish reformers had actually asked Rousseau for advice, and followed it, creating a unified educational system. By 1800, 200 secular schools were created in Poland and there were new textbooks in Polish, in science and other languages. Though Poland was politically destroyed, the education mission had laid the foundations for the continuity of Polish literature and culture.

The Netherlands was among other countries that had a good system of education with both religious and secular schools.

Orbis Pictus

Jan Amos Komensky was popularly known as Comenius. Born in Moravia in 1592, Comenius knew many languages, and had varied interests. He was a bishop of a religious sect known as the Czech Brethren and an educator. He wrote on spirituality, politics and education, and some of his books were so popular that they had hundreds of versions in different languages. Among these was *Orbis Pictus* or *Orbis Sensualium Pictus* (The World of Things, Obvious to the Senses) drawn in pictures, a book for children written in 1658.

Illustrations on a page from Orbis Pictus *by Comenius*

It is a kind of encyclopedia on different topics with 150 chapters comprising woodcut illustrations and a descriptive text. It was first published in Latin and German, and in English in 1659. A four-language version, including French, was published in 1666. It also appeared in other languages and was updated over the years.

Comenius laid the foundations for the new educational theories of Froebel, Pestalozzi, Montesorri, Dewey and others. He said: 'Not the children of the rich and powerful only, but boys and girls alike, rich and poor, in all cities and villages should go to school.'

Hornbooks

A hornbook was used to teach children in England from around 1450. A hornbook usually had one page of vellum or, later, paper, pasted on leather, wood, bone, ivory or even stone, and attached to a handle. The page was about 4x6 inches (10x15 cm). The sheet had a transparent cover made of horn or mica, so that it would not tear. There were different types but some had the alphabet in capitals and small letters, followed by the Lord's Prayer, and then Roman numbers from 1 to 9.

Hornbooks were used in Britain and America but their popularity declined after 1800, when books with pictures became popular.

MAGIC AND THE OCCULT

Reason was increasingly being used in philosophy and literature, but at the same time there were other trends. There was a deep interest in magic, the occult, alchemy, divination, astrology, witchcraft, ghosts and fairies. As for miracles, even the Church recognized and was interested in them.

Rosicrucianism, literally 'rosy cross', was the term for a secret group said to have been founded in the 14th century, but revealed to more people in the 17th century. They studied the hidden mysteries of the world. Several subgroups soon arose.

Roshen Dalal   51

Freemasons were another secret group that soon became widespread.

The Kabbalah, which had both Jewish and Christian forms, was a system of understanding hidden mysteries. Tarot cards developed as a method to foretell the future around this period.

Nostradamus

Michel de Nostredame (1503–66), known as Nostradamus, was a noted healer who wrote his prophecies in quatrains (four-line verses) towards the end of his life. They have been interpreted in many ways and thought to predict the future.

But there was also a fear of the unknown, and a resistance to the development of individual power.

In Europe and in other parts of the world, women were often labelled as witches and killed. This was both an attempt to control women, or at times to obtain their property.

BOOKS

Print and paper were other revolutionary developments, and books contributed to the spread of knowledge.

In 1455, the first true book printed in Europe was the Gutenberg Bible. By 1500, about 35,000 separate editions of books (called incunabula) were published. Between 1500 and 1600 there were 1,50,000–2,00,000 separate editions. Apart from the Bible there were other sacred texts, grammars, histories and classics. After 1600, the number of books multiplied further.

A new clearer typeface was soon used, invented in Italy and based on Florentine manuscripts.

Literature

From the 16th century, literature in regional languages increased. Italian was one of the earliest regional languages used, but books in French, Spanish, Portuguese, Dutch, Polish,

German and English multiplied. Writing also continued in Latin. Among the noted writers in Latin was Conrad Pickel, alias Celtis (1459–1508), who was the first poet laureate of the Holy Roman Empire.

Doktor Faustus

In Germany, Johann Wolfgang von Goethe wrote *Doktor Faustus* in 1657. The theme is of being saved by love from a pact with the devil. Doktor Faustus was actually a real person educated in various universities in Germany, who died in 1541. He claimed he could perform miracles and that he was associated with the devil. Several books were written with this as the theme, some even in the 20th century. An earlier work on the same theme was Christopher Marlowe's play *Faust* written in 1594.

Wanderers

Picaresque novels on vagabonds or wanderers became popular around this time. *Guzman de Alfarache*, by Mateo Aleman, was a picaresque novel in Spanish, published in two parts in 1599 and 1604. This was widely read and translated into French, Italian, Spanish and English. It is the story of Guzman, a picaro (vagabond or beggar), and his travels from Seville to Rome. It revealed the secret world of vagabonds, beggars and other travellers who had no fixed home. They had their own rules and laws, and even their own secret language. There were books on vagabonds in other languages as well.

Don Quixote

Among other books of this period was *Don Quixote*. A book in two parts written by Miguel de Cervantes Saavedra (1547–1616), it is very well known.

The book is funny, but is actually a commentary on the oddities of people and the world.

Utopia

Thomas More wrote *Utopia* in 1516. It means 'No Place'. It was translated into English in 1551, and into French, German, Italian and Spanish. Utopia is a world without property, a world of equality, of universal education and religious tolerance. Other Utopian books of the period were *New Atlantis* by Francis Bacon and *The Commonwealth of Oceana* by James Harrington.

ART AND ARCHITECTURE

In early Renaissance architecture, architects attempted to revive classical styles, but brought in new elements. Classical architecture is a broad term for architectural forms of this period, which had its origin in ancient styles.

Mannerism was a style that used classical elements in unusual and dramatic ways. Palladian architecture is named after Andrea Palladio (1518–80). This style also used classical elements in unique ways. His type of villa had widespread appeal. Palladio also designed churches. He wrote *Quattro Libri della Architectura* (The Four Books of Architecture), which was published in Venice in 1570.

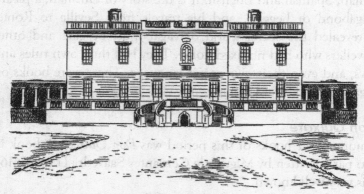

The Queen's House in Greenwich (1616–35) was a Palladian-style villa designed by Inigo Jones for the wife of King James I of England

In both art and architecture, the first half of the 17th century is known as the Baroque period. By the early 18th century, baroque styles were replaced by rococo. Baroque and rococo styles were also called classical, though they have entirely new elements. Neoclassical architecture developed from 1750 to 1850. Art, sculpture and music broadly followed the same trends. Baroque art was characterized by contrasting light and shadow. Rococo was more decorative and less dramatic.

Architects and artists

There were numerous wonderful architects and artists of whom only a few are mentioned here.

Inigo Jones (1573–1682) was a great architect in England. Among Italian architects, Gianlorenzo (Giovanni Lorenzo) Bernini (1598–1680) created the canopy over the altar of St Peter's church in Rome, while Francesco Borromini (1599–1667) designed several churches. Bernini was a great artist, sculptor and architect. Among his many sculptures were the *Abduction of Proserpina*, *The Fountain of Four Rivers*,

Saskia in Bed, *a drawing by Rembrandt of his wife Saskia who died in 1642*

and the *Ecstasy of St Theresa's*. Apart from the canopy, he designed other aspects of St Peter's including the Cathedra Petri (chair or throne) in marble, gilt, stucco and bronze. He also designed a number of palaces and three churches.

Architects were often engaged in religious architecture.

Among artists, Rembrandt van Rijn (1606–69), Jan Vermeer or Johannes Vermeer (1632–75), Jan Steen and Frans Hal were world-famous painters from the Netherlands.

Flemish painters included Peter Paul Rubens (1577–1660) and Anthony van Dyck (1599–1641).

Diego Velásquez (1599–1660) was an important Spanish painter.

MUSIC AND DANCE

Music, too, followed the same broad trends as art and architecture, with baroque, rococo and classical styles. George Frideric Handel (1685–1759) was one of the greatest musicians of the later Baroque period.

The German musician Ludwig van Beethoven (1770–1827), Joseph Haydn (1732–1809) and Wolfgang Amadeus Mozart (1756–91)—both from Austria—were among the best classical musicians of this time.

Opera was a new development in music. The first opera, *Dafne*, was composed by an Italian, Jacopo Peri (1561–1633), but does not exist today. It was enacted on the stage in 1594. Claudio Monteverdi (1567–1643) and Francesco Cavalli (1602–67) were other composers of operas.

Choral music, known from early days, further developed at this time. The violin as an instrument evolved from the earlier viola.

The Bach family

Johann Sebastian Bach (1685–1750) was a great composer from Germany. He was an organist and composed organ and other music. He was famous throughout Germany and later throughout the world. He came from a great musical family, in which there were at least 40 musicians over a period of 200 years. His son, Karl Phillip Emmanuel, was also well known.

Dance

Folk and other dances were always known but the Baletto dance began in the late 15th century in Italy, and spread to France. In Paris, Jean Georges Noverre (1727-1810) was a great ballet master. Ballet reached its height later in Russia.

SCIENCE AND MATHS

There were enormous developments in science.

Scientific methods, or ways of arriving at true knowledge, began to be used. These included reason, comparison and observation.

Nicholas Copernicus (Nikolaj Kopernik, 1473-1543) from Poland had put forward the theory that the earth and other planets moved around the sun. This was not an entirely new theory, but because of the influence of the Church, it was generally believed that the earth was the centre of all existence. Copernicus's theory was published at the time of his death, but did not achieve much prominence until the time of Galileo. Tycho Brahe (1546-1601), a noted astronomer, made astronomical measurements of the solar system and the stars. He did not totally accept Copernicus's theory. Johannes Kepler, Brahe's assistant, used Brahe's work to explain laws of motion and the movement of the planets.

Galileo Galilei (1564-1642), an Italian scientist, used a telescope to look at the skies for the first time. He realized that the earth moved around the sun, and discovered the four moons of Jupiter. But he was imprisoned for his scientific discoveries. He was forced by the Inquisition to deny his beliefs.

Isaac Newton (1642-1727), professor at Cambridge University, laid the basis for the laws of physics. His main contributions were:

He put forward the theory of gravity.

He also discovered that white light was composed of rays of coloured light.

He discovered calculus, a new branch of mathematics, though Leibniz had made an independent discovery of this.

Though he made these discoveries in 1665–67, they were published in 1687. In 1705, he was knighted by Queen Anne. Newton was considered the greatest example of progress through science. The English poet Alexander Pope (1688–1744) wrote:

'Nature and nature's laws lay hid in night / God said, "Let Newton be" and all was light.'

People felt that through the use of analysis and reason, everything would be known.

There were several other scientists and mathematicians from various European countries. In the Netherlands Christiaan Huyghens (1625–95) experimented with light and saw that it travelled in waves.

Antoine Lavoisier (1743–94) introduced a new theory of combustion. In 1662, Robert Boyle, an English scientist, formulated a law stating that the volume of gas is inversely proportionate to its pressure. The Swedish botanist Carl Linnaeus (1707–78) classified plants and animals.

John Napier, a Scottish mathematician, discovered logarithms in 1614.

GLASSES

Reading glasses were made by 1300. They often consisted only of a single lens held in front of the eye; sometimes there were two lenses. Initially they did not have the rods that rest behind the ears, but were held or fixed to a hat.

Evangelista Torricelli invented the barometer in 1643. He was an Italian.

MEDICINE

The Belgian scholar Andreas Vesalius published a text on anatomy in 1543 called *De Humani Corporis Fabrica* (On the Fabric of the Human Body), which was a great advance on existing knowledge. This had seven books, dealing with bones, muscles, the brain and other parts of the body. The English physician William Harvey discovered the circulation of blood in 1616, while Antoni van Leeuwenhoek (1632–1723) of the Netherlands studied the composition of blood.

Edward Jenner (1749–1823), an English physician, experimented with the first vaccination for smallpox in 1796, and successfully developed this vaccine. This was the first experiment with immunization.

PARACELSUS—A UNIQUE DOCTOR

Theophrastus Bombastus von Hohenheim (1493–1541) was a German-Swiss doctor. He was known as Paracelsus. He was one of the first to believe in practical observations to understand the human body, instead of relying on ancient texts. He also believed in holistic medicine and links between the environment, psychology, the supernatural and physical disease. He wrote a number of books. The most important was *Opus Paramirium* (Work beyond Wonders). His ideas were not accepted at that time, but contributed to a more scientific approach to medicine and to new ways of thinking.

7
France
1500–1799

In 1500, France was under the Valois dynasty, which succeeded the Capets in 1328. The Valois kings reduced the power of the feudatories and increased that of the kings.

The Valois ruled till 1589, when they were succeeded by the Bourbons.

THE VALOIS DYNASTY

The kings of the Valois dynasty after 1500 were:
Louis XII (1498–1515)
Francois I (1515–47)
Henri II (1547–59)
Francois II (1559–60)
Catherine dé Medici (regent, 1560–63)
Charles IX (1560–74)
Henri III (1574–89)

SOME ASPECTS OF THE VALOIS KINGS
Louis XII

Louis XII was the son of Charles, Duke of Orleans, and was the second cousin of the earlier French king Louis XI. He married Jeanne, daughter of Louis XI, and became the king when Charles VIII died without a male heir. Then, he had his marriage to Jeanne annulled by the Pope, and married Charles's widow, Anne of Brittany. This was a political alliance to ensure that Brittany remained with France. After Anne's death he made another political marriage to the eighteen-year-old Mary Tudor, sister of Henry VIII of England, but died soon after. Louis XII fought wars with Italy, but finally lost territory there. Within France he was popular, and called 'the father of the people'. He reduced taxes and reformed the judiciary.

Francois I (Francis I) and Henry II

Francois I was the son of Charles d'Angoulême. Louis XII had no surviving son. Francois I was his cousin, and was married to his daughter Claude. During his reign there were great cultural advances. He patronized art and literature and had a number of grand buildings constructed. Leonardo da Vinci (1452–1519), a great Italian sculptor, artist, architect and engineer, left Italy to live in France during the reign of Charles VIII. He had a special relationship with Francois I. He was given the title 'The King's First Painter, Engineer and Architect'. He designed buildings, an ideal town, and several other items, including a mechanical lion. When he died, Francois said, 'For each of us, the death of this man is a bereavement, since it is impossible that we will ever see his like again.'

Benvenuto Cellini, a master goldsmith, and the artists Rossi and Primaticcio, contributed to art and decoration. Attempts were made to acquire paintings and sculptures of great artists such as Michelangelo, Titian and Raphael, and France gained a valuable art collection. The royal library was expanded. Francois himself loved reading. In 1539 he made French the language of administration. Before this Latin had been used. Francois also began the French exploration of North America, but was not politically successful in Europe. Too much money was spent on wars and buildings, and France now faced an economic crisis.

Henri II fought wars against Austria, and was involved in persecuting the Huguenots (French Calvinists). After him there were some years of chaos and conflicts.

Religious wars
France fought a series of religious wars from 1562 to 1598. The wars were between Catholics and Protestants. While the kings and most of the population was Catholic, the Protestant Huguenots had grown in power.

Catherine dé Medici
Catherine dé Medici was the widow of King Henri II of France, who died in 1559. She became the regent of their son Francois II and after he died, of their younger son Charles, who was ten years old at the time. Later Charles tried to rule independently. He was a Catholic but was influenced by Admiral Gaspard de Coligny, who was a leader of the Huguenots. At this time, Marguerite, the daughter of Catherine, was about to get married to Henri of Navarre, a Huguenot. The marriage was to take place in Paris. Catherine first tried to get Coligny assassinated, but when that failed she decided to massacre the Huguenots, many of whom had come to Paris to attend the wedding.

St Bartholomew's Day
The massacre took place in 1572, and began on 24 August, which was St Bartholomew's Day. Coligny and about 20,000 other Huguenots were killed, both in Paris and in the rest of France.

The war of the three Henris
Henri III, another son of Catherine, became the king of France after the death of Charles in 1574, and was also a Catholic.

His heir was Henri of Navarre, who was descended from King Louis IX and was a Protestant. The third Henri was the Duke of Guise, who was the leader of the Holy Catholic League. The Duke of Guise persuaded Henri III to ban Protestantism. Henri of Navarre then fought against the king, and won some battles. Meanwhile Henri the duke, who actually wanted to be king himself, occupied Paris. Henri the king had to escape to Blois, but there he made his own plan. He asked the duke to come for a meeting, and once he was there killed him. The Holy League army attacked the king to take revenge. The king then made peace with Henri of Navarre, and heading their two armies they moved towards Paris to take it back from the League. But on the way the king was assassinated by a monk named Jacques Clement.

SOME VALOIS ODDITIES

Catherine made a rule that only women with thin waists would be acceptable at court. Hence women started wearing corsets, that squeezed their waists to make them seventeen inches (43 cm) or less!

Henri III liked to dress as a woman. He had young men as his attendants. They were known as Les Mignons (the darlings).

THE BOURBONS
Henry IV

In 1589, Henry, king of the small state of Navarre, became Henry IV and began the Bourbon line of kings in France. But peace could not be established until he himself became a Catholic in 1593, after which he had the support of the people of France. However, by the Edict of Nantes in 1598, he granted some privileges to Huguenots. This ended the religious wars.

Assisted by Maximilien de Béthune, duc de Sully, Henri improved agriculture, protected forests and encouraged education. He made Paris a grand city with tree-lined roads, bridges and canals. He had the Grande Galerie of the Louvre constructed. One mile (1.6 km) long, and 100 feet (30 m) wide, this was built along the river Seine. Hundreds of artists and craftsmen lived and worked on the lower floors, on his invitation, and this continued for another two centuries.

But though Henry IV was loved and popular, he, too, was assassinated in May 1610. The assassin was Francois Ravaillac, a Catholic fanatic.

Louis XIII, XIV, XV

Louis XIII, XIV and XV together ruled for 164 years.

Louis XIII (ruled 1610-43)

Henry IV's son Louis XIII was only nine years old when Henry died, and his wife, Marie dé Medici, was the regent for the next seven years. Louis XIII took actual power in 1617, and exiled his mother, but the two were reconciled in 1622. Later she attempted a coup, and was again exiled.

France, under the Bourbons, tried to gain power in Germany. The Catholic Bourbons fought against the Catholic Habsburgs, but allied with Dutch Calvinists and Danish and Swedish Lutherans, who supported the Protestant princes of Germany.

Cardinal Richelieu began to play a major role in France. He was close to Marie dé Medici, and became the chief minister in 1624, and later the prime minister. He was responsible for the aggressive French foreign policy. He strengthened the power of the king, and reduced those of the Huguenots (French Calvinists). 'Intendants' or royal officials of the king were appointed in the provinces. Taxes were increased and the peasants suffered, but rebellion was suppressed. Richelieu led France into the Thirty Years' War.

Louis XIV (ruled 1643–1715)

Louis XIV was only five years old when he became the king, but he continued to rule over the next seventy years. At first his mother, Anne of Austria, was his regent, helped by Giulio Mazzarini (Cardinal Mazarin). Mazarin was his main instructor. France was affected by the last phase of the Thirty Years' War, in which Lorraine, Burgundy and part of eastern France were badly affected. The Parlement of Paris, a corporation of lawyers, were against new taxation and led a rebellion in Paris in 1648, later named the Fronde. A second Fronde was led by noblemen in 1653. The monarchy survived, but Louis lost trust in the nobles. Mazarin died in 1661, after which Louis ruled independently. Jean-Baptiste Colbert was his financial advisor.

At this time France had the highest population in Western Europe along with good economic resources. The French Church was independent of the Pope but under the king. The intendants or administrators were centrally appointed and the court was glamorous and luxurious. France had also built a good army and navy.

Louis fought four wars, in which many lives and much money was lost. His wife was Maria Theresa, the daughter of Philip IV of Spain. Louis invaded Spain, claiming the Spanish Netherlands and Franche Comte on her behalf. He next waged war against the Dutch. Peace was signed in 1668 and 1678 respectively. These two wars led to small gains in territory.

Louis was keen on acquiring territory in Germany and on becoming the Holy Roman Emperor, but did not succeed. He claimed part of the Palatinate, a German state, and started an invasion in 1688. This was called King William's War or the War of the League of Augsburg. King William of Orange was ruling with his wife Mary in England. Members of the League were the Holy Roman Emperor, Leopold I; the king of Sweden, the king of Spain, the electors of Bavaria, the Palatinate and

Saxony joined in 1689 by England. The War of the League of Augsburg took place between 1689 and 1697. The war ended with the Treaty of Ryswick. By this, most of the territory earlier conquered by France was returned.

France next joined in the War of the Spanish Succession (1701–13), and was to some extent successful. (See Chapter 3.)

Louis's internal and foreign policies were connected. He was against Protestants, and Huguenots were exiled or pressured to convert. Four hundred thousand Huguenots, many of them craftsmen, left the country during his reign.

The Sun King

In France royal power reached a height under Louis XIV. Louis was called the Sun King, because of his prestige and glory, and also because he once took part in a court ballet playing the role of the sun. French prestige reached a height with the building of the grand palace at Versailles, later replicated on a smaller scale in many parts of Europe. Louis set up academies to promote art, architecture and science. The Comedie-Francaise was a theatre established in 1680. Among the great playwrights were Molière (1622–73) and Jean-Baptiste Racine (1639–99).

VERSAILLES

Versailles was once a small building, the hunting Lodge of Louis XIII. Louis XIV converted it into a huge palace, and moved his government there in 1682. Five thousand courtiers lived there, and 5000 servants nearby.

The Palace of Versailles took 47 years to build. It cost the equivalent of 150 million pounds. This huge palace was 3158 m long. In it were the Grand Apartments of the king and queen, including the huge Hall of Mirrors, with 17 mirrored arches, each consisting of 21 mirrors. The Hall of Mirrors overlooked rectangular pools which reflected sunlight into the hall. Wonderful gardens were made with numerous decorative fountains and an orangery. Though Louis was against the Dutch, he bought millions of tulip bulbs from them every year for Versailles.

Louis XV and XVI, too, lived in the palace and added to it. The chapel and opera were built during the reign of Louis XV. The palace was deserted after 1789, but in the time of Louis-Philippe, who came to power in 1830, it was made into the Museum of the History of France. Many items were added to the display at the museum, including more paintings and sculptures depicting events and personalities of France.

Front view of the Palace of Versailles

The Hope Diamond

The Hope Diamond was a symbol for Louis XIV. It was cut in such a way that when mounted on a gold background, a gold star representing the sun could be seen. The diamond was blue in colour. Blue and gold were the colours of the king.

Louis XV (ruled 1715–74)

After Louis XIV, his five-year-old great-grandson became Louis XV, while Louis's nephew, Philippe II of Orleans, was the regent. France faced a major defeat at this time, in the Seven Years' War (see Chapter 4). Louis XV eventually died of smallpox.

Louis XVI (ruled 1774–92)

Louis XV was followed by his grandson, Louis XVI. It was during his time that the French Revolution took place.

THE FRENCH REVOLUTION (1789)
The background

The French Revolution had a number of mixed causes. New ideas brought in a spirit of criticism regarding the ways in which governments ruled. These ideas influenced the people, but did not cause the revolution.

France had a large population. Trade was good. Businessmen and craftsmen were numerous. Peasants owned two-fifth of the land and were engaged in agriculture over most of France. On the whole, the people did not want revolution, but reforms.

The main cause of the revolution was financial. When Louis XVI came to the throne in 1774, France was faced with a financial crisis, mainly because of expenditure on wars fought earlier. Louis XVI immediately tried to bring in financial reforms, but his attempts were opposed. Finally he decided to ask the Estates General to raise money. The Estates General was an elected national assembly. It had last met in 1614. It had three estates or sections. The First Estate consisted of the clergy; the Second Estate of the nobles; and the Third Estate of the middle class and peasants. The higher clergy and nobility had special privileges and tax exemptions, as well as their own law courts. It was difficult for the king to remove these rights, which had existed for generations. Nobles had the highest posts in the army and government. Some bishops, too, had become nobles. The privileges of these groups were resented by merchants, traders, lawyers, other middle class people and rich peasants. The burden of taxes was on them.

In 1789, elections were held for the assembly. Louis had decided that the Third Estate would have as many members as the first and second estates combined, but the manner of voting had not been made clear.

To add to the problems, France was faced with price rise, poor harvests in 1787 and 1788, and peasant riots (jacqueries) in 1789.

After being elected, the Estates General met in May. Before this, local areas were asked to prepare cahiers or lists of grievances. The main demands were a reduction in taxes, limits on the powers of ministers and freedom of the press. The Third Estate wanted voting on proposals by simple majority, which would give them adequate power. But the two higher estates would not allow the third estate to have equal voting rights. Though the king claimed absolute power and rule by divine right, in reality his power was limited by the whole feudal structure of rights and privileges. He was not able to make the necessary changes to give the Third Estate more power. Each estate only had one vote. This meant that the two higher estates could outvote the common people.

The revolution

On 17 June 1789 the Third Estate, led by Comte de Mirabeau and Emmanuel Sieyès, named itself the National Assembly. Louis wanted to dismiss the assembly, and prevented them from using the meeting hall. On 20 June they met at a tennis court, and vowed to frame a new constitution for France. Now they were joined by a number of liberal nobles and some clergy from the two higher estates. Observing the mood of the people, on 27 June the king asked the rest of the clergy and nobles to join this assembly and renamed it the National Constituent Assembly. But neither the queen nor the Comte d'Artois (later Charles X) favoured the idea. Louis was persuaded to bring foreign regiments to Paris, and to dismiss Jacques Necker. Necker was the finance minister, one of the main people who had worked to give power to the Third Estate.

The people felt betrayed by these new developments. A number of people in Paris joined together and attacked the Bastille, a fortress-prison, on 14 July 1789. This marked the beginning of the French Revolution. Louis withdrew the troops and reinstated Necker. On 4 August in the National Constituent Assembly, the clergy, nobles and middle classes themselves gave up their privileges. The assembly introduced a number of reforms. They then began to draft the constitution whose preamble began with the significant Declaration of the Rights of Man and of the Citizen.

Painting depicting the fall of the Bastille, a prison in Paris, on 14 July 1789

But in Paris the people were hungry and desperate. A large group of women accompanied by some men reached Versailles, and tried to capture the king. He was rescued, but confusion followed. Were the common people becoming too powerful? Some nobles resigned, and others went abroad. The rest continued with the drafting of the constitution, and its first draft was approved by Louis on 14 July 1790. It had made radical changes in the existing structure, reorganized the administration and abolished all hereditary titles. But poor people were still not allowed to vote, as voters had to be property owners. The power of the king was reduced, and to help finances, a type of paper currency called assignats, which was backed by land, was introduced. The final draft of the constitution was yet to be prepared, but those without property felt their needs had not been met.

Leopold II, Holy Roman Emperor and brother of Marie Antoinette, the wife of Louis XVI, as well as other kings of Europe were against what was happening in France. Louis tried to escape from the country in June 1791. He was helped by his allies Austria and Prussia, but he was captured, brought back to Paris and allowed to live in the Palace of the Tuileries. After a brief period, Louis was reinstated by the Constituent Assembly, which wanted to restore order in the country. He accepted the new constitution, the Constituent Assembly was dissolved, and a newly elected National Assembly took its place on 1 October 1791. There were many divisions, groups, and differences of opinion in this new assembly. Among the groups, the Feuillants wanted a constitutional monarchy, that is, the king would rule with limits on his power. The Girondins and Montagnards were in favour of a republic, but had their own differences. Meanwhile the Holy Roman Emperor and Prussia threatened to attack. In April 1792 the National Assembly declared war on the Austrian part of the Holy Roman Empire. Austria invaded France, and in July, Prussia and Sardinia joined in the war against France.

In August people reached the Tuileries in Paris, killed the guards and imprisoned the king. In a battle against the Prussians, the French gained victory at Valmy. On 21 September the National Convention abolished the monarchy and on 22 September, declared that France was a republic.

The First Republic

The Girondins, Montagnards and Marais were three groups in the National Convention. At first the Girondins became powerful. Louis XVI was accused of treason and executed on 21 January 1793.

In 1793, the Jacobins became powerful, and killed the Girondins. Maximilien Robespierre, the head of the Committee of Public Safety, unleashed a 'reign of terror'. Thousands of people were executed, and more than 2,00,000 arrested. In July 1794, Robespierre himself was executed.

In 1795, a new National Assembly with two houses was formed, the Council of Five Hundred and the Council of Ancients. They elected a Directory, consisting of five men to be their leaders.

THE COALITION WARS TO FIGHT FRANCE

There were three coalition wars against France. The first coalition: 1792-99. Austria, Britain, the Netherlands, Piedmont, Prussia and Spain joined together to fight against France. France won several battles, and conquered the Netherlands. Prussia, Spain and Austria agreed to a peace.

We will look at the next two coalitions and the rise of Napoleon in Chapter 24.

8
Great Britain
1500–1800

The Tudor dynasty governed England from 1485 to 1603. Henry VII was their first king. The Tudors were originally a Welsh family and had ruled over Wales.

THE TUDORS

Two noted Tudor sovereigns were King Henry VIII and Queen Elizabeth I.

Henry VIII (ruled 1509–47)

Henry VIII was the second son of Henry VII. Henry VIII became king when he was just 18. He was young, red-haired and handsome, and loved to dance. He was also well educated and spoke four languages.

Henry fought unsuccessful wars against France, but managed to defeat an invading Scottish force. He built a strong navy, increasing its strength from five to fifty ships.

He is remembered for having six wives (in succession, not all together!) and for making the English Church independent of the Pope. This happened because Henry VIII wanted to dissolve the first of his six marriages, but the Pope did not agree to this. With the support of the Parliament, Henry made himself the head of the Church of England, which was then separate from the Catholic Church of Rome. After this some monasteries and other Church properties in England were sold. All the monks and nuns living in them had to leave. Most of them had no place to go and some became beggars.

HENRY VIII'S WIVES

Catherine of Aragon: married in 1509; divorced 1533. She was the widow of Henry's elder brother, Arthur. Catherine had five children, of whom only one girl, Mary, survived.

Anne Boleyn: married in 1533; executed in 1536. Henry married Anne for two reasons. Anne was young and pretty, and in addition, Henry had hoped for a son. He wanted to get a divorce from Catherine but the Pope did not allow this. Henry ignored the Pope, divorced Catherine and married Anne. The Pope's power in England came to an end. Henry became the head of the English Church. But Anne did not bear a son. She had a daughter named Elizabeth. Henry later accused Anne of being unfaithful to him, and had her beheaded.

Jane Seymour: married in 1536; died in 1537. Before her death Jane had a son, named Edward. She died of natural causes.

Anne of Cleves: married in January 1540; divorced July 1540; Anne was a German princess. Henry married her in an attempt to regain friends and allies in Europe. Many European kings were against him for breaking with the Pope. This marriage did not work, but Henry took care of Anne financially as long as he was alive.

Edward and Mary

After Henry's death, his son Edward became king, as Edward VI in 1547, though he was still a child. He died in 1553 of tuberculosis. During his reign, the kingdom was controlled by the duke of Northumberland, John Dudley, who was also Lord Chamberlain, and by Edward Seymour. A marriage was arranged between John Dudley's son and Lady Jane Grey, a great-granddaughter of Henry VII, and granddaughter of Mary, the sister of Henry VIII, from her second marriage. John Dudley wanted to retain power and persuaded King Edward to designate Lady Jane Grey his heir. This was done but she was able to rule only for nine days. The Privy Council (the king's advisors) that had initially accepted her succession rejected it when Mary, daughter of Catherine of Aragon and Henry VIII, gained support. Mary then became queen. Lady Jane Grey, her husband and father-in-law were later executed. But Mary did not prove popular. She married Philip II of Spain, and tried to bring Catholicism back to the country. Queen Mary had a number of Protestants killed and this turned people against her. They called her 'Bloody Mary'. After her death in 1558, Elizabeth, daughter of Anne Boleyn, became queen.

Elizabeth I (1558–1603)

Elizabeth was a remarkable ruler. She had a difficult childhood, as her mother was executed when Elizabeth was just two-and-a-half years old. She was cared for and educated by her stepmother Catherine of Parr, and later had special tutors. Thus Elizabeth knew several languages, wrote poetry and played the virginals, a keyboard instrument. She remained unmarried, though there were some courtiers and princes she was close to.

In the time of Elizabeth I, the independence of the Church of England was reestablished by the Act of Supremacy of 1559. The Act of Uniformity, also passed in 1559, indicated the form of worship and other practices of the Church of England. The principles of the new Church of England were formulated in the Thirty-nine Articles of Religion in 1563. These together are known as the Elizabethan Religious Settlement.

Anglicanism, the term for the main type of religion in England, then became a blend of various Protestant and Catholic influences. Calvinism was the dominant religion in Scotland, where it

Portrait of Elizabeth I, painted around 1592

was introduced by John Knox. There it came to be known as Presbyterianism.

During Elizabeth's reign there were battles with Spain and France.

Her reign, however, has been called a 'Golden Age' because of the great literature composed at this time, and the new trends in art, architecture and music. Theatre, too, flourished. William Shakespeare, perhaps the greatest of all writers in English, lived during her reign. Edmund Spenser (1552–99), Philip Sidney (1554–86) and John Donne (1572–1631) were other great poets of this age.

WILLIAM SHAKESPEARE (1564–1616)

Shakespeare composed a number of plays and sonnets. His works are applicable to different times and situations, and this accounts for his popularity even today. *As You Like It, Twelfth Night, Hamlet, Othello, King Lear, Julius Caesar* and *Macbeth* are among his many plays.

Mary, Queen of Scots

James V, king of Scotland, died in 1542. He was the son of James IV and Margaret Tudor. His six-day-old daughter Mary became the queen. Mary's mother was French, hence she was brought up in France, and was a Catholic. When she was sixteen years old, she was married to the dauphin, who would later be Francois II of France. But he died just two years later.

Mary returned to Scotland in 1561. There she married Lord Darnley, who was also a Catholic and her cousin. She became friendly with David Rizzio, an Italian who was her secretary, and was also a good musician, but he was killed in 1566. She then became friendly with the Earl of Bothwell, James Hepburn. It was believed that Lord Darnley had a role to play in the death of Rizzio. Now Darnley was killed in 1567, as somehow his house blew up, and it was thought the Earl of Bothwell had a hand in it. Mary then married Bothwell, but a revolt started, and Mary had to abdicate. The son of Darnley and Mary became the next king, James VI, but he was still a baby. Mary went to England, hoping that Elizabeth I, who was her cousin, would protect her. But Mary soon became suspected by the Protestants to be involved in a plot to kill Queen Elizabeth and was executed in 1587.

THE STUARTS

The Stuarts were the next dynasty to govern England. They had been in power over Scotland since 1371. James I was the first king of this dynasty to rule over England after the death of Elizabeth I. He was also known as James VI of Scotland. Thus a personal union of Scotland and England took place in 1603. Both countries had the same king, but were not politically united.

James's second son Charles I ruled England and Scotland from 1625 to 1649, followed by Charles II. Charles married Henrietta Maria, daughter of the king of France, in 1625. The people of England did not like this union as Henrietta was a Catholic.

THE PARLIAMENT

The English Parliament had gradually been growing from the time of the first signing of the Magna Carta in 1215. By 1500, the Parliament was already divided into two houses, which later became known as the House of Commons and the House of Lords. The knights and burghers (representatives of towns) formed the lower house, while nobles and clergy made up the upper house. The lower house had less power than the upper. However, the authority of both houses was restricted whenever there was a strong king or queen on the throne. There were often

The Puffin History of the World

conflicts between the king and the Parliament. These conflicts reached a height at the time of Charles I.

The Parliament in those days did not meet regularly. After becoming king, Charles called Parliament a few times. In 1628, the Parliament laid down some new rules called the Petition of Right. This constitutional document stated that the king could not bring in new taxes without the consent of the Parliament. Among its other aspects was the protection of people against imprisonment without sufficient cause. The king agreed to the petition but then he dissolved the Parliament and continued to rule without it. Eleven years passed before Charles desperately needed money and called the Parliament again. There was a rebellion in Scotland, and Charles needed the Parliament's help to raise taxes for the war. In November 1640, the Parliament met and put forward a number of demands. They insisted that it should be called every three years. It should not be dissolved without its own consent. This Parliament is called the Long Parliament.

Charles agreed. He had no option. In January 1642, however he led some soldiers into the Parliament and tried to arrest some leaders. The soldiers could not find those they went to arrest, but the people became angry. Some members of the Parliament thought there was a plot to bring back the power of the Pope, and had two of the king's men executed.

Very soon a civil war started.

THE PURITANS

Puritanism, a form of Protestantism, was growing in England and America. Early Puritans were mostly Anglicans. They disapproved of rituals and lived a plain and simple life. They wanted to impose their ideas on royalist Anglicans and other Protestant groups. There were a number of Puritans in the Parliament. (See later for more on the Puritan way of life.)

THE CIVIL WAR

The civil war is sometimes called 'the English Revolution' or 'the Puritan Revolution'. However, it was not just an English civil war as three countries were involved. It is now also called the War of the Three Kingdoms.

The war lasted from 1642 till 1651. The beginnings can be traced to Scotland, where there were conflicts and a rebellion against England. In Ireland there was a Catholic rebellion in 1641.

There were several periods of fighting between the Parliamentarians in England, also called the Roundheads, and the Royalists or supporters of the king, also called Cavaliers. The two main phases of the civil war were from 1642 to 1646 and from 1648 to 1649. Oliver Cromwell was one of the leaders of the Roundheads, and played a major role in the struggle.

The Roundheads got their name because many wore their hair cut short, close to the scalp. Royalists usually wore their hair in long ringlets.

The Roundheads were mainly Puritan or Presbyterian Protestants. Though King Charles was a Protestant, he followed the elaborate religious ceremonies of the Church of England, which were close to Catholicism.

At this time there was no full time army. Both sides had to recruit and train soldiers. At first neither side could gain an advantage. Then the Parliamentarians formed the New Model Army which was well trained and efficient. In 1645, the Parliament defeated the Royalists in the Battle of Naseby. By 1646, Charles was captured. Charles still remained the king but now there was confusion about the next course of action. Many Parliamentarians wanted to negotiate with him.

Even in captivity, Charles managed to organize more battles against the Roundheads. Cromwell and other senior leaders decided that Charles could not be trusted. They removed all the people in Parliament who still wanted to negotiate with him. The remaining Parliament was called the Rump Parliament. It decided to execute Charles. This was done on 30 January 1649.

LOVE OF ART

Charles I did not have much success as a monarch. But he was a great patron of art, architecture and theatre. He commissioned works of art by various artists, including Anthony van Dyck (1599–1601) who painted his portrait. Charles also collected art by famous artists including Titian and Rembrandt and built up a a collection of over 1750 paintings. The architect Inigo Jones (1573–1652) designed buildings for him. Charles promoted masques, dramas performed by masked players. Such masques included dances and were often performed at the court.

THE COMMONWEALTH

Then in March 1649, the Commonwealth or Republic was proclaimed. Fighting continued with King Charles II and his supporters and those of the Rump Parliament. Charles II, the son of Charles I, had been accepted as king in Scotland, and some parts of Ireland and England. He had been in exile, but returned to Scotland and then invaded England in 1651. The Parliamentarians gained victory in the Battle of Worcester in September 1651. Charles II escaped to France.

Ireland and Scotland

In Ireland the Confederates supported the Royalists of England. They were defeated by Cromwell in 1649. Civil war in Scotland took place from 1644 between Royalists and Covenanters. The Covenanters were Scottish Presbyterians who were committed to maintaining Presbyterianism in Scotland.

Reasons for the civil war

Historians cannot agree on why the civil war took place. Neither religion nor constitutional differences can explain these years. Some have seen the civil war as a class struggle, a confrontation between the common people and the nobles. Others have seen it as a conflict between the court bureaucracy and the rich landowners who paid the taxes. There were all these elements but no single cause. Localities and even families were divided in this war.

THE SEALED KNOT

During the time of the Commonwealth, the Sealed Knot was a secret society that tried to bring back royalty. They made eight attempts between 1652 and 1659, but failed. Today the Sealed Knot is a society that re-enacts battles of the civil war.

Oliver Cromwell

Cromwell, born in 1599, was a Puritan belonging to a farming family, educated at Cambridge. He became a member of Parliament in 1640. During the civil war he served as a military leader. He trained a cavalry regiment. They proved to be very efficient and came to be known as the Ironsides. He was initially a moderate, but later was part of the Rump Parliament and involved in the decision to execute Charles. In the early years of the Commonwealth he put down a rebellion in Ireland. He became the supreme commander of the English army. In 1653, the Rump Parliament decided to fight a war against Holland. The New Model Army did not like this, as Holland was a Protestant country. Cromwell led the army into London and removed the Rump Parliament.

Lord Protector of England

Another Parliament was formed, popularly called The Parliament of Saints, as it was mainly made up of Puritans. Oliver Cromwell became Lord Protector of England, that is, the head of the government. Taxes paid to the Church were abolished and civil marriage was introduced. There were rebellions by the Sealed Knot and other societies. In 1655, Cromwell divided the country into eleven provinces. Each was headed by a major general, a military governor, who functioned like a dictator. Cromwell also introduced the 'Reformation of Manners'. He wanted people to be pious and sober. Dancing was banned at weddings. Theatres were closed. Even Christmas was not to be celebrated. The common people did not like this, though this was actually the Puritan way of life. But England was successful in military exploits abroad. The army and navy were large and efficient. Jamaica was captured from Spain in 1655 and Dunkirk in 1658 during the Anglo-Spanish War of 1654–60. Cromwell was allied with France during this war.

WEAPONS

Muskets, cannon, pistols, swords and pikes were the weapons used in war. Full armour was not worn at this time, but breastplates and helmets were used.

Cromwell died in 1658. He was followed by his son Richard who ruled for only nine months.

Charles II

In 1660, England was without a king or ruler. Charles II, who was in France, was asked to return and become the king. He ruled till 1685. During his rule, his brother James was made the lord high admiral. However, James became a Roman Catholic in 1572. The Test Acts of 1673 and 1678 were passed. These said that no Catholics could be appointed to public offices. James resigned from his post as lord high admiral.

James II (ruled 1685–88)

Even though James was a Catholic, he became the king, as James II. He then appointed Catholics in the administration. And though Parliament was much stronger at this time, he dismissed it. James became very unpopular. In 1685, he suppressed a revolt in England and another in Scotland. Some members of Parliament united and invited William III of Orange to invade the country. After some struggles and minor conflicts, James left for France. This took place in 1688–89 and has been called the Glorious Revolution, as it represented the will of the people. It has also been called the Bloodless Revolution.

James returned to Ireland from France in 1690, along with some troops, but could not succeed in winning back the throne. He died in France in 1701.

Mary and William

Mary was a daughter of James II. However, Mary was a Protestant. She was married to William III of Orange (from Holland), who was also of the same faith. She and her husband now ruled England jointly. Scotland accepted the new rulers, but Ireland had to be subdued by war. Mary died in 1694 of smallpox. William III governed till 1702.

The Bill of Rights was passed in 1689. It stated that no Catholic could become king or queen. Even the wife or husband of a Catholic was disallowed. The Bill of Rights gave Parliament more authority, and restricted the power of the king. It was an important step towards constitutional government. Other Acts were the Toleration Act of 1689 and the Triennial Act of 1694. The Act of Settlement was passed in 1701. The Act again stated that Catholics could not become king or queen. These acts together formed the basis for future government.

Anne

Anne, who was Mary's sister, was also a Protestant and became the last Stuart ruler. She ruled from 1702 to 1714. Anne's son, the duke of Gloucester, died before her. According to the Act of Settlement, if Anne died without an heir the throne would go to Sophia, though there were many closer relatives. Sophia was a granddaughter of James I. She was a Protestant and the electress of Hanover. This was to prevent the Catholic descendants of James II from returning to power. After Anne's death, Sophia's son George I, elector of Hanover, became the king as Sophia had already died.

Stuarts in exile

The Roman Catholic Stuarts in exile wanted to return as kings, even after James II had died. Charles Edward, the grandson of James II, made attempts to invade England and regain the throne, but did not succeed. He died in 1788.

Plague and fire

England was affected not merely by wars and conflicts, but also by plague and fire. A great plague swept across London from the end of 1664, lasting more than a year. Over 75,000 people died, while others left London and took refuge in the countryside.

Not long after this, a fire broke out in the city of London in September 1666. Thirteen thousand houses and 80 churches were destroyed. At this time most of the houses were made of wood, and roads were narrow. After this most of the houses were rebuilt with brick and stone. There were no fire engines in those days. People used to put out fires with buckets of water, but this conflagration was too large. King Charles II ordered some houses to be blown up, so that a fire gap would be created, that is, the fire would not spread from one building to the next. This was done in certain areas,

LITERATURE

Great literature continued to be composed in England. Among the major poets there were John Milton (1608-74) and John Dryden (1631-1700). William Blake (1757-1827) is still known for his mystical poetry.

Satires include *A Tale of a Tub, Gulliver's Travels* and other books by Jonathan Swift (1667-1745). Daniel Defoe (1660-1731) is remembered for *Robinson Crusoe*. Samuel Johnson (1709-84) compiled *A Dictionary of the English Language*. The era of the romantic poets began after 1789. (See Chapter 25.)

Samuel Pepys (Pepys is pronounced 'peeps')

Samuel Pepys (1633-1703) worked in the government in the admiralty, which was in charge of the navy. He made the navy strong. But he is remembered for the diary that he wrote between 1 January 1660 and 31 May 1669. This journal is in shorthand, uses symbols, and was only deciphered and read in 1820. He describes life in London, including the great plague and the great fire. The original diary had 3012 pages.

but the blaze died down only after four days when the wind direction changed.

HOUSE OF HANOVER

George I was the first Hanoverian king of Britain. The Hanoverians ruled England till 1901. Hanover was in the present region of Germany, and at that time was part of the Holy Roman Empire. George became Elector of Hanover in 1698 and king of Britain in 1714. George spoke German and never learnt English, and was not liked in England. However, he had good ministers to help him. Among them was Robert Walpole. These administrators made the position of the House of Hanover secure.

Miniature portrait of King George I of England, painted in 1718

George I was succeeded by his son George II in 1727. He, too, was born in Hanover and considered a foreigner by the people of England. There were numerous rebellions during the reigns of these two kings. George III, grandson of George II, became the king in 1760. He was born in England and was more popular, though he rarely kept good health. He was followed by his son George IV in 1820.

SCOTLAND

After James I became king of England in 1603 (he was already James VI of Scotland) the two countries had one monarch, but the governments remained separate. Scotland had rejected Catholicism. Presbyterianism, a form of Protestantism, was its state religion. In 1707, an Act of Union was passed, joining both countries, which now came to be known as the United Kingdom of Great Britain. They would have one Parliament, but there would be separate judicial systems. The Churches would also be separate.

Among the great writers of Scotland were George Buchanan (1506–82) who wrote on Scottish history and the poets, Allan Ramsay (1686–1758), and Robert Burns (1759–96), who is the national poet of Scotland.

IRELAND

England attempted to impose her policies, language, and religion, on Ireland. The people of Ireland wanted the freedom to follow Roman Catholicism, and to live in their own way. As a result, there were numerous conflicts between Ireland and England, and a series of rebellions. Notable among them was the Nine Years' War from 1594–1603. Entire villages were destroyed along with crops, and many in Ireland died of starvation.

During the time of James I, English law was imposed and the Irish Parliament lost all independence. But rebellions continued. By the Plantation of Ulster, the English had been settled in parts of Ireland. In 1641, the Irish managed to drive them out of there, and thousands of English were killed. Conflicts continued and Ireland supported James II at the time of the Glorious Revolution. To ensure Irish support, Charles III concluded the Treaty of Limerick (1691), allowing the Irish some freedom of religion, and restoration of land. The English Parliament was against this treaty, and influenced the Parliament in Ireland. Irish trade was suppressed and the economy declined. Many Irish left and migrated to other countries, including Spain and France. Irish Protestants went to America. The struggle continued, and people in Ireland were inspired by the French and American Revolutions.

The prime minister of Britain, William Pitt the Younger, felt that a legislative union with Britain, along with rights for the Roman Catholics in Ireland, would do away with the threat of the constant revolts. The Act of Union was passed by the Irish Parliament and the union of Britain and Ireland became a reality on 1 January 1801.

WALES

Wales had been conquered by King Edward I of England in 1284, but was not united with England. By the Act of Union of 1536, part of Wales came under England, while another Act of 1543 merged the rest of Wales. People from Wales were elected to the Parliament in England, and English became the official language.

However, there were attempts to maintain and promote the Welsh language, and books in Welsh were brought out in the 16th and 17th centuries. A Welsh Bible was published in 1588. Among the notable works in Welsh is Morgan Llwyd's *Llyfr y Tri Aderyn* (Book of the Three Birds, 1653), a mystical and psychological work, and Ellis Wynne's *Gweledigaetheu y Bardd Cwsc* (Visions of the Sleeping Bard, 1703). Poetry, too, flourished, and in the 18th century free verse came into use. William Williams of Pantycelyn (1717–91) wrote both prose and poetry, and is known for his long poems and hymns in Welsh and English. Among his poems were *Golwg Ar Deyrnas Crist* (A View of Christ's Kingdom). Ann Griffiths (d.1805) composed mystical hymns.

9
West Central Asia and Russia

Central Asia is a vast region that can broadly be divided into two parts: east Central Asia, including Tibet and the Xingiang region of China, and west Central Asia, consisting of the present countries of Kazakhstan, Kyrgyzstan, Tajikistan, Turkmenistan and Uzbekistan. Between 1450 and 1500 there were numerous small states in west Central Asia.

In the early 16th century, there were several empires struggling for control along the borders of Central Asia. Among them were the Safavids of Iran, Muscovy (Russia), various Mongol groups, and the Manchu of China. Within Central Asia, there were khanates or small kingdoms under Kazakhs, Uzbeks and other groups.

In about 1470, some Kazakh groups settled in the present region of Kazakhstan. They were led by Jani Beg and Girey. Kasim Khan, son of Jani Beg, controlled the Kipchak steppes. Under him were over a million warriors.

SHAIBANID DYNASTY

The Shaibanid dynasty was also in Central Asia. The Uzbek Shaibanids were descended from Shiban, the fifth son of Jochi, who was the eldest son of Genghis Khan. Muhammad Shibani, a leader of the Shaibanid dynasty, moved into Samarkand in 1500, pushing out the descendants of Timur. He was also a writer and poet. He was connected with the Yasawiyya sufis and called himself 'imam of the age'. He was allied with the Ottomans, but was killed in 1510 in Merv, in a battle with the Safavids.

The Timurids briefly regained Transoxiana, but the Uzbeks reoccupied it in 1512. Shibani's successors ruled Samarkand, which from 1557 was known as the Amirate of Bukhara. The khanate of Khorazm, later known as the khanate of Khiva, was founded at Urgench (in present Turkmenistan) in 1512.

THE CARAVAN TRADE

Indian merchants controlled the caravan trade between India, China, Iran, Afghanistan and Central Asia. Some caravans to India consisted of 40,000 animals carrying loads. At the time of the Mughal emperor Aurangzeb, 1,00,000 horses were imported every year from Bukhara and Afghanistan. Trade from Russia, too, passed through Central Asia.

DECLINE OF THE UZBEKS

The Uzbek khanates constantly fought against one another. This led to their eventual decline. With the opening of sea routes, the overland caravan trade, too, was slowed down and the economy suffered. The khanates were always under threat from Russia to the north and Iran to the west. The Astrakhan dynasty ruled Bukhara from 1599 to 1785. Farghana separated from Bukhara, and formed the khanate of Kokand in 1710, when Shah Rukh of the Ming Uzbek clan declared his independence. Later, Alim Khan founded a new khanate in Kokand in 1798.

Mir Masum of the Mangit Uzbek clan married a princess of

the Astrakhan dynasty. The Mangits or Mangudai then reigned over Bukhara from 1785 to 1920, when it became part of the Soviet territory. In the 18th century, other new khanates and dynasties were established. The Kongirat or Hongirad Uzbek family founded a dynasty in Khiva and the rulers took the title of khan in 1804.

RUSSIA
In Russia, the kingdom of Muscovy (Moscow) was growing in power.

The Tsars
Ivan III
Under Ivan III (ruled 1462–1505) Muscovy emerged as a powerful state. Ivan had added Novgorod and Tver to its territories, and refused to pay tribute to the Mongols, thus ending their dominance. He invaded Lithuania-Poland, and took over some border towns. By 1500, Muscovy or Russia had become a great European power.

Vasili III Ivanovich
Ivan was succeeded by Vasili III (ruled 1505–33). Vasili took over Pskov in 1510, Smolensk in 1514, and Ryazan in 1521, thus further expanding the kingdom of Muscovy.

Ivan IV Vasilyevich (ruled 1547–84)
Ivan IV succeeded Vasili III in 1533, but at that time was only three years old. Initially his mother was the regent, but she soon died. He was then taken care of by boyars (nobles). They often neglected him and were cruel to him, and Ivan's disturbed childhood caused him to develop a cruel temperament. Though Ivan III had already called himself tsar, Ivan IV was the first to use the title officially, when he began to rule in 1547.

Marriages

Ivan IV married Anastasia Romanovna. She died in 1560, and Ivan became imbalanced after that. The couple had three children. Their first son, Dmitri, drowned in 1553. Ivan IV himself killed his second son Ivan in 1582, in a fit of temper, though he immediately regretted it. The third son, Fyodor I Ivanovich, became the tsar on his death. Ivan III married six more times. Another Dmitri, the child of his seventh wife Maria Nagaya, was the only other surviving child at the time of Ivan's death.

Expansion of territory

Ivan further expanded his territory, and annexed the khanate of Kazan in 1552 and of Astrakhan in 1556. In 1571 and 1572 he had to defend his territories from the Tatars of Crimea. He fought what is known as the Livonian War (1558–83). This aimed at the control of territories in the present region of Estonia and Latvia. Russia had initial successes, but finally lost territory. From 1581 to 1583, most of the Ob river basin, that is part of Siberia, was occupied.

Administration

Ivan IV also reformed the administration and tried to remove corruption. He created a new law code in 1550. In 1556, he divided Russia into two parts. One part, the oprichnina, was under his own control. The other part, zemschina, was under a council of boyars. But Ivan indirectly controlled even the zemschina through the oprichniki, a kind of secret or personal police. He began to have people tortured and killed, accusing them of various crimes without any real evidence. After a rebellion in Novgorod he killed most of the people there between 1569 and 1570.

In 1581, he passed a law restricting the movement of peasants, thus laying the basis for serfdom. He entered into trade treaties with England.

Ivan IV is remembered for his terrible acts, but at the same time he laid the foundation of a strong Russian state. In later years he lost his mental balance. He died in 1584.

Fyodor I (1584–98)

Fyodor I, the son of Ivan IV, was mentally weak. His brother-in-law Boris Godunov was the regent. In 1597, a law was passed which legalized serfdom. Russia continued to grow and prosper at this time. But Fyodor had no children, and Ivan's son Dmitri from his seventh wife had died in 1591. It was thought that Godunov had got him killed.

Even so, after Fyodor's death, Boris Godunov was elected the tsar.

Smutnoye Vremnya—the time of troubles

Boris Godunov died in 1605. Though Dmitri had died, there was a mystery surrounding his death, and some believed he was alive. Hence a false Dmitri, who called himself Dmitri I, was supported by Poland and Lithuania, and became the tsar. One year later he was killed. The boyars chose Prince Vasili Shuysky, a boyar, as the next tsar. The peasants and Cossacks did not like this, and another false Dmitri, Dmitri II, launched an attack from the south. Meanwhile Sigismund III, of Poland invaded from the west. Sweden sent troops to help Vasili. After some years of fighting, Vasili was removed from the throne in 1610. Wladislaw, the son of King Sigismund of Poland, was a candidate for the throne. A Polish army reached Moscow in his support. But a Russian army finally defeated the Poles in Moscow in 1612. Then a Zemsky Sobor (National Assembly) was called, which elected Mikhail (Michael) Fyodorovich Romanovna as the tsar. Michael was a boyar, and was also the great-nephew of Anastasia, the first wife of Ivan III.

THE ROMANOVS

The Romanov dynasty ruled Russia for 300 years.

Mikhail Fyodorovich (1613–45), Aleksei I (1645–76) and Fyodor III (1676–82) were the first three Romanov tsars. At this time laws were passed which gave landlords even greater control over the serfs. More and more serfs began to run away to escape their poor conditions. Many went to regions along the lower Volga, Don and Dnieper rivers, where there were Cossack settlements. In 1670, Stenka (Stephen) Razin, a Cossack, led a peasant revolt, but it was finally suppressed. In 1654, the Cossacks of Ukraine, at that time under Poland, started a revolt and accepted Aleksei I as the ruler. Russia then fought a war against Poland (1654–67) and won. Smolensk and east Ukraine, in which Kiev was located, once again became part of Russia.

The Ukraine Orthodox Church was allied with Constantinople, while the Russian Orthodox Church was independent. To bring the two together, the Russian patriarch named Nikon introduced reforms in the Russian Church. But this led to a schism or split in 1654. In 1667, those who would not accept the reforms, known as the Raskolniki or old believers, were not allowed to be part of the Russian Church. Many were tortured and killed, others escaped.

The main event during the reign of Fyodor III was a war against the Ottomans in which Russia was victorious.

Ivan V and Sophia

Pyotr Alekseyevich, or Peter I, tsar from 1682 to 1725, was born in 1672, and was the half-brother of Fyodor III. From 1682 he became joint tsar with his half-brother Ivan V, until Ivan died in 1696. Ivan's sister Sophia acted as the regent as Ivan was mentally weak. Sophia lived in the Moscow Kremlin, where women were kept in seclusion in a separate part of the palace known as Terem. She was already influential at the court when her brother Fyodor was ruling (1676–82). Peter was a strong personality, 6 ft 8 inches (203 cm) tall.

Pyotr (Peter) I

In 1689, Peter took over power. He sent Sophia to a convent and continued as joint ruler with Ivan. However, his mother Natalya became the power behind the throne until her death in 1694. Ivan died a natural death two years later.

Eudoxia Lopukhina was Peter's first wife. Peter married her in 1689 and divorced her in 1698. He also had a long relationship with Anna Mons, the daughter of a Dutch merchant. In 1707, he married Marta Helena Skowroñska, who later became the empress Yekaterina (Catherine) I.

Bronze statue of Peter I located in St Petersburg, completed in 1782

Peter fought a number of wars. Azov was conquered from the Turks in 1696. He took part in the Great Northern War (1700–21) and captured territory for Russia.

The army was reorganized, a navy founded and court functioning changed. Peter began the construction of ships for the Russian navy in 1695. In 1696, the navy was successful in a war in the Sea of Azov against the Ottomans. In 1697, Peter visited England, France, Germany and the Netherlands to look at conditions there, and returned after almost two years with many new ideas.

Modernization

Russia was modernized. At Peter's court, more Westernized clothes were worn. He ordered the boyars to cut their beards, and those who retained them had to pay an annual beard tax of 100 rubles. Trade expanded, there were more manufacturing industries, and new roads and canals were constructed. There were new educational institutions, including some for technical training. Science began to develop, and Peter supported Galileo's theories. Industry and trade flourished. A census was held for the first time and the population was counted. A postal service, too, was inaugurated. There was tolerance and freedom in the practice of religion.

A new calendar, the Julian, was used from 1700, instead of the traditional Russian calendar.

St Petersburg

Despite initial losses, territory was acquired in the great Northern War (1700–21). By the Treaty of Nystad, Russia acquired Livonia, Estonia, Ingria, part of Karelia, and some Baltic islands. Among the areas earlier taken from Sweden was a marshland region, where Peter began the construction of St Petersburg in 1703. Because of poor working and living conditions, many workers died. By 1714, 35,000 stone buildings were erected here. St Petersburg became the new capital of Russia. It was a great centre of art and culture. In 1721, Muscovy was renamed Russia, and Peter took the title of emperor, instead of tsar.

After Peter I (1725-62)

After Peter's death in 1725, there were a number of rulers.

Peter's son Aleksei had already died in prison after he was

arrested for a plot to overthrow his father. Peter's second wife Catherine came to the throne, but died two years later. There were several other rulers. Among them, Peter's youngest daughter Elizabeth provided a strong administration from 1741 to 1762. She was followed by a nephew, Peter III, but he was killed and succeeded by his wife Catherine.

Yekaterina (Catherine) II (ruled 1762-96)

Catherine II was also known as Catherine the Great. She waged several wars and expanded the empire. Among them were the Russo-Turkish wars fought between 1768 and 1774 and between 1787 and 1792. Ochakov, a Black Sea port, and other territory in the Crimea and elsewhere were acquired. Other wars against Poland led to three partitions of the region, and huge territorial gains of around 4,68,000 sq km.

Catherine further modernized the Russian court, and French became the court language. St Petersburg came to be called 'The Venice of the North'. Catherine initially wanted to improve the conditions of the serfs, but the nobles opposed this. After the French Revolution of 1789, she was afraid of similar problems in Russia, and so dropped all liberal policies. In fact, a great peasant rebellion led by a Cossack, Ivanovich Pugachev, had taken place earlier in 1775 and been suppressed.

Pavel (Paul) I

Catherine's son Paul I (ruled 1796-1801) succeeded her. He joined in the Second Coalition Wars against France, and passed laws in favour of the serfs. Paul was killed in 1801 by a group of nobles.

LIFE OF THE PEOPLE

In Russia nobles and higher classes began to live in great luxury. The peasants and serfs survived in poor conditions. Some aspects of the lives of the people are given below:

Clothes

Russian tsars and emperors wore richly decorated crowns and were seated on elaborate thrones to indicate their power. Up to the 17th century these were often made by Turkish or Persian craftsmen, though later Russian craftsmen were usually used. For instance, the throne of Aleksei Mikhailovich had an inner base of sandalwood, covered with gold and silver plates, and inlaid with turquoise, diamonds and other precious and semi-precious stones. When Ivan and Peter ruled together, a two seated-silver throne was created for them. Their clothes, caps, swords, and all the other items they wore or carried, were also elaborate.

Russian boyars or noblemen wore fur hats. Cossacks and Turkics wore bashlyks or cone-shaped hoods on their heads, and later these became popular with Russians, too. There were also different types of hats and caps, worn for protection from the cold. These usually covered the ears and head. Men wore long tunics or shirts over trousers, and boots. Valenki boots, made of wool felt, began to be worn from the 18th century. Women in rural areas wore long tunics with straps, over vests or undershirts. Married women wore headdresses known as kokoshniks, while those of unmarried women were slightly different. During the 18th century, middle-class women were influenced by European fashion styles.

Food

Food continued to include porridge, soups, stews, various meats and traditional items such as pirogi and kasha (see Volume 1), but in addition, new food items were introduced through contact with other areas. Though potatoes reached Russia by the end of the 18th century, they were not a popular food at this time. In the markets of St Petersburg at the time of Catherine II, wheat and wheat products, barley, oats, rye, beef, mutton, pork, poultry, wild game, butter, eggs, milk, oil, fruits and vegetables, both dried and fresh, sugar and nuts could be bought. In addition there were wines from France and Hungary, raisins, cheeses from England and the Netherlands, coffee and tea, imported fresh fruits like apples and watermelons, along with herbs and spices. In the court and palaces of the rich, chefs from France and Italy prepared special items. The main vegetables were cabbage, beets, onions and garlic.

Languages used

Russian was the main language used at this time. Mongol and Turkish words, as well as Persian and Arabic which had become components of Turkish, became part of Russian by the 14th century, and the Turkish language was used at court by the 15th century. Russian noblemen, during the 15th to 17th centuries, sometimes took on Tatar (Turkish) surnames. Russian words for a number of foods as well as other items were borrowed from Turkish. Some of these words in Turkish were originally in another language.

Books

Among the notable books of this time is the *Nikon Chronicle*.

It is a 16th century collection of East Slavic chronicles, named after Nikon, a patriarch (head) of the Russian Orthodox Church. This collection was made at the time of Ivan IV. It can be called the official Russian history of that time. An illustrated version was published in the 1560s and 1570s.

An autobiography, *The Life of The Archpriest Avvakum* (1672–75), translated only in the 20th century, is a good description of those times. Among other noted writers was Aleksandr Nikolayevich Radishchev, whose book *Journey from St Petersburg to Moscow* (1790) is considered his best. But after its publication he was sent to exile in Siberia.

Some other aspects

Moscow State University was founded in 1755 with the help of Mikhail Vasilyevich Lomonosov (1711–65), a noted scientist, chemist, astronomer and writer, and a scholar of the Russian language. Lomonosov wrote poetry, as well as a history of Russia. Mosaic art was revived through his efforts.

A porcelain factory was constructed outside St Petersburg, and produced beautiful articles. Russia was also known for mosaics and work in precious and semi-precious stones.

ENTERTAINMENT

Entertainment in the cities included masquerades, balls and theatre. Bylini, or epic folk songs, were composed and sung. Bylini is also called starina (what is old) by peasants. Bylini comes from the word bylina, meaning 'what happened'. Bogatyrs, a sort of superhero, were the chief characters in the bylini. Svyagator, a giant warrior, was one of the bogatyrs.

Skomorokhi were professional storytellers. It was said that they sang their stories so beautifully that they cast a spell on the listener. Because of this, Tsar Aleksei banned them in 1648.

10
India
1500–1800

In north India various dynasties of sultans had been ruling from CE 1206. Their territories had been steadily declining. The last of the sultans was the Lodi dynasty.

THE MUGHALS

Defeating the last Lodi sultan, as well as coalitions of Rajput princes, Babar founded the Mughal dynasty in India in 1526. Originally from Farghana in Central Asia, Babar had conquered the region of Afghanistan after having lost his own kingdom.

In India Babar defeated Ibrahim Lodi at Panipat to the northwest of Delhi in 1526. In 1527, he won the Battle of Khanua, followed by the Battle of Ghaghara in 1529. In these three battles Babar had vanquished most of the rulers of north India. Before he had time to consolidate his territories, he died in 1530.

Humayun and Sher Shah

Babar was succeeded by his son Humayun, who had to fight many battles to try and hold on to his territories. In 1540, he was overpowered by the Afghan Sher Khan, who then took the title

Sher Shah. Humayun escaped to Iran. Sher Shah and his successors ruled till 1555, when Humayun succeeded in reoccupying Delhi. He died soon after, after a fall from the steps of his library, and was succeeded by his thirteen-year-old son, Akbar.

Akbar and later emperors

Akbar (ruled 1556–1605) was the greatest Mughal emperor who extended Mughal rule over much of north India. He was known for

The Mughal emperor Akbar

his liberal policies, and for founding a new religion, Tauhid-i-ilahi. This new faith combined the best elements of various religions, but did not continue after his death.

Jahangir (1605–27), Shah Jahan (1628–58) and Aurangzeb (1659–1707) were the next Mughal rulers, after which the dynasty began to decline.

At the time of the later Mughals, there were devastating invasions of Nadir Shah (1739) and the Afghan Ahmad Shah Abdali (1761).

Art, architecture and crafts

Miniature painting flourished at the time of Jahangir. Shah Jahan was known for his magnificent architectural marvels, the greatest of which is the Taj Mahal, built entirely of white marble. Crafts included fine pottery, brocade, embroidered silks and other textiles.

Agriculture

Crops grown included rice, wheat, barley, lentils and sugar cane, fruits and vegetables. Grapes, melons and plums were introduced by the Mughals from Kabul (Afghanistan). The Portuguese had begun establishing settlements on the west coast from 1500, and papayas, pineapples and cashewnuts were introduced by them, along with tobacco. Coffee was grown from the 17th century. Potatoes were introduced but overall growing conditions were not suitable for them.

Cities and markets

Under the Mughals there developed great cities and wonderful markets. Trade too expanded. Lahore, Agra, Delhi and Ahmadabad were among the large cities. But numerous wars, as well as the grand buildings made particularly by Shah Jahan, took a toll on the economy.

HOW BABAR BECAME KING

Babar wrote his memoirs in Turkish, known as the *Babar Namah*.

It begins with this sentence: 'In the month of Ramzan, in the year 899 (June 1494) in the province of Farghana, in my twelfth year, I became king.'

Babar goes on to describe Farghana and its capital Andizhan. The river Andizhan passes through Farghana. The country has plenty of grain, wonderful fruit, melons, grapes and pears. Then he describes his family, his father, uncles, brothers, sisters, mother and grandmother. The descriptions are realistic. For instance, about his father, Umar Shaykh Mirza, Babar says that he was short and fat, with a round beard. And when he had to fasten his tunic, he had to hold in his stomach; if he let it go, the ties often broke.

Umar Shaykh ruled in Farghana, while in Samarkand to the west reigned his elder brother Ahmad Mirza. Sultan Ahmad Mirza and Sultan Mahmud Khan of another kingdom combined their armies together to fight Umar Shaykh. But just at this time he fell down a ravine and died, when he was flying his doves from the top of a fort. Umar was just 39 years old.

And Babar became king.

These memoirs are full of wonderful descriptions of everything Babar saw and did, and how he finally reached India.

OTHER KINGDOMS

There were independent kingdoms in various parts of India, as well as local rulers and minor chieftains. Some of the kingdoms acknowledged the Mughal emperor as the supreme ruler. Among the kingdoms were those of Avadh, Bengal, Hyderabad and Mysore. There were many more.

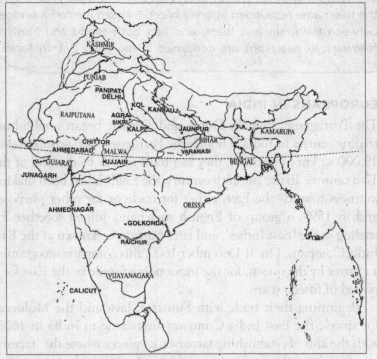

Mughal empire at the end of the 17th century

Marathas and Sikhs were two groups who were gaining in power. Maratha expansion began under Shivaji who inherited his father Shahji's estate in 1647. The Marathas challenged Mughal power but were defeated by the Afghan invader Ahmad Shah Abdali in 1761.

The Sikhs, originally a religious group, gradually created their own kingdom in north-west India.

SIKHISM

The Sikh religion was founded by Guru Nanak (1469–1539) who was followed by nine other gurus. The Sikh religion believes in an eternal God, who has no form. God could be called by any name, but the true name resounded in one's heart. Sikhism formed a bridge between Hinduism and Islam, and had both Hindu and Muslim followers. Its teachings are contained in the *Guru Granth Sahib*.

EUROPEANS IN INDIA

The Portuguese, French, Dutch and English began establishing trading centres in India. Though the Portuguese had acquired over 19,000 sq km of territory, they lost most of this by the end of the 17th century. In the late 16th century, the English had been making journeys towards the East, either for trade or for other purposes and in 1599, a group of English merchants joined together for trading in the 'East Indies', and later came to be known as the East India Company. On 31 December 1600, this company was granted a charter by the queen, for the monopoly of trade in the East for a period of fifteen years.

Beginning their trade with Sumatra, Java and the Moluccas for spices, the East India Company first came to India in 1608, with the aim of establishing factories, or places where the 'factors' or officials of the company would reside. With the permission

The Taj Mahal

of the Mughal emperor Jahangir, the first factory was set up at Surat in 1613, though not before a battle with the Portuguese who had already occupied the region. Additional factories were soon established in west, east and south India. Among the most important were those in Bombay and Madras. The Dutch had trading settlements along the coasts which were gradually conquered by the British.

The British focus then turned towards the Mughals and other Indian rulers. Conflicts began with the Mughal emperor, and in Bengal. By 1690, agreements were made which gave them trading rights. Further rights were granted in 1715. The Battle of Plassey of 1757, won by bribery, gave the British control over Bengal, and the Battle of Buxar, of 1764, provided control over Avadh. The Mughal emperor, Shah Alam II, at that time in exile, had found refuge at the court of Shuja-ud-daulah, nawab of Avadh. Shah Alam had also participated in the Battle of Buxar. In the meantime the British and the French were struggling to gain control over south India. The English and the French fought a number of fierce wars, involving local rulers as well, before the French were finally defeated. The Marathas, and the states of Hyderabad and Mysore were all involved in this struggle.

Hyderabad

In 1713, the Mughal emperor Farrukhsiyar appointed Qamruddin, a noble, as the governor of the Deccan. Gradually Qamruddin asserted his independence, though he still acknowledged the Mughal emperor. He received the title Asaf Jah and founded the Asaf Jahi dynasty in 1724. The Asaf Jahis were known as nizams, the term for a governor.

The large area over which they ruled was known as the state of Hyderabad, and existed till 1948.

HOW THE ASAF JAHIS GOT THEIR FLAG

One day Qamruddin went to meet a Sufi saint, whose name was Hazrat Nizamuddin Aurangabadi. Qamruddin was quite hungry when he reached there and so the saint gave him a plateful of kulchas (flat bread), of which he ate seven. Aurangabadi therefore predicted that there would be seven kings in the dynasty, and he was later proved right.

Though there were three more rulers, they did not enjoy the title Asaf Jah. Because of this prediction, the Asaf Jahis had a unique flag. It was yellow, with a blue kulcha (type of flat bread) in the middle of it.

The British did not take over Hyderabad, but a Resident and British troops were stationed there. Hyderabad had to pay two and a half million rupees every year for their upkeep.

Mysore

Mysore was a large independent state, ruled by Hyder Ali followed by his son Tipu Sultan. After the third Anglo-Mysore War, fought from 1790 to 1792, Tipu Sultan had to surrender half his dominions and pay an indemnity to the British.

Three wars (1772–1818) against the Marathas further consolidated British territory.

Thus by 1800, the British were the dominant power in India. The French and the Portuguese retained small territories on the west coast and south India respectively.

The role of the British government

The East India Company had originally come to India for trade purposes. Later it started governing territories in India. At this time the British government began to impose restrictions on the Company. A Board of Control was set up in 1784 which regulated the Company's actions.

The Company also lost its exclusive right to trade in India.

Robert Clive, a portrait

ROBERT CLIVE (1725–74)

Robert Clive had a key role in establishing British power in India. He was at first a clerk in the East India Company, but then joined the Company's military service. He was noted for his strategic skills. In 1757, he along with Admiral Watson won the Battle of Plassey and recaptured Calcutta from Siraj-ud-daulah, the nawab of Bengal. Clive then entered into intrigues to replace Siraj-ud-daulah with Mir Jafar. Clive also became the governor of Bengal. He stayed in England between 1760 and 1765 and was given the title of Baron Clive of Plassey in the Irish peerage.

He returned to Bengal in 1765 as governor and commander in chief. The Battle of Buxar had just taken place and Clive had introduced political changes by which the East India Company became the real ruler of Bengal. Clive also recognized Shah Alam II as emperor of India, and in return was granted the right to collect revenue and administer civil government in Bengal, Bihar and Orissa. After making large sums of money, Clive retired in 1767. In England he was accused of corruption though his service to his country was also recognized.

Clive later became depressed and ended his own life.

11

The Ottoman Empire 1500–1800

The Ottoman Turks established a vast empire.

THE BEGINNINGS

A kingdom was founded near the Black Sea coast around 1300 by a Turk named Osman. This later expanded and covered a huge territory. One of the greatest Ottoman achievements was the conquest of Constantinople in 1453 from the declining Byzantine empire.

AFTER 1500

The empire continued to expand after 1500.

The Sultans
Salim I (ruled 1512–20)

Salim I succeeded the sultan Bayazid II in 1512. Two years later the Ottomans defeated the Safavids and captured the Iranian capital of Tabriz. During the years 1516–17 they conquered Syria and Egypt, ending the Mamluk sultanate in Egypt and began to exercise control over Mecca.

Sulaiman I

Sulaiman the Magnificent (ruled 1520-66)

Salim's son was Sulaiman I. He came to be known as Sulaiman the Magnificent in western countries. This name was given to him for two reasons. Firstly, the empire reached the height of its power and extent at this time, and secondly, his court was grand and luxurious. Sulaiman I made the administration more efficient, introduced new laws and reformed old ones. As a result, he was called Kanuni, which means 'the lawgiver'. Islamic law is contained in the Sharia, a collection of teachings on Islam. However, under the Ottomans there were other laws as well. These additional laws developed gradually. Under Sulaiman these laws received their final form, and no further changes were made to them.

Sulaiman made several conquests. He occupied Belgrade (Serbia) in 1521. He defeated Hungary in 1526. In 1529 he started a siege of Vienna (Austria) but withdrew in the winter. In 1538 the Ottoman troops led by Khayr ad-din (Barbarossa) defeated the combined forces of Venice.

He conquered Baghdad and the area around it, then under Iran in 1534. Next he captured Transylvania, the region of present Romania.

The Knights of St John

The navy helped to expand Ottoman power. The island of Rhodes was captured from the Knights of St John in 1523. These knights were a military order who also owned land. (See Volume 1 for more on these knights.) The knights then moved to Malta. But the Ottomans under Sulaiman attacked them here too in 1565. The Turks crossed the seas and besieged the island.

  The Puffin History of the World

Jean Parisot de Valette, the head of the order, led the knights. Ships and troops from Sicily came to their aid. The Turks were crushed. A new city and capital was founded in Malta. It came to be known as Valetta.

Death at Szigetvar

Sulaiman was known for his courage in battle. He made various conquests. In 1566 he died during the siege of the Szigetvar fort in Hungary.

Salim II

Salim II (ruled 1566–74) succeeded Sulaiman. At this time, Austria paid tribute to the Ottomans after the Peace of Adrianople in 1568.

Defeat at Lepanto

In 1570 the Ottomans invaded Cyprus and took it over. Cyprus was at that time under Venice. Venice had been fighting against the Turks for many years. The Turkish fleet, based at Corfu, attacked other regions, and reached close to Venice. Now Venice asked for help from other European powers. A large fleet was organized by Pope Pius V. It included ships from Venice, Genoa, Spain and his own Papal States. Together, this fleet known as the Holy League consisted of 208 oar-propelled galleys and six galleases.

Each ship was loaded with a number of guns. The fleet of the Holy League fought against 230 galleys of the Turks in the Gulf of Lepanto (now known as the Gulf of Corinth) near Greece. The Turks were defeated in 1571 and lost most of their vessels. Their naval power was reduced, and Turkish control over the Mediterranean came to an end.

Though the Turks soon acquired more ships, their navy did not regain its former strength.

TYPES OF SHIPS AT THIS TIME

Galleys: ships that used oars and had sails. They included merchant ships and war galleys.

Galleases: larger ships. They had more sails and oars than a galley.

Carrack: ships that were deep and broad with three to four masts, and both square and other sails. They were used as merchant ships and for exploration.

Caravel: sailing ships smaller than a carrack, also used in long voyages of exploration.

Galleon: ships that were long and narrow. Used in war, they were faster and easy to manoeuvre.

Frigate: warships of many types are called frigates. In the 17th and 18th centuries, the term was used for sailing ships that were fitted with guns.

Fusta or galliot: ships that were like small galleys, using both oars and sails.

Murad III (ruled 1574–95)

At the time of Murad III, several territories were gained from Iran. He also acquired territory in Georgia and Yemen. However corruption during his reign led to some decline.

LATER DAYS

Iran recovered most of her territories, including Baghdad, at the time of the Safavid ruler Shah Abbas I. The Ottomans regained these territories in 1639. They held power over the vast empire till around 1680, but after this a decline started. In 1683, they were defeated in an attempt to capture Vienna. In 1687 Venice seized Athens from the Ottomans.

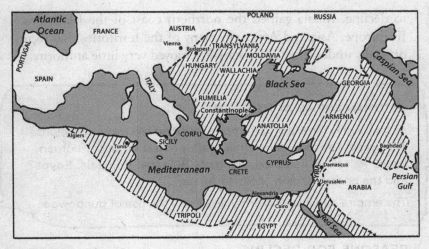

The Ottoman empire
1580

The extent of the Ottoman empire

Ahmad III (ruled 1703–30)

The Ottomans won the battle of Prut against Russia in 1711. Azov, which had been conquered, was returned to the Ottomans. But meanwhile the Safavids threatened to invade.

Ahmad's rule was unpopular because of the luxurious style in which he and his nobles lived. A revolt by the janissaries led him to abdicate. (Janissaries were the elite soldiers who guarded the sultan and his household.)

Mahmud I (ruled 1730–54)

Mahmud I was placed on the throne by Ahmad III. Mahmud was Ahmad's nephew.

After this there were many more defeats, and by 1792, much territory was lost to Austria and Russia. The Ottoman power began to decline. Russia gained the northern coast of the Black Sea. In Europe, Asia and Africa, in many of the territories that were officially under them, they actually enjoyed very little authority.

> **OTTOMAN EMPIRE AT ITS HEIGHT**
>
> At its height, the Ottoman empire included the present regions of Turkey, Greece, Macedonia, part of Arabia, Syria, Jordan, Israel, Palestine, Lebanon, Hungary, Bulgaria, Romania, Egypt and the coastal region of North Africa.
>
> The empire had a strong army and knew the use of gunpowder.

REASONS FOR DECLINE

Many causes are said to be responsible for the Ottoman decline. For one thing, the empire had become too large to control. Maintaining the boundaries through war was proving expensive. New types of weapons were used against them, and stronger fortresses had to be built. There were revolts in various parts of the empire, and local rulers and officials increased their power. European states, too, had grown in prominence and this contributed to the Ottoman defeat.

The sultans lived in great luxury in their palaces and did not pay much attention to governance.

The pashas and other local governors began to grow more powerful.

RELIGION

Islam was the official religion in the Ottoman empire. After 1517, the sultan was also known as the khalifa. Khalifa (caliph) is the term for a religious head of an Islamic group. However, even though they followed Islam, Ottomans were usually tolerant of other religions. Different religions in the empire were given protection.

Among them were large groups of Orthodox Christians, Catholics and Jews. Islamic law was not enforced on non-Muslims, who were free to follow their own beliefs. The millet system gave minority groups some power over their own communities. This system provided separate legal courts for the personal law of religious minorities. There was an Orthodox Christian millet headed by a patriarch, an Armenian Christian millet, as well as other millets.

By the devshirme system, some non-Muslim male children of the empire had to be handed over to the government. These boys had to adopt Islam, and were in theory slaves, but actually often held high positions.

FRATRICIDE

Under Sultan Salim, fratricide, that is, the killing of brothers, started. It continued among successive sultans until 1595. Whenever a new sultan took power, he would lock up all his brothers. As soon as the reigning sultan had a son, his imprisoned brothers would be killed. All the sultans who came to the throne followed this practice.

LITERATURE, ART AND ARCHITECTURE

Books were written in Persian, Turkish and Arabic. Arabic was used mainly for works on science and religion and philosophy. Painting and music flourished particularly during the reigns of Sulaiman I and Salim II.

Numerous mosques, madrasas (schools) and tombs were constructed.

The Ottomans had their own court architects, who designed their buildings. Koca Mimar Sinan (1490–1588) was the greatest Ottoman architect. Among his remarkable creations are the Sulaiman Mosque in Istanbul and the Selimiye Mosque in Edirme. His pupils designed another grand mosque, the Sultan

The Blue Mosque

Ahmad or Blue Mosque of Istanbul, constructed between 1609 and 1616. The mosque has one main large dome, eight small domes and six minarets. The inside is decorated with blue tiles.

During the reign of Ahmad III baroque and rococo art and architecture styles were used.

Royal officials were also in charge of designing carpets, textiles, tiles and metal items, which were made in special workshops. Paintings too were stylized. Other Ottoman crafts included stained glass, silver and goldwork as well as glazed and decorated pottery.

Items were imported from other regions.

ISTANBUL AND OTHER CITIES

Across the vast Ottoman empire were many ports and cities. Istanbul, earlier known as Constantinople, was the largest city. Coffee from Yemen, textiles and spices from India, woven fabrics from North Africa, and fine silks were among the main commodities. There were coffee houses in many cities, which became centres for holding discussions and for the exchange of ideas.

Trade took place across the empire, from Europe to Africa, and all kinds of products reached Istanbul. Cairo and Damascus were among the other large cities. Each region had its own special products and items of trade. Goods traded included silk and other textiles, Chinese porcelain, indigo and other dyes, spices, musk and rhubarb.

Istanbul was one of the names used for the city at the time of the Ottomans and even earlier. But the Ottomans continued to use other names, such as Konstantiniyye, even on their coins. It was only after 1930 that Istanbul became accepted as the only recognized name of the city.

KARAGOZ AND HACIVAT—SHADOW PUPPET THEATRE

According to a story, Karagoz, a man from a village, and Hacivat, from a city, were constructing a palace in Bursa. They made so many jokes that all the other workers kept laughing, and could not do any work. The supervisor had their heads cut off, but strangely they did not die. Karagoz and Hacivat just picked up their heads and went away somewhere else.

These two characters were depicted in a form of puppet shadow theatre, popular at the time of the Ottomans. Other characters in the plays were from different Ottoman regions, including Greeks and Armenians. Karagoz puppets are made from leather, and the images are projected on to a white screen using a lamp. Different sounds, songs and dialogue form part of the plays.

Hacivat and Karagoz

12

West Asia: The Safavids and Other Dynasties

The Ottoman Turks ruled part of West Asia, but there were a number of other dynasties as well.

THE SAFAVID DYNASTY

The Safavid dynasty ruled Iran from 1502.

The Origins

Shaikh Safi al-din was a Sufi saint who lived in the 14th century in Azerbaijan. He founded a Sufi order, which acquired many followers. Junayd Safi, a leader of the order, who lived in the 15th century, went to east Anatolia and married into the Turkoman clan. The Aq Qoyunlu Turkomans ruled part of Iran at this time. Junayd's grandson Ismail defeated the Turkoman ruler, and in 1501–02, became the ruler of Azerbaijan and Iran as Ismail I.

Ismail I

Ismail I was a follower of the Isna Ashari Shia sect. He claimed descent from Ali, the Prophet's son-in-law, and thus became both the imam (religious leader) and the ruler. Ismail's rule

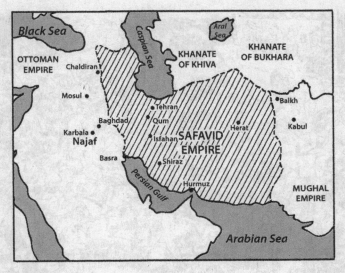

 Area of the Safavid empire

The Safavid empire

extended over neighbouring regions, including Armenia and part of Afghanistan. He formed an army of Turkmen, known as the kizilbash (red heads) as they wore red turbans with twelve folds, representing the twelve imams (See below.)

The Ottoman empire was to the west and the Uzbeks to the east. Ismail conquered part of the regions of present Iraq and Turkey, but then faced defeats from both the Ottomans and the Uzbeks. Within the empire there were conflicts between the Turkoman and Iranian nobles. Ismail died in 1524 at the age of thirty-six, and was followed by Tahmasp I (ruled 1524–76).

Abbas I (1588–1628)

Abbas I created a strong kingdom. He allowed the Ottomans and Uzbeks to occupy some territories, thus establishing a temporary peace. Then he created an efficient and well-trained army. He

Ismail I leads his forces in battle

conquered Baghdad in 1603, and made further conquests going on to control territory up to the Indus region in present Pakistan. At Mashhad in Khorasan he built a shrine to Ali al Riza, the eighth imam of the sect, who died in 818. He moved the capital from Qazvin to Isfahan in 1598. Isfahan soon became a grand city, with a population of around 5,00,000.

The later rulers

After Abbas I, the Safavids declined. Hussain I governed from 1694 to 1722, was religiously inclined, but not a strong ruler. In 1722, an Afghan, Mir Muhammad, who had been a vassal of the Safavids, captured Isfahan and killed Hussain. Shiraz became the new centre of government. Russia and the Ottomans conquered some regions. Tahmasp II succeeded Hussain, though the power remained with Mir Muhammad. Nadir Shah defeated Mir Muhammad acting on the behalf of Tahmasp in 1729.

Tahmasp made Nadir the governor of most of east Iran. Nadir Shah made himself the regent in 1732, and removed Tahmasp, making the latter's son, Abbas III, the ruler, though he actually had little power. In 1736, Nadir Shah took control himself, and the Safavid dynasty came to an end.

NADIR SHAH

Nadir Shah was of Afsharid Turkoman origin. He now ruled over Iran. Under him the state grew in strength and could withstand invasion. He created a powerful army and acquired ships from the British, giving Iran her own navy. In 1738, he conquered Afghanistan. From here he attacked the Mughal empire in India, and devastated the capital of Delhi. He brought back so much wealth from this invasion that he did not have to collect taxes in Iran for three years. He extended his empire into parts of Central Asia. However, Nadir Shah began to gradually lose his mental balance, and became suspicious of everyone. He was assassinated in 1747.

AFTER NADIR SHAH

After Nadir Shah's death the empire disintegrated. Different states arose in Afghanistan, Azerbaijan, north-west Iran, Khorasan and Mazandaran.

Nadir Shah's grandson Shah Rukh, who was blind, ruled Khorasan and part of Iran. While Shah Rukh continued to rule at Khorasan till 1795, Muhammad Karim Khan occupied much of Iran, and founded the Zand dynasty in 1750, though at the same time he placed a puppet Safavid ruler on the throne. In 1796, Agha Muhammad Khan of the Qajar dynasty took over both Iran and Khorasan. The Qajar dynasty ruled till 1925.

ISFAHAN

In the 17th century, Isfahan was a great city, located along the Zaindeh Rud river. Mosques, palaces, madrasas and tombs were

The Masjid-I Shah

built across the city. Among the beautiful mosques were the Masjid-i-Shah, and the Masjid-i-Shaikh Lutfullah, which is built of blue tiles. The mosques had domes and tall minarets. In Iran, minarets were gradually not used for the call to prayer. Another structure, known as a 'guldasta' (literally bouquet), a balcony shaped something like a small hut was constructed for this. Many of the buildings were decorated with tiles in different colours. These mosques can still be seen. Wonderful gardens were laid out, and an arched bridge was built across the river. Broad roads and canals were built. Literature and art flourished.

ART AND CRAFT

A number of artists illustrated books with miniature paintings. Bihzad was one of the greatest painters, who created landscapes and illustrated books. In the 16th century, one of the best artists was Ali Reza Abbasi, who painted both portraits and group scenes.

In the 17th century, European styles influenced Iranian painting.

Weaving, metalwork, pottery and carpets were among the other crafts.

ARABIAN PENINSULA

The Ottomans had a hold over the Arabian Peninsula. The Portuguese, and later other European powers tried to gain power particularly over ports in the coastal areas which were located on important routes.

The Hejaz region to the west is the area which includes the holy cities of Mecca and Medina, and was under the Ottomans from 1517 to 1916. The sharifs of Mecca were the local rulers.

Najd is located to the east of Hejaz, and forms the central part of the peninsula. West of Hejaz is the Tihamah, the coastal region along the Red Sea. Southern and eastern Arabia form two more regions. Najd and Yemen in the south are among the areas with fertile land.

Oman is located to the south-east. The Portuguese gained control over Muscat which is in the region of Oman in 1507. They extended their control over other areas. Muscat remained an area of conflict between the Ottomans and Portuguese. The Yaruba or Yarubid dynasty ruled Oman from around 1624 to 1742. They belonged to the Ibadi sect of Islam and were originally from Yemen. Nasir bin Murshid bin Sultan al Yaruba (ruled 1624–49) founded the Yarubid dynasty, and was its first imam. He unified the different groups in the region, organized an army, and captured some forts and towns from the Portuguese. The Portuguese were finally driven out of Muscat and Oman in 1650 by Sultan bin Saif al Yarubi (ruled 1649–88). Under Sultan bin Saif and succeeding rulers, the east coast of Africa, too, was conquered from the Portuguese. The Yarubids were replaced by the Al Said dynasty in 1749, that continue to rule till today.

After 1500, both the Mamluks and the Portuguese attempted to gain control over Yemen. The Mamluks succeeded but soon lost control to the Ottomans. However, the Yemen highlands remained relatively independent, under the Zaidi Shia group. The Zaidis and Ottomans fought for control. Al Mansur al-

Qasim founded the Zaidi kingdom. Though this faced many ups and downs it continued to exist till 1962.

The early 19th century saw the rise of the Wahhabis in the region. (See Chapter 30.)

ARAB SLAVE TRADE

The Arab slave trade began in the 7th century. Between 700 and 1900, between 14 and 20 million slaves were sold.

THE ISNA ASHARI AND OTHER SECTS

Islam is broadly divided into two groups: Sunnis and Shias.

There are a number of Shia sects who believe in various imams. Ali, the son-in-law of Prophet Muhammad, was the first imam.

The Isna Ashari sect has twelve imams, and therefore is popularly called 'the twelvers'. These imams were historical figures, but they believe that the twelfth imam did not die and remains are still hidden in the world till today. This imam was Muhammad al-Muntazar, who lived in the 9th century. The Zaidi sect believe in the imam Zaid ibn Ali (d. 740), whom they consider the fifth imam. The Ibadi sect is neither Sunni nor Shia.

13

China and Korea
1500–1800

The Ming dynasty had come to power in 1368, overthrowing the Mongolian Yuan dynasty. The Ming began to decline around 1450, though its rule continued till 1644.

THE MANCHU

The Jurchens, later known as the Manchu, spoke Tungusic and lived on the borderlands of China. Once nomadic, by the 15th century, they had established agricultural settlements in south Manchuria. The Jianzhou, a federation of Jurchens, were traders who lived on the borders of China and Korea.

Nurgaci

Around 1582, after a conflict among various rival Jianzhou leaders, Nurgaci (also spelt Nurhaci), a young Jianzhou leader, gained power. In 1616, he founded the Later Jin (meaning golden) dynasty of which he was the khan or leader. He had been given the title of khan by the Mongols.

Nurgaci organized the army into units called 'banners'.

He invaded China in 1621 and took over Shenyang, a regional

capital of Liaodong province. He renamed the city Shengjing, while its Manchu name was Mukden. Nurgaci settled there and constructed palaces and other buildings, but died after being wounded in a battle in 1626.

Hong Taiji

Nurgaci's son Hong Taiji, also known as Abahai, then became the khan. He captured the capital of Lighdan of the Chakhar khaganate. In 1636, he inaugurated a new empire, combining the Jin and Chakhar regions. He himself gave the dynasty its new name, Qing (the pure). He also introduced the name 'Manchu' for the Jurchen people of his kingdom. Though the origin of the word is not clear, this name was considered to mean 'superior' or 'senior'. Hong Taiji made Korea a protectorate of the Qing, and continued to invade Ming territories.

At Mukden, he organized a Chinese-style government, and civil service. Examinations for the civil services were held in three languages: Chinese, Manchu and Mongolian. Hong Taiji died in 1643.

The Shunzhi Emperor (ruled 1643–61)

Manchu princes chose Hong Taiji's five-year-old son Fulin, later known as the Shunzhi emperor, as the next emperor. Two regents were appointed, Dorgon, who was a son of Nurgaci, and Jirgalang, a nephew of Nurgaci. Dorgon was the main authority until his death in 1650.

In China a rebel leader Li Zicheng started a revolt and in 1644 even captured Beijing. Some of the generals of the Ming dynasty thought of asking the Manchu to help them defeat the rebels. The Manchu agreed to help them, but instead they themselves took over Beijing. However, they took quite some time to gain control over the whole of China. This could be completed only in the reign of the Kangxi emperor.

The Kangxi, Yongzheng and Qianlong Emperors

Shunzhi died at the age of 22 of smallpox. His seven-year-old son Xuanye succeeded him in 1661. He was known as the Kangxi emperor from 1662. Initially his grandmother and other regents controlled the empire, but later he took over the administration himself. During his reign, the Kangxi emperor gained control over the whole of China, Taiwan, Tibet, Mongolia and Manchuria. He put down rebellions and made the empire prosperous

Portrait of the Kangxi emperor

and peaceful. He was succeeded by the Yongzheng emperor (ruled 1722–36). The Yongzheng emperor introduced administrative and tax reforms. In 1729, he set up an Office of Military Finance to deal with any urgent matters. This was known to foreigners as the Grand Council. The Grand Council had an average of seven members, including Chinese and Manchu, and sometimes Mongolians.

Yongzheng was followed by the Qianlong emperor (ruled 1736–96). Qing power was now at its height. Central Asia up to the Pamirs and Chinese Turkestan came under their control.

LIFE AT THE TIME OF THE MANCHU

The Emperors

The emperor was considered the 'son of heaven', who had a divine right to rule. There were numerous ceremonies performed at the court and in society.

In the summer the emperors moved to their court in Inner Mongolia. There they focused on physical activities, hunting,

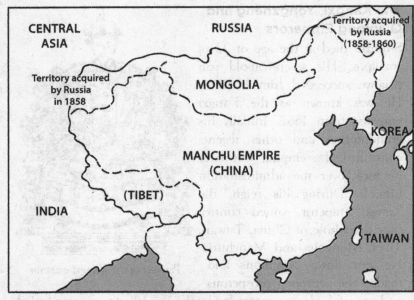

The Manchu empire

riding and shooting. They tried to keep northern Manchuria for themselves, free of the Chinese. A ditch was dug across hundreds of kilometres and willow trees planted along it to prevent people from crossing to the north.

Government

Manchus held the top military posts in China. Manchu military banner units were positioned at all strategic points. There were Chinese troops within the provincial forces. They mainly guarded routes and protected areas from bandits, but were not trained like the Manchu troops.

To deal with civil administration there were more Manchu officials at Beijing, but less in the provinces. Chinese and Manchu presidents together governed each of the six ministries or boards at the centre. The Imperial Household department was a secret department distinct from these ministries. It had its own staff and was financed by huge funds obtained from trade and taxes.

The Manchu language continued to be used. There were documents in Manchu that the Chinese could not read. Initially marriage between the Manchu and the Chinese was banned. Gradually this changed. Chinese men also had to follow the Manchu rule of shaving the front part of the hair, and wearing their hair in a pigtail.

Laws

Laws were based on the concepts of morality prescribed by Confucius. The Qing Legal Code contained 436 main statutes and over 1900 subsidiary ones. There were laws regarding marriage, inheritance and various aspects of administration. There was a hierarchy of courts, and different types of punishments including death and exile.

SHENGYU

The Sacred Edict (Shengyu) was issued by the emperor Kangxi in 1670. It consisted of 16 maxims, each of seven characters, which were guidelines for daily conduct. Commentaries, and variations and translations of these followed, and they were taught in different regions, with modifications to suit the audience. In 1724, the Yongzheng emperor expanded these to 10,000 characters. These moral guidelines were a way to bring unity in different areas.

Art, architecture, literature and music

There was a royal painting academy, as well as individual artists who developed their own styles. Large buildings, including temples and palaces were built. Palaces had golden roofs and white marble staircases. Red paint was used to add a touch of colour.

Literature enjoyed royal patronage. Under the Kangxi emperor, the *Kangxi Dictionary* was brought out. An encyclopedia in 5020 chapters was published. At the time of the Qianlong emperor there were a number of publications including the *Complete Library of the Four Treasuries*, which contained 3697 books. It consisted of four important categories—history, philosophy, classics and literature. But the Qing also suppressed books they did not like, especially those critical of them.

Chinese opera developed. Western music was introduced. Kangxi himself was taught to play the spinet by a Western musician. Plays and operas were enacted in villages and towns.

Crafts

Among crafts, glazed and enamelled porcelain were produced on a large scale. At Jingdezhen there was an imperial porcelain manufacturing industry with 1,00,000 workers. There were at least 300 kilns which functioned even at night. At Suzhou there was an imperial silk manufacturing centre. In 1685, this was provided with 800 looms and employed 2330 workers. By the 18th century, a number of textile factories had been set up. There was also metalwork, carvings in jade, fine furniture, lacquer and gilt work. Blown glass items were made. There were household industries in silk and tea.

Merchant guilds were formed.

Agriculture, towns and trade

There was an increase in grain supply, partly because of an expansion in cultivated area. Different varieties of rice were introduced from the south and double cropping was practised. Corn (maize), sweet potatoes, peanuts and tobacco were introduced from the Americas. There were several towns and ports. Market towns were known as zhen.

Domestic trade was in agricultural and farm products. Canals were one of the main methods of transport. Items traded internally included raw cotton, as well as cotton yarn and cloth, ceramics, tea, timber, rice, salt, sugar, silk, iron and matches.

The Ming had prohibited sea trade, but the ban was not really followed. It was officially removed in 1567. Even during late Ming and early Qing days, about a hundred Chinese ships traded every year with South East Asia. These further increased.

After 1600 the British and Dutch East India companies traded with China. China exported tea, silk and porcelain; imports included silver, woollen textiles and later opium from India. By the end of the 17th century millions of porcelain items were being sent to Europe.

But after 1759 restrictions were placed on trade. Guangzhou (Canton) was the only port from which European trade was allowed. The Canton trade with Europe was organized by the government and supervised by government officials.

Another aspect of Chinese trade were imports of silver in the 16th and 17th centuries from Japan and the Americas. About ten million dollars' worth of silver reached China every year. This led to a rise in prices, an economy where money was increasingly used, and more commerce. A reduction in silver imports in the mid 17th century led to a fall in prices. Thus China was already a part of an international trade network.

There was also a good banking system.

RELIGION

The Manchu had their own local gods and shamans (priests) but had been influenced by Tibetan Buddhism, even before reaching China. In this form of Buddhism, many deities were worshipped. Within China the Manchus continued with their original forms of worship, but also introduced new Chinese elements.

The traditional Chinese reverence for ancestors was

maintained. Neo-Confucian principles were followed and promoted. These included maintaining a hierarchy with respect for elders and superiors. This helped to maintain order. Other forms of Buddhism were also practised as well as Daoism.

Guandi and Ma Zu

Some local or folk religious cults were promoted to bring a sense of unity between rural areas and cities. Guan Yu was a guardian deity of a founder of the three kingdoms that existed from CE 162–220. He became popular as the god of wealth, literature and of actors, protector of temples and of secret societies. Later he came to be known as Guandi. Another local deity who became important was Ma Zu, a goddess of fishermen and sailors, who in 1737 was made the Empress of Heaven (Tian Hou). This helped to integrate people from local cultures into the mainstream.

The Daoist deity Xi Wang Mu ('Godmother of the West'), dated 1725. This was a decoration on a porcelain plate.

Missionaries

In the 17th century, Jesuits and other missionaries reached China. Apart from works on Christianity, the Jesuits brought out over a hundred books on Western science and technology, which influenced China. China also had an impact on Europe in the 18th century. Chinese philosophy had an effect on that of Europe, and Chinese gardens, architecture, ceramics and other artefacts also inspired styles in Europe.

Europe in the 18th century was really impressed by China. But it was Europe that moved beyond it. In 1750 the pre-industrial societies of China and Europe looked similar, but there were great differences in terms of the underlying society and culture.

By the end of the 18th century the population in China was growing. The Qing government found it difficult to collect taxes and provide for the needs of the people, particularly when there were disasters such as floods, drought or famine.

FOOT BINDING—A THREE-INCH GOLDEN LOTUS

Once, in the 10th century in China, there was an emperor who had a favourite concubine. She once constructed a stage in the shape of a lotus. Then she tied her toes below her feet, and danced on the lotus with bound feet. The emperor liked this performance a lot. That's how, it is said, foot binding started as a practice and was widely copied by others.

It was thought that women were beautiful only if their feet were very small. The size should be just three inches (7.6 cm). But how could a woman have three-inch long feet? Between the ages of five to eight up to when they were 13 to 15, the feet of young girls were bound with long strips of cloth, with the four small toes being turned under. This continued until the feet stopped growing. Foot binding probably started for court ladies and the nobility in the 10th century, but later even peasants and farm women followed this practice in some areas.

Manchu and Mongol women did not bind their feet; this practice was followed only by the Chinese. In the 19th century, almost 50 per cent of Chinese women had bound feet. Amongst upper classes it was done by almost all. The Qing emperors tried to stop foot binding but it continued. In 1912 it was abolished and declared illegal, but even after this some continued the practice in order to ensure good marriages.

It was totally abolished only after 1949.

KOREA

In Korea the Choson or Yi dynasty was ruling from 1392. The country was prosperous and peaceful up to 1592. In 1592 the Japanese invaded Korea, but were defeated by 1598 with the help of the Ming dynasty of China.

In 1627 and 1636 the Manchus invaded Korea and made it a protectorate. After this in the 17th and 18th centuries, Korea remained relatively peaceful, with a good administration. Government officials were appointed from Confucian academies. But the economy was changing, money began to be used as a form of exchange, and some people became very rich. The dynasty remained in power till 1910, but saw further changes in the 19th century.

Korean art was influenced by China, but developed in its own way as well. Delicate blue and white porcelain was produced, as well as thicker, brightly-painted pottery.

TIBET

Tibet came under the Qing dynasty, but at the same time was governed by its own kings. Buddhism was the main religion, but there were diverse Tibetan Buddhist sects. Gushi Khan, ruler of the Khoshot Mongols, defeated Desi Karma Tenchong (ruled 1622–42) of the Tsangpa dynasty of Tibet, and offered power to Lobzang Gyatso of the Gelug sect. Lobzang Gyatso, the fifth Dalai Lama, became the gyalpo or king of Tibet and governed from 1642 to 1682. Lobsang Gyatso made Lhasa the capital. After this Dalai Lamas of the Gelug sect became rulers of Tibet until 1959.

Dalai Lama

Dalai Lama was actually a title given by the Mongols. Dalai means 'ocean wide' or wide-ranging.

Lama Sonam Gyatso of the Gelugpa or Gelug sect went to visit the Mongol leader Altan Khan in the Ordos-Suiyan region in 1578. Altan Khan praised him for his learning and gave him the title 'Dalai Lama', because of his wide and vast knowledge. The Gelug sect then conferred this title on two of their earlier chief lamas, Gedun Deb and Gedun Gyatso. Thus Lama Sonam Gyatso became the third Dalai Lama.

The Potala, the main residence of the Dalai Lama in Lhasa

MONGOLIA

The Mongols in the region of Mongolia ruled independently but remained under the Manchu dynasty of China. They adopted Tibetan Buddhism in the 16th century. A Mongol khan ruled from Urga (now Ulaanbaatar). In 1650 he was known as a Living Buddha.

14
Japan
1500–1868

In Japan the period 1500–1868 had several centres of power. The emperors enjoyed little authority themselves. Real power was in the hands of the shogun or supreme military commander. His centre of administration was called the bakufu (tent government). The daimyo were military clans who formed the local rulers. Each daimyo ruled over a territory known as a han.

BEFORE 1500

In the second half of the 15th century, there were numerous conflicts in Japan.

Shoguns of the Ashikaga family ruled, but their power had declined, and the daimyo were virtually independent within their respective territories. Within the daimyo hans, forts and castles were built.

AZUCHI-MOMOYAMA PERIOD
Oda Nobunaga

After almost a hundred years of conflict in Japan, Oda Nobunaga (1534–82), one of the daimyo, started bringing other daimyos under his control. He made Yoshiaki Ashikaga the shogun in 1568, but when Yoshiaki tried to assert his power, he removed him in 1573. The period of Ashikaga shoguns had ended.

Buddhist sects in their monasteries had lived independently, but Nobunaga destroyed their power and brought them under his control. He built castles at strategic points, and introduced a single currency in the areas he conquered.

One of his own generals, Akechi Mitsuhede, killed Nobunga by treachery in 1582. Another of his best generals, Toyotomi Hideyoshi, then killed Mitsuhede.

Toyotomi Hideyoshi

Hideyoshi continued Nobunaga's work of unifying the country. In 1585 Hideyoshi received the title of kampaku (regent). He had the whole country surveyed. This was useful to assess the areas for taxation, and also to understand how to bring in unity. During the survey he realized that within the hans of the daimyo, there were just too many weapons. In 1588 he ordered all peasants to surrender any swords and armour in their possession. He promised that these would be melted and used to make a huge Buddha statue at Kyoto.

Hideyoshi at first appointed his nephew Hidetsugu as his successor, but later he had a son who was named Hideyori. Hideyoshi then got his nephew and his family killed, and asked his chief daimyo to support Hideyori. On his deathbed in 1598, he appointed five daimyo regents for his young son. They were assisted by five commissioners.

This period is named Azuchi-Momoyama because of two great castles, one built by Nobunaga at Azuchi, and the other by Hideyoshi in Momoyama district. (See later for more on castles.)

  The Puffin History of the World

TOKUGAWA RULE—THE EDO PERIOD

Tokugawa Ieyasu was the most powerful daimyo regent, but he was attacked by one of the commissioners, Ishida Mitsunari. In 1600 they fought a battle at Sekigahara and Ieyasu won. In 1603 he received the title

Tokugawa Ieyasu

of shogun from the emperor. His bakufu or centre of government was Edo (modern Tokyo), while the emperors remained at Kyoto. Ieyasu and his descendants continued to hold power till 1868. Ieyasu gave up the title of shogun in 1605, but remained the real ruler till his death in 1616, though Tokugawa Hidetada became the shogun. Ieyasu focused on reforming the administration.

Bakuhan system

The Tokugawa bakufu and the daimyo ruled jointly, and this was known as the bakuhan system. It was a form of feudalism in which the daimyos became feudatories.

About one quarter of Japan came directly under the shogun. These were known as tenryo lands and included Nagasaki, Edo, Kyoto and Osaka. These lands were six times larger than that of any daimyo. Apart from these there were over 260 daimyo han of varying sizes.

At Kyoto the emperor did not move out of his palace area. At Edo, the shogun lived in a castle. After 1651 he too hardly moved out except for special occasions and ceremonies. But he made a rule that all the daimyo should spend alternate years at Edo. The daimyo powers were thus controlled, as they could not spend all their time in their own lands. There were other limits on their power. They could not even marry without the shogun's permission. They were no longer allowed to fortify their territories. They could not build large ships.

The Tokugawa also made laws to regulate Buddhist monasteries and Shinto shrines. They tried to regulate the lives of people in the cities. Music halls and theatre were controlled. Excessive expenditure on festivals, fancy clothing, food and other items were discouraged.

A closed country

The Portuguese reached Japan in the 1540s, and were followed by the Spanish. Their missionaries converted some of the Japanese to Christianity. By 1600, there were about 3,00,000 Christians in Japan. Japanese leaders tried to control the influence of the foreigners. In 1639 laws were passed, which led to Japan being closed to outsiders. According to these laws, Japanese could not travel outside the country. Christian missionaries and most of the European traders were driven out of Japan. External trade could only take place through Nagasaki, foreigners were not allowed anywhere else. For over 200 years after this, the Dutch and Chinese were the only foreign groups living in Nagasaki. But there was some trade with China and Korea through other regions. Japan started changing around the 18th century, with more foreign influences. In 1720, Shogun Yoshimune allowed European books and study. In 1858 Japan signed a trade treaty with the US, marking the end of Japan's isolation.

Tempo reforms

In the first half of the 19th century Japan faced many problems. In the Tempo era (1830-44) there were poor harvests, and revolts in both rural and urban areas. Administrative reforms were then introduced from 1841 with the agreement of the daimyo. These are known as the Tempo Reforms. The reforms did not bring about much internal benefits.

ECONOMY

After 1600 Japan increasingly had a money economy with trade and credit facilities. A money economy is one in which money is used, instead of barter or other mediums such as gold or silver.

Living standards rose. Like everywhere there were differences between rich and poor. Even villages had shops and farmers were not badly off, but there were several landless labourers who were quite poor.

Agricultural production increased. Better seeds were used and double cropping practised.

More rice, wheat, millet, soybean, barley and cotton were grown. There were new crops like tobacco, ginseng, sugar, potatoes, sweet potatoes and tea. Pumpkins and sweet corn also reached Japan.

Fish, rice and vegetables remained the main items in food, but the new crops grown added variety to the diet. Tempura (fried seafood) probably originated in Portugal, but began to be eaten in Japan. Luxury foods like sugar were used.

Sericulture was practised. Vegetable oils and dyes were made.

Edo, Osaka and Kyoto were three of the largest cities of the world. The first had a population of over a million, and the next two about 5,00,000. There were also about 50 provincial centres each with a population of more than 10,000. In the cities artisans and craftsmen produced gold, silver, copper, wood and metal items, including items of steel. There were beautiful textiles, toys and puppets, musical instruments, books, pottery, lacquer work and other items. The cities had good markets. Weaving and dyeing techniques were perfected.

There was internal trade but no direct commerce between Japan and Europe. The Portuguese at Macao were intermediaries for trade with China. Chinese silk was exchanged for silver, lacquerware, swords and copper from Japan. As mentioned above, Nagasaki was another significant centre of foreign trade.

ART AND LITERATURE

Art

Sculpture and painting showed new trends. Gateways and walls were decorated with flowers, animals, birds and various designs. Two great artists were Hasegawa Tohaku (1539–1610) and Kano Eitoku (1543–90). The Kano School of Painting was founded by Kano Masanobu (1434–1530) and his son Motonobu (1476–1559). They used gold and bright colours in their paintings.

There were several new styles and schools of art. Among them, Ukiyo-e (meaning 'floating world') was a style that included coloured woodblock prints and paintings on paper and silk. Scenes from the towns and amusement centres were often depicted. One of the prominent artists was Suzuki Harunobu (1725–70), who created artistic coloured calendars. Later, landscapes were painted in Ukiyo-e and in various styles. One of the greatest artists was Katsushika Hokusai (1760–1849), known for his series of woodblock prints called *Thirty-six Views*

Ogata Korin's Irises, painted on screens in 1701

of Mt Fuji. Ando Hiroshige's (1797–1858) *Fifty-three Stages of the Tokaido*, consisting of scenes on the road from Edo to Kyoto, was among other wonderful prints.

Literature

Among the interesting writers Ihara Saikaku (1643–93) wrote novels and stories on the new trends in Japanese life. Chikamatsu Monzaemon (1653–1724) composed over 130 plays for Kabuki and Bunraku. Many of his plays focus on the conflict between duty (giri) and emotions (ninjo). Popular literature began to be written. The haiku, a form of poetry in 17 syllables, was perfected at this time. Matsuo Basho (1644–94) invented the classic haiku form. Other great haiku masters were Kobayashi Issa, Yosa Buson (1716–84) and Shiki.

KOBAYASHI ISSA (1763–1827)

Issa was the name under which Kobayashi wrote. It meant a 'cup of tea'. It is said he was called 'one cup of tea' because he just stopped to have a cup of tea before moving on in his travels. Issa was constantly travelling from place to place.

Issa had a tragic life. His mother died when he was only three, his stepmother hated him, and the grandmother, who loved him, passed away when he was only 14. After his father died, he managed to get rights to half the property, and in 1814 he married Kiku, but their three children didn't survive long. Kiku too died in 1823 giving birth to the fourth child. Issa married again, but he died in 1827.

He wrote over 20,000 haiku. He wrote about his own life, as well as about nature, plants, toads, frogs, snails and insects. Issa had great compassion for all creatures, including fleas and flies. He also made drawings to accompany his haiku.

Here is a haiku he composed:

'Don't chase, don't chase, children!
That flea has kids.
Don't swat the fly,
wringing hands,
wringing feet. ' (Trans. David G Lanoue)

He also wrote haibun (prose interspersed with haiku) and renku
(verses in collaboration).

ARCHITECTURE

The typical Japanese style house was first made at this time. It
had wooden outer walls, a tiled roof, tatami floors and sliding
internal walls. Stone was not usually used in buildings. But one
of the first stone buildings was the Nijo castle, built by Nobunaga
in 1575. To build it he used the stone from idols broken up
in Buddhist monasteries. Around the castle was a moat, filled
with water in which swam several birds. A drawbridge had to
be lowered to cross the moat. Soon other stone castles too were
erected. Hideyoshi built one at Osaka that had a keep (tower)
seven storeys high. In it there were rooms filled with gold, silver,
silk and other items.

THEATRE

There were two main types of theatre at this time, Kabuki and
Bunraki. Kabuki was performed by actors. It reached its height
in Edo in the 18th century. It was accompanied by grand scenery
props and costumes, and orchestras.

Bunraku was a form of puppet theatre. It is also known as
Ningyojoruri, and was founded in Osaka in the Edo period. One
person narrates the story, while music, songs and chants often
accompany the performance. The shamisen, a stringed instrument,

flutes, and percussion instruments are used. Bunraku puppets are half the size of real people. The puppeteers manipulate them with their hands. The puppeteers can be seen by the audience, but are dressed in black, indicating they are not to be looked at.

Kabuki and Bunraku both depict love stories, stories of heroes, and of historical events.

Noh theatre also continued. (See Volume 1.)

IKEBANA AND THE TEA CEREMONY

Ikebana, the art of flower arrangement, and the tea ceremony, which had originated earlier, continued to develop in this period.

RELIGION AND PHILOSOPHY

Neo-Confucian philosophies were used in government and promoted in society. Buddhism and Shintoism as well as local deities remained popular. Suika was a new form of Shinto with Confucian elements. Shingaku combined worship of the goddess Amaterasu and other Shinto deities with both Neo-Confucian and Zen Buddhist elements. Zen Buddhism, and earlier Buddhist systems such as that of Nichiren Daishonen, continued to evolve. Zen Buddhism was reflected in art and literature. There were several other new sects as well. But local temples were the most popular. For instance, in 1771, two million people visited the Amaterasu shrine at Ise. In 1830 there were five million pilgrims to the shrine.

HOKKAIDO

Hokkaido, a large island to the north, was still outside the direct control of the shogun. Soon Russians started visiting it and exploiting the resources there. In 1799 it came under the direct control of the bakufu.

WARRIORS

The samurai were military warriors who were originally part of private armies. These warriors still survived across Japan. They could be easily recognized as they carried two swords and wore a distinctive hairstyle. But in this period the samurai were educated, and were not only warriors. Some performed special functions, such as serving in the tea ceremony. There were also a number of samurai who were known as rōnin, that is, they were not under any lord.

There were also ninja warriors, who were trained in martial arts. They were often employed as assassins or spies.

THE LAST SHOGUNS

After 1850 the shoguns followed some policies that angered the people. Some nobles asked the emperor Mutsuhito to overthrow the shogun. He did so and moved to Edo in 1868. He took the name Meiji, meaning 'enlightened rule', and remained the emperor till 1912. This is known as the Meiji period. (See Chapter 30.)

15

South East Asia: Myanmar, Thailand, Laos, Cambodia and Vietnam, 1500–1800

South East Asia saw many conflicts and changes in territory at this time. New kingdoms rose and fell.

MYANMAR

In Myanmar the kingdom of Bagan declined by 1287 and a number of small states were established. Among them were the Ava, Prone, Hathanwady, as well as the Shan and Arakan states. There were constant wars up to around 1550. Arakan states continued to exist till 1785.

Taungoo dynasties

The Taungoo dynasty named after the place of Taungoo, south of Ava, was founded in 1486 by King Mingyinyo. Mingyinyo's son, Tabinshwehti, gradually began to conquer most of Myanmar, but he was killed in 1551. Bayinnaung, who was his brother-in-law,

Bayinnaung: a statue located at Yangon in Myanmar

succeeded him, and extended the territories. He conquered Manipur in north-east India in 1560, and Ayutthaya in Thailand in 1569. The Taungoo now reigned over a very large area, but could not hold on to its newly- conquered territories.

Another Taungoo dynasty, also known as the Nyaungyan dynasty, began to rule in around 1597–99. This dynasty became strong under King Anaukpetlun (ruled 1605–28) but after this, began to decline. The Taungoo dynasty finally ended in 1752. Maha Dhammaraza, who ruled from 1733 to 1752, was the last king. The Taungoo were Burmans, horsemen from the north, who had first entered the region in the 9th century CE. (See Volume 1.) Among other groups in Myanmar, were the Mon people with their capital at Bago (Pegu). They had been conquered by the Burmans, but asserted their independence and defeated Dhammaraza in 1752.

Konbaung dynasty

Another dynasty, the Konbaung dynasty (1752–1885), arose in the north, and under king Alaungpaya gradually established control over the whole area. As the Konbaung armies reached lower Burma, many Mon people fled to Thailand. The armies also defeated the French and the British, who had supported the Mon. The Konbaung began expanding their territories. They established their rule all over Myanmar and to regions beyond. In 1767 Ayutthaya was taken over. Chiang Mai too had been conquered in 1558. Both these regions were in Thailand.

Throughout this period, Theravada Buddhism remained the

The following places are shown on the map:

TIBET

AHOM

MING

MANIPUR

KOSHANPYE

Pagan · Ava

Kengtung

Arakan
mrauk U ·

Dai La

TAUNGOO EMPIRE

MyedeMong Pai
· Taungoo

Cheingmai

LAN XANG
Luang Prabang

VIETNAM

Prome

LANNA
· Sukhothai

Xiangkhouang
Wiang-Jun
(Vientiane)

· Thaton
Dagon · Pegu

Champassak

AYUTTHAYA
Ayutthaya

Tavov · Nakhon Pahom

KHMER

CHAMPA
· Panduranga

Gulf of Thailand

Andaman Sea

South China Sea

The Taungoo empire

main religion. The Konbaung dynasty re-established relations with Sri Lanka, which followed the same faith.

THAILAND

The kingdom of Ayutthaya, with its capital city of the same name, existed in Thailand from 1350 to 1767. The Portuguese ambassador Duarte Fernandes reached there in 1511.

In 1700 Ayutthaya was one of the largest cities in the world, with a population of one million. In the 18th century, the Konbaung dynasty of Myanmar attacked the kingdom. The capital was captured in 1767. The last king, Ekkathat, went into hiding and finally died of starvation. The city was burned, destroyed and looted.

General Taksin, later King Taksin, founded a new capital at Thonburi, and reunited the kingdom. However, he lost his mental balance and Gen. Chakri helped him administer the kingdom. As King Rama I, Gen. Chakri started the Chakri dynasty in 1782. He founded a new capital known as SiaYuthia, also called Bangkok. In the 1790s, the Myanmarese were pushed out of Siam (Thailand).

The country was known as Mueang Thai to its people, and Siam or Sayam to outsiders. Europeans called Ayutthaya the kingdom of Siam. 'Siam' is thought by some to come from the Sanskrit word 'shyama', though others consider this unlikely.

Wat Chaiwatthanaram

There were several Buddhist temples in Thailand. Among them is Wat Chaiwatthanaram, on the west bank of the Chao Phraya river, near the old city of Ayutthaya. It was constructed in 1630 by the king Prasat Thong, and was the royal temple where he and his successors performed religious ceremonies. It is built in Khmer style on a rectangular platform, with a central prang (tower) 35 m high, and four other prangs. This Buddhist temple was deserted in 1767.

The remains of Wat Chaiwatthanaram

Chiang Mai, a city in northern Thailand, was the capital of the independent kingdom of Lanna. It was conquered by Myanmar in 1558. It became part of Thailand in 1775. Today it is a prosperous city with more than 300 Buddhist temples. Some of them date back to the 13th century.

LAOS

In Laos, there were different groups of people. The Kha were among the earliest, followed by the Lao and Tai. The kingdom of Lan Xang (meaning 'million elephants') existed from 1354 to 1707. The capital was at Muang Swa, which is the present city of Louang Phrabang.

Lan Xang reached its greatest extent in the 16th century. At this time Chiang Mai was briefly conquered. Though in Thailand, this kingdom was then under Myanmar, from 1558 to 1775. This led to numerous conflicts with Myanmar. The capital was shifted to Vientiane in 1563.

King Souligna Vongsa (ruled 1637–94) brought peace and prosperity to the region.

But after his reign there was again conflict. One of his nephews tried to take over the throne, with the help of a force from Vietnam. Others opposed him. As a result, three kingdoms emerged in Laos by 1713—Louang Phrabang, Vientiane and Champasak. In 1778 Vientiane was occupied by Thailand, and the other two kingdoms also had to acknowledge Thailand's rule.

CAMBODIA

After the fall of the Khmer kingdom in 1432, Cambodia experienced a period of chaos and confusion. Moving away from Angkor, some of the Khmer people set up a new kingdom at the present site of Phnom Penh. Here, two rivers, the Mekong and Tonle Sab, met. Through the Mekong delta, routes connected the region with China and India.

King Ang Chang (1516–66) was a strong ruler who set up a new capital at Lovek, also known as Longvek. This city too was on the banks of the Tonle Sab river, and developed into a prosperous centre. In the markets were precious and semi-precious stones, items made of metal and ivory, textiles and lacquerware. Traders and merchants from different regions, including China, Japan,

Spain, Portugal, and later England and the Netherlands, lived there. Lovek was captured by Thailand (Siam) in 1594. After this most of Cambodia remained under Thailand's rule for around 300 years. The Khmer king Chetta II married a Vietnamese princess in 1620 and Vietnam began to exercise influence over the region.

THE STORY OF PHNOM PENH

It is said that once Duan Penh (Lady Penh) found a floating log of wood in the Tonle Sap river and brought it out of the water. Inside were five statues, four of the Buddha and one of the Hindu deity Vishnu. She constructed a shrine on a hill for these statues. Phnom means 'hill', and hence the place came to be called Phnom Duan Penh and the area around it Phnom Penh. As it was a sacred place, the Khmer people made it their capital when Angkor was conquered.

VIETNAM

In Vietnam, the Le dynasty came to power in 1428 after defeating the Chinese Ming dynasty. The first king was Le Thai To, who had earlier been known as Le Loi. By the end of the 15th century the kingdom had expanded to the south and conquered the kingdom of Champa, but then a decline set in. In 1527 a general called Mac Dang Dung took control of much of the country, with the support of China.

Two clans, the Trinh and the Nguyen, helped the Le dynasty reconquer the region by the end of the 16th century. But actual power was with the Trinh clan.

In about 1620 the Nguyen were granted some land in the south. Their centre was at Hue. The Trinh in the north had their centre at Hanoi.

By the 18th century, there were feudal lords who controlled large areas.

The Tay Son brothers

In 1777 there was a peasant revolt. It was led by three brothers of Tay Son village in Binh Dinh province. They were of the Ho clan, but took the name Nguyen. They led a rebellion in which the existing Nguyen rulers were killed, defeated the Trinh and united Vietnam in 1789. The Tay Son aim was to take over the property of the rich, and give it to the poor. They opened the storehouses and distributed the stocks of grain free. They removed all taxes, and burnt tax and land registers. Many people joined their movement, including peasants, scholars and merchants.

One of the brothers ruled for a few years. Nguyen Nhac, the eldest brother, made Qui Nhon the capital in 1773. In 1778 he proclaimed himself the emperor Thai Duc. By 1786 the Trinh dynasty was defeated, and Vietnam was united after 200 years. The brothers recognized the Le emperor as the overall sovereign, but governed as three kings in the north, south and centre of the region. The Le emperor went to China in 1788. Helped by a Chinese army, he seized Thang Long and was recognized as king of Annam. But in 1788 Nguyen Hue, the second Tay Son brother, took the title emperor QuangTrung and defeated the Chinese army of 2,00,000 men. He set up a new capital at Phu Xuan, near present Hue, and provided a good administration till his death in 1792.

The Portuguese reached Vietnam in 1516 and in the 17th century established a trading port, but were then expelled.

The Nguyen dynasty

Then Nguyen Anh, a nephew of the last Nguyen lord, gathered supporters to fight against the Tay Son leaders and the third Tay Son brother. He was helped by French and other forces.

Nguyen Anh captured Phu Xuan in 1801 and Thang Long in 1802, and started the Nguyen dynasty in 1802. He was known as the emperor Gia Long.

THE TWO SNAKES

There are many stories about the Tay Son brothers. According to one story, when Nguyen Hue and his troops were marching down a road, two giant snakes blocked their path. Nguyen Hue then prayed to the snakes and to the supreme Snake Spirit. He said that if the Snake Spirit wanted his success, he should let them pass and help him, otherwise, the spirit should kill him but let his troops return safely.

The two snakes allowed them to pass. They even accompanied the troops to make sure they reached safely. And they brought Nguyen Hue a black-handled dragon knife, which they carried in their mouths and presented to him. This knife would ensure his future victory in war.

16

South East Asia: Philippines, Malaysia, Indonesia, Brunei, Papua New Guinea, 1500-1800

European inroads began in this area of South East Asia.

THE PHILIPPINES

The Philippines has 11 main islands and thousands of others. The islands have a volcanic origin, and have tropical forests, with a diversity of flora and fauna. Volcanic eruptions and earthquakes take place frequently in these islands.

The Mayon volcano on Luzon Island has erupted 30 times since 1616.

From the 14th century Islam began to spread to some of the islands. There were numerous states ruled by various types of rulers, including sultans, huangs, rajas, datus and lakans.

Ferdinand Magellan reached here in 1521. (See Chapter 1.)

He was killed on the island of Mactan, near the island of Cebu. Lapu-Lapu, the leader of the warriors who killed him, is still revered as a hero.

Spain claimed the islands in 1542 and named them Islas Filipinas, or in English, the Philippines. They were named after Philip, who was later Philip II of Spain. At this time a small, temporary Spanish colony was set up there.

THE BOXER CODEX

The Codex is an illustrated manuscript written around 1590. It describes the various groups in the Philippines when the Spanish reached there, and contains paintings of how they looked. The groups include Tagalogs, Visayans and other Philippine people, along with foreigners living in the Philippines. The artist is not known, but was probably Chinese.

Tagalog royal couple, depicted in the Boxer Codex

Miguel López de Legazpi led a Spanish expedition here in 1564–65, and the Spanish gradually increased their hold over the islands. Manila became the capital and administrative centre in 1571–72. Legazpi then became the first Spanish governor-general. Missionaries converted people to Catholicism, and the area was unified. Churches were built in baroque and other styles, and patron saints were adopted. From 1565 the area was part of the Viceroyalty of New Spain. (See Chapter 21.) A sea route linked Manila to Acapulco, Mexico. From Acapulco ships reached Spain.

In the 17th and 18th centuries, Manila was a great city and a flourishing centre of trade. Silk, spices and other products from China, Japan, Brunei, the Moluccas, and India reached Manila. Silver from New Spain paid for these items. The trade lasted till 1815. New food crops such as corn, tomatoes, potatoes, chilli peppers and pineapples were cultivated. The European population increased. Tobacco was grown for export. New animals too were introduced.

Spain ruled the region for 333 years, during which time they faced internal revolts and attacks from outside, including by the Dutch and English.

However, the Spanish did not gain full control of the highlands. In addition, some areas in the south remained free of Spanish rule. Among them were the Sulu and the Maguindanao sultanates.

Maguindanao Sultanate

This sultanate ruled parts of the Mindanao island and remained independent till 1888. It was established by Sharif Muhammad Kabungsuwan of Johor. At its height the sultanate controlled the whole of Mindanao as well as surrounding islands.

The Maranao people were among those who lived on the Mindanao island. Though they were Muslims, they followed a number of Hindu traditions. They had their own epic, *Darangen*, a version of the Ramayana, the famous Indian epic. Singkil was their traditional folk dance, in which dancers step between crossed bamboo poles. Kulintang, a form of music, including percussion instruments, accompanied the dance, which depicted scenes from the *Darengen*.

Sarimanok Garuda, derived from the sacred bird Garuda of Hindu tradition, is still the symbol of the Maranao people.

MALAYSIA

Malacca was a sultanate established on the Malaysian mainland in CE 1400. Its capital was conquered by the Portuguese in 1511. At this time the ruling sultan was Mahmud Shah. His sons then formed the two new sultanates of Johor and Perak. The Portuguese also set up settlements on Ternate, Ambon, Solor and other islands.

Achin (Aceh), based in Sumatra, was among the states competing for power. Wars were fought between the Portuguese, Johor and Aceh. In 1641 Malacca was conquered by the Dutch. The Dutch too fought wars with Johor and Achin. In the north there were other kingdoms, including Perdis, Kedah and Kelantan. These kingdoms were influenced by Thailand.

In 1786 the sultan of Kedah leased the island of Penang to the British East India Company. The British then gradually increased their influence in the region.

BORNEO

Borneo, a large island, is today under Malaysia, Brunei and Indonesia. In the 15th and 16th centuries, northern Borneo was under the sultanate of Brunei, while the southern part came under the kingdom of Majapahit. Sultan Bolkiah (ruled 1485–1524) made Brunei a strong state, extending his territory up to Johor. The Spanish made attempts to conquer Borneo, but failed. Meanwhile pirates were based in Borneo, and remained active from there.

INDONESIA

Islam gradually became the religion of Indonesia, spreading over Sumatra and Java in the 16th century. But aspects of earlier religions continued.

Different sultanates were established here. In Java the sultanate of Demak Bintoro lasted from 1475 to 1568. It was followed by that of Pajang, which was conquered in 1588 by the sultanate of Mataram. Surabaya was another kingdom in east Java. Sultan Agung (ruled 1613–46) of Mataram expanded the territories and conquered Surabaya. The Mataram sultanate declined by 1680.

The Sultanate of Banten lasted from 1526 to 1813. Around 1525 Sunun Gunung Jati from the Cirebon (Kesultanan) sultanate captured the Banten port from the Sunda kingdom. Cirebon in the Java region declined after 1677 and the Dutch gained control after 1807.

One of the gates of Kota Gede, the former capital of Mataram sultanate, Yogyakarta, Indonesia

The Dutch East India Company (VOC) was set up in 1602. After 1610 it became the main European power in Indonesia. The city of Sunda Kelapa, present Jakarta, was captured in 1619 and renamed Batavia. Dutch control began to spread through Java. In 1641, the Dutch conquered Malacca from the Portuguese. In 1800, The Dutch East India Company was dissolved, and the Dutch East Indies became a territory directly under the Netherlands.

The Samundera Pasai sultanate existed from the 13th century. It was conquered by the Portuguese in 1521.

The Ternate sultanate, established in 1257, reached its height in the 16th century. It covered eastern Indonesia, and part of the southern Philippines. Along with Tidore, it produced the largest amount of cloves in the world. The Portuguese attempted to gain control over Ternate, followed by the Spanish. However, the Dutch allied with the Ternate rulers. By the end of the 17th century, Ternate was under the Dutch, but the sultans retained some independence. The same line of sultans still rule as constitutional monarchs today.

The Aceh sultanate, which existed from 1496 to 1903, had its capital at Kutaraja, the present Banda-Aceh. It came into conflict with the Johor sultanate in Malaysia, and Malacca, also in Malaysia under Portuguese control. Spices, including pepper, nutmeg and cloves grew in the region, and contributed to its wealth. Aceh reached its height in the 16th and 17th centuries. Though it continued to exist after this, smaller states within the region were largely independent.

Malayu (known as Malay by Europeans) was the literary language of Aceh and several other states of Malaysia and South East Asia. It was also the spoken language of many states and was influenced by the languages of India. Traders from India were prominent up till the 17th century, particularly in Aceh. Pepper, tin and elephants were exported from Aceh. Textiles from India were highly prized both in Aceh and in the rest of South East Asia. Aceh was also the centre of Islamic and particularly Sufi literature. Among the books was *Hikayat Aceh*, written in praise of Iskandar Muda, a sultan of Aceh. Aceh was also ruled by a number of sultanas, women rulers. There were a hundred eunuchs and a thousand women in the palace as attendants to each sultana.

LANFANG REPUBLIC

This was formed in 1777 in west Kalimantan, Indonesia, by Chinese settlers who had come to the region for trade. It was actually under the Manchu rulers of China, but was virtually independent. The republic came under the Dutch in 1884.

Pagarayung was another kingdom in western Sumatra, located in the Minangkabu highlands. It was established around 1350, and existed till 1833, though its power declined after 1800.

THE STORY OF NUTMEG

The nutmeg tree, *Myristica fragrans*, mainly grew in the Banda Islands, part of the Maluku (Moluccas), also known as the Spice Islands. At the beginning of the 17th century, the Dutch East India Company (VOC) took over the islands from the Portuguese. In order to have a monopoly of the spice, they banned the export of nutmeg trees. Before exporting nutmeg the nuts were made infertile by dipping them in lime. And when local people protested, all the males over the age of 15 on the island were killed. In 15 years after the arrival of the

Dutch, the population dropped from 15,000 to 600. Nutmeg was used as a spice, incense and medicine. One Banda island named Run was under the British, but the Dutch received this in exchange for a trading post, now known as Manhattan.

Pierre Poivre from France managed to take a few nuts out in 1769. They were planted in Mauritius, and from here the British East India Company brought the nuts to different places and the trees began to grow in India, Malaysia, Singapore, Grenada and the West Indies.

17

Africa: Continuity and Change 1500–1800

In Africa there were different levels of development and numerous states and territories. Some groups still lived by hunting, while others lived in cities.

THE OTTOMANS

The Ottomans began gaining control over North Africa. In 1517, they conquered Egypt from the Mamluks. In 1529, Algiers (Algeria) came under the Ottomans, followed by Tunisia, in 1534. In 1551, Tripoli (present Libya) was conquered.

However, Ottoman power in these regions was limited, and gradually declined.

In Egypt, the Mamluks still remained as administrators in a subordinate role, until Napoleon's invasion in 1798.

In Algiers, the first dey or local ruler was appointed in 1671. In 1718, the tenth dey of Algiers, Ali Chaouch, was given the title of pasha, further increasing autonomy.

In Tunisia, the dey or local governor was assisted by an officer called bey. Murad bey (d. 1631) began the hereditary succession of beys, increasing their power. His successors held power till 1702, when Murad bey II was assassinated by a cavalry officer named Ibrahim al Sharif, who held the offices of both dey and bey. After an invasion by Algiers in 1705, a new dynasty of beys arose, founded by Husain Ali, who pushed back the invaders and defeated the dey of Tunisia.

Tripoli had earlier been ruled by Egypt, but in 1510 was occupied by Spain. Spain handed Tripoli over to the Knights of St John who controlled it from 1523 to 1551. Then it was captured by the Ottomans and administered by a pasha or governor. Ahmad Karamanli killed the Ottoman governor in 1711, and established himself as a semi-independent ruler. Under the Karamanli dynasty, Tripoli was virtually independent till 1835, when the Ottomans again brought it under their command.

FUNG SULTANATE

In about 1500 the Fung or Funj Sultanate was established with its capital at Sennar on the Blue Nile. It was a successor of the Alwa Christian kingdom. The Fung was located in northern Sudan, to the west of Ethiopia, and gradually expanded its territory further, ruling a large part of north-east Africa up to 1821. From Egypt, the Ottomans fought against the Fung, but could not defeat them.

Fung sultans, who had the title Mek (meaning sultan), adopted Islam in 1523, but indigenous religions continued to coexist.

In the 16th century its army had several cavalry units. Horsemen wore armour and used long swords in battle. Sennar at this time was a rich centre of trade. The sultanate began to decline in the 17th century. In 1821 it was conquered by Egypt, which was still under the Ottomans.

ETHIOPIA

The region comprising the present countries of Ethiopia, Eritrea and Somalia was ruled by a number of different dynasties and kingdoms. The Amhara or Solomonid dynasty began to rule Ethiopia from CE 1270. They claimed that they were descended from King Solomon and Queen Sheba. Apart for a few brief periods, this dynasty ruled up to 1974.

However, Ethiopia was not free of problems and conflicts. The Ottomans occupied some coastal regions from 1516 to 1846. A war was fought against the Adal sultanate from 1527 to 1543. This sultanate was located in the Horn of Africa. Imam Ahmad of Adal, the virtual ruler of Adal, conquered part of Ethiopia. In 1541, Ethiopia obtained Portuguese support, while Adal was helped by the Ottomans. The war lasted till 1543, when Ahmad was killed. After this, the emperor Galawedos (ruled 1540-59) restored order in Ethiopia, but was troubled by raids by the Oromo people. In 1559 he was killed in another battle against Adal. His younger brother Minas (ruled 1559-63) succeeded him. Between 1563 and 1597 Sarsa Dengel was the king of Ethiopia. Sarsa Dengel reorganized the army and made a peace agreement with the Ottomans in 1589.

Another notable king was Fasilidas, also known as Basilides, who ruled from 1632 to 1667. He established his capital at Gondar. The city became a great centre of art and architecture, where several castles, palaces and churches were built. Numerous scholars and merchants lived here. His son Yohannes I succeeded Fasilidas in 1667. In 1682 Yohannes's son Iyasu (Jesus) I came to the throne. Under him, art and architecture flourished. His reign has been called the period of the renaissance of Ethiopian culture. At the same time, he fought several battles against the Oromo. After his death in 1706, Ethiopia faced increasing problems. Iyasu II, also known as Adyam Saggad, ruled from 1729 to 1755. He built a palace in Gondar and churches in Qusqwam and Ayazo near

Fasilidas's palace at Gondar

Gondar. His second wife was from an Oromo family. Their son Iyoas became the king after Iyasu II's death.

The Oromo then began to dominate Ethiopia. Ethiopia broke up into several local or feudal kingdoms though a line of Ethiopian kings continued. Wars took place among these feudal rulers, and continued till 1855. Even at this time of disunity, religion was a factor of unity.

The main religion was Monophysite Christianity, also called Coptic Christianity, which was part of the Orthodox Christian Church.

MOROCCO

In the 15th century the Portuguese and Spanish began to control the coastal areas of Morocco. But the Saädi dynasty, also called the first Sharifian dynasty, ruled in Morocco, from 1549 to 1654.

In 1578 the battle of al Kasr al-Kabir took place. The Portuguese king Dom Sebastian invaded Morocco with a large force, but after a fierce struggle was defeated and killed. The sultan Abdul Malik led the Moroccan forces. He too was killed in the battle, but his brother Ahmad, now called al-Mansur (the victorious) became the sultan. This battle is important in history, as it led to the decline of Portugal. The Portuguese were driven out from Agadi, Safi and other ports of Morocco. In 1591 the kingdom of Songhe was invaded by Morocco, and controlled through pashas based in Timbuktu. Overall the rule of Ahmad al-Mansur (1578–1603) was a time of Moroccan strength. Art and architecture flourished.

Arabs and Jews migrated to the country in the 16th century, after they were expelled from Spain, and Morocco benefitted by their presence.

The second Sharifian dynasty began in 1660. Ismail al-Hasani (ruled 1672–1727) was the most important king of this dynasty. His reign was prosperous and peaceful, but after this there was disorder for some time.

Miknas (Meknes), containing the sultan's palace, is called the Moroccan Versailles. It is an important Sufi centre.

MALI AND SONGHE

Mali and Songhe were two empires in western Africa. By 1500 Mali had declined, and part of it was taken over by Songhe. Askia Muhammad (ruled 1493–1528) was the greatest of the Songhe rulers. Timbuktu in Mali was a prosperous city that came under the Songhe. The Songhe empire declined by the end of the 16th century, after its invasion by Morocco in 1591. The region broke up into small kingdoms. Among these were the kingdoms of Macina, Segou and Gonja.

Timbuktu

In the 16th century Timbuktu under Songhe had a population of 40,000. Trade across the Sahara passed through here. The Sankore mosque and madrasa in the city was important from the

14th century. It had a huge library and thousands of students. Islamic scholars lived there. Timbuktu had grand markets where gold, textiles and other items were sold.

A number of old manuscripts have been found from Timbuktu. According to some estimates about 7,00,000 manuscripts have been discovered from various parts of the city. Most have not yet been studied and many have been destroyed. The manuscripts are on different topics including art and science, while some are short letters. Most belong to the 16th–18th centuries, though there are both earlier and later documents dating from the 13th–20th centuries. The manuscripts are mainly in Arabic, but there are some in Songhe and Tamasheq languages.

LEO AFRICANUS (1494–1554)

Leo Africanus, whose real name was al-Hasan ibn Muhammad al-Wazzan, was born in Granada, but soon after moved to Fez, where he grew up. He studied at the University of Al Karaouine and later travelled to different places, sometimes on diplomatic missions. He was captured by Spanish corsairs (pirates) in 1518, and in 1520 was freed and baptized in Rome.

He wrote a description of Africa, based on his own travels. This is divided into nine books. The first book is an introduction. The next seven describe kingdoms and regions: Marrakesh, Fez, Tiemcen, Tunis, Numidia, Sub-Sahara and Egypt. He first dictated his account in Arabic, and then in Italian. It was published in Italian and translated into French, English, Latin and other languages. It provided Europeans with an insight into Africa, a continent they still knew little about. In English, the book was called *A Geographical Histoirie of Africa*. A BBC documentary has been produced on Leo Africanus, and a fictionalized account of his life was written by Amin Maalouf.

BENIN

Benin was in the region of present southern Nigeria, and was different from the modern state of Benin. Benin was founded by the 13th century, and was also known as Edo. The founders claimed to be descended from the Yoruba. The kings were known as Oba. The empire expanded under Oba Esigie (ruled 1504–50). Benin city was the capital. It was well laid out with broad roads and had several wooden buildings.

The Portuguese had reached Benin before 1500, while English traders arrived there in 1553.

Palm oil, spices, ivory, and textiles were among the items of trade. In the 17th century the Dutch reached there. Dutch visitors to Benin city commented on its cleanliness. Olfert Dapper, a Dutch trader, said Benin city had wonderful palaces and houses. There were long galleries with wooden pillars covered in copper. Battle scenes were engraved on these. The craftsmen of Benin made beautiful brass, bronze and ivory statues, wall plaques and fine jewellery. Ivory was used to create images and figurines. Two ivory leopards, symbolizing power, were placed beside the king on special occasions. Leopards in fact stood as a symbol of royal power not only in Benin but in several parts of Africa.

Benin started participating in the slave trade in the 18th century. At this time the kingdom was involved in wars and disputes.

In the 1890s the British took over Benin and in 1897 forced the Oba to submit to them. However he retained his traditional title and hereditary line.

BORNU

Bornu, also known as Kanem-Bornu, was a kingdom in the Sudan region that existed from the 8th to 19th centuries, but began to decline after 1650. It actually began as the Kanem empire, which lasted till 1376. The Saifawa dynasty ruled from CE 800. The capital was intitially at Njimi. The Bulala people pushed the Saifawa out of the Kanem region. The Saifawa then founded the new empire of Bornu, with the capital at Ngazargamu. By the end of the 15th century, the Bulala were defeated and Njimi was reconquered.

Idris Alooma (probably ruled 1571-1603) was the most powerful king of this dynasty. He had an efficient army. He bought weapons from the Ottomans, and organized a camel corps. He improved the system of administration and built a number of mosques. Trade crossed through North Africa to the Mediterranean. Slaves, ivory and cotton were among the exports, while salt, horses and guns were included in the imports. A line of Saifawa kings continued until 1846, but the last few kings had no real power, and the empire had declined by 1800.

PIRATES AND SLAVES

North Africa, particularly the region of Tunisia, Algeria, Morocco and Tripoli, was a base for sea pirates. These are known as Ottoman pirates or Ottoman corsairs, as most of this area was under the Ottomans. They are also called Corsairs of Barbary, Barbary being a name Europeans used for this region. (It comes from Berber.) These pirates sailed across the seas and captured ships, and landed in towns and villages of Europe. They even reached Iceland, Newfoundland and Ireland. Most of the pirates were Arabs of North Africa, but some Europeans too joined them. After 1650, their power was reduced, as European kingdoms and orders of knights attacked them, but even so between 1500 and 1815 they captured about one million people, mainly European Christians, and sold them as slaves in North Africa and West Asia. Some of the slaves were freed through ransom, but others lived and died in terrible conditions. Pirate activities ended after 1815. This was because some European countries made treaties with the pirates. There were also some European conquests of the region.

18

Africa: Other Kingdoms 1500–1800

In this chapter we look at some more kingdoms and peoples of Africa.

THE HAUSA

In the area of Nigeria, there were several city states of the Hausa people. Among the states were Daura, Gobir, Rano, Katsina, Kano, Zazzau and Biram. In the 16th century, Kano was the largest state. Kano had been founded in the 10th century, but became a sultanate in 1349. Berber traders were among those that lived here. Metal, gold and ivory items were produced as well as textiles. *The Kano Chronicle* provides an account of the Kano kingdom and sultanate as well as an idea of other Hausa states. The *Chronicle* was composed in the 19th century, but is based on earlier oral traditions. Hausa states continued to exist till the 19th century.

YORUBA AT OYO

The Yoruba people existed in south-west Nigeria. Initially their centre was at Ife, but later it moved to Oyo. Between 1600 and

1800, Oyo was the centre of an empire, which controlled the surrounding city states. Most of the city states were headed by an oba (priest-king) who was elected, and a council of leaders. The Oyo king was known as the alafin. The main region of the Yoruba extended between the Volta and Niger rivers. Oyo expanded to the east, north and south-west, and in the first half of the 18th century, gained control over Dahomey, which paid the Oyo king an annual tribute. The tribute included cowries, coral and guns. The Alafin's power began to decline after 1750. Oyo was defeated by the states of Borge and Nupu in the 1780s. By the first half of the 19th century the power of Oyo declined further and smaller states became independent.

The Yoruba were known for their wooden carvings and sculptures, as well as for weaving textiles and for metalwork and beadwork. Doors, verandah posts and deities were among the items carved in wood. The remains of the Old city of Oyo, enclosed in mud walls, can still be seen.

AKWAMU AND DENKYIRA

The present state of Ghana is located in west Africa. The Gulf of Guinea is to the south. In medieval times there were many states in the region. The Gunja, Buna and Wa states were formed in the north, and Denkyira and Akwamu in the south. Between 1677 and 1702, the state of Akwamu expanded its territories under the king Ansa Sasraku. Denkyira was prominent after 1620.

ASANTE

The Asante, also known as Ashanti, were people of Akan origin. Between the 10th and 12th centuries, they settled in small states in the southern region of modern Ghana. Initially they were under Denkyira. In the 17th century the Asante clans came together under Osei Tutu (ruled 1690–1712). Osei Tutu was the ruler of a small state with its capital at Kumasi. In 1701, Denkyira was defeated. Opoku Ware, (ruled 1720–50) further expanded the kingdom.

Asante people speak the Twi language, also known as the Akan language. The Asante have several traditional proverbs and stories. According to one story, Osei Tutu brought down the Golden Stool from heaven, through which he received his authority. Asante kings wore gold jewellery. Wooden carvings wrapped with gold foil were crafted. Special silk cloth was woven, with thread taken from European textiles. They also made elaborately carved gold weights.

In the Asante religion, the supreme creator is known as Nyame, the deity of the sky. He had several abosom or children, who mainly represented powers of nature. The Asante had their own typical music.

FON STATE (DAHOMEY)

The Fon or Dahomey (Abomey) state was founded in c. 1650 under Wegjaba or Houegbadja. He had twin children, a boy named Akaba and a girl Hangbe, as well as another son, Dosu, also known as Agaja.

After the death of Houegbadja, Akaba ruled Dahomey from 1685 to 1716. The state expanded. Akaba died in the Oueme river valley, though it is not known if this was a result of a battle or of smallpox. His sister Hangbe took control, planning that Akaba's son, Agbo Sassa, would take over the throne. However, Agaja defeated them and became king in 1718.

After 1718, Agaja continued to increase its territories. Around 1727, Agaja conquered the small coastal states, of Alladah (also called Ardrah), Ouidah (Whydah) and Jakin, and created a centralized monarchy. He founded a new capital at Abomey. Ouidah was a major port of trade with Europe.

Dahomey was involved in the slave trade. Ardrah (Porto Novo) was developed as a port for this trade.

MADAGASCAR—THE HOLY ISLAND

The island of Madagascar was settled by a number of different groups. It was once covered with tropical forests in which different types of animals and birds lived. Among these were elephant birds (Aepyornis maximus), which could not fly and were around 3 m tall. Their eggs could have a diameter of 1 m. There were several species of lemurs, larger than those that exist today, as well as types of fossa (a carnivorous animal) and the Malagassy hippopotamus. As people began to plant crops and clear the forests, the wildlife declined. The elephant bird became extinct in the 17th century.

ANCESTORS

Honouring ancestors was very important in Madagascar. Madagascar has elaborate carved posts erected above tombs, with animal capitals or groups of humans. Post-shaped funerary monuments were constructed in a variety of styles in several other parts of Africa, including Ethiopia, Sudan, Tanzania and Kenya.

Madagascar grave posts

The Arabs set up trade centres by the 10th century. In the 16th century rice was among the crops grown, and large herds of cattle were kept. The French founded trading centres in the 17th century. By this time Madagascar had a number of kingdoms that had become rich through trade. From 1774 to 1824 it was known both for its slave trade and for its pirates.

JAMES FORT

Kunta Kinteh Island, earlier known as James Island, is located on the river Gambia. The island was occupied by the Portuguese in the 15th century, and called St Andrew's Island, but about 200 years later was bought by the duke of Courland (The duchy of Courland was a vassal state of Poland-Lithuania.) Jacob Fort was built in 1651 on the Gambia estuary island by Courlanders, and used for trade between Latvia and Lithuania, and Africa. In 1661 it was captured by the British, and renamed James Fort. It was Britain's first success in Africa. Gold, ivory and slaves were transported from here. Later it came under France. The island was abandoned in the 1830s, as it was no longer profitable.

TWO IMAMATES

Some Islamic kingdoms were ruled by imams, and are referred to as imamates. The Futa Djallon imamate was founded in the Guinea region, in 1725. The imamate lasted till 1896, when it was taken over by the French. The city of Timbo was the capital. In 1775, the Futa Turo imamate was founded in the Senegal region. This led to the decline of the Denianke dynasty in the region. Both these imamates were founded by Fulani Islamic groups, leading up to the formation of the Fulani empire.

KONGO

In the 14th century the Kongo kingdom was established in the region of present Angola and the Republic of Congo.

It was founded by King Wene. The next kings were elected from members of the royal family. Kongo had a number of tributary kingdoms. Among them was Ndongo. In the late 15th century, the Portuguese began to settle in Kongo, and occupied the coastal region. In 1491, the king was converted to Catholicism, and took the name Joao I. He was succeeded by Afonso I (ruled 1506–43). War slaves were traded in the markets of Kongo, but with the arrival of the Portuguese, the international slave trade began.

The city of Luanda was founded on the coast by the Portuguese in 1576, and developed into a Portuguese colony. By 1665 several provinces of Kongo became independent. By the end of the 17th century, the French, Belgians and Portuguese had occupied the kingdom. The independent kingdom of Ndongo fought against the Portuguese in the 17th century.

In 1621, Mbandi Ngola Kiluanji (Ngola was a title of the king of Ndongo) sent his sister Nzinga to make peace with the Portuguese. The peace treaty was not honoured, and in despair King Ngola committed suicide. Nzinga became the regent for his son. She fought against the Portuguese and allied with the Dutch, but finally lost. Queen Nzinga then conquered and ruled the kingdom of Matamba. Nzinga is still remembered in Angola, and a statue of her stands in Luanda.

LUBA AND LUNDA

According to tradition, the Luba kingdom was founded around 1500 by Kongolo (meaning 'rainbow'). After some time, Mbidi Kiluwe (Mbidi the hunter) and his people came to Kongolo's land. Kongolo welcomed them and, and married his two half-sisters to Mbidi. Later there was a quarrel, and one of his sister's sons, Kalala Illunga, took over the kingdom. The Luba kingdom was not centralized, hence there were constant conflicts, and breakaway states were often formed.

Around 1600, one son of the dynasty founded the Lunda empire. This empire too broke up into different states. (As this is a traditional account, some scholars believe the Luba and Lunda kingdoms were founded later, around 1585 and 1665 respectively.)

These various states are grouped together under the term Luba-Lunda states. Bemba, Kasanje and Kazambe were among them. Kazambe became a powerful state. Between 1750 and 1850 it controlled southern Katanga and part of the Zimbabwe plateau. The states existed till 1887–89.

Royal stools and Lukasa boards

Each Luba king had some royal items, including a stool with a kneeling woman beneath, bow stands, and spears, which were often also decorated with women figures.

Lukasa were carved boards, on which beads were glued in a particular pattern. Court historians used these to narrate history, the beads serving as memory devices.

Buli was a village where a number of carved bowls and stools were made.

A Luba stool

EAST AFRICAN CITY STATES

Along the coast of East Africa, were a number of cities and towns involved in trade with West Asia, China and India. These were under the Kilwa sultanate, though they enjoyed some autonomy. Among the cities were Kilwa, Malindi and Sofala. The islands of Mombasa, Pemba, Mafia, Zanzibar, Mozambique, Comoro, also came under the Kilwa sultan. By the 15th century, the power of the Kilwa sultans had declined. Their ministers, known as emirs or viziers, often held the real authority. Emir Ibrahim murdered the sultan and assumed power himself, but many of the cities then asserted their independence. The Portuguese reached the region from 1497, and gradually tried to gain control over the prosperous cities and more importantly over their trade. In 1505, they burned Kilwa, and the Swahili city ports began to decline. Trade too declined as the Portuguese were unable to maintain the extensive sea trade that had once taken place. The Portuguese also began to penetrate the Zambezi valley. Later, many of the small states came under the sultanate of Oman. Oman also conquered Zanzibar and other places along the east coast from the Portuguese. Oman was helped by the Ajuran sultanate that existed in Somalia. In 1749 the Al Said dynasty came to power in Oman. They took over the east Africa coastal cities. In the 19th century, the sultan of Oman began to live mainly in Zanzibar. Palaces and mosques were built in the city.

THE CHRONICLE OF KILWA

Around 1520, the *Chronicle of Kilwa* was written in both Arabic and Portuguese. According to the stories in the Chronicle, the Kilwa sultans came from Shiraz in Persia in the 10th century. The Chronicle records the names of the Kilwa sultans up to around 1450.

BUNYORO AND BUGANDA

In the region of modern Tanzania, Rwanda, Burundi and Uganda, were a number of kingdoms ruled by the Bachwezi people. Luo people migrated into the region from the area of Sudan. In the Uganda region, Bunyoro, Ankole, Buganda and Karagwe were among the states founded. Bunyoro was important until around 1750. After this Buganda rose in power. Buganda's king was known as the Kabaka. In Rwanda-Burundi, the Bachwezi, also called Tutsi Bututsi or Bahima, formed the ruling class from around 1500. The people were Bantus.

Roshen Dalal   181

MUTAPA EMPIRE

The Mutapa (Munhumutapa) empire was established in the 15th century, but weakened in the 17th century with the rise of the Rozvi empire.

This empire was located north of Great Zimbabwe on a plateau overlooking the Zambezi river. According to a story it was founded by one of the Shona people from Zimbabwe. He had been sent to the north to search for salt. The Mutapa residents were divided into the Shona elite and the ordinary people. The Shona owned huge herds of cattle, while the peasants herded sheep and goats. Cereal crops were grown in the kingdom. Gold mines were located here and the gold trade formed part of the economy. Wooden palisades surrounded their buildings. Traders from Africa's east coast came to trade. The Mutapa empire began to decline in the 17th century. Near the Zambezi the Portuguese organized chiefdoms that attacked Mutapa, and they even killed the Mutapa king in 1633. Finally the Mutapa kingdom was replaced by the Rozvi empire, under Changamire.

ROZVI EMPIRE

The Rozvie empire (1684–1834) was set up on the Zimbabwe plateau by Changamire Dombo. He brought the entire Zimbabwe region under his control. Cities were constructed with buildings of stone, as well as of clay. Polychrome pottery was made. The Rozvi maintained an efficient army. Warriors were armed with spears, bows and arrows. Agriculture, cattle farming and gold mining formed part of the economy. There was trade in gold, ivory, copper and other items.

The main centres of the empire included Danamombe (also spelt Danangombe), Khami, Zinjanja and Naletale.

Danamombe (earlier known as Dhlodhlo) was the capital. Khami was earlier the capital of the kingdom of Butua, a Torwa state founded by Shona people. Butua succeeded Great Zimbabwe in south-west Zimbabwe, and later came under the Rozvi empire. The Rozvi power declined when the Nguni invaded the region and the Ndebele came there in the 1830s.

Khami

Khami is located west of the Khami river, 22 km from the city of Bulawayo on a hilltop. The remains of the ancient city cover an area of about 108 hectares. Khami was abandoned in the 19th century. It has walled structures. The chief's residence was to the north. The people lived in huts made of daga, a type of clayey soil found in the region. Huts were often decorated with friezes and surrounded by granite walls. The walls too were decorated, and there were long passages and galleries. There were trade links with regions beyond Africa. Items found at Khami include Spanish silver and Chinese porcelain. A large granite cross was probably fixed there by the Portuguese.

Remains of a wall at Khami

THE CAPE OF GOOD HOPE

At the southern end of Africa, the Cape of Good Hope was an important point on the trade route to the east.

The Portuguese had sailed around the Cape of Good Hope in 1488 (Bartholomew Dias) and 1497 (Vasco da Gama), but did not establish a settlement there.

Others too followed the same route, including the Dutch. The Dutch ship, *Nieuwe Haarlem*, of the Dutch East India Company, was shipwrecked there in March 1647, and the survivors built a small fort and lived at the Cape for a year. One year later they were rescued, but returning to the Netherlands, they suggested that the Dutch East India Company should start a trading settlement there.

In 1652, the Dutch established a settlement at Cape of Good Hope, with 90 Calvinist settlers, led by Jan van Riebeeck. They built a fort of wood and clay, and between 1666 and 1679, a larger fort called the Castle of Good Hope, that still exists. They bought some land from the local Khoikhoi people. Gradually a number of semi-independent farms were established in the area. The number of farms reached 435 by 1731. But these farms were controlled by a small proportion of the population. After 1688, French Huguenots began to settle here, but were absorbed into the Dutch way of life. Dutch was the only language taught in schools. Agriculture and trade formed the basis of the economy at Cape Town. Slave labour was used.

By the end of the 18th century, Cape Colony was occupied by numerous settlers known as Boers, from the Dutch word for farmer. They had different origins, but all had to speak Dutch and practise Calvinism and thus developed a common cultural identity, calling themselves Afrikaners. Most slaves and servants in the region were blacks, the masters Europeans.

During the Napoleonic wars the Cape first passed to the British (1795–1803), then to the Batavian republic (1803–06) and again to the British in 1806.

TRADE

Before 1750 Africa had long-distance trade networks across the oceans, with trade mainly in luxury goods such as gold, salt, beads and leather. In 1750, various parts of Africa had different economies. It gradually was drawn into the world economy along with India, Russia, the Ottoman empire and the Americas.

THE SLAVE TRADE

There was both internal and long-distance trade in slaves. Within Africa, war captives could be sold as slaves, but they often rose to high positions, and were in a different category from other types of slaves. It was the trans-Atlantic slave trade that led to misery, exploitation and death for Africans. In order to make profits, African countries, particularly in west and Central Africa, were themselves were involved in this trade. Initially slaves went to Europe and to Portuguese and Spanish settlements in the Atlantic islands. The first lot in Europe were sold in Lisbon in 1444.

From the mid-16th century slaves reached Brazil, the Caribbean islands and North America. Some Europeans had been enslaved by Ottomans and Africans by Arabs, but never to the same extent. In the interiors of Africa, 'slave hunts' took place, and Africans were chased, hunted and caught in order to be sold. Thousands died even while being transported in ships, as slaves were chained together in extremely unhygenic conditions, with little space to move or breathe. Families were generally separated, and not only men, but also women and children were sold.

Between 1650 and 1750 the trade in slaves tripled. The decline in the slave trade after 1750 was partly because it was no longer profitable. As colonies were established, Africans were required within Africa, to work and produce raw materials for world trade. It was not cost-effective to capture and transport slaves to work in other distant parts of the world.

Between 1650 and 1900, historians estimate that at least 28 million Africans from western and central Africa were transported as slaves, though these figures are controversial. Because of the misery imposed by slavery and the sheer numbers that died, the slave trade has been called the Black Holocaust.

At one time it was thought that the slave trade profits led to European industrialization, but this is now not considered correct.

EUROPEANS

The Portuguese were the first Europeans to enter Africa in the 15th century. They tried to impose Catholicism on various groups, and interfered in the affairs of local kingdoms. They also began the Atlantic slave trade. Gradually the French, Dutch, the British and other European powers entered Africa. By the end of the 19th century all of Africa was controlled by European nations. (See Chapter 35.)

MUNGO PARK (1771–1806)

Though Europeans had occupied parts of Africa, many places in the interior remained unknown. European explorers tried to find out more about the interior of Africa. Among the explorers was Mungo Park.

Mungo Park was born in Scotland. He studied medicine and botany at the University of Edinburgh, and in 1793 was appointed as assistant surgeon on a ship, the *Worcestor*. He sailed to

Mungo Park

Benkulen in Sumatra, and on his return, described some rare Sumatran fish and plants.

In 1794 Park joined the African Association to assist in explorations in Africa. In 1796, after many adventures, he became the first European to reach the Niger river at Segou. Returning to Scotland in 1797, he wrote *Travels in the Interior of Africa*, a book that became very successful.

In 1805 Mungo Park led an expedition to discover the terminal point of the river Niger. Many members of the expedition died from fever or dysentery. Mungo Park made a special canoe and continued in it down the Niger, with a few helpers. But soon after Yauri, the canoe rammed into a rock, and was stuck there. From the nearby riverbanks, arrows were shot at them, and Mungo and others jumped into the river. He and three others drowned, while one slave on the canoe survived. Mungo is remembered as one of the greatest explorers who provided accurate descriptions of his journeys and of the places he visited.

19
North America

'There was a time when our people covered the whole land, as the waves of a wind-ruffled sea cover its shell-paved floor. But that time has long since passed away, with the greatness of tribes almost forgotten. ' Chief Seattle.

Chief Seattle was a Native American chief who lived between around 1780 and 1866. His words quoted above reflect the tragedy of Native Americans.

THE NATIVE AMERICANS

North America had a number of people and numerous cultures before the arrival of the Europeans. Today the early inhabitants are called Native Americans or sometimes American Indians. In Canada they are often called First Nations, First Peoples, or indigenous people. It is not known how many people lived in North America when the Europeans reached there, as there are widely different estimates from 8.4 million to 112 million. There were approximately 700 indigenous societies of North America. Each of these had cultural and other differences. Over 700 different languages too were spoken. Among the various groups, far north were the Arctic people known as the Inuit or Eskimos, and the Aleuts. Groups in Alaska included Inuits, Athabascan, Haida and others. Together they are known as Alaska natives. Hawaii had entirely different settlers, who were of Polynesian origin.

Other groups across North America included the Tlingit, Nakota, Cree, Mikmaq, Penobscot, Tsimshian, Black foot, Hidatsa, Mandan, Sioux, Cheyenne, Iroquois, Shawnee, Delaware, Niska, Gitkan, Tsimshian, Salish and many more.

Each of the hundreds of Native American societies had their own histories and ways of life. To describe them would take many volumes, and only a brief picture can be provided here.

By 1500, these many groups lived in different ways. Some of them continued to live largely by hunting animals and gathering foods from the wild, along with some amount of agriculture. Bison, elk, moose, caribou, deer, beaver, porcupine, bear, birds, rabbits and waterfowl were among the creatures hunted. Other groups lived in agricultural villages and some in urban centres or towns. There was trade and exchange among the various groups or clans. Each had its own stories and legends, and its own ceremonies and ways of life.

Agriculture was practised in most of the regions. The main crops were corn (maize), beans and squash, melon and sunflowers along with tubers. Agricultural techniques were quite advanced. For instance, Native Americans grew 30 varieties of corn, which had been adapted to different environmental and climatic conditions.

Some made complex and large houses, beautiful pottery, simple weapons, baskets and other items. Even those who were primarily agricultural often hunted. Clothing could be made from skins, and other parts of the animals were used to make implements and various items. Weaving was a highly developed skill. Songs, dances and art were advanced. However, they did not use the wheel, the plough, or iron. On the whole Native groups in North America did not have a writing system, though they may have had systems of notation.

All the groups had close kinship and family connections. Their societies had a hierarchy and a chief or leader, with political power. Nobles or leaders owned items such as masks and crests used in ceremonies, which others did not have. Religious and other rituals were important, and there was some similarity in religious beliefs. Marriage, birth, death and coming-of-age rituals were celebrated by all. Potlaches or public feasts were often held. Groups met for trade, exchange and social functions. Polygyny was practised, and in very few cases, polyandry. Groups such as the Iroquios, Cherokee and several others had matrilineal/matrifocal societies. In these societies, inheritance was from mother to daughter. However, such societies were not matriarchies, as men continued to be chiefs.

SOME EARLY WRITING SYSTEMS

Wiigwaasabak scrolls are birchbark scrolls with geometric shapes and patterns that contain information. They were used by the Ojibwa, a group of the Anishinaabe-speaking people, a branch of the Alonquian language family of North America (Canada), at least from 400 years ago. Their Midewiwin Society keeps scrolls and records of events.

Mi'kmaq hieroglyphic writing was used by the Mikmaq of the east coast of Canada by the 17th century or earlier.

Lifestyles

Here we take a brief look at some variations in lifestyles in different parts of North America around 1500. Variations in the lifestyle of different groups were largely based on climate and terrain.

In the northern coasts of Alaska and Canada, extending to about 300 km north of the US border, the region was too cold for agriculture. Most of the people lived by hunting and fishing. Along the north-western coast of the Pacific coast extending from southern Alaska to northern California, there were some villages. Wooden houses were built in these. Items were traded with other regions.

Other groups of people lived in the plateau region, which included parts of Idaho, Oregon, Washington, Montana and an adjoining part of Canada. Fish from the rivers, camas (edible plants) and other naturally-growing plants were eaten and dried for consumption in winter. People lived in villages, but there was a market town on the lower Columbia river for trade. In the mountain slopes and valleys of Utah, Nevada and California, the lifestyle included hunting, fishing, gathering wild nuts and seeds, and some agriculture.

In the North American plains there were grasslands extending from Canada to Mexico. Here herds of bison (buffalo) roamed. Within the plains there were different types of terrain. By 1500 many Native American groups settled in villages and towns along the rivers. Various crops were grown. Bison were hunted and used for food. In the eastern United States and Canada, extending southwards from Minnesota and Ontario, there were some large settlements including villages and towns. Cahokia in Illinois was perhaps the largest, with a population of over 20,000.

In the south-west there were both villages and towns. Some of their towns had huge structures, temples and roads. The people here were termed Pueblos by the Spanish.

The south-east region included the area north of the Gulf of Mexico along the Atlantic coast, extending towards the west to central Texas. Here in 1500, there were both towns and villages. Broadly, eastern, midwestern and south-western parts of the present US had societies that practised agriculture, along with some food-gathering, hunting and fishing.

Below, we provide an idea of the life of one of the groups, and of one village.

The Natchez

The Natchez were one of the hundreds of Native American groups. They lived in villages near the Mississippi, near the present place Natchez, and the Natchez Bluffs. They spoke a language that is considered an isolate, that is, not related to any other Native American language. Their beliefs were somewhat different from other Native American groups. They kept a fire burning in their temples and worshipped both sun and fire. The Great Sun was the leader of the tribe. There were about 5000 people in a unified group.

The location of the Emerald Mound

Among the Natchez centres is the site of Emerald Mound. The huge mound measures 230 m by 133 m, with a height of 11 m, and was used as the main ceremonial centre of the Natchez. Remains of tools, pottery and animal bones have been found here. Around 1680, the centre moved 19 km south-west, to the Grand Village of the Natchez.

The French explorer René-Robert Cavelier, Sieur de La Salle reached here in 1682. He and the members of his expedition were the first Europeans to come in contact with the Natchez. The French settled in the region in 1716, with their centre at Fort Rosalie. They joined with the Choctaw in 1729 in a war against the Natchez, after which the latter declined.

Ozette—a buried village

Ozette, a village on the Olympic peninsula (Cape Alva) in Washington, was occupied from around 400 BCE to about 1920. But part of the village was buried in mud around CE 1750 (or according to some dating methods, 1560).

Just like Pompeii and Novgorod (see Volume 1), this part of the village is well preserved, and tells us about life at the time. The Makah people lived here. The village had houses made of wood planks. The houses faced the ocean and were in two rows. Like Novgorod, the houses and objects beneath the mud were preserved because of waterlogging. The planks of the houses were found, along with objects including fishing nets, baskets, ropes, tools made of wood, bone and antler, and other items. More than 55,000 objects have been found. Most of these were made of wood. There were also 40,000 remains of structures, and one million animal remains. The people lived mainly by fishing. Most of them caught and ate ordinary fish, but one important family ate salmon, halibut and whale. This family lived in the largest house, with many decorated items.

20

North America (continued)

After Christopher Columbus reached the Caribbean Islands (see Chapter 22) and other parts of the Americas, more Europeans began exploring and settling in these regions.

A DISCOVERY OR A CONQUEST?

Columbus was not the first European to reach there, the Vikings, Irish, and even the Welsh had visited before him. And of course the Americas were not discovered by him—they had been occupied by other people for thousands of years. For these reasons, historians no longer refer to his arrival as the 'discovery of America'. Instead his visits are referred to as an encounter or meeting of cultures, or a conquest.

America was a name given to the area by Europeans. The continents were not named after Columbus, but after another explorer, Amerigo Vespucci. (See Chapter 21.)

THE FIRST EUROPEANS AFTER COLUMBUS

The early settlers in North America were mainly the Spanish, French and English. The Swedish and Dutch also founded some settlements. Among these early settlers, Jacques Cartier (1491–1557) of France founded Montreal in Canada in 1536. More French settlements were established in the Canada region after 1604, including Quebec in 1608. French settlements along the St Lawrence river were grouped together as the colony of New France. Cartier met the Huron people in this region. As their term for village was kanata, the French called the whole region Canada. The French expanded further in the Mississippi valley region, a territory then called Louisiana. By 1712 the French controlled Louisiana and a large part of eastern Canada.

The Spanish and the French struggled for control over Florida and California. Early Spanish settlements in Florida did not survive. In 1565, Pedro Menendez founded St Augustine in Florida. The French had already reached the region and there was a nearby Huguenot settlement that he destroyed. He hanged all the inhabitants. After three years Dominique de Gourges, a Huguenot, reached there and did the same to the Spanish garrison.

In 1584, a fleet was sent from England by Sir Walter Raleigh. Its aim was to found a settlement on Roanoke Island in Virginia. This settlement, however, did not survive long.

An English settlement was founded at Jamestown in 1607. In 1624 it came under the British government.

Meanwhile in 1620 the ship *Mayflower* from Plymouth, England, reached Cape Cod Bay in Massachusetts, after a voyage lasting 65 days. Though 102 people had started out, during the journey, five died and two were born. Hence 99 individuals reached the new land. The area where they settled had already been named New Plymouth. The people were mostly Puritans from England; some were earlier in exile in the Netherlands, where they had gone because of persecution in England. This group was later called 'the Pilgrim Fathers' (the term was first used in 1799). They governed themselves by the Mayflower Compact,

The signing of the Mayflower Compact, a later painting

an agreement considered the first constitution. The English then founded more settlements including Maryland in 1634 and Rhode Island in 1636. Slightly later, in 1682, Pennsylvania was founded by William Penn. This area was named New England. Towards the south, there was a settlement in the Carolinas, established in 1665.

Meanwhile the Dutch West India Company founded a settlement on the Hudson river in 1623 at present Albany, then known as Fort Orange. They also founded New Amsterdam (later New York).

Peter Stuyvesant was the last Dutch governor of New Amsterdam. The English and Dutch fought wars over this region. Dutch settlers did not help in its defence, and the English captured it in 1664.

The Swedish founded a settlement at Delaware in 1638.

By 1750, the main European occupants of North America were the British and the French. The British controlled an area along the east coast from New England in the north to Georgia in the south, that later would form the core of the USA. The

British also had occupied parts of Canada, including some territory around Hudson Bay, and Nova Scotia. France held a large part of Canada, as well as of the later USA.

WAR BETWEEN FRENCH AND BRITISH

The Seven Years' War (1756–63) was fought both within and outside Europe. The North American part of the war is also known as the French and Indian War.

The war in America actually started before the continental Seven Years' War, and was fought between France and Britain. The French were helped by some members of the Huron, Ojibwa and other Native American groups. The British were supported by some of the Iroquois and Cherokee, though a war with the Cherokee in 1758 ended the latter's support. The war began with a dispute over territory. The first minor battle was fought near the French Fort of Duquesne in 1754. After this the British sent a force in an attempt to seize the fort, but were defeated. The French gained more victories, but the British then won a battle at Lake St George in 1755. In 1756, after the Seven Years' War began in Europe, the French focused on the European war, while the British sent more troops to America. British forces moved north, captured Louisbourg in 1758, advanced towards the St Lawrence river and after a fierce battle captured Quebec. The French commander Marquis de Montcalm and the English general James Wolfe were both killed in this conflict, but the British retained Quebec and moved towards Montreal. Montreal too was captured in September 1760, and all of New France came under Britain. Meanwhile the Seven Years' War continued elsewhere.

The Peace of Paris was signed in 1763 between Britain and France who was allied with Spain. Britain gained Canada, French territory east of the river Mississippi and the region of Florida. Through a secret treaty with France, Spain acquired

Louisiana, French territory west of the Mississippi and the island of Minorca.

QUEBEC

In 1791 Britain divided Quebec into French Lower Canada and English Upper Canada. The latter was inhabited mainly by refugees from the American War of Independence.

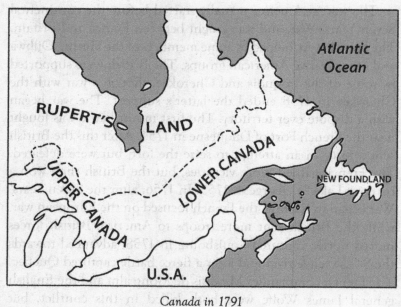

Canada in 1791

EFFECTS OF EUROPEAN CONQUEST

The European conquest of North America had serious effects on the Native Americans. Firstly, they were exposed to new diseases for which they had no immunity. The diseases included smallpox, pleurisy, typhus, mumps, measles and chickenpox. People died in thousands from these. Sometimes diseases were even deliberately spread among them. Wars killed thousands more. For instance, during the Pequot Wars, which the English and Native allies fought against the Pequot tribe, hundreds of Pequot villagers including children were killed in Mystic, Connecticut in 1637, and the village was burnt to the ground.

Europeans made treaties with the Native Americans, but went against the terms of agreements whenever they liked. Native Americans were gradually deprived of their lands. As time passed they were increasingly removed from where they lived, and sent to 'Indian territories'. Their children were sent to boarding schools, the aim being to kill 'the Indian' aspects in them. Westerners believed in their own superiority. In fact they introduced the concept of Manifest Destiny. This was the belief that it was the destiny of the Europeans who came to North America to conquer and settle the land. This concept was linked to one that the lands were generally unoccupied, though now it is believed that occupation was more widespread than was earlier presumed.

Native Americans had always lived in harmony with nature, never taking more than they needed. But with the coming of the Europeans their ways changed.

Horses and guns did not exist in North America when the Europeans arrived. Later, Europeans brought them there. After Native Americans began to use them, they could hunt migratory bison better. The meat and fur of bison and other animals were important to trade with Euro-Americans. Women prepared the hides. Polygyny increased. Social status came to be dependent on the ownership of horses and the number of wives a man had. Native Americans also began hunting beavers in large numbers for the fur trade, as well as other animals.

Crops such as sugar and cotton reached the Americas for the first time and flourished there.

Native American women generally occupied an inferior position, but some women became involved in hunting and warfare. It was an individual choice, and they were called 'Big Hearted Women'.

Changes were also introduced by new laws, which affected both marriage and adoption. Marriages between Native Americans and European settlers were not recognized. Adoption had been common in the past. Those who did not have children easily adopted them. Adoption of war captives had taken place earlier, as well as adoption of adults into the clan.

Several Native Americans converted to Christianity. In the New England area they had to live in Praying Towns. There were rules of conduct, including no long hair, and no sex without marriage. Joint families were not allowed. Polygyny was not recognized.

But things were different in the French territories. Jesuits in New France encouraged mixed marriages to make the Native Americans Catholics and French citizens.

SLAVERY

African slaves (see Chapter 18) reached North America in large numbers. This had long-lasting consequences.

BENEFITS TO THE WORLD

European settlements in the Americas introduced new food items to the world. Among these were cocoa, tobacco, haricot beans, tomatoes, capsicum peppers, potatoes, maize and turkey.

According to the anthropologist Jack Weatherford, 70–75 per cent of the world's food and resources came from the Americas.

Gold and silver were found in South and Central America. Europeans came to look for these in the north too; instead they discovered wood, fish, animal skins and new foods, which in the long run were more profitable.

ANNE BRADSTREET (1612–72)

The Americas soon had new literature, art and culture.

Anne Bradstreet is considered the first American poet. She was the first woman writer in English in North America. Bradstreet was born in England in 1612. She reached America as part of the Puritan migration in 1630. Both her father and husband became governors of Massachusetts. They also helped in founding a college in 1636, which later became Harvard University.

Anne's collection of poems, *The Tenth Muse Lately Sprung Up in America*, was published in 1650.

21

South and Central America 1500–1775

U p to 1500, South and Central America were occupied by numerous groups of people.

But with the arrival of the Spanish and the Portuguese, these civilizations declined and a new era began.

POPULATION

The population of South America before the arrival of the Spanish and Portuguese has been calculated in different ways. According to some accounts it was about 60 million. Others feel it was much higher, with that of Central Mexico alone being 25 million.

THE GREAT CIVILIZATIONS

At the time the Europeans arrived in the region, there were the great but declining civilizations of the Mayas, Aztecs and Incas. (For more about these, see Volume 1.)

Maya

The Maya civilization covering part of the region of Central America and Mexico, originated around 1500 BCE, and continued beyond CE 1500. It included some areas of Guatemala, Honduras, Belize, and Mexico's Yucatán Peninsula. The civilization was organized into city states, all of which had a similar culture. After CE 900 a decline started, but several city states were still flourishing. Among them were Chichen Itza, Mayapan, and Iximche. Different Maya groups ruled here. The Maya people also lived in rural areas around these cities.

Aztecs

The Aztecs settled in the Valley of Mexico in the 13th and 14th centuries CE. The main Aztec group is also known as the Mexica. By CE 1500 the Mexica Aztecs ruled over a large area. All the nearby states acknowledged their supremacy and paid them tribute. Their territory was divided into 38 provinces.

Montezuma II (also known as Motecuhzuma) was the Aztec king from 1502 to 1520.

Montezuma, a portrait

Incas

The Incas controlled a large empire. Their main city was Cuzco in the present region of Peru. Another grand city was Machu Picchu in the Andes Mountains.

In the second half of the 15th century, the empire expanded and covered the coastal region from northern Ecuador to Chile, a distance of 4800 km.

No modern weapons
Even in these grand civilizations, which were highly advanced in terms of art, architecture and culture, there were no modern weapons. They did not use horses either.

OTHER SETTLEMENTS
There were other settlements across South and Central America.

Apart from these civilizations there were other groups of people living in different ways. In Central America and in present Columbia and Venezuela, there were villages, organized into kingdoms ruled by chiefs. Here there were priests, warriors, ordinary people and slaves. There were some towns, as well as temples and larger buildings made of wood and mud. In other areas there were small villages as well as semi-nomadic groups.

THE FIRST EUROPEANS
Christopher Columbus reached the mainland of South America on his third voyage in 1498, and sailed along the coast of Central America in 1502. He had earlier reached the Caribbean islands.

AMERIGO AND AMERICA

Amerigo was from Florence. He joined both Spanish and Portuguese expeditions, which reached the coasts of Venezuela and Brazil. He was the first who referred to South America as 'mundus novos', a new land. A German geographer, Martin Waldseemuller, made a map of the area in 1507, and called Brazil 'America', based on Amerigo's name. Later the whole continent was called America. But the Spanish still called the area Las Indias, because of Columbus's mistaken idea that this was India. The native people too were therefore called Indians. Of course, it was a new world only for Europeans, as innumerable people had lived here from very early times.

After this several Portuguese and Spanish groups arrived in the region.

Meanwhile several Spanish explorers reached South America. Among them was Amerigo Vespucci, originally from Italy. The continent of America was named after him. There were also early German colonists, who had received some territory from Spain, but this was later taken back by Spain.

THE SPANISH

Vasco Núñez de Balboa (1475-1519) of Spain, was one of the first Europeans to reach the Pacific Ocean from the east in 1513. He had earlier been part of a group that explored the north coast of South America and settled first in Santa Domingo and later in Darien (Panama) in 1510. But the many quarrels among these early explorers and settlers, led to him being executed. Pedrarias Davila, who had Balboa executed, founded Panama City in 1519. From here he made further explorations.

Diego Velazquez, who had conquered Cuba, sent two expeditions in 1517 and 1518, to explore the Mexican region. He requested permission for further exploration, but meanwhile Hernan Cortes, (1485-1547) who had been a soldier and administrator in Hispaniola and Cuba, set off with a small force from Cuba.

Despite the guns, horses, and ferociousness of the Spanish soldiers, each conquest took some time and involved many hazards. One example of the Aztec conquest is given below.

Hernan Cortes reached the Aztec territories in 1519. He founded Veracruz, a settlement on the coast of the Gulf of Mexico. The Aztec king, Montezuma, sent messengers with gifts, but asked the Spanish to leave. Cortes meanwhile realized there were groups in the Aztec empire who resented Aztec rule. As he and his group approached the capital, they were impressed by the towns and villages, with their grand buildings of stone, built on reclaimed land.

Montezuma at first welcomed Cortes, but was taken hostage. According to a story Montezuma thought Cortes was the god Quetzalcoatl, but this account, which was narrated by the Spanish, is now thought to have been invented. Montezuma just did not realize how dangerous the Spaniards were. Cuitahuac became the next Mexica king, and Montezuma died in captivity. Montezuma is described as being of good height, well proportioned, and slim. His hair was just over his ears, and he had a short black beard. He was very neat and clean, and bathed every day.

Cortes gathered together other local people to fight against Cuitahuac, but this was not necessary. The Spanish had brought with them germs and diseases that were so far unknown. A smallpox epidemic began, and Cuitahuac died. Cuauhtemoc (Guatemotzin) was the next king, but in 1521 he as well as the city of Tenochtitlan was captured by the Spanish. The Aztec empire came to an end. Cortes began to rule over Aztec territories, that he named New Spain. He was appreciated and honoured by the Spanish king. In 1527, he was replaced by an audencia (council of royal officials). In 1535, a viceroyalty was established under Antonio de Mendoza, who was a good governor.

Further conquests

Western Honduras was part of the Maya civilization. After gold was found there, different Spanish groups fought for control. Finally Pedro de Alvarado gained control in 1539.

The first Spanish settlers reached Nicaragua in 1522. The Panama region did not have grand settlements but was influenced by both Maya and Inca cultures. The Spanish explorer, Rodrigo de Bastidas, reached the area in 1501. Ferdinand V of Castile gave Panama and other lands to Diego de Nicuesa, another Spanish explorer. As we saw in Chapter 1, Vasco Núñez de Balboa founded a Spanish settlement at Darien, (the earlier name of Panama) and later reached the Pacific Ocean. Pedrarias Dávila, who actually got

Balboa killed in 1517, founded Panama City in 1519. With this as the base, he tried to bring Nicaragua and Honduras, in which there were Maya city states, under his control. Three Spanish groups from Panama, Hispaniola, and Mexico began to fight for control over Central America. Finally, Pedro de Alvarado, a captain of Cortes, conquered Guatemala and El Salvador. In Nicaragua he met an expedition sent by Pedrarias Davila.

Christopher Columbus sailed past Costa Rica in 1502, and gave it its name, meaning Rich Coast. Costa Rica did not have any great empires before the Spanish conquest, but its native people fought and resisted Spanish occupation. Juan de Cavallon in 1561, followed by Juan Vásquez de Coronado in 1562, were the first to establish Spanish settlements in the region of Costa Rica. Most of the natives died of disease or in battles or escaped to other areas.

The Spaniard Francisco Pizarro, who was at Panama, obtained permission from the Spanish government to conquer Peru. He started with a small force in 1530 from Panama and reached Ecuador, and then went overland to Tumbes. There he learnt that the Incas were facing a crisis. Huayna Capac, the emperor, had died of smallpox. His son Huascar and Huascar's half-brother Atahuallpa, began to fight for the throne. With just a small force of 100 men, Pizarro defeated and captured Atahuallpa, who was leading a vast army of thousands. Atahuallpa offered a huge amount of gold in return for his freedom. Pizarro accepted but treacherously killed Atahuallpa. Huascar had already been killed by Atahuallpa's troops. Inca power was destroyed, and a relative of Huascar was put on the throne. Spanish control extended over

Atahualpa, the 14th Inca, a portrait of the 16th century

their territories in Peru, Bolivia and Chile. However, the Incas continued to hold a small area in the northern provinces of Quito (Ecuador), led by the general Ruminavi (also spelt Ruminahui).

Pizarro became the governor of Peru, and was granted the northern territories by Spain. His associate Diego de Almagro was allotted the southern territories, but Pizarro fought against him over Cuzco, the Inca capital. Finally Diego was captured and killed. Pizarro and his brothers ruled over Peru, but Francisco was killed by the followers of Diego Almagro, and his brother Hernando was imprisoned in Spain for 22 years. The Spanish government did not approve of the actions of Pizarro and his brothers. After more turmoil and conflict, Spain controlled the territory from the 1550s.

Meanwhile Manco Capac, who had been set up by the Spanish as a puppet ruler, founded an independent territory in the northwest in Vilcabamba. This continued under Manco's successors, Titu Cusi and Tú*tac Amaru, until it was conquered by the Spanish in 1572.

The Spanish reached the Maya region in the Yucatán Peninsula in 1527, and began to occupy the cities. This conquest took some time, and the last Maya state was annexed in 1697.

Spanish control

Gradually the Spanish gained dominance over most of South America, while the Portuguese controlled Brazil. By the 17th century only Guiana was not in their possession and remained under the control of Great Britain, France and the Netherlands.

Spanish South and Central America was divided into two parts. One part was under the viceroyalty of New Spain, with the capital at Mexico City, and the other under the viceroyalty of Peru, with the capital at Lima. Within these two viceroyalties there were smaller administrative units under audencias (a court of law). The audencia territories had their own names and boundaries and were further subdivided into provinces. For example, the audencia at Santiago de Guatemala, governed the kingdom of Guatemala, which contained the provinces of Guatemala, Chiapas, Nicaragua, El Salvador, Honduras and Costa Rica.

Apart from the other audencias, there were two important ones at the viceroyalty capitals. Belize came under New Spain, but in 1683 an English group from Jamaica settled near the river Belize. This group remained there, and in the 19th century, Belize came under the British. The viceroyalty of New Granada was created in 1717, and that of Rio de la Plata in 1776.

As in North America, thousands of Native Americans died through wars and diseases. Those who remained lived in poor conditions under the rule of Spain. The Spanish lived in towns and cities in the region, but there were not many of them.

Spanish missionaries attempted to convert the remaining Native Americans to Christianity (Catholicism). In residential areas Indians and Spanish lived separately and had different forms of local government. Some Native Americans were resettled in villages called congregaciones, where they were supposed to live a European Christian lifestyle. Centres of education, as well as hospitals, orphanages and other shelters were set up by Christian missionaries. As so many Native Americans had died, their numbers were insufficient to work as labour in mining or agriculture. The import of black African slaves started, and black Africans soon formed a large part of the population. According to estimates, 50,000 Africans were imported up to 1595, and another 1,32,600 from 1595 to 1640. New groups developed as children were born of Spanish and Native American alliances (called mestizos), Spanish and blacks (creoles), blacks and Native Americans (zambos).

ECONOMY

As the population increased, by the late 18th century most of the blacks were freed from slavery and worked for wages.

Gold and silver were exported from South America, and were

an important part of the Spanish economy. But the yield from mines began to decline, and silver also had to be used to build defences in South America. Wheat, meat, sugar and wine, began to be produced. Textiles, metal, wood and leather crafts, attained high standards. Tobacco was grown in the 18th century.

There were trade links from Apaculpo in New Spain to Manila in the Philippines and beyond.

> Hacienda: the term for a large estate in South and Central America.

INCA GARCILASO (1539–1616)

Inca Garcilaso de la Vega, earlier known as Gomez Suarez de Figueroa, was the son of a Spanish soldier, Captain Garcilaso de la Vega y Vargas and a woman of the Inca royal family, Palla Chimpu Oclo. She was the granddaughter of the Inca emperor Tupac Inca Yupanqui (1471–93). Inca Garcilaso was born in Cuzco in 1539. His parents had a long-term relationship but could not

Spanish and Portuguese America in 1784

marry because of the prevailing political circumstances. He was well educated, and knew both Spanish and Quechua. When he was 20 years old, he went to Spain, and later wrote about the Incas and the Spanish in North and South America. His works included an account of Hernando de Soto's exploration of North America in 1539–43, and of the Inca empire and early Spanish conquest. His books are still read and studied, though they are a mixture of fact and fiction. (Another person called Garcilaso de Vega was a poet of the Spanish Renaissance.)

THE PORTUGUESE

In Brazil there were native people of four main language groups, Tupi, Ge, Arawak and Carib. The Tupi were the most numerous. They were mainly in the southern Amazon basin. The Arawak and Carib were along the Amazon and tributaries, and the Ge were in the interior. All these groups mainly had simple agriculture, supplemented by hunting and fishing. Some lived in temporary villages in huts made of wood and grass. Decorated pottery and baskets were among the items made. Warfare was frequent, but battles were fought only with bows and arrows and clubs.

Pedro Álvares Cabral landed on the coast of present Brazil in 1500. He claimed this territory for Portugal, but it was some time before Portuguese settlements were set up there. The Portuguese began to occupy the region from 1530. Portugal already had a number of other overseas territories in Asia and Africa.

When the Portuguese reached Brazil they did not find much to interest them.

However, there was a dyewood called 'brazil' which they began to export. And this gave Brazil its name. By the end of the 17th century the Portuguese had found gold in the Minas Gerais province in east central Brazil, and diamonds in 1727. Native Americans and African slaves were made to work in the mines under poor conditions.

22

The Caribbean Islands

The Caribbean islands, located east of Central America, consist of hundreds of islands which today are grouped into 27 territories. Out of these 13 territories are independent, the others under various European powers. The independent territories are Antigua and Barbuda, the Bahamas, Barbados, Cuba, Dominica, Dominican Republic, Grenada, Haiti, Jamaica, St Lucia, St Vincent and the Grenadines, St Kitts and Nevis, Trinidad and Tobago. (For the names of more islands see Volume 1.)

Each island has its own unique history and cultural heritage.

Some of the Caribbean islands were occupied from around 5000 BCE. When Europeans reached the region a little before CE 1500, there were different groups of native people living there. These groups mainly lived by farming, fishing and hunting. Some of the islands had large territories under a leader known as a cacique. Routes to Peru and Mexico passed through the islands.

Columbus's arrival changed their history.

CHRISTOPHER COLUMBUS

Christopher Columbus, known in Spanish as Cristobal Colon, made four voyages in his attempt to reach India.

The island where he first landed was known as Guanahani. This was thought to be the island later named San Salvador, while recent research suggests his first landing was at Samana Cay Island. Both these are in the Bahamas. Columbus found the islands very beautiful, but did not discover gold. The search for gold was one of the reasons for his expeditions. He then reached Colba (later known as Cuba), and next another island that he named Hispaniola (this today contains Haiti and the Dominican Republic). He thought there must be gold here, as the women wore ornaments of gold. Here he met a chieftain called Guacanagari, and with his help established a small Spanish settlement. It was named Navidad (the Nativity). Twenty-one Spanish people remained there, while Columbus returned to Spain.

He began his second expedition in 1493, with seven ships and 1500 men. When he returned to Navidad, he found all the Spaniards there had been killed, as they had misbehaved with the

Christopher Columbus embarking on his first voyage

native people. Moving further east, he then founded a settlement called Isabela, under his brother Diego. Protests and revolts from the local people of Hispaniola were suppressed with guns. He returned to Spain in 1496.

The 3rd voyage started in May 1498, and Trinidad was reached in July. He then reached the coast of Venezuela, but did not realize he was exploring a whole continent. It was Amerigo Vespucci who first understood this, following the same route as Columbus.

In Hispaniola he found the Spaniards fighting, at the new town of San Domingo that had been set up. He and his brother Bartholomew were arrested by a royal official and sent back to Spain in 1500. In 1502, Nicolás de Ovando was sent from Spain as the governor.

Columbus's fourth voyage was from 1502 to 1504. He reached the Central American coast and sailed along Honduras, Nicaragua, Costa Rica and Panama. His son Diego was appointed governor of Hispaniola. Columbus died in 1506.

THE BAHAMAS

The Bahamas form an archipelago consisting of about 700 islands and islets, though only 40 of these are occupied. The largest island is New Providence, on which the capital Nassau is located. The islands do not have much fertile land. Vegetation is mainly scrub and pine, along with hardwood trees like mahogany. Coffee also grows wild.

A branch of the Taino, the Lucayan, lived in the region when Columbus reached here. The Lucayan and Taino spoke Arawak languages. The Lucayan lived mainly in the 19 largest islands of the archipelago. The total population was around 40,000. In a few years almost the entire population was transported as labour to other islands. Only 11 people remained there in 1520, and soon there were none.

For another 130 years, the islands had no human habitation. Thick forests grew. By the Treaty of Paris, they were given to Britain in 1783. From 1648, the British from Bermuda began to settle in some of the islands, though many returned to Bermuda after a while. The new settlers included whites, slaves and free blacks. These early settlers lived mainly by fishing and hunting. They also used wood for houses and material from shipwrecks. After a conflict with the Spanish, the islands were almost totally abandoned in 1684, but again settled in by people from Jamaica in 1686. Conflicts continued with the Spanish. The islands also became a base for buccaneers and pirates. (See below.) The British Proprietors from Carolina in North America appointed the governors from 1670 to 1717. The Proprietors were nobles who had been granted this region by King Charles II of England. As a result of this, the Bahamas came directly under the British. After this, for a few years the Bahamas were under the newly independent America, and then again under Spain, but became a British colony in 1787. By this time, not a single descendant of the original inhabitants remained.

HISPANIOLA

The population of Hispaniola at the time of Columbus's arrival is not known. Estimates vary from eight million to 50,000. When Columbus reached Hispaniola in 1492 he found that the inhabitants were peaceful and helpful. The Spanish called them Tainos, and Columbus wrote that they were 'such an affectionate and generous people and so tractable that there are no better people or land in the world.' But Columbus was not trying to make friends, he was looking for wealth, gold and control over the region. Apart from the Taino, there was a rival group known as the Carib. There were five territories on the island of Hispaniola at this time, each ruled by a chief. These were Marien, Magua, Maguana, Jaragua and Higuey.

On his second voyage to Hispaniola in 1493, Columbus brought along 1500 people to settle there, and insisted that every 'Indian' over the age of 14, should supply him with a certain amount of gold every three months. But there was not much gold there, and they could not do so. Many had their hands and feet cut off as punishment, and bled to death. Other local people died of various diseases. By around 1512 there were only 28,000 people, and by 1542, only 200.

As the local people had declined in number, slaves were imported from Africa for labour. The Spanish too found it difficult to live there, and moved to South America. All kinds of people then occupied the island, including pirates and refugees from the law. (See Buccaneers on the next page.) French adventurers, too, were among them.

Part of Hispaniola was ceded to France by the Peace of Ryswyk in 1697. It was known as Saint Dominique, and later Haiti. Haiti was a French colony at the time of the French Revolution.

Toussaint L'Ouverture

Influenced by the revolution in France, African slaves led by Pierre Dominique Toussaint-Breda (1743–1803) started a revolt. He was known as Toussaint L'Ouverture as he always found an opening (ouverture) in battles.

In 1793, France abolished slavery and the revolt ended. After a civil war Toussaint became the ruler of Haiti in 1801, but was defeated by Napoleon in 1802, who even reimposed slavery. Toussaint was transported to France and died there in prison. But in 1804 Haiti declared independence.

Meanwhile, the Spanish part was called Santo Domingo. Spain did not take much interest in it, and it too was ceded to France in 1795, but later once again came under Spain. The people asserted their independence in 1821, but in 1822, Haiti annexed it. Finally, Santo Domingo became independent as the Dominican Republic in 1844.

BUCCANEERS

After 1605, the northern part of Hispaniola was abandoned by the Spanish. All sorts of people escaped to this region and began to live there. Among them were runaway slaves, servants, soldiers and sailors. They lived in the deep forests. Goats and cattle brought there by the Spanish were now in wild herds, and these people killed them for food. They cooked the meat over a type of barbecue known as a boucan, and thus they came to be known as buccaneers.

CUBA

Cuba lies to the south and south-west of the Bahamas and is the largest Caribbean island. This too is part of a limestone platform. The soil is fertile and there were once thick forests including palms, pines, oaks, cedar and mangroves. There are also a number of small animals, birds of all kinds, more than 10,000 types of insects, crocodiles, snakes and other creatures. The Cuban flag has three colours: blue, red and white. The trogon, a bird with feathers of the same colours, was therefore chosen as the national bird.

Like the Bahamas, the simple life of the people here suffered with the arrival of Christopher Columbus and the later Spanish. The Cubans today are descended from the Spanish settlers and the Africans brought in as slaves, apart from a few ethnic minorities. There are no descendants of the original inhabitants. The Ciboney were the earliest residents, followed by the people known as Arawak. When Columbus arrived there, they referred to themselves as Tainos. The Tainos lived by fishing and farming, and made boats, pottery, ropes, baskets, and various items from wood. They also wove cloth. Cassava was the main crop, but maize, tobacco, cacao, beans and spices were also grown. Tools were not only made of wood, but of stone, shell and coral. Thus the Tainos were not backward, but they soon all died from diseases and exploitation by the newcomers.

Cuba was actually conquered by Diego de Velazquez de Cuellar in 1511. The towns of Barcoa, Cuba and Havana were established. African slaves were brought to work on plantations. Sugar plantations were set up in the 16th century. Tobacco was grown, and coffee was introduced in 1748. Though there were no indigenous inhabitants left, by 1800, Cuba was quite prosperous.

JAMAICA

Jamaica, to the south, has hills, mountains and a number of trees and flowering plants. There are numerous and diverse birds. Christopher Columbus noticed the island on his second voyage. The Arawak were the local people, but once again after it was occupied by Spain in 1509, the local people died out. The first Spanish settlement and capital was St Iago de la Vega (later called Spanish Town). As in other islands, African slaves were imported for labour. Jamaica was conquered by the English in 1655, and transferred to England by the Treaty of Madrid in 1670. After this there were a number of English settlers on the island. Plantation crops were grown including sugar and cacao, as well as other crops. Jamaica became one of the largest slave-trading centres. In 1692, there was an earthquake which affected Port Royal, where there was a huge slave market. After this the town of Kingston was founded.

TRINIDAD

Trinidad had seven Native American groups, including the Arawak, Chaima, and Carib. Columbus reached there in 1498, and later a Spanish governor was appointed in 1530. However, there were attacks by the Carib, and it was difficult for the Spanish to live there. There were also Dutch, French and British raids on the island. Britain conquered Trinidad in 1797, and it became a colony of Britain in 1802 by the Treaty of Amiens.

OTHER ISLANDS

Though it is not possible to describe in detail the history of each of the island groups, their history was somewhat similar to those described above. The native people were all destroyed. Slaves were imported, and plantations established. The islands were used to make profits for the colonial powers.

PIRATES AND SLAVES

At this time pirates roamed through the seas. They captured ships and the goods that were carried. Pirates lived a free life, and were among the first liberators of slaves. When they captured a slave ship, they allowed the slaves to join them, and treated them with equality. All the slaves were happy to be freed from their chains. Even the crew of the slave ships were happy to join them, as they too were not treated well. One-third of the pirates were black. Pirate captains were often elected. They had their own laws under which black, white, English, French or Native American were all equals. There were also women pirates. Between 1680 and 1725, about 10,000 men and some women operated as pirates, and belonged to no country.

By 1727, most pirates had been defeated or killed. As a result the number of slaves transported across the Atlantic rose.

John King—the youngest pirate

John King was an upper-class boy around the age of ten, a passenger along with his mother on a ship called the *Bonetta*, in the year 1716. The ship's captain was Abijah Savage. The *Bonetta*, moving towards Jamaica, was attacked by a pirate ship led by Sam Bellamy. The passengers and crew were not harmed, but the ship was looted for several days. And young John King just insisted on becoming a pirate. His mother tried to stop him. Initially the pirates did not take him seriously. The ship's captain tried to discourage him. But John said he would throw himself overboard if he was not allowed to join the outlaws. He said his father did not like him. And he even attacked his mother. Finally his mother agreed, and John became the youngest pirate. Unfortunately, Sam Bellamy captured another ship, a few months later, the *Whydah*. Sailing on this ship, he and most of his fellow pirates, including young John, were killed in a shipwreck. The remains of the *Whydah* and of John have recently been found, and are now in a museum.

BLACKBEARD (1680–1718)

Blackbeard (Edward Teach) from England was one of the most famous pirates, but was killed in a battle.

He had a very long black beard which gave him a ferocious appearance. Though he captured a number of ships, he never harmed his captives. These two aspects accounted for his fame. His ship, *Queen Anne's Revenge* was found and excavated in 1997. More than 15,000 objects from there are preserved.

Several stories and films have been based on him,

Blackbeard, from an engraving of 1736

and his ghost is said to haunt the seas. He was killed in a battle on 22 November 1718, by soldiers who had been sent to capture him, by Alexander Spotswood, the governor of Virginia.

The Puffin History of the World

23

Australia, New Zealand and Adjacent Islands 1500–1800

A ustralia had been occupied from very early times, at least from around 60,000 BCE. There were of course changes in technology and culture over the years, but the lifestyle remained simple, until the Europeans reached the area.

At the time of European occupation indigenous Australians were between 3,00,000 to one million, according to various estimates.

The original inhabitants were then called aborigines. Aboriginal people refer to themselves by the name of the tribe or clan to which they belong, or the name of their language. There were once separate 'nations' and 600 language groups. Different dialects were used within each language group. At the time when Europeans began to settle here, the tribes spoke about 250 different languages.

Aborigines had their own customs, rules and ways of life. They also interacted with those of other countries or clans. Among the many clan groups are the Pintupi, Pitjantjara, and the Warlpiri, which is also a language, the Anmatyerr or Alyawarre, and the Arrernte. The Ngunnawal, Eora, Dieri are among the many others. The Palawah live in Tasmania.

There was no written language, though art and painting were quite advanced. Songs and dances were quite elaborate, and were linked with religious and other ceremonies. Houses were simple, usually made of bark, branches and leaves or bushes. People also lived in caves and natural shelters. In a few places there were houses with circular stone walls covered with branches or leaves for the roof. There were weapons and tools of stone and wood. Metal was not used at all. Items were also made of precious stones, shells, seeds and feathers.

Food included yams, edible roots, fruits, berries, seeds, coconuts, nuts, some wild vegetables, insects, birds and wild animals. Dingoes were the only domesticated animal in Australia. Torres Strait islanders also tamed pigs.

There was trade with New Guinea via the Torres Straits islands, as well as with other Indonesian islands. Canoes were used for short sea journeys. Traders from Malaysia, China, and Arab traders from Africa, probably reached Australia before the Europeans. However, the way of life did not substantially change till the Europeans arrived.

TERRA AUSTRALIS

Europeans had not seen Australia, but based on logic, they felt that such a land must exist. They felt there had to be some southern counterpart to the northern lands of Europe and Asia. They called this unknown land Terra Australis, or 'Great Southern Land'. Geographers had presumed that such a land existed, and they called it Terra Australis Incognita, 'the unknown southern land'.

FIRST EUROPEANS IN AUSTRALIA

The Dutch who had occupied some ports in Indonesia were the first Europeans to reach Australia. William Jansz, a navigator from the Netherlands, was employed by the Dutch East India Company. He sailed from the Netherlands to Java, and to the port of Bantam where the Dutch were based. From there he set sail in his ship *Duifken* (Little Dove) in 1606. He wanted to reach New Guinea, which, he heard, had plenty of gold. He did reach the southern coast, and then turned towards the south. He landed on Cape York Peninsula in northern Australia. He called the area New Holland. He also explored the Gulf of Carpentaria. They saw some of the local people, and some of his men were killed in a conflict with the aborgines. But Jansz did not realize that a strait separated Australia and New Guinea. He believed that the two lands were connected.

From Batavia, further expeditions were sent by the Dutch. In 1616, an expedition led by Dirk Hartog landed at Shark Bay in western Australia. In 1626 and 1627, Peter Nuyts explored the south coast of Australia. On a second voyage in 1644 Tasman (see below) went around the coast of north Australia.

But the Dutch did not settle there.

THE BRITISH

William Dampier, an English buccaneer, reached north-west Australia in 1688. Returning to England, he wrote a book called *Voyages* describing his travels. He received funds for another expedition, explored the west coast in 1699–1700, and wrote a detailed account of it. He was quite critical of both the land and the people, hence even the English did not try to occupy the new land.

As Britain's power increased, she began to gain interest in Terra Australis. Despite the fact that many had already reached Australia, explorers were not convinced that this was really the unknown southern continent.

Captain James Cook of Britain (1728–79) confirmed that Australia was indeed the unknown southern continent. It was then called New Holland. Cook arrived on its eastern coast after reaching New Zealand. In April 1770, he reached a bay where there were innumerable different plants. He called it Botany Bay. He was the first European to see a kangaroo. The Royal Society of Britain was still not convinced that the land Cook found was Terra Australis. It was only after his second voyage, that this discovery was confirmed.

In Britain the prisons were overcrowded. The British thought of sending some convicts to the new land. This would also help Britain to claim the territory for herself. A British settlement began in Botany Bay in 1788. This settlement was called Sydney. Its earliest residents were the 759 convicts, sent to this unknown land along with their guards. There were also officials to administer the region, which was called New South Wales. Smallpox, measles and tuberculosis began to affect the aboriginal people. Many died in a smallpox epidemic in 1789. Did smallpox spread by accident? Some historians have suggested that the British deliberately introduced it when they had no ammunition and were faced with local hostility.

After some time more immigrants came from Britain. The first free British reached Australia in 1793.

Soon whalers from Britain and America settled on the coasts, killing the huge whales for profits.

Botany Bay, *a watercolour painted in 1788 by Charles Gore*

Convicts continued to be sent to Australia till 1868. About 1,37,000 men and 25,000 women convicts had been sent till then. When their sentences were over, they settled in Australia.

James Cook

James Cook was a British explorer in the Royal Navy.

He took part in the Seven Years' War and at this time mapped the coast of Newfoundland. He made three voyages, recording islands and coastlines in maps for the first time. In the first voyage from 1768 to 1771 he went to Tahiti, New Zealand and Australia.

His second voyage was from 1772 to 1775. Once again he was asked to find Terra Australis; he almost reached the Antarctic mainland, then went to Tahiti and New Zealand, and also landed at several other islands.

During his third voyage, from 1776 to 1779, Cook's main aim was to see if a passage linked the Northern Atlantic Ocean to the Pacific Ocean. He stopped at several Pacific islands before looking for the northern passage. From Tahiti, he reached the Sandwich Islands, now the called Hawaiian Islands. Altogether he remained around the Hawaiian Islands for four months; one month in January 1778, and three months from November 1778 to February 1779. In January 1779, he anchored in Kealakekua Bay at the large island of Hawaii. After staying there a month, Cook and his ships set out again. However, a mast of one of the ships broke, and they returned to Hawaii for repairs. A quarrel broke out, and Cook tried to take the king of Hawaii as hostage. He was then killed by the king's supporters.

Captain James Cook, a portrait by Nathaniel Dance-Holland, c. 1775

Cook's voyages added greatly to the European knowledge of the Pacific. However, though celebrated in Europe, attitudes towards him in Hawaii are mixed. As in other areas where the Europeans went, diseases reached Hawaii.

NEW ZEALAND

The first European, Abel Janszoon Tasman of the Netherlands, reached the islands of New Zealand in 1642. Before that Maoris, of Polynesian origin, were the only people settled there. Zeeland then became a territory of the Netherlands. A Dutch map-maker named it New Zealand. Captain James Cook of Britain reached here on his first voyage in 1769. Soon after this, a French expedition under Marion Dufresne arrived in New Zealand. A conflict with the Maoris led to his death in 1772, along with that of his own crew and around 300 Maori. From the 1790s, the British, French and Americans began trading with Maoris. They provided guns and metal tools, in return for wood items, flax and food.

Up to and beyond 1800 New Zealand remained free of large-scale European settlements, but there were some individual settlers. The Maoris lived in wooden houses, and surrounded their settlements with enclosures known as 'pa'. These pa could be small, or could be as large as 40 hectares. Within the large pa there were several houses as well as areas for storage. When Europeans visited, the Maoris were still living in pas. One large fortified pa was at Ohinemutu at Roturua in North Island. It had obviously been constructed for defence. (For more on their lifestyle before the arrival of Europeans see Volume 1.)

TASMANIA

Abel Janszoon Tasman reached Tasmania in 1642, which at that time he named Van Dieman's Land. Van Dieman was the governor of the Dutch East Indies, who had sent the expedition. Tasman also explored New Zealand and the northern coasts.

NEW GUINEA

Portuguese and Spanish explorers reached New Guinea early in the 16th century. It was reached by other Portuguese in 1526. The Spanish explorer Luis Vaez de Torres reached New Guinea in 1606, a few weeks after the Dutch explorer Jansz. Luis passed through the Torres Strait, which was later named after him. He therefore knew that New Guinea was an island, but this information somehow did not become common knowledge for the next 150 years.

THE HAWAIIAN ISLANDS

The Hawaiian Islands consist of an archipelago of eight major islands, as well as smaller ones. These islands in the north Pacific Ocean, are 3000 km away from any continent. At the time Cook reached there, approximately one million people lived in all the islands. They were ruled by chiefs. The islands sometimes had conflicts with one another.

Westerners began to settle in the islands soon after Cook's voyages. By 1790 many Europeans lived in the islands. Diseases affected the native population, forests were cleared for plantations and their way of life changed. Many of the native birds and other creatures became extinct in the 19th century. King Kamehameha I united the islands under his rule. He became the king of the main island of Hawaii in 1782, and brought the others under his control by 1810. He tried to preserve old customs and traditions. At the same time he increased the prosperity of the kingdom through trade with Europe and America.

FIJI AND TONGA

Tasman also reached the Tonga and Fiji islands. Tasman found an advanced culture at Fiji. Jewellery and other items were crafted here.

Tonga is made up of 176 islands. Tonga had earlier been

reached by other Dutch explorers, and later by James Cook, who called them the Friendly Islands. Around 1600, the main Tui Tonga dynasty was replaced by the Tui Kanokupolu dynasty. There was a period of unrest which ended in the 19th century. After Cook's voyages many of the islanders became Christians.

EASTER ISLAND

In 1722, Jacob Roggeveen, a Dutch navigator, landed on Easter Island, and saw the huge stone statues there. Later research showed these were built from around CE 700. (See Volume 1 for more on these.)

Oval stone houses were built around CE 1500. In the 1600s, tupa, or stone towers with inner rooms began to be built. Statue building ended in the 1680s. Both population and resources declined, and a civil war started. Roggeveen also reached the Samoa Islands.

OTHER DISCOVERIES

In 1525, the Portuguese Diego Gomez de Sequeira probably located the Caroline Islands and the Palau Islands near New Guinea.

Spain began some explorations from Peru. The Spanish explorer Alvaro de Mendana de Neyra set off from Peru and arrived at the Ellice Islands and the Solomon Islands to the northeast of Australia in 1567. However, after returning, he could not pinpoint their correct location, and they were rediscovered only after 1760.

In another expedition in 1595, Alvaro discovered two more island groups, the Marquesas Islands and the Santa Cruz (Nderic) Islands. He died of fever while trying to capture the latter. The Marquesas Islands as well as others made beautiful carved items of wood.

24

The Rise of Napoleon

Napoleon Bonaparte of France changed the course of European history, through a series of conquests across Europe.

Born in 1769, Napoleon joined the French army in 1785. At the time of the French Revolution he returned to his homeland, the island of Corsica, and was involved in revolutionary struggles there. After a conflict with Pasquale Paoli, a Corsican leader, Napoleon again went to France. He successfully led the French Republican forces against Toulon, which had been occupied by the British, and which was against the Republic. In 1796, he was appointed commander of the French Army of Italy. After a number of successful campaigns, Napoleon led an invasion of Egypt in 1798-99. Napoleon won against the Mamluks, who were under the Ottoman empire. However, he was defeated by a British fleet in the Battle of the Nile.

France at this time was governed by a directorate or committee (known in French as the Directoire). Napoleon joined with others in overthrowing the Directorate and setting up a government of three consuls. He himself became the first, or supreme consul in November 1799. By a new constitution, that had been partly written by Napoleon, he became the only consul, First Consul for Life in 1802. In 1804, he proclaimed himself emperor.

EUROPE AGAINST FRANCE

As we saw countries in Europe feared the rise of France, and joined together to fight against her. These are known as the coalition wars. The first coalition lasted from 1792 to 1799. (See Chapter 8.) The second coalition was from 1799 to 1802. Britain actually had not withdrawn from the war, and now allied with Austria, Russia, Portugal, Naples and the Ottoman empire. France initially suffered some defeats but then gained victories. A peace was signed in 1802. A third coalition, too, was formed. In 1803, Britain once again began a war against France. In 1804, she was joined by Austria, Naples, Russia and Sweden. Spain formed an alliance with France.

Napoleon's main battles are listed below:

1800: Napoleon defeated Austria at Marengo.

1805, October: Battle of Trafalgar; Napoleon lost to the British. In this sea battle, a French and Spanish fleet was destroyed by British ships, led by Horatio Nelson.

1805, December: Battle of Austerlitz, considered his greatest victory. Napoleon defeated Austrian and Russian forces. By the Treaty of Pressburg, France gained most of central and western Europe. The Holy Roman Empire was dissolved, and new states of Holland and Westphalia were formed. Over the next five years Napoleon's close relatives or those loyal to him were made kings of various countries including Holland, Westphalia, Spain, Italy, Naples and Sweden.

1806: France started a blockade of Britain, preventing other countries from importing British goods.

1806: Battles of Jena and Auerstadt; France invaded and defeated Prussia.

Battle of Trafalgar

1807: Battle of Friedland; France defeated Russia.

1808: Austria rejoined the war but was defeated.

1808–14: the peninsular war, fought in Spain and Portugal. In 1808, Napoleon attacked Spain and Portugal. His brother Joseph was made king of Spain. Spain asked Britain for help. British troops reached Spain through Portugal. Napoleon gained a victory at Corunna in northern Spain, but after more years of fighting, he lost the Battle of Toulouse in 1814.

1809: Napoleon defeated the Austrians at Wagram.

1812, June: Russia attempted to avoid the blockade of Britain. Napoleon invaded Russia with 6,00,000 troops. He defeated the Russians at Borodino, and marched towards Moscow. The Russians burnt the city of Moscow and left it devastated. Moscow was captured by Napoleon. The freezing cold winter was setting in. As Napoleon's troops advanced, they found there was no food. They starved and froze too because of inadequate clothing. The French troops had to retreat. As they withdrew in the fierce cold, they came across many lying on the road who had frozen to death. Only a few thousand of the French troops returned home.

1813: Battle of Dresden; Napoleon won.

1813, October: Napoleon was defeated in the Battle of Leipzig, by Prussia, Russia and Austria.

1814, April: Napoleon abdicated; he was exiled to the island of Elba.

1815, March: escaping from Elba, Napoleon returned to France and regained control. Louis XVIII, the king of France, fled when Napoleon arrived. But Napoleon did not remain long in power. He was vanquished in 1815 in the Battle of Waterloo in Belgium by the allied forces.

After this Napoleon was exiled to the island of St Helena, where he died in 1821.

THE CONGRESS OF VIENNA (1814–15)

Napoleon's numerous victories had changed Europe. France had become the most powerful nation. The Congress of Vienna was a meeting of the representatives of the states of Europe. Its aim was to ensure peace in Europe, and to restore the balance of power. The Congress began in 1814. When Napoleon returned to power, there was a break. It reconvened after Waterloo in 1815. Its main provisions were:

(i) A German confederation of 39 states was created. This replaced the Confederation of the Rhine and the Holy Roman Empire.

(ii) Prussia received half of Saxony.

(iii) Austria gained most of North Italy, but lost the Netherlands.

(iv) The Austrian Netherlands were given to the United Provinces. The United Provinces lost the Cape of Good Hope.

(v) Sweden lost Finland but received Norway.

France had to give up the territories that had been conquered by Napoleon. The Congress also looked at some of the other concerns of Europe. Slavery was condemned. It had already been banned by Britain, and gradually other countries did the same.

ADMINISTRATION

Napoleon was not just a great general, but also an efficient administrator. He centralized the government. In 1804, he brought in reforms in law through 'Code Napoleon'. The Code was actually drawn up a team of lawyers but Napoleon too was involved in the discussions. The Code included some of the new ideas introduced by the French Revolution. It ensured equality for all men and freedom of religion. Women however, were not equal and could not own property. This Code was Napoleon's most long-lasting legacy. It included 2281 articles. Though modified and modernized, it still forms the basis for law in European countries.

Napoleon also founded the Bank of France in 1800.

Roman Catholicism became the state religion of France but under Napoleon, France was tolerant towards other religious groups.

Portrait of Napoleon

SOME ASPECTS OF NAPOLEON'S PERSONAL LIFE

Napoleon was born in Ajaccio, the capital of Corsica, an island to the south-east of France and west of Italy. It comes under France, but is just north of Sardinia, an island under Italy. The Corsican language has similarities with French, but is not identical.

Casa Buonaparte, the home where Napoleon was born, is today a museum.

Corsica was under Genoa from 1349, but after a brief period of independence, came under France by 1770. After the French Revolution it was occupied for brief periods by Britain, but was returned to France in 1796, and again in 1814.

Napoleon married Josephine de Beauharnais in 1796. She always remained his greatest love. This was her second marriage. They divorced in 1809. Though he still loved Josephine, Napoleon wanted a son and heir, and she could not give him one. In addition he had heard rumours that Josephine was not faithful to him.

In 1810, he married Marie Louise of Austria. It was a political alliance. At this time she was only 19, and Napoleon was 41. Napoleon was a good husband to her. A son was born to them in 1811. When exiled to Elba, he named his son Napoleon II as his successor. Marie took the boy to Austria at this time, but after Napoleon's defeat in the Battle of Waterloo, some of his supporters, made Napoleon II the emperor. However, he was soon deposed. In any case he was still a child. In 1830, King Charles X was removed from the throne of France. But Napoleon II by this time was ill with tuberculosis and died in 1832.

Marie Louise married twice more after Napoleon's death.

Another woman of the same name, Marie Walewska, a Polish countess, had a loving relationship with Napoleon, and was believed to have given birth to his son, Alexandre, in 1810. However, Marie's husband, acknowledged the boy as his own.

NAPOLEON'S LEGACY

Napoleon's strength and exploits found a place in history, literature, art, and music.

The writers Stendhal and Honore de Balzac praised him, while Tolstoy condemned him. In his novel *War and Peace*,

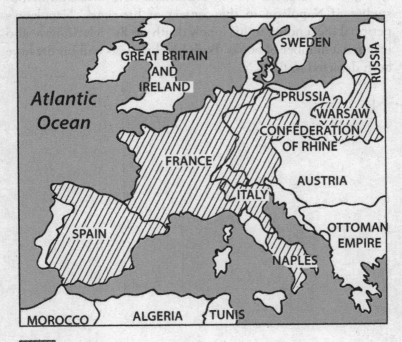

/////// Territory under Napoleon in 1812

Napoleon's conquests up to 1812

Tolstoy (1869) described the Battle of Borodino in which the Russians lost 42,000 men, and Napoleon, 32,000. The great musician Beethoven wrote his *Eroica Symphony* with Napoleon in mind, but later lost his regard for Napoleon, and did not dedicate the symphony to him. Tchaikovsky composed the *1812 Overture*, a musical description of Napoleon's armies retreat from Moscow. Antoine-Jean Gros (1771–1831) gained renown as a painter through his portrait of Napoleon and the depiction of scenes of Napoleon's battles. Anne-Louis Girodet-Trioson (1767–1824) who painted imaginative and legendary subjects, also created an oil on canvas entitled *Ossian Receiving the Ghosts of Napoleon's Generals* (1801). Historians have made numerous studies of Napoleon in the context of his times. Napoleon's personal life, ending in his lonely death on St Helena, have also inspired a number of books. Both his conquests and his life have been depicted in films.

25

Europe: Technology, Science and Culture 1800–1914

After 1800, Europe began to race ahead of the rest of the world, particularly in the field of technology and science.

INDUSTRIAL REVOLUTION

The Industrial Revolution refers to a time when new machinery was invented, leading to an expansion and growth in industry. This process began in Britain but soon spread to other parts of Europe.

The origins of the Industrial Revolution can be traced to the 16th century. There were several new inventions in the 17th century and more in the 18th and 19th centuries. By the early 19th century, these began to lead to a total change in the way of life. Factories replaced trees and meadows. New factory towns emerged. Smoke from the factories often polluted these towns and people lived in unhealthy conditions.

New technology

New technology was a major aspect of the Industrial Revolution. We will look at some of its aspects here.

Spinning and weaving

The flying shuttle, used in weaving cloth, invented by John Kay (1704–80) and the spinning jenny, invented by James Hargreaves, were early machines that led to more efficient spinning and weaving. The shuttles made it possible for wider textiles to be woven, while the spinning jenny had several spindles in one frame. In 1769, Richard Arkwright created a water-frame, in which water power was used for spinning.

Around 30 years later, spinning machines which worked fast were invented, and thus more textiles could be produced in a shorter time. The new machines were quite large and factories were built to house them. Soon after 1800, all spinning and weaving was done in factories in England.

Carpet loom in a factory in Bridgetown, Glasgow

The invention of the sewing machine in 1830 by Barthelemy Thimonnier of France was another major innovation.

Steam

Steam engines brought in a revolutionary change. There were some engines that ran on steam in the 1600s. These were used to pump water. A more efficient steam engine was designed in 1769 by James Watt. A company was formed to make them. Coal was used in these engines. Some factories were located near coal mines. Steam engines began to be used to pull wagons on fixed tracks. The first mobile steam engine, called 'Puffing Billy', was made in 1813, at Tyneside in northern England. It was used to bring coal from a mine to a loading point on the river Tyne.

James Nasmyth made a steam hammer (1842), which could bend iron bars. It could also be used for delicate work. It could crack an egg on a wine glass, without breaking the glass.

Railways

George Stephenson then used a steam engine to pull coaches with passengers. This led to the first passenger railway, which began in Britain in 1825. The Liverpool and Manchester railway opened in 1830. By 1835, there were railways in North America and in parts of Europe. Austria, Canada, France, Germany, Italy, Spain, Poland, Switzerland and Russia soon had railways. The South Carolina railway was one of the first in the US. The Ramapo was an American engine of the mid-1800s.

Coal, iron and steel

Coal was needed for the steam engines. Coal mines were established. Both adults and children worked there in poor conditions. Iron, too, was required, and there were a number of iron works. Iron ore began to be extracted using coal, whereas in the old days, charcoal, made from wood, had been used. The use of coal for this was begun by Abraham Darby and his son in the 18th century. Iron production then increased. Steel, too, began to be produced. Though steel production had taken place in ancient days, a new and cheaper way of making steel was invented by Henry Bessemer of England in the 1850s.

Steamships

Steam engines were used in ships. The first trial steamship was constructed in 1801. In 1803, the *Charlotte Dundas* was a functioning steamship used for towing boats. Steamships started being used to cross the Atlantic in the late 1830s.

A new type of worker

As inventions increased, machinery began to be used in place of animals and humans for various processes. Though people were still required to work on machines, the nature of their work was different. Work in factories was subdivided into small units. The work was usually repetitive and not creative. Each worker performed the same task over and over again, which could be as simple as fitting or turning a screw.

But some of the work was really hard. For instance, small wagons filled with coal had to be pushed and pulled along tracks in low tunnels in mines. Children were often employed for this task.

Puffing Billy

Working hours

In the 19th century factory acts began to be passed to limit the working hours of adults and children. But until that happened they had to work up to 16 hours a day.

The Luddites

Many craftspeople and workers were against the new machines. This was because they were being displaced, and were losing their jobs.

In England there was a group known as the Luddites. They joined together to smash the machines in textile factories. The Luddites were active in 1811 and 1812, and to some extent up to 1820. The Luddites claimed to be led by one Ned Ludd, also called King Ludd. It is not clear whether he was a real or mythical person. According to some accounts, Ned was a weaver who once broke two weaving frames. Others were inspired by this story, and though Ned was not heard of again, they used his name in protests against machines.

Gradually trade unions were formed to help the workers.

SOME OTHER IMPORTANT INVENTIONS

In 1782, Aime Argand, a Swiss scientist, designed an efficient oil lamp, which had a glass chimney and a wick, and did not smoke. At first, fish oil was used in these, followed by vegetable oil, and finally after 1850, mineral oil. Gas lamps were also used.

William Farraday created a gas burner in 1855, which was modified by a German chemist, Robert Bunsen. This was known as a Bunsen burner, and provided a hot and steady flame. Bunsen burners are still used in laboratories for experiments involving heating and combustion.

The electric telegraph was developed in the 1830s by Charles Wheatstone and William Fothergill of England. However, Samuel Morse, an American artist and inventor, developed the most efficient system. In 1840, it received a patent and was named after him. The Morse Code, used to send messages, was a system of dots, dashes, and spaces, representing letters of the alphabet. The messages could be conveyed by electric pulses, or by a visual such as flashing lights of different durations. From this, an international Morse Code was introduced in 1851, which was used until 1999.

In 1895, the Italian Guglielmo Marconi invented wireless telegraphy, or radio. Among other forms of communication, the telephone was developed by Alexander Graham Bell in 1876. It was later modified by others.

Benjamin Franklin's (1706-90) experiments helped to understand electricity. At that time electricity was called 'electric fluid', and two types, vitreous and resinous, were believed to exist. Franklin showed the two were actually the same. He renamed them 'positive' and 'negative', terms that are still used today. By flying a kite in a storm, he also proved that lightning is a form of electricity.

In 1800, Volta, an Italian scientist, made an electric battery or cell. In 1832, an electric motor was developed by William Sturgeon of Britain.

The American Thomas Alva Edison invented the first commercially viable light bulb in 1879, and the first power station was set up in 1881-82. America first used the DC (direct current) system, while the AC (alternate current) system was developed by Nikola Tesla (1856-1943) and George Westinghouse (1846-1914).

An electric car, running on a battery, was made in the 1880s. In Germany, Karl Benz made a two-cylinder car engine in 1879 followed by a three-wheeled car in 1885. In 1885, Benz became the first company to sell motor cars.

His car company made one of the first four-wheeled cars in 1893. Meanwhile, another German engineer, Gottleib Daimler, along with Wilhelm Maybach, made a four-wheeled car in 1889, and started the Daimler Motor company in 1890. Between 1893 and 1897, Rudolf Diesel, a German, developed a diesel engine.

The first American petrol-driven car was made by Charles Duryea and J. Frank Duryea in 1893.

Airships which flew with engines were an earlier development than aeroplanes. Airships were also called dirigibles, and were lighter-than-air aircrafts. A bag containing gas was used to lift the airship. Though there were earlier designs, Henri Giffard, a French engineer, created the first successful airship in 1852. Different types of airships continued to be made in the 20th century, and are still used for observation, sightseeing, or other purposes.

THE WRIGHT BROTHERS

Who was the first to construct and fly a heavier-than-air plane? Most people seem to think it was the Wright Brothers. The Wright brothers Wilbur (1867–1912) and Orville (1871–1948) are believed to have built the first aircraft. Its first flight undertaken by Orville, on 17 December 1903, was at Kitty Hawk, North Carolina. It covered 37 m and lasted for 12 seconds.

But there are other claimants for the first flight, including Clément Ader, Gustav Whitehead, Richard Pearse and Karl Jatho. For instance, according to newspaper reports, Gustav Whitehead, a German immigrant in Connecticut, USA, flew the first powered and controlled flight, at a height of 50 feet on 14 August 1901. His aeroplane model was named No. 21. In memory of this model, you can have a No. 21 breakfast at a restaurant in Connecticut, US. It includes an omelette with hamburger filling and German apple pancakes!

In 1827, the first photograph was taken by Nicephore Niepce of France. In 1895, the Lumiere brothers invented a film projector.

Among other great inventions around this time was the phonograph (record player), made in 1877 by Thomas Edison.

As seen above, Edison also developed a light bulb. Among his numerous other inventions, were the motion picture camera.

SCIENCE

There were constant advances in science happening at this point in time. Charles Darwin (1809–82) introduced the theory of evolution, and completely changed the thinking of the Western world, which had earlier believed in religious ideas of creation. (See Volume I for more on his theory.)

Louis Pasteur (1885–95), a French chemist and biologist, had many discoveries to his credit, though he is primarily known for the technique of pasteurization, a heat treatment that stops milk and other liquids from spoiling. He also proved that disease is carried by microbes, and developed a vaccine against rabies in 1885. He improved and developed the technique of inoculation initiated by Edward Jenner.

Pierre and Marie Curie discovered the element radium and in 1903 were awarded the Nobel Prize for physics along with Antoine Henri Becquerel. (The first Nobel prizes were given in 1901.) In Japan, a doctor named Hanaoka Seishuis is considered the first to use general anaesthesia in surgery.

ART, LITERATURE AND MUSIC

The dominant style in art, literature and music in Europe from 1800 to 1850, is termed romanticism. Though romanticism was not something that originated during this period, it reached its peak at this time. Romanticism focused on deep feelings and emotion, rather than reason and the intellect. Works were inspired by nature and by the imagination, and also focused on love, beauty, and death. There were numerous Romantic poets and novelists in all European languages. It is not possible to name or describe them all, but a verse, given below, provides an example.

'She lived unknown, and few could know
When Lucy ceased to be;
But she is in her grave, and oh,
The difference to me!'
(from 'The Lost Love' by William Wordsworth)

Romanticism also had a dark side, and included horror and accounts of the supernatural. Romantic artists painted landscapes and portraits, but also imaginatively depicted historic events, as well as myths and fantasies. Francisco Goya (1746–1828) of Spain is considered the greatest romantic artist. Goya's paintings included portraits, religious frescoes, depictions of war, myths, and other themes. Among his works are 11 small paintings titled *Fantasy and Invention*, as well as a series known as *Black Paintings*. *Saturn Devouring His Son*, a dark and gloomy painting, is one of the latter.

Painting of Degas, The Dance Class

In music, the later works of Beethoven and Franz Schubert (1797–1828), who are termed 'classical', moved towards romanticism. (See Chaper 6.) Romantic musicians included Robert Schuman (1810–56), Hector Berlioz (1803–69), Frederic Chopin (1810–49) and Franz Liszt. Like other Romantic works, such music too explored nature, deep emotions and mysticism. Music was used to try and reach spiritual heights and to transcend the world.

Impressionism

Impressionism is a form of art that uses colour and light to provide a natural and luminous effect. In France, Paul Cezanne, Edgar Degas (1834–1917), Claude Monet and Pierre Renoir were artists who used this style in the 1870s and 1880s. Later they developed different individual ways of painting. Degas, a French artist, created paintings, sculptures, prints and drawings, but is particularly known for his paintings of dancers.

Realism and individualism

Realism was another style in art, where items were depicted realistically. In post–impressionist art, colour and light were used but artistic styles were individual. Great artists of this period included Vincent van Gogh (1853–90), Paul Gauguin (1848–1903) and Henri de Toulouse–Lautrec (1864–1901).

MODERN DANCE

The basic principles of modern Western dance was first put forward by Francois Deisarte (1811–71), followed by Jacques Dalcroze (1865–1950), who was Swiss, and the Hungarian Rodolf Laban (1879–1958). Dance further developed in the USA both before and after the world wars. Isadora Duncan of the early 20th century, is considered the founder of modern American dance.

FAIRY TALES AND CHILDREN'S LITERATURE

In Europe, and in other parts of the world, books began to be written especially for children. Fairy tales were collected, put together and illustrated. Jacob Grimm (1785–1863) and his brother Wilhelm (1786–1859), who were German linguists and academicians, published a popular collection of fairy tales. *Hansel and Gretel*, *The Frog Prince*, *Snow White*, and several others were part of their collection. These stories were appreciated all over the world, and have been translated into more than 160 languages.

The Danish author Hans Anderson (1805–75), wrote dramatic fairy tales, which made him famous. Among them was the long story *The Snow Queen*. The Danish artist Vilhelm Pedersen (1820–59), a naval officer, was the first to illustrate the tales. A totally different kind of writing, which was realistic, was *Heidi*, the story of a young girl and a goatherd, by the Swiss writer Johanna Spyri (1827–1901). There were, of course, many other books and stories.

An illustration from The Snow Queen

NEW IDEAS IN ECONOMICS

Europe was now involved in world trade. Colonies were set up in Asia and Africa and used to market products from Europe. These changes and developments led to new economic theories.

Adam Smith

Adam Smith (1723–90) was a noted economist and philosopher who put forward some very influential ideas. His work, *The Wealth of Nations*, is considered the first modern text on economics. He believed in the free market which he said would lead to prosperity for everyone.

In his personal life Adam Smith was quite absent-minded. While thinking of something else, he once tried to boil bread and butter instead of tea leaves to make a cup of tea. He then remarked that it was the worst cup of tea that he had ever drunk!

Adam Smith never married. He lived with his mother.

Capitalism

Capitalism is an economic system that is interpreted in different ways. In general, it implies private ownership of industries, and buying and selling in a free market. Prices would depend on competition in the market. Profits would lead to the accumulation of capital (i.e. money), which would be used to make more money. It was believed that capitalism would lead to advances in all spheres, material, scientific and artistic, and these advances would gradually spread through the world. Nation states with democratically elected representatives would be formed, which would guarantee property and civil rights.

However, many criticized this system, saying that its benefits remained in the hands of a few. There are several different kinds of capitalism, which form part of economic theories.

Communism

Karl Marx (1818–83) was one of the greatest thinkers of the modern world. His ideas influenced the development of communism and socialism all over the world. He also wrote on capitalism.

Marx was a German but he lived mostly in London after 1849. Some of his books were written along with Frederich Engels. *The Communist Manifesto*, which they co-wrote, as well as other writings, look at history in terms of 'class struggle'. A class is a group of people who have the same way of living. In the modern world the two main classes are the workers, who work in factories (also called the proletariat) and the bourgeois (the capitalists). The capitalists are the owners of the factories who benefit from this ownership, making large amounts of money.

Marx and Engels believed that capitalism was an unfair economic system, which would one day be destroyed. Capitalists would be overthrown and the proletariat (workers) would become the ruling class. The communists, those who understand the nature of class struggle, would initially be the leaders and allies of the proletariat, who would take over state power through a revolution. This is called the 'dictatorship of the Proletariat'. But at a later stage, this dictatorship would end and all would be equal. No one would own private property.

Their ideas were further developed by thousands of people. Among the most important were Lenin, Stalin and Trotsky of Russia (see Chapter 38) and Mao of China (see Chapter 46).

Communist ideas were obviously feared by capitalists.

26
Europe
1815-1900

The Congress of Vienna of 1814–15 restored peace in Europe. (See Chapter 24.) The 'Congress System' functioned for several years after this, during which the 'Concert of Europe' met regularly and decided European issues. The Concert consisted of the European nations of Britain, Austria, Prussia and Russia.

Meanwhile, ideas of nationalism were growing. There were a number of diverse groups in various countries, and many of these wanted independence. The Ottoman empire had several such groups.

GREEK INDEPENDENCE

Greece was among the territories that wanted independence, and a Greek revolt against Ottoman rule began in 1821. The Ottomans obtained help from Muhammad Ali of Egypt, but France, Britain and Russia joined together to defeat the Turkish fleet in 1827 in the battle of Navarino Bay. Later, Russia won more victories. The Treaty of Adrianople was signed in 1829, and the war ended. Greece was given independence in 1832, but its king was chosen by the European powers.

Lord Byron

The great poet George Gordon, more commonly known as Lord Byron, went to Greece to support their movement for independence. In 1824, he died of malaria there. In Europe, he was considered a hero and a symbol of freedom.

FRANCE

In France, the monarchy was restored after 1815. All Napoleon's relatives were exiled. The younger brother of Louis XVI ruled as Louis XVIII. He was a constitutional monarch, as his powers were limited by a new parliament. After his death, his brother ruled as Charles X from 1824. After a revolt in 1830, Charles X abdicated. Louis Philippe, another member of the Bourbon family, came to the throne. France was affected by the revolutions of 1848. Though there was some political instability, France became an industrialized nation and was economically powerful. Railways began to be constructed and the number of cities increased. Free education was provided for all boys.

THE REVOLUTIONS OF 1848

In 1848, a series of revolutions spread across west and central Europe.

In some areas the aims were nationalistic—freedom from foreign rule. In others there was a desire for reforms, for more rights and benefits. Sometimes the two aims were combined. Poor harvests and unemployment contributed to these revolutionary movements, which took place in Italy, France, Austria–Hungary, the German states, Switzerland and Denmark. In England and Ireland there were demonstrations and demands for change. The revolutions in the various countries were not connected, and were not planned. They occurred spontaneously. Most of them were suppressed by force by the end of 1849. Nevertheless, the revolutions did bring in some changes.

In February 1848, the revolt in France led to King Louis Philippe being removed. The Second Republic was established in France on 24 February 1848.

Charles Louis, the nephew of Napoleon, returned to France from exile. He was elected president of the republic. In 1852, he declared himself Emperor Napoleon III and ruled till 1870. He lost power after his defeat by Prussia.

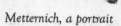

In Austria, the conservative chancellor, Prince Klemens (Clement) Wenzel von Metternich, was forced to resign. Hungary, which was under Austria, at first proclaimed independence. Though Austrian rule was restored, a 'dual monarchy' was created. The same ruler was emperor in Austria, but king in Hungary. Denmark received a new constitution. In the Ottoman empire some Balkan states were granted reforms.

Metternich, a portrait

THE UNIFICATION OF ITALY

Italy had geographical unity but was politically disunited. There were independent states under princes while other areas were under foreign powers. In 1848, much of Italy was under Austria. The Pope ruled the states under the Church.

In 1831, Charles Albert of Savoy became the king of Piedmont–Sardinia, an independent state. He was sympathetic to nationalist ideas. Some writers and thinkers urged all Italians to unite and support him, so that he could overthrow Austria. There were several secret societies, including the Carbonari (literally

The Puffin History of the World

'charcoal-burners'), which wanted unity. They were founded by rural charcoal burners, which gave them their name. People from different levels of society, including nobles soon joined them. The Carbonari consisted of a number of groups, subdivided into smaller units or cells. As a secret society they had special initiation rituals and used terms known only to them. 'Buono cugini' meaning 'good cousins' was the code word for members.

Guiseppe Mazzini was another leader of the movement for unity. He led a group called 'Young Italy' which was in favour of a democratic republic. Others wanted a federation of states, with the Pope as the leader.

In 1858, Piedmont-Sardinia was independent and took the lead in liberating other Italian states. Piedmont began to mobilize its army in 1859, but Austria asked it to disband. Comte de Cavour, prime minister of Piedmont, declared war on Austria. France supported Piedmont, which took over Lombardy. The states of Parma, Modena, Tuscany and Romagna joined Piedmont. France received Nice and Savoy, which were part of Piedmont, as a reward for its aid.

In 1860, Guiseppe Garibaldi, who had once been in the Carbonari, defeated the kingdom of Naples. He allied the southern Italian states as well as Sicily with Piedmont.

Garibaldi and his followers wore red shirts, and hence were popularly called 'redshirts' ('camicie rosse' in Italian).

In 1861, the kingdom of Italy was formed. Victor Emmanuel of Piedmont was its first monarch. In 1866, another war took place. At the end of this Austria surrendered Venice. The Papal States remained independent till 1870, when they and Rome became part of Italy. Italy was now unified.

THE UNIFICATION OF GERMANY

The German states were joined together by a Confederation, but each one was virtually independent. Prussia and Austria were the most powerful. Otto von Bismarck, prime minister of Prussia from 1862, aimed to unite the German states under Prussian leadership. In 1864, Prussia and Austria joined together and annexed Schleswig-Holstein, which was under Denmark.

But Prussia and Austria then fought against each other. In 1866, after a seven-week war, Prussia defeated Austria in a battle fought near Koniggratz and Sadowa in Bohemia.

Austria then remained out of the German confederation.

Bismarck

Franco-Prussian war (1870-71)

As Prussian power grew, France was uneasy. Bismarck wanted a war with France, hoping that this would lead the German states to unite under Prussian leadership. Keen to provoke a conflict, he first suggested that Prussia would support a German prince as king of Spain. Then he altered a telegram sent by King Wilhelm of Prussia to include a passage insulting to France. France declared war but was not well-prepared. Paris was under siege for 132 days, before it surrendered in January 1871. The main French army and Napoleon III had already been defeated. By the Treaty of Frankfurt, Prussia received the territories of Alsace and Lorraine from France. France also had to pay 5000 million francs to Prussia. This war completed the unification of Germany. Germany was now an empire under Kaiser Wilhelm II

The Puffin History of the World

(Emperor William II) of Prussia. Germany included 25 former states, of which the largest was Prussia.

After this war, the Third Republic was founded in France, which lasted up to 1940.

SWITZERLAND AND THE NETHERLANDS

The United kingdom of The Netherlands

During the Napoleonic wars, France had occupied the Netherlands, as well as Belgium and Luxembourg. After the Congress of Vienna, these were joined together in the United Kingdom of the Netherlands, under King William I. However, Belgium started a revolt in 1830 and became a separate kingdom in 1831. The French–speaking areas of Luxembourg were granted to it. Luxembourg enjoyed some autonomy from 1839. It became fully independent in 1867.

Switzerland

In 1815, Switzerland was a union of 22 small city states called cantons. (See Volume 1.) In 1847, a civil war started when the Roman Catholic cantons created a league called the Sonderbund. This was defeated by federal forces, and a new constitution was drafted in 1848, which increased the power of the federal government. After another new constitution it became a unified federal state in 1874.

We will look at more states in the succeeding chapters.

27

Great Britain and Ireland 1800–1914

As we saw in Chapter 8, George I was the first of the Hanoverian kings of Great Britain.

LATER HANOVERIAN RULERS

George III of Hanover was the king of Great Britain and Ireland from 1760 to 1820. America gained independence from Britain during his reign.

George III suffered from health problems, and became blind in 1809. Though he continued as king, his son became the regent from 1811, and was then crowned as King George IV in 1820.

William IV came to the throne in 1830. He was the brother of George IV. William had ten children by his mistress, the Irish actress Dorothea Jordan. Later he married a German princess, Adelaide of Saxe–Meningen.

In 1837, Victoria, daughter of the Duke of Kent and the niece of William, became the queen. She was only 18 at the time. She had an extremely long reign till her death in 1901. She was not the ruler of Hanover, which went to William's brother Ernest Augustus. She married Albert of Saxe-Coburg-Gotha in 1840. After her death the British crown passed to the house of Saxe-Coburg-Gotha. This was renamed the House of Windsor in 1917.

THE PARLIAMENT

Britain did not have a written constitution. From the time of the signing of the Magna Carta in 1215, the Parliament developed and changed only through various acts and agreements. The two houses of Parliament, the Lords and the Commons, already existed in 1800, but their nature was different from what it is today. The House of Lords had more authority. The Reform Bill of 1832 gave more men the power to vote in Britain and removed some of the problems in constituencies. (A constituency is an area from which candidates are elected.) The Reform Acts of 1867 and 1884 further increased the number of people who could vote. At the same time these acts reduced the dominance of the House of Lords.

Sir Robert Walpole, the Lord of the Treasury in 1721, is usually considered the first prime minister, though there was no exact date for the creation of the office of prime minister. As there was no written constitution, the powers of the prime minister grew gradually. By around 1835 the prime minister gained more power. He was the head of the government, and was assisted by other ministers. Early political parties, the Whigs and the Tories, emerged in the 17th century. Later, the Whigs came to be known as the Liberal Party, and the Tories as the Conservatives. Two prime ministers, the Liberal, William Gladstone and the Conservative, Benjamin Disraeli made many important decisions in the second half of the 19th century. Gladstone was the prime minister from 1868 to 1874, from 1880 to 1885, in 1886, and again from 1892 to 1894.

Disraeli served as prime minister for a brief period in 1868, and later from 1874 to 1880.

ECONOMY

Britain's prosperity reached new heights in the 1860s and the standard of living rose drastically. But by the end of the 19th century the USA and Germany had more manufactured goods and were producing more steel. However, Britain remained first in shipbuilding, shipping and banking.

THE GREAT EXHIBITION

As we saw in Chapter 25, the Industrial Revolution began in Britain. An exhibition was held in London in 1851 in Hyde Park to showcase the progress industry had made.

The Crystal Palace, designed by Sir Joseph Paxton, was specially built for this exhibition. This iron and glass building was the largest building to have ever been constructed till that date. It was 563 m long and 124 m wide. It used 400 tonnes of glass, 4000 tonnes of iron and 6,00,000 planks of wood for the floorboards. It was designed as a temporary structure, and prefabricated (ready-made) units were used. This grand show exhibited various kinds of machinery, locomotives, musical instruments, raw materials, porcelain, art objects, and much more. Each nation showcased its products and prizes were awarded in two categories, for innovation (Council Medal) and for excellent workmanship (Prize Medal). There were 13,937 exhibitors, and 3088 received medals, out of which only 170 were Council Medals. The exhibition lasted for 14 weeks and about six million people viewed it. The queen herself visited it 40 times. The building was removed from Hyde Park after the exhibition and reassembled in Sydenham in south London, but burnt down in 1936.

NEW LAWS FOR CHILDREN

Industrialization had its positive and negative aspects. At first labour conditions were very bad. After 1800, numerous laws

Children working in a cotton mill

were passed to regulate and improve the condition of workers in factories. There were also new laws to protect children working in factories and mines. The laws gradually limited the working hours of children and women and prevented the employment of young children.

Among the various acts, the Ten Hour Act of 1847 stated that no child should work more than ten hours a day. And by the Factory Act of 1874, no child under the age of ten was to be employed in any factory. Lord Shaftesbury (1801–85), was one of the main reformers who worked to end child labour.

SCHOOLS

Though schools already existed, more were set up from the 1860s. Elementary education acts passed from 1870 onwards, gradually made education compulsory up to the age of 13 in both England and Wales. There was a similar act in Scotland. Schools had two objectives, to provide academic learning and to get children to learn polite and proper behaviour.

OTHER DEVELOPMENTS
Slavery
Slavery had already been banned in 1807, and in 1833 an act was passed by which slavery was abolished everywhere in the British empire.

Workhouses
By the Reform of the Poor laws, in 1834, workhouses were set up for the unemployed, which were often worse than prisons. The great writer Charles Dickens (1812–70), wrote about these in his novel *Oliver Twist*, the story of an orphan who stays for some time in a workhouse. Here is a passage from the book:

> 'They established the rule, that all poor people should have the alternative (for they would compel nobody, not they) of being starved by a gradual process in the house, or by a quick one out of it.'

After 1850, a number of people tried to improve the conditions of the poor. Among them was William Booth, who founded a mission in 1865, later called the Salvation Army. His programme of reforms later spread to other parts of the world.

Equality for Catholics
The Catholic Emancipation Act was passed by Parliament in 1829 though it was opposed by the king. It gave Catholics more rights and equality with Protestants in England and Ireland. A Catholic could become a Member of Parliament but still could not become king or queen.

The Corn Laws

Corn Laws were introduced to regulate the import and export of grain, mainly of wheat. Such laws were first passed in the 15th century, and modified in succeeding centuries. The Corn Law of 1815 banned wheat imports until the price of domestic wheat rose. Another law in 1828 allowed imports but maintained the high prices through duties. As a result, bread became very expensive. Landlords supported these laws, but merchants wanted free trade. Farmers and workers too were against these regulations because of the rise in prices. An Anti-Corn Law League was founded in 1839 in Manchester. In Ireland, the poor lived mainly on potatoes. In 1845–46, the potato crop failed, and there was famine in Ireland. The British government did not provide adequate relief, and around one million people died. Around two million Irish emigrated to America. The Corn Laws were revoked in 1846. Free trade was allowed, export duties removed, and import duties greatly reduced, and totally abolished by 1869.

But the Irish famine continued till 1851, reaching a peak in 1847.

Postage

In 1840, the first postage stamp was introduced in Britain. Before this mail was stamped by hand with an ink stamp, and the transport cost was collected at the delivery point. As many refused to pay, it led to losses for the postal department. Creating a postage stamp solved this problem. Soon postage stamps began to be used in other parts of the world.

FOREIGN POLICY

Britain at this time was a major European power. It was involved in maintaining the balance of power in Europe, through negotiations as well as participation in Congresses and in wars.

It also had vast colonies all over the world, though the American colonies were lost to it by now. Among the most important colonies was India, which in 1858, came under the British crown. In 1877, Queen Victoria became the 'empress of India'.

CULTURE

Art, music, theatre and literature were part of life in Victorian England. Among artists, two great landscape painters were John Constable and J.M.W. Turner.

Punch and Judy puppet shows became popular in the 19th century. These shows did not have set stories but consisted of short episodes that varied according to the puppeteer and changed over time. Punch, his wife Judy, the Baby, a crocodile and a policeman were the main characters. There was entertainment in music halls, as well as comedies, pantomimes, operas and theatre. Several museums were set up. The British Museum dates back to 1759, while the National Gallery, Natural History Museum, Science Museum, Victoria and Albert Museum and the Tate Gallery were founded in the 19th century. Madame Tussaud of France established a wax museum in London. It soon became a popular tourist attraction

There were too many great writers to list here. Among them were the poet, Alfred, Lord Tennyson, who is considered one of the best poets of this time. *The Lady of Shallot*, *Maud*, and *Morte d'Arthur* are some of his well-known poems. H.G. Wells was a versatile author, writing books on history and politics, as well as novels. He is best remembered for science fiction portraying both the past and the future. Though Charles Dickens is considered the greatest novelist of this time, there were many others including women writers. Among the women novelists were Jane Austen, the three Bronte sisters, Charlotte, Emily and Anne, as well as George Eliot. Special literature was written for children.

ALICE'S ADVENTURES IN WONDERLAND

The Reverend Charles Lutwidge Dodgson was a mathematician who wrote complex books on trigonometry and algebraic geometry. Under the name Lewis Caroll, he astounded all who knew him by writing *Alice's Adventures in Wonderland* (1865) and its sequel *Through the Looking Glass and What Alice Found there* (1871). These entertaining fantasies remain popular even today.

Sir John Tenniel (1820-1914) illustrated Carroll's works. He was British and was also a political cartoonist. He drew

Illustration from Alice in Wonderland

cartoons for the British magazine *Punch*, and also illustrated Aesop's Fables.

Nursery rhymes

James William Elliot put together a collection of nursery rhymes, *National Nursery Rhymes and Nursery Songs*, in London in 1870. Though these rhymes were and still are popular with children, they originally had hidden meanings. As the original meaning was often lost, there were different interpretations of each rhyme. For instance, according to one interpretation of the rhyme beginning 'Humpty Dumpty sat on a wall', it refers to a cannon in Colchester at the time of the Civil War. In 1648, a cannon in the walled town was known as Humpty Dumpty. The royalists were defending the town, but a Parliamentary cannon knocked down the wall, and the royalist cannon fell. All the king's men, i. e. the royalists, tried to put it on another wall, but could not as it was too heavy.

According to some the rhyme beginning 'Ring a ring o'roses' refers to the plague that destroyed half the population of Europe between 1347 and 1351. (See Volume 1.)

IRELAND, SCOTLAND AND WALES

As we saw in Chapter 8, the union of Britain and Ireland took place on 1 January 1801. However, Irish protests against England started soon after this. These increased after the Irish famine that began in 1845. The Irish Republican Brotherhood was founded in 1858 with the aim of creating an independent republic. A similar group, the Fenian Brotherhood, was formed by the Irish living in the United States. Both groups were often referred to as Fenians. The Fenians organized protests and bomb blasts. A Home Rule movement started in the 1870s. One of its main leaders was Charles Stewart Parnell. The Liberal prime minister, Gladstone, was in favour of granting Home Rule to Ireland but did not receive sufficient support for this in Parliament. Home Rule would provide autonomy, but not complete independence. There were also a number of secret societies involved in struggles for independence.

The London Irish Literary Society was founded in 1891, and the National Literary Society in Dublin in Ireland in 1892. The great poet W. B. Yeats (1865–1931) was one of the main members. The aim of these societies was to promote the Irish language and Irish literature and theatre.

Scotland, which had joined with Britain in 1707, was by this time industrially well-developed.

However, the Scots wanted to show that they had their own identity, different from the English. Tartan, a type of material with geometric designs, was worn as kilts (a pleated knee-length garment) by some Highland Scottish clans. Each clan wore a different tartan pattern. In the 19th century, more clans began to wear tartan kilts. Many of the tartan designs were actually created at this time. Bagpipes, too, came to be associated with Scotland. The pipes are believed to have originated in mainland Europe, and then spread to the British Isles, at first to England. When adopted by Scotland, their popularity increased to such an extent that there was a piper in every town, and a tradition of hereditary pipers. Pipers accompanied all Scottish military regiments.

Wales had been united with England for a long time. As in Ireland and Scotland, there were groups keen to promote a Welsh identity. A Welsh national movement too existed. Its activities led to Welsh being taught in schools in Wales from 1889.

THE TITANIC

The *Titanic* was a British ship which sank on 14–15 April 1912. It was a 46,000-tónne liner, on its very first voyage from Southampton to New York. This was the largest ship sailing at that time. Just before midnight the ship hit an iceberg. This created a hole 90 m wide in her side. Two hours and 40 minutes later the ship sank. There were 2224 passengers on the ship, and lifeboats were insufficient. Though many were saved, 1513 were drowned.

After this tragedy, new international rules were formulated for the safety of ships.

28

The Expansion of Russia and Decline of the Ottomans 1800–1900

As seen in Chapter 9, the kingdom of Muscovy (Russia) was steadily expanding, both into Central Asia and beyond Siberia. Several wars against the Ottomans enabled Russia to gain more territory. Meanwhile east European states were struggling for independence from the Ottomans.

CENTRAL ASIA

There were a number of khanates in Central Asia that often fought against one another, and gradually came under Russian control.

By the 18th century Russia had occupied the Kazakh region. After 1860, Russia occupied the Uzbek states, and extended control up to the borders of Iran and Afghanistan. Of the khanates in the region, Kokand was annexed to Russian Turkestan in 1876. Russia conquered Khiva in 1873, and the following peace treaty ceded territory to Russia, though Khiva retained part of its territory. Finally Khiva came under the Soviet Union in 1919 and became the Khorazm Soviet Republic in 1920. The Mangits or Mangudai reigned over Bukhara from 1785–1920, when it became part of the Soviet Union. (See Chapter 9 for more on these states.)

ABAI

Central Asia had a number of writers and poets, whose works were mainly in Persian and Turkish or in various other Turkic languages. Among the best and most philosophical was Abai Kunnanbaiuli (1845–1904). Abai was a Kazakh of the Trobikty clan. He turned away from the violence he had witnessed and became a poet and philosopher who wanted Kazakhs to live in unity and avoid unnecessary conflicts. His main work is the *Book of Words*, containing both philosophy and poetry. He also translated the works of Russian and European writers into Kazakh. Abai is still considered a hero in Kazakhstan. Two novels have been written about him, and a film has been made on his life. Statues of him can be found in several Kazakh cities.

Here is a verse from one of his poems:

'My soul craves friendship, seeks it daily,
My heart is aching for it, and while I
Have never known a friend who'd not betray me,
I sing a hymn to friendship for all time. '

RUSSIA

In 1800, Russia already covered a huge area. By 1900, territories had expanded further.

The emperors

Alexander I (1801–25), was the son of Paul I and the grandson of Catherine.

Nicholas I (1825-55), the younger brother of Alexander I
Alexander II (1855-81)
Alexander III (1881-94)
Nicholas II (1894-1917)

Alexander I

Alexander I joined in the third coalition against France but, in
1807, allied with France instead by the Treaty of Tilsit. By this
treaty, Russia was free to fight against Sweden and Turkey. It
had acquired Georgia in 1801 after a war with Iran, and now
gained many more territories including Finland and the Aland
Islands after the Russo-Swedish war from 1809 to 1809, and
Bessarabia, from Turkey (Russo-Turkish war, 1806-12). After
another war with Iran in 1806, Russia gained Dagestan, Baku
and other areas. But relationships with France changed again and
Napoleon invaded in 1812. The invasion was bad for Russia, but
worse for France. (See Chapter 24.) Alexander then again turned
against France, and joined in the final defeat of Napoleon. By
the Congress of Vienna of 1815, Russia gained some territory.

Nicholas I

Alexander died suddenly in 1825, and Nicholas, his younger
brother, became the emperor. Meanwhile young people in Russia
were being influenced by ideas in Western Europe and wanted
modernization.

There was a revolt in December with demands for a
constitutional monarchy, but this was suppressed. There were
other revolts and a number of secret societies that wanted reforms
and the removal of serfdom.

Nicholas did not bring in reforms but focused on expanding
the empire. A war with Iran in 1826 gained him part of Armenia
with the city of Yerevan. He supported the Greek struggle for
independence and participated in the victory at Navarino Bay in

1827. A Russo-Turkish war followed and ended in the defeat of the Ottomans. The Treaty of Adrianople (1829), was in Russia's favour. Russia aimed to increase control over the declining Ottoman empire, while Britain, France, Prussia and Austria tried to prevent Russia from becoming too powerful.

The Crimean War (1854–56)

Russia invaded the Ottoman empire in 1853 and occupied Moldavia and Wallachia. Russia wanted its warships to be allowed to pass through the Dardanelles Straits, which was under the Ottomans. Russia claimed its aim was to protect Christians in the Ottoman empire. After trying and failing to bring peace, Britain and France allied with the Ottomans. In September 1854, France and Britain attacked Sevastopol, a Russian naval base in the Crimea. They won battles at the Alma River, Balaklava and Inkerman. At Balaklava, before achieving victory, 670 horsemen of the Light Brigade charged at the Russian artillery because of wrong orders, and most of them died. (Alfred Tennyson, the poet laureate, wrote a poem on this, the second verse of which is given

THE CHARGE OF THE LIGHT BRIGADE BY ALFRED TENNYSON (SECOND VERSE OF THE POEM ON THE BATTLE AT BALAKLAVA DURING THE CRIMEAN WAR)

'Forward, the Light Brigade!'
Was there a man dismay'd?
Not tho' the soldier knew
Someone had blunder'd:
Theirs not to make reply,
Theirs not to reason why,
Theirs but to do and die:
Into the valley of Death
Rode the six hundred.'

Florence Nightingale

here.) There was a break in fighting, but Sardinia joined Britain and France in 1855. Sevastopol was again attacked and captured.

Austria threatened to join the war hence Russia agreed to peace. The Treaty of Paris was signed in 1856. The Ottomans received some territories from Russia. Warships of Russia and other countries were not allowed to enter the Black Sea. The safety of Christians in the Ottoman territories was guaranteed by the allies. Russia had to return the Danubian territories and part of Bessarabia.

The Lady with the Lamp

Florence Nightingale (1820–1910) was a British nurse who supervised and organized nursing during the Crimean War in the British barracks at Uskudar (Turkey) and Balaklava. The wounded were dying in hospitals because of poor hygiene and infections. Florence Nightingale helped to change this. As she went around at night with a lamp checking the condition of the soldiers, she came to be called 'the lady with the lamp'. She wrote several books on nursing and even founded a training institute for nurses. She is considered the founder of nursing as a profession.

Alexander II

While the Crimean War was being fought, Nicholas died and Alexander II came to the throne in 1855. During his reign Poland was further integrated into Russia, and more territories were gained.

Poland

Poland had been divided among Austria, Russia and Prussia by three partitions in the 18th century. (See Chapter 5.) By the Treaty of Tilsit of 1807, Napoleon created the Duchy of Warsaw out of the Polish territories under Prussia. This was in return for help by the Polish people in his wars. In 1809, Western Galicia from Austria was added to the Warsaw duchy. But the Congress of Vienna made some changes. Part of the duchy of Warsaw became the kingdom of Poland, under the Russian emperor. Krakow was made a city republic. Other areas were under Prussia and Austria. A Polish revolt in 1830–31 was suppressed. There were several more revolts. After a rebellion from 1863–1864, the Russian language was imposed, and there was an attempt to integrate the Polish kingdom with Russia.

Congress of Berlin (1878)

Another Russo–Turkish war was fought from 1877 to 1878. Russia made gains by the Treaty of San Stefano. However, other European powers met at Berlin and insisted on the modification of the treaty. By the Congress of Berlin, Serbia and Montenegro gained independence from the Ottomans. Bosnia and Herzegovina, formerly under the Ottomans, was given to Austria–Hungary. Overall the Ottomans lost a lot of territory. Russia too could not retain all that she had gained.

Russian expansion

Russia continued to advance in other areas. Siberia and Kamatchka had been conquered in the 17th century, and new settlements began in these regions. By 1858, the northern part of the island of Sakhalin and the Amur region came under Russia.

Internal reforms

Alexander was not just involved in wars, but also focused on internal reforms. Serfdom was abolished in 1861. Elected district councils known as zemstvos were set up in 1864. The Russian State Bank was set up in 1866.

Alaska was sold to the USA in 1867.

Assassination

Alexander was assassinated by a bomb in 1881, and succeeded by his son Alexander III.

Alexander III

Alexander III inaugurated a programme of Russianization. The power of the zemstvos declined during his reign. It was also a time when Jews were persecuted. Most of Russia remained rural, though industries developed in the 19th century. Industrialization was helped by the expansion of railways. There were about 32,000 km of railway tracks by 1890. The Trans-Siberian railway was begun. Iron, steel, coal and textiles were the main industries. By the 19th century factory workers amounted to 1.4 million. They lived in very poor conditions. Several secret societies existed, including Marxist and revolutionary groups, who plotted to overthrow the emperor.

In foreign policy, Alexander made a secret agreement with France in 1894, the Franco-Russian Alliance. This was a political and military pact, an agreement to ally if threatened by other powers.

Nicholas came to the throne the same year. We will look at his reign in Chapter 38.

LIFE IN BATISHCHEVO

Aleksandr Nikolaevich Engelgardt, a young intellectual, had to leave St Petersburg in 1870, because of his involvement in radical gatherings. He was sent to Batishchevo in Dorogobuzh

 The Puffin History of the World

district of Smolensk Province where he wrote an account of the way of life there, and about the difficulties the peasants faced. In the villages. People ate mainly rye bread and soup, and as their stock of rye diminished, they made bread without removing the chaff. Later in the season, they often went hungry. In the summer wild mushrooms, buckwheat, kasha and potatoes, soup and salted beef, and lard, were eaten. The potato was an important food source at this time. However, the potato had become a popular food only recently. In fact in 1843, there were riots when peasants were asked to grow potatoes.

RUSSIAN CULTURE

Russian literature, music and ballet flourished. Alexander Pushkin, Ivan Turgenev, Gogol, Leo Tolstoy (1828–1910) and Fyodor Mikhailovich Dostoyevsky (1821–81) were among the great writers of this time.

Russia had a rich tradition of oral literature, including folk and fairy tales. A. N. Afanasiev (1826–71) compiled an anthology of Russian fairy tales. He collected around 600 stories. He was the librarian of the archives of Moscow, and had written several scholarly articles. He was also a specialist in Slavic languages. His works were an inspiration for writers and musicians, including the musicians Rimsky Korsakov and Stravinsky. Korsakov's compositions *Sadko*, and *The Snow Maiden* were based on these tales, as was Stravinsky's *Firebird*.

Among other musicians, the works of Tchaikovsky are celebrated everywhere. *Swan Lake* (1876), *Sleeping Beauty* (1890) and *The Nutcracker Suite* (1892), are some of his most famous compositions. Ballet developed in Russia as Sergei Diaghilev (1872–1929) set up the Ballet Russe. (See Chapter 6 for the origins of ballet.)

BABA YAGA

There are many stories, cartoons and films about BabaYaga in Russia and East Europe. She appears in Afanasiev's fairy tale collection and in other sources.

Baba Yaga is a witch who lives in a strange house without windows and with a hidden door. The house, which is at the edge of a forest, stands on chicken legs! To enter the house a magic phrase is necessary: 'Turn your back to the forest, your front to me'.

Baba Yaga travels on a broomstick made of birch. Sometimes she kidnaps and eats children; at other times she helps strangers.

Baba Yaga

THE OTTOMANS

By 1800, the Ottomans were in decline. (See Chapter 11.)

Salim III (ruled 1789–1807), tried to bring in reforms. He reorganized the administration, and introduced the nizam-i cedid, or the New System. He was followed by Mahmud II (ruled 1808–39), who strengthened central power. He created a modern and efficient army and brought in administrative and legal reforms.

The Puffin History of the World

Tanzimat (1839-76)

Tanzimat is a Turkish term meaning 'reorganization'. After Mahmud II's reforms there was further reorganization and reform from 1839 to 1876. The aim was to make the empire strong enough to resist both external invasions and internal problems. Apart from creating a strong central government, there were new educational institutions. Railways and telegraph were introduced. Freedom of religion was guaranteed. Abdul Macid (ruled 1839–61), began the process of Tanzimat.

A new constitution

Abdul Hamid II became the new sultan in 1876. The same year, a new constitution was introduced. This ended the Tanzimat period.

But after the Russo–Turkish War of 1877–78, the constitution was suspended. Abdul Hamid used a secret and terrifying police force to put down all protests.

The Armenian Massacre

From 1895 to 1896, a massacre of Armenians occurred. Abdul Hamid did not intervene to stop it.

The Young Turks

There were many groups who wanted reforms. These came to be called the 'Young Turks'. The Committee of Union and Progress was one such group founded in 1889, which became the most important later on.

DOLMABAHCE AND YILDIZ PALACES

Palaces, mosques and other structures continued to be built in Ottoman territories.

The Dolmabahce Palace was built in baroque style between 1843 and 1856, in the Besiktas district of Istanbul, along the Bosphorus strait. It had over 300 rooms, many decorated with huge chandeliers and mirrors. There were bannisters made of red crystal. A simple and plain palace was built at Yildiz in 1877. Sultan Abdul Hamid carved many of the wood cabinets in the palace himself. The Dolmabahce Palace was the administrative centre from 1856 to 1887, and from 1909 to 1922. The Yildiz Palace was the centre from 1887 to 1909.

Dolmabahce Palace

Ottoman Decline

'The Sick man of Europe'

Because of their declining power, the Ottomans were sometimes referred to as the 'Sick man of Europe'. Several states formerly under the Ottomans gained independence including Serbia, Montenegro, Romania and Bulgaria. Egypt was under British control. However, the Ottomans still controlled Greater Syria (including present Syria, Turkey, Albania and Iraq), as well as part of the Arabian Peninsula.

ROMANIA

Moldavia and Wallachia joined together forming Romania in 1859. Its autonomy was recognized by the Ottoman empire in

1861. Romanian independence was recognized by the Congress of Berlin in 1878, though Russia acquired Bessarabia, part of east Moldavia.

BULGARIA

Bulgaria was under the Ottoman empire. By the 19th century, Bulgaria was economically prosperous, but wanted independence. Nationalism was growing. In 1876, a Bulgarian uprising against Ottoman rule was suppressed. After the Russo-Turkish War, by the Congress of Berlin Bulgarian territory was divided into three parts. Part of it became an autonomous principality under the Ottomans; a second part, Eastern Rumelia, also gained some autonomy under the Ottomans. Macedonia, which had once formed a part of the Bulgarian empire, remained under the Ottomans. The autonomous principality could choose its own king, though with the approval of the European powers. Alexander of Battenburg, a German but a nephew of Alexander II of Russia, was chosen. Eastern Rumelia started a revolt in 1885 and was joined with Bulgaria in a 'personal union' under Alexander. However confusion followed. Serbia attacked Bulgaria but was defeated. Alexander of Battenburg was kidnapped and a pro-Russian government set up. Stefan Stambuloff, a Bulgarian, overthrew the pro-Russian government, and Prince Ferdinand of Saxe Coburg-Botha was chosen as the new king. Stambuloff was actually the main power in Bulgaria, till he was assassinated in 1895. Ferdinand declared Bulgaria fully independent with himself as the tsar in 1908.

29

British Expansion in South and West Asia

After 1800, British control over South and West Asia increased.

INDIA

In India, British rule was becoming hateful to many different groups.

The British tried different methods to gain control of the areas still under Indian rulers. Lord Wellesley, the governor general from 1798, introduced the 'subsidiary alliance'. According to this, the Indian ruler had to pay an amount (a subsidy) to the British for the maintenance of British troops in his own state. This was supposedly for his protection, but in practice the ruler lost all independence.

Wars too were fought which, by 1848, had brought most of India directly or indirectly under British control. To bring more areas under direct control, Lord Dalhousie, governor general from 1848 to 1856, introduced the Doctrine of Lapse. According to this, if an Indian ruler died without a son, his state would 'lapse', that is, come under the British. Adopted sons were disallowed from inheritance.

There were other reasons for discontent. The army and police were reorganized, but top posts remained with the British. In the army there were no Indian officers. In addition there were economic problems. Artisans suffered as the Indian textile industry was ruined. This was because the British forcibly exported raw cotton and sent finished cotton products to India. In general, the economy was ruined by a 'drain of wealth' with money from taxes and other income being sent to Britain.

Benefits to India included the construction of roads and railways and the improvement of communications through posts and telegraphs. As some elite Indians acquired a Western education, Western philosophy and concepts of equality and freedom began to spread. Reform movements started in India, among them the Brahmo Samaj founded by Raja Rammohan Roy in 1828. Roy wanted to modernize India and combine the best of Indian culture with reason and science. He fought to improve the condition of women, and to prevent sati, the immolation of a woman on the funeral pyre of her husband. The Arya Samaj, founded in 1875 by Swami Dayananda Saraswati, was another reform movement. It aimed to combine Vedic learning with Western scientific ideas, and also worked to reduce caste restrictions, and to improve the position of women in society.

The Revolt of 1857

Widespread resentment led to a revolt against the British in 1857. The revolt began as a mutiny in the army. The immediate cause was a new Enfield rifle. The sipahis (soldiers) had to remove the top of the cartridge with their teeth. According to rumours these cartridges were coated in pig and beef fat. The sipahis included

The Rani of Jhansi, who fought bravely against the British

Muslims and Hindus. Muslims as a custom do not eat pigs, and Hindus do not eat cows.

In March, a soldier called Mangal Pandey attacked his officers when asked to use these cartridges. He was hanged. In April, more soldiers refused and after they were sentenced a mutiny broke out at Meerut on 10 May 1857. Other military units and thousands of ordinary people joined in. The revolt spread across north India and Bahadur Shah Zafar, the powerless Mughal emperor, was proclaimed the emperor of India. After initial successes the revolt was finally suppressed. The last Mughal emperor was exiled to Rangoon (Yangon) in Burma, where he died in prison.

Capture of Bahadur Shah Zafar, the last Mughal emperor

The British government now took over India, removing the East India Company. For the next 90 years Indians struggled to unite, organize and win independence. A sense of nationalism awakened, and the Indian National Congress was founded in 1885. This led the independence movement in the coming years.

EXPANSION OF BRITISH COLONIES

Using India as their base, the British began to expand their territories.

The Portuguese, followed by the Dutch, gained control over part of Ceylon (Sri Lanka), but it was taken over by the British in 1802. In 1815, the British removed the last king, Sri Vikrama Rajasimha (ruled 1798–1815), and brought the entire island under their control. Cinnamon was exported from here and coffee plantations were introduced. After the vast coffee crops were ruined by a leaf disease, tea, rubber and coconut plantations were set up. Labour from India was imported to work on the plantations.

Bhutan, an independent kingdom, made a treaty with the British in India in 1865. In return for financial help, Bhutan agreed not to make raids along the border.

Nepal held some territory in northern India. The British fought a war against Nepal from 1814 to 1816. It was concluded by the Treaty of Sagauli. Nepal retained internal autonomy, but did not try to encroach on Indian territories. In foreign policy it was guided by Britain.

In the east, Britain finally gained control over Burma (Myanmar) in 1885, after fighting three wars.

THE GREAT GAME

The struggle between Britain and Russia for the region of Afghanistan and Iran is known as the 'Great Game', because of the constant manipulations and attempts of the two countries to gain control in the region.

Afghanistan

In Afghanistan, Ahmad Shah Abdali (Durrani), a general of Nadir Shah, gained control after Nadir's death. (See Chapter 10.) His empire extended into east Iran and north India, but had collapsed by 1818. Dost Muhammad Khan, an Afghan, came to power in east Afghanistan in 1835. The British asked him to remove a Russian representative who was stationed at Kabul. When he refused, a war took place from 1839 to 1842. A British army removed Dost Muhammad and placed Shah Shujah on the throne. In 1841, Shah Shuja was overthrown by Dost Muhammad's son, Akbar Khan. The British resident in Kabul was killed. The British Indian troops surrendered in Kabul but were massacred when retreating. Another British army reoccupied Kabul but later withdrew. Dost Muhammad regained

Dost Muhammad of Afghanistan

the throne. In 1855, Dost Muhammad concluded a treaty of friendship with Britain.

Another war took place from 1878 to 1880, when Amir Sher Ali had a Russian alliance. He was deposed by British Indian forces. Yakub Khan was placed on the throne but after another revolt was replaced with his nephew Abdur Rahman Khan. The British gained control over the Khyber Pass and some other areas of Afghanistan. Afghanistan did not have clear boundaries but these were fixed in 1893. After this Russia did not enter Afghanistan. Britain continued to try to gain more control in Afghanistan, and another war was fought in 1919. This had no clear result and Britain then left Afghanistan alone.

Iran

In Iran the Qajar dynasty was ruling from 1794. The first ruler, Agha Muhammad Khan, was crowned Shah in 1796, but was assassinated in 1797. His nephew Fath Ali Shah ruled from 1797 to 1834. An Iran–Russia war from 1804 to 1813 led to a Russian victory. Russia gained Georgia. Another war was fought with Russia from 1825 to 1828. Russia temporarily occupied Tabriz, and gained control over the South Caucasus region. In 1848, Nasiruddin became the shah. The administration was reformed by the prime minister Mirza Taqi Khan. Iran was modernized and western style education was introduced. The Dar al Funun, the first modern university in Iran, was established. However, the shah was persuaded to believe that Mirza Taki was a threat to the throne, and so he was exiled and later killed.

Since its defeat against Russia, Iran had been attempting to gain control over Herat and other areas of western Afghanistan. In the period 1856 to 1857, Britain attacked Iran to push her out of the region. Britain succeeded though some amount of Iranian influence remained till 1863. Trade concessions were granted to Britain. After a long reign, Shah Nasiruddin was assassinated in 1896.

British influence spread to south Iran and the Persian Gulf, and Russian to north Iran. In 1907, this influence was formalized and an Anglo–Russian Convention was signed. By this Iran was divided into spheres of British and Russian influence.

Art and architecture

Architecture and art flourished at the time of the Qajar dynasty. Fath Ali Shah had life-size portraits and paintings made, and both large and miniature portraits continued to be made later. In the latter half of the 19th century, some artists such as Sani al Mulk and Kamal al-Mulk created paintings in European styles. Rock-relief sculptures, in the styles of the Achaemenid and Sasanian dynasties, again began to be made. A royal museum was opened by Shah Nasiruddin.

DIFFERENT SECTS AND NEW RELIGIONS

Ismaili

The Ismaili is a Shia sect of Islam. It believes that Ismail (d. 760) was the seventh and last imam, and will return as the mahdi or messiah.

In 1840, the Aga Khan, the head of the Ismaili sect, started a revolt against the shah in Iran, but was defeated and escaped to India. The head of the Ismaili sect then continued to live in India.

A new religion—the Bahai

Sayyid Ali Muhammad (1819–50) of Shiraz called himself the 'Bab' or gateway to the truth, and started the Babi movement. He wrote a book called *Bayan* (Declaration or Explanation) which he felt should replace the Quran. He was executed at Tabriz. One of his chief disciples, Mirza Husain Ali (1817–91), founded the Bahai religion in Iran. He was called Bahaullah (glory of god). The Bahai religion believes in one god, and teaches people to unite and maintain love for all beings in the universe. Today it is followed by many diverse peoples across the world.

30

China and Japan: The Decline of the Qing Dynasty and the Meiji Restoration

CHINA

In 1800, the Qing (Manchu) dynasty was still in control in China. Their territories extended beyond China to Central Asia, Taiwan and Tibet. In fact, at this time they had the largest empire in the world. The population was steadily growing. There were some advances in agriculture yet these were insufficient to meet the food requirements of the people. There were wonderful crafts but industrialization had not taken place.

The opium wars

Opium from India reached China through British and Indian traders, and was sold at Guangzhou, the only port open for external trade. As opium imports increased, the Chinese government was worried for two reasons. Silver was used to pay for the opium, and as large amounts of the metal were used for this, its value reduced. In addition, opium smoking was destroying the health of the people of China. High prices led to corruption and violence. At Guangzhou, the Chinese were stopped from trading, and the foreigners confined to the factories, until they surrendered their opium. This they did, but soon a war took place from 1839 to 1842. There were several battles along the south-east coast. Britain won because of her strong gunboats. The Treaty of Nanjing ending the war was signed in August 1842.

This was the first of the unequal treaties that China signed.

By this treaty, the Qing gave Hong Kong, then a barren island, to the British. Five ports were opened for trade, Guangzhou (Canton), Xiamen (Amoy), Fuzhou (Foochow), Ningbo (Ningpo) and Shanghai. The British could trade with anyone they liked at the five ports, and live wherever they liked. Twenty-one million silver dollars were paid as compensation to the British. The Qing also agreed to set up 'a fair and regular tariff'. The British in return promised to withdraw all their troops from Nanjing and the Grand Canal. A supplementary treaty was signed in October 1843. By this, British citizens came under their own laws, and not those of China. Also Britain would have the same privileges granted to any other foreign power. Treaties were also signed with the USA and France in 1844.

Each treaty port had a separate section for the foreign residents, with a club and a church. The Chinese did enter these areas as workers, servants and shopkeepers, but they were under foreign control.

A second war against the Qing resulted in the treaties of Tianjin in 1858. An Anglo-French invasion in 1860 concluded the treaties.

The Qing government became weaker, the treaty system continued to expand and more and more ports were opened to foreigners.

Education and modernization

The Chinese tried to have a two-fold method of learning, with Chinese studies remaining important, but Western studies being used for technical and scientific learning. Jesuit missionaries translated a number of works, including many on science, into Chinese. An interpreters' college was set up at Beijing in 1862. Yet some objected to teaching Western subjects as they said Western sciences actually borrowed from ancient Chinese systems. They also felt railways, telegraph and other modern technology would disturb the harmony between man and nature (fengshui). However, the Kaiping coal mines were opened to the north of Tianjin in 1878, and the first regular railway was founded in 1881.

REBELLIONS

The Qing government found it difficult to collect taxes and provide for the needs of the people, particularly when there were disasters such as floods, drought or famine. There were also several internal rebellions. Among them were:

The White Lotus Rebellion (1796–1804)

The White Lotus Society was a religious group that was formed in the time of the Yuan dynasty. It promised that the Bodhisattva Maitreya would come as a messiah, the Ming dynasty would be restored, and there would be peace and prosperity in China. A series of rebellionsspread in the northern mountainous border regions, but was suppressed by 1804. A rebellion of the Eight Trigrams, another secret society, took place in 1813.

The Taiping Rebellion (1851–64)

This was started by Hong Xiuquan, a Chinese who became a Christian, in the region of Guanxi to the west of Guangzhou.

His followers were trained in battle and by 1850, numbered at least 20,000. On 11 January 1851, Hong's 38th birthday, he proclaimed himself the king of the Heavenly Kingdom of Great Peace (Taiping Tianguo). The sect did not wear the Manchu pigtail, and kept their long hair open. They were fierce in battle, and a civil war started across China. In 1853, the Taiping captured Nanjing, and made it their Heavenly Capital. The Taiping leadership was against gambling, the use of intoxicants and foot binding, and gave women more privileges. Women supported them, and some even served in the army.

Meanwhile the Qing had other problems. Beijing was occupied by Anglo–French forces in 1860. The Taiping moved towards Shanghai. In 1861, the Qing emperor was removed, and the Empress Dowager, Cixi, took over power as regent. Under her were two Manchu leaders, Prince Gong and the Grand Councillor Wenxiang. They tried to bring order. On the one hand they accepted the unequal treaty system. On the other they brought more Chinese into prominent positions. Zeng Guofan, a Chinese Confucian scholar, reorganized the army. All these policies together managed to crush the rebellion by 1864.

Hong Xiuquan

The Nian Rebellion (1853–68)

Almost simultaneously with the Taiping rebellion, the Nian rebellion was taking place in the north-east. The rebels there had fortified villages. They fought on horses, and plundered areas for food.

THE EMPRESS CIXI

The empress Cixi (1835–1908), was the consort of the Chinese emperor Xianfeng. Her son, Tonghzi (ruled 1861–75), came to the throne when he was a minor, and she ruled as regent. After Tonghzi's death, she made her nephew, Guangxu, the emperor and ruled as his regent till 1889, and again from 1898 till her death. She was a strong ruler, and extremely conservative, but in later years attempted to modernize the country.

Other rebellions

There were also rebellions by Islamic groups, from 1855 to 1873 in the south-west and from 1862 to 1873 in the north-west. Many people were killed in these rebellions and battles.

POPULATION DECLINE

According to some estimates the population was around 410 million in 1850, but after all these conflicts, had dropped to 350 million in 1873.

WAR WITH JAPAN

A war with Japan took place between 1894 and 1895 over events in Korea. Korea was traditionally linked to China, but had been recognized as an independent state by Japan in 1875. Within Korea there were differences among reformists and traditionalists. In 1894, the Donghak, a Neo-Confucian sect, began a rebellion. The Donghak were nationalists, and were against Western culture. They were joined by peasant armies and together defeated some government troops. China sent troops to help the Korean government, at their request. Japan too sent forces, though without being asked. A war began between Chinese and Japanese

The Puffin History of the World

troops, as both wanted to control Korea. Japan won. By the Treaty of Shimonoseki, Japan received Taiwan, the Pescadores (Penghu) Islands, and the Liaodong Peninsula of Manchuria. Russia, France and Germany made Japan return Liaodong. However, China had to pay an indemnity and open four more ports for foreign trade.

THE YIHETUAN MOVEMENT: THE BOXER REBELLION

The Yihetuan (Society of Righteousness and Harmony), often translated as 'Boxers', started a rebellion in 1900. They developed out of several secret societies that trained in martial arts.

They supported Chinese values and culture, and were against foreigners, Christians and missionaries.

The Boxers attacked Europeans and Chinese Christians in Beijing and other cities. The foreign legations in Beijing were besieged for 55 days, until an international force of several European countries and the USA reached Beijing to rescue them. A large number of non–Christian Chinese were killed. The Qing was asked to pay a huge amount of money in compensation. However, much of the money was returned or not taken at all. European officials were persuaded that this was a local uprising without the support of the Qing.

ATTEMPTS AT REFORM

The Qing government realized it had to make changes to survive. From 1901, a period of reform started. The old examination system was abolished in 1905, and modern education established. At Beijing new and modern government ministries were founded in 1906.

In 1908, a programme was started which would bring in a constitutional government within nine years. A new system of self-government was set up. There was also a programme for the centralization of government power.

SUN YAT-SEN: A REPUBLIC IS FORMED

However, opposition to the Qing dynasty continued. Sun Yat-Sen (Sun Zhongshan), from a peasant family of China, became a doctor in Hong Kong in 1892. In 1894, he left his career as a doctor and focused on organizing a revolution against the Qing government. In 1905, the Tongmenghui (United Revolutionary League), a Chinese group based in Tokyo in Japan, chose Sun Yat-Sen as their leader. On 10 October 1911 there was a revolt at Wuchang in China. Many provinces then declared independence from the Qing. The Chinese Republic was founded at Nanjing on 1 January 1912. Sun Yat-Sen was the provisional president. In March 1912, Yuan Shikai, a military leader, was chosen as president of the new republic. The Qing emperor abdicated.

Yuan Shikai proclaimed himself emperor in 1915, but died in 1916 and the republic was reestablished under Sun Yat-Sen and the Kuomintang, the Nationalist Party he had founded in 1911.

JAPAN: THE MEIJI RESTORATION (1868–1912)

In Japan there was resentment against the shoguns after the signing of a trade treaty with the USA in 1858. This was followed by trade concessions to other European countries. With an ill-equipped army, Japan was not in a position to resist.

Some of the samurai turned against the shogun. They wanted a strong Japan without Western interference. In the name of the emperor the samurai attacked foreign ships. They were defeated but clashes began between the samurai forces and the shogun. Both groups imported and used Western guns. The shogun, Tokugawa Yoshinobu, resigned in 1867. He aimed to gain support of the daimyo to become the leader again. Soon after this, radicals reached the emperor's palace in Kyoto, and proclaimed the restoration of the rule of the emperor.

A war took place between some of the samurai supporters of the emperor and the shogun's forces, resulting in a victory for the emperor Mutsohito. He took the name Meiji, meaning 'enlightened government', and remained the emperor till 1912. This is known as the Meiji period. The capital was moved to Edo and renamed Tokyo. In 1871, all the daimyo lands came under central rule, and new provinces were created. Many of the daimyo were appointed as governors in the new provinces. Having seen the level of development in Europe, Japan created a strong army and navy. Railways were constructed and industrialization began. A new constitution was introduced in 1889. This set up a Parliament with two houses, though the emperor's power was supreme. In 1890, new codes of law were drawn up. These were based on Western systems.

Japan won a war against China during 1894 to 1895. By 1899, all unequal treaties with the European powers were changed. During 1904 to 1905 Japan won a war against Russia. In 1910, they annexed Korea. Japan had shown it was equal to any European power.

Japan had thus totally changed during the Meiji period. This period came to an end with the death of the Meiji emperor in 1912. The new emperor, Taisho, was not strong. During his reign, Japan was involved in the world war.

The emperor Meiji and family

31

South East Asia after 1800

South East Asia increasingly came under the influence of European powers.

MYANMAR

After the Second Anglo-Burmese War of 1852, Lower Burma, which was then under King Bagan, came under the British. Mindon and Kanung were Bagan's half-brothers. They overthrew Bagan and tried to retain northern Burma.

King Mindon Min (ruled 1853-78) struggled to maintain control. Mindon also founded a new capital at Mandalay. Helped by his younger brother Kanaung, he tried to reform the administration and modernize Myanmar. The army was strengthened and officials were paid a fixed salary. He sent scholars to Europe and America to find out about new machinery and technology. For the first time coins were made by machines and steamships were used for trade.

King Mindon had a number of queens and about 110 children from them and from other women. Shwepayagyi was the main queen, but another queen, Hsinbyumashin, wanted her daughter and son-in-law to be the next rulers. Her son-in-law Thibaw was actually one of Mindon's sons. Hsinbyumashin managed to get most of the other sons killed, and Thibaw came to the throne in 1878. But in the Third Anglo-Burmese War, he was defeated. In 1885, the British gained control over the whole of Myanmar.

Kuthodaw Pagoda

King Mindon had the Kuthodaw Pagoda constructed at Mandalay. This temple contains the entire collection of Pali Buddhist scriptures written on marble slabs. Each stone slab was placed in a small stupa.

Kuthodaw Pagoda, the main shrine

THAILAND

King Rama I (ruled 1782–1809) of the Chakri dynasty revived the Thai kingdom, known at that time as Siam. Ayutthaya once again flourished. A treaty with the British in 1826 led to British influence in the region. King Mongkut (ruled 1851–68) began the modernization of the country. This was continued by his son Chulalongkorn. In 1893, there was a boundary dispute with France, who controlled Vietnam, Laos and Cambodia. Thailand had to surrender Cambodia and Laos, east of the river Mekong.

LAOS

The region of Laos, including the three former kingdoms of Vientiane (Vien Chan), Louang Phrabang and Champasak were under the rule of Thailand (Siam). The kings were appointed by Thailand, and had to pay tribute to that country. Each of these kingdoms had a commissioner from Thailand who exercised some control. In 1827, Chao Anou (Anouyong) the king of Vientiane, led a force against Bangkok in Thailand but was defeated. Vientiane was annexed and garrisons were placed in Champasak in 1846 and in Louang Phrabang in 1885. Thailand then expanded towards the hill states of the north-east, which were jointly controlled by Vietnam and Louang Phrabang.

France already had a protectorate over Vietnam and protested against this. In 1886, France entered into discussions with Thailand. They wanted the boundary between Thailand and Vietnam defined. They got permission to establish a French vice consul in Louang Phrabang, and then increased control over it. This formally came under France in 1893. France obtained the rest of Laos territory in 1904, and in 1907 territory from Thailand. Though under French protection, Louang Phrabang continued to have some autonomy under its own kings. Kham Souk, also known as Zakarine, ruled from 1895 to 1904, though he was regent for his father from 1888. The other former Laos kingdoms were governed by French officials. When Laos finally gained independence, Louang Phrabang's king, Sisavang Vong or

Vatthana, became king of the whole territory. Louang Phrabang was the royal capital until 1975.

CAMBODIA

Around 1800, Vietnam and Thailand (Siam) both aimed to control Cambodia. Meanwhile in 1863, Cambodia came under the indirect control of France. Cambodian kings still ruled but under the guidance of French officials.

VIETNAM

In 1802, the Nguyen dynasty was established by Nguyen Anh who defeated the Tay Son, and became the emperor Gia Long. The north and south were now united and the whole region was renamed Vietnam. However, the French began to have an influence over the country. Catholic missionaries were not liked by the local people. The Nguyen dynasty continued to rule in name, but in actuality the French gained control. In 1861, the French occupied Saigon (now Ho Chi Minh City) and by 1883 France controlled Vietnam.

PHILIPPINES

The Philippines was under Spain. (See Chapter 16.) It was initially ruled by the viceroyalty of Mexico. In 1821, Mexico gained independence. The Philippines then came directly under Spain. From around 1890, a nationalist movement started to gain freedom from Spain. Among the main leaders was José Rizal. He was executed in 1896 and more protests started. Emilio Aguinaldo led a rebellion against the Spanish government in 1896. A Spanish–American war took place in 1898. (See Chapter 34.) Emilio helped the Americans. He then temporarily became president of the new republic, but it was soon taken over by the US.

By the Treaty of Paris, signed in December 1898, Spain granted the Philippines to the US, on payment of 20 million dollars in compensation. Protests against US occupation began. In the following years hundreds of thousands of Filipinos died, but by 1903 the protests largely died down. Aguinaldo, leading the protests, was arrested by USA in 1901. He was released after promising support to USA. In 1902, William Howard Taft was appointed as the United States governor of the Philippines. (He was later the president of USA.) A Parliament with two houses was set up. In 1907, the first Philippines assembly met. The Filipinos desired complete independence, but this was granted only after the Second World War in 1946.

JOSÉ RIZAL

José Rizal was not just a political leader, but a writer. He wrote two novels against Spanish rule, *Noli me tangere* (1886) and *El filibusterismo* (1891). These were later translated as *The Social Cancer* and *The Reign of Greed*.

José Rizal

MALAYSIA

By 1800, the British controlled the island of Penang, Province Wellesley and Malacca and soon extended their hold on Malaysia. Malacca was taken from the Dutch in 1795, returned in 1818 and again restored to the British in 1824. Sir Thomas Stamford Raffles, an employee of the East India Company, took over Singapore in 1819. There were still a number of independent Malay states, many of which had disputes with one another. The British persuaded them to accept a resident, an official who would provide them with advice. By 1895, the British controlled the places mentioned above, along with Perak, Selangor, Negeri

Sembilan and Pahang. In addition there was some control over Johor to the south. The four northern states of Perlis, Kedah, Kelantan and Trengganu were taken over from Thailand in 1909. Johor was totally under the British by 1914. These states together later formed west Malaysia.

Borneo was mainly under Brunei. The sultan of Brunei gave some land to an Englishman named John Brooke, and also granted him the title of Raja of Sarawak. John and his successors were known as 'white rajas'. They expanded the state which then had the same boundaries as Sarawak today. The sultanates of Brunei and Sulu also allotted land on lease to a British trading company, known after 1881 as the British North Borneo (Chartered) Company. North Borneo and Sarawak were British protectorates by 1888.

> Protectorate: a territory militarily or diplomatically protected, but which maintains autonomy.

INDONESIA

Diponegoro, a Java prince, led a revolt against the Dutch from 1825 to 1830. After this the Dutch directly controlled some parts of Java and Sumatra. Crops were grown for export. This led to a decline in rice cultivation, and famines took place. Coffee, sugar, tobacco and rubber were grown; oil and tin were the other exports. Gradually more areas were taken over by the Dutch, including the Celebes, Moluccas, Lesser Sunda Islands and part of Borneo. Aceh was conquered in 1908, and Bali in 1909. Railways and roads were made, and ships crossed the seas between islands, leading to closer contacts between them. Western-style educational institutions produced some highly educated Indonesians, who led the movement for independence. In 1912, the nationalist group Sarekat Islam was set up, which by the end of the First World War had a huge membership. The Indonesian Communist Party (PKI) organized revolts in 1926 to 1927.

The Indonesian Nationalist Party (Partai Nasional Indonesia), founded in 1927, led the movement for complete independence. Independence was proclaimed after the Second World War in 1945, but was finally granted only in 1949.

MT TAMBORA

Mt Tambora, a volcano in Indonesia, had a huge eruption in April 1815. This led to the death of more than 10,000 people, and created tsunamis across the Java Sea. Debris from the explosion remained in the atmosphere for several months, and led to the cooling of parts of the earth. Its effects extended to China, Tibet and parts of Europe and North Africa, and even caused famines and failure of crops there. The crater of the volcano today is 4.8 km across and 914 m deep, a totally barren area.

A SPECIAL TYPE OF ART: BATIK

Art, literature, music and dance had many different forms in this region. One special technique of painting and designing textiles, using wax, originated in Indonesia. At first designs were in white, with an indigo background; later several colours were used. The cloth is then dyed in stages, with wax covering the area to be kept free from the dye. Batiks were introduced in Europe by the Dutch in the 17th century, and were well known by the 19th century.

32

Africa
1800-1900

I n 1800, there were numerous groups and kingdoms of
   African people. Each group occupied a certain territory and
   had a distinctive language and culture. By the end of the 19th
century, European control had spread over the continent. The
slave trade gradually declined.

Here we will look at some of the kingdoms and the main
developments.

EGYPT

Egypt was invaded by French forces under Napoleon in 1798,
though they did not gain control of the whole area. A new struggle
for power began between the Ottomans and the Mamluks.
Finally in 1805, an Ottoman governor, Muhammad Ali,
became the governor of Egypt with local support. Muhammad
Ali defeated all opponents and ruled almost independently. He
conquered Al Hijaz (in present Saudi Arabia) in 1819 and Sudan
between 1820 and 1822. He improved industry, organized and
provided training for the army, and sent Egyptians to Europe
to learn new technology.

The Ottomans were still ruling Syria. Muhammad Ali and his son Ibrahim Pasha invaded Syria and defeated them. They moved towards Istanbul, but fearing that Egypt was becoming too powerful, Russia, France and Britain came to the help of the Ottomans. Muhammad Ali could not advance further. Britain was interested in the region, as it was searching for new markets to sell its machine-made goods. Muhammad Ali died in 1848. His son Ibrahim Pasha succeeded him, but did not live long. Said Pasha took over from him. His nephew, Ismail Pasha, became the governor in 1863. He received the title of Khedive, or viceroy. Ismail modernized the country, and contributed to the building of the Suez Canal that was opened in 1869. This canal connects the Mediterranean Sea with the Gulf of Suez. However, Ismail borrowed money from European banks for this, and Egypt soon faced a financial crisis. France and Britain began to control Egypt's finances in 1876, and Ismail abdicated in 1879. His son Taufik Pasha was the next governor, but some army officers in Egypt wanted to remove him and end Ottoman control. Taufik asked the British for help, and Britain took control of Egypt in 1882.

The Suez Canal provided Britain the shortest route to India. Taufik and his successors remained governors, but the real ruler was a British consul general. Despite protests, British dominance was maintained. In 1904, the French recognized the British occupation of Egypt, and the British recognized the French occupation of Morocco. Meanwhile Egypt's grain cultivation was reduced. Instead cotton was cultivated as this was needed by the British textile mills.

SUDAN

The Funj kingdom at Sennar in the Sudan region was conquered by Egypt after a war from 1820 to 1822. Between 1884 and 1898, Muhammad Ahmad ibn as Sayyid Abd Allah, who proclaimed himself the Mahdi, ruled. (Mahdi is a term meaning 'the guided one', a messiah or great spiritual leader). In 1882, he led the people against Egyptian rule and defeated Anglo-Egyptian troops. The British sent General Charles Gordon, who had been governor of Sudan on behalf of the Ottomans, to supervise the withdrawal of these troops. He was besieged in Khartoum for 10 months, and was killed in January 1885. The Mahdi died soon after this but was succeeded by Abdallah at Taaisha, who ruled for another 13 years. In 1898, the British destroyed Mahdi power in the battle of Omdurman. The British began to rule Sudan along with Egypt.

In other parts of North Africa, the city of Algiers was occupied by the French in 1830, followed by the rest of that country in 1834. Tunisia came under French occupation in 1881. Tripoli remained under the Ottomans.

ETHIOPIA

Ethiopia had broken up into small kingdoms. In 1855, Ras Kassa, a leader from the north-west of Ethiopia, defeated some feudal rulers and became the emperor Tewedros II (ruled 1855–68). Britain invaded Ethiopia in 1867. In 1868, Tewedros killed himself to prevent his capture. After a few years of confusion, in 1872, Dejaz Kassai, governor of Tigre province, became the emperor Yohannes IV (ruled 1872–89). Yohannes resisted an invasion by Egypt but was killed in a war against Sudan. Menelik II (ruled 1889–1913) was the next emperor. He moved the capital to Addis Ababa.

Meanwhile Italy was trying to occupy Ethiopia. In 1889, Menelik signed the Treaty of Wichali (Ucciali) with Italy. In 1896, Italians invaded Ethiopia but were defeated at Aduwa. Ethiopia remained free of European rule.

THE FULANI EMPIRE

The Fulani were Muslims who were earlier nomadic. Between 1804 and 1811, they organized what is known as the Fulani Jihad.

Several Fulani kingdoms were established in West Africa. Usman dan Fodio, a Fulani reformer, conquered the Hausa lands of most of north Nigeria and united them into an empire. The first ruler was Amir al Mumenin, Muhammad Bello, and the capital was at Sokoto. The area they ruled is called the Sokoto Caliphate or the Fulani empire.

By the 1860s, Sokoto dominated the Hausa lands as well as areas beyond. Within the empire, however, individual emirates had considerable autonomy. In north Nigeria, the Sokoto were defeated by the British between 1900 and 1903.

TUKOLOR

As we saw in Chapter 17, the Songhe empire was succeeded by the smaller kingdoms of Macina, Segou and Gonja. Seku Ahmadu, a Fulani Muslim, defeated the Segou empire (also known as the Bambara empire) and conquered part of the territory in 1818. This formed the kingdom of Macina which grew into an empire including the region around the river Niger from Jenne to Timbuktu.

Macina followed strict Islamic laws. New mosques were built without too much decoration, and 600 madrasas were founded. In 1852, Al-haji Umar, an Islamic scholar of the Tijanniya Islamic sect, began a series of conquests from Upper Guinea. In 1861, he conquered the rest of the Bambara empire, and made Segou his capital. In 1862, he took over Macina. By the time of his death in 1864, he had created the large Tukolor empire. The empire lasted till 1890, when it was occupied by the French.

OTHER KINGDOMS

There were other Muslim states, as well as great kingdoms such as the Asanti, Dahomey and Oyo. All these gradually came under European rule.

ZULUS

In South Africa, the Zulus created a strong state. The Zulus were a group of the Nguni people. From around 1810, Chaka or Shaka, a Nguni leader, began to organize and unite the various Nguni tribes. By 1825, after fighting several battles, Shaka created a large empire. Warriors were trained and grouped into disciplined impis or armies. They used assefais or light spears when fighting. People were also grouped into amabutho or regiments on the basis of age and gender. Dingane, Shaka's half-brother, murdered him in 1828, and became the king and ruled until 1840. The Zulu empire existed until its defeat by the British in 1887.

Zulu conquests displaced several groups who moved to different areas, forming new kingdoms. Among them were the Sotho kingdom in present, Lesotho, and the Gaza empire.

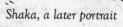
Shaka, a later portrait

THE MFECANE

Mfecane, meaning 'crushing or scattering', refers to conflicts in South Africa between 1815 and 1840. (According to other accounts, 'mfecane' comes from the Xhosa language, from the terms 'ukufaca', which means to become thin with hunger, and 'fetcani', which means starving intruders.) It was a period of change, migration and conflict. As groups migrated they tried to dominate the people in the new territories, and wars and conflict resulted. The mfecane was once considered to be caused mainly by Zulu aggression which displaced people in South Africa. However, recent analysis shows that reasons were complex. Drought and overgrazing were the main causes of the migration of farmers and pastoralists. Another cause was the expansion of Europeans into the region.

CAPE COLONY

The Dutch controlled Cape Colony. But at the time of the Napoleonic Wars, the British gained control of it in 1806. It came formally under Britain in 1814. The Dutch, known as Boers, continued to live in the region. During 1835 to 1837 the Boers moved from Cape Colony to Natal. Natal was conquered by the British in 1843. The Dutch Boers then moved to Orange Free State and Transvaal.

In 1877, Britain obtained Transvaal from the Boers, after an agreement with them. But in December 1880, the Boers again asserted their independence and defeated the British in two battles, at Laing's Nek and Majuba Hill. On 5 April 1885, the Treaty of Pretoria was signed. By this, Transvaal's independence was agreed to, but foreign affairs remained under Britain.

Gold was discovered in Transvaal in 1886. People from different countries went there to try and grab some gold for themselves. They were known as Uitlanders (foreigners) and did not have the same rights as Boers. They decided to revolt. Cecil Rhodes, the prime minister of Cape Colony under the British, promised to help them with a force led by Dr Leander Starr Jameson, a British administrator and politician. The Uitlander revolt was called off, but Jameson attacked the Boers without permission. The attack failed, and he was sent to jail, while Cecil Rhodes (1853–1902) had to resign.

The Boer War

The Boers attacked the British in October 1899. The towns of Mafeking, Ladysmith and Kimberley were besieged in Cape Colony and Natal. As the British sent more troops the Boers were outnumbered. They continued to attack with guerilla warfare before their final defeat in May 1902. The Peace of Vereeniging ended the war. The Boer territories of Transvaal and Orange Free State were acquired by the British. These were incorporated into Natal and Cape Colony in 1910 and formed the dominion of South Africa.

SCRAMBLE FOR AFRICA

Meanwhile, European explorers penetrated deep into Africa, and European nations struggled amongst themselves and against the local rulers for control over the continent.

Around 1880, what came to be known as the 'Scramble for Africa' began among the European countries. At the Conference of Berlin (1884–85), the European powers along with USA met and decided on their spheres of influence within Africa. No African state was represented at the conference.

By the end of the 19th century most of Africa was parcelled out among various European powers. Britain, France, Spain, Portugal, Germany, Italy and Belgium controlled various parts of Africa. Only Ethiopia and Liberia remained independent. Liberia was a state set up in 1822 by the American Colonization Society for freed slaves.

SOME EXPLORERS

Gradually most of Africa was explored by Europeans, and the sources of the great African rivers were discovered. We had already looked at Mungo Park's efforts in Chapter 17.

Among the other explorers was the German Henrich Barth (1821–65) who described his travels in five volumes, *Travels and Discoveries in North and Central Africa 1857–58.*

Richard Burton and John Hanning Speke of Britain located Lake Tanganyika and Lake Victoria in 1848.

David Livingstone, a Scottish doctor and missionary, was one of the greatest explorers who crossed the river Zambezi, and saw the Victoria Falls in 1853–56. He

David Livingstone

was involved in many more explorations, and was also against the slave trade. After he had been missing for some time, he was met at Ujiji on Lake Tanganyika by another great explorer, Henry Morton Stanley, in 1871.

James Augustus Grant and Sir Samuel White Baker were among other British explorers. Grant helped Speke in discovering the source of the Nile, while Baker was involved in exploring the Upper Nile.

THE SLAVE TRADE

During the 19th century, the slave trade was banned in most parts of the world. There had been numerous laws in earlier centuries imposing some kind of ban. By the 19th century the movement against slavery grew. This was partly on moral grounds, and partly because it was no longer economically profitable. Countries in Europe and the Americas gradually passed laws against slavery.

Slavery continued to some extent, and in different ways in the 20th century, but the mass transport of black African slaves had stopped.

LITERATURE

New types of literature developed at this time. Among these were secular and Black African literature, Swahili poetry, works on travel and exploration, as well as novels.

A great Swahili spiritual poem, 'Utendi Wa Inkishafi' (The Soul Awakening) describes the vanity of earthly life. In contrast, *The Story of an African Farm*, a novel by Olive Schreiner, a white South African, written in 1883, looks at the reality of life in South Africa.

33

North America—the formation of Canada and the USA

The territories that would later become Canada and the US developed in entirely different ways.

CANADA

By the Treaty of Paris of 1763, England gained New France (Quebec). At this time there were four main regions in Canada. The large area around Hudson Bay, also known as Rupert's Land and the Northwestern Territories nearby, were relatively unoccupied. Here the Hudson Bay Company as well as other companies were involved in trade in fur. The Newfoundland area had small fishing settlements. Nova Scotia, Prince Edward Island, which was a part of Nova Scotia till 1769, and Quebec were well settled. However, Quebec had a French population in the north, and an English population in the south. Another province, New Brunswick, was created out of Nova Scotia in 1784. Quebec was divided into Upper and Lower Canada in 1791. There were mainly British in Upper Canada, and French in Lower Canada.

In 1840, Upper and Lower Canada were unified. Canada became a self-governing dominion of the British empire in 1867. At this time Canada was a federation consisting of Nova Scotia, New Brunswick, Quebec (Lower Canada) and Ontario (Upper Canada). A Parliament was set up and Sir John Alexander Macdonald became the first prime minister. Rupert's Land and the Northwestern Territory were bought from the Hudson Company in 1870, and added to Canadian territories. Next, British Columbia became part of Canada in 1871 and Prince Edward Island in 1873. The Canadian Pacific Railway helped in uniting the vast land.

The indigenous people in Canada were gradually pushed into reservations, areas that were reserved for Native Americans. However, their treatment was better than in the US and they were given money and facilities for farming.

THE USA

The War of American Independence (1775–83)

After the Seven Years' War in 1763, Britain had acquired several French territories, and was the main power in North America. The American colonies had their own laws, but finance and trade was under Britain. During the Seven Years' War the British discovered that the colonies ignored the Navigation Acts, which provided rules for import and export, and made trade deals on their own. They did not fully support Britain in the war effort. After the Seven Years' War, Britain maintained an army in North America.

Britain thought that the American colonies should contribute to the expenses both for the war, which had left them in debt, and for the army. They passed various acts to raise money, including the Stamp Act in 1765. According to this, special stamped paper had to be bought and used for all official documents. There were protests against this, and also a boycott of British goods. The colonies believed there should

  The Puffin History of the World

be 'no taxation without representation'. The Stamp Act was removed, but other taxes were imposed on various imports from Britain, leading to more protests.

Finally, all taxes except on tea were removed, but even this was not acceptable to the colonies.

The Boston Tea Party

Ships carrying tea were in the Boston harbour. On 16 December 1773, some colonists entered the ships and threw the tea out. This came to be known as the Boston Tea Party.

The British closed the port of Boston and introduced laws which the Americans called 'Intolerable Acts'. These were laws meant to restore order.

In 1774, the colonies held the First Continental Congress, a meeting of representatives of 12 of the colonies, at Philadelphia, and asked for the laws to be repealed. When this was not done they decided to boycott British goods. They also collected guns and other weapons and stored them at Concord nearby. British troops were sent to destroy this hoard. On 19 April 1775, near

The Boston Tea Party

Lexington, Massachusetts, on the way to Concord, the two groups met, and a war began.

The war

The colonial forces besieged Boston. In June 1775, a battle was fought close to Bunker Hill near Boston, which was won by the British, but at great cost.

In May 1775, the Second Continental Congress began.

On 4 July 1776, it issued the Declaration of Independence which was mainly written by Thomas Jefferson. It stated that they were free of British rule.

But the war continued. Several battles were fought. Among them, in 1777 the British won a battle at Brandywine Creek in Pennsylvania. But soon after this, they lost a battle at Saratoga, New York. France and later Spain joined the war in support of the colonists.

The final defeat of the British was at Yorktown, Virginia on 19 October 1781.

The Treaty of Paris was signed on 3 September 1783. This recognized the independence of the United States. Thirteen former British colonies in North America became the United States of America. These were: Connecticut; Delaware; Georgia; Maryland; Massachusetts; New Jersey; New Hampshire; New York; North Carolina; Pennsylvania; Rhode Island; South Carolina and Virginia.

George Washington

George Washington, who had led the army that defeated the British at Georgetown, became the first president of the USA after an election in 1789.

By 1900, the number of states had risen to 45. Between these two dates, several events took place.

Another war
There was another war between the USA and Britain from 1812 to 1815, over attacks on US ships and sailors. There was no clear win and the Treaty of Ghent signed at the end of 1814 restored the situation before the war. However, a battle was fought at New Orleans after this, in which the British had to withdraw. This war gave the USA confidence and there were no further wars with Britain. In 1818, the United States and Britain agreed on an unfortified border between Canada and the United States along the 49th parallel.

Louisiana purchase
Louisiana was a large territory located between the Mississippi and the Rocky Mountain. It was under France, but after the Seven Years' War was acquired by Spain in 1763. France again took it over in 1800. In 1803, Napoleon, as first consul of France, allowed the US to buy this for a payment of 15 million dollars. By acquiring this, the area of the United States was doubled.

Other additions to territory
Florida, earlier under Spain, was added to USA in 1813 to 1819. Texas had gained independence from Mexico in 1836. The USA annexed it in 1845. A war took place with Mexico, after which the USA added California, Nevada, Utah and New Mexico to its territories. More territory was bought from Mexico in 1853, and Alaska was bought from Russia in 1867.

The Homestead Act
The Homestead Act of 1862 encouraged further settlement. According to this, new settlers could claim up to 160 acres of

The Chrisman sisters in front of a sod house. They were among the women who claimed and owned land.

land for themselves, provided they lived there and developed the land for agriculture. The land title would be finalized after five years. This led to US citizens occupying uncultivated land. While farming was promoted through this, many also misused the act and claimed the timber, water resources, or minerals on the land. The plus point of this act was that it allowed both African Americans and women to claim land. Before this act, about 128 million acres had been granted to railroad companies, and this limited land availability.

While the act benefitted many, it was disastrous for Native Americans, who had once lived across this land.

Despite many difficulties, some of these plots of land grew into farms, and groups of farms became towns.

CIVIL WAR (1861-65)

A civil war took place mainly on the question of slavery. It was the southern states that extensively used slave labour in cotton plantations and farms. The northern states had industries without slave labour, and had abolished slavery. Abraham Lincoln (1805-65), a Republican, became president in 1860, and was in favour of limiting slavery. Eleven southern states who wished to preserve slavery left the American Union of States and formed the Confederate States of America. The states in this were Alabama, Arkansas, Florida, Georgia, Louisiana, Mississippi, North Carolina, South Carolina, Tennessee, Texas and Virginia.

A war between the two groups began in April 1861.

The Confederates won some early victories but lost the battle of Gettysberg in 1863. The Union troops also managed to block the southern ports. After many more fierce battles the Union won the war by May 1865. Over 6,00,000 died in the war.

After the war the Confederate states were gradually readmitted to the Union. This was completed by 1870. The US was reunited but bitterness remained between the two groups.

ABOLITION OF SLAVERY

On 1 January 1863, Lincoln abolished slavery. This became part of the US constitution in December 1865. Lincoln also spoke in favour of giving black people the right to vote. But many did not like his views and actions. Abraham Lincoln was shot on 14 April 1865, and died on the 15th. He is remembered as a great statesman who believed in the values of liberty and equality.

Abraham Lincoln

Slaves were now free, but it was a long time before they got equal rights.

NATIVE AMERICANS

The Indian Removal Act of 1830 led to Native Americans in the South East of the United States, being pushed west of the Mississippi River.

In the south-east were five Native American groups that were called the 'Five Civilized Tribes'. These were the Chickasaw, Choctaw, Cherokee Nations, Muscogee Creek and Seminole. These tribes had been part of the Mississippi culture, with well-developed agriculture, and had lived in large towns even before the Europeans arrived. There was confusion in attitudes towards Native Americans. Were they citizens with equal rights? Or were they separate nations, with whom treaties and agreements had to be made by the American government? President George Washington had recognized them as separate and signed treaties with them, but President Andrew Jackson was against this. He said, 'What good man would prefer a country covered with forests and ranged by a few thousand savages to our extensive Republic . . . ?'

After the 1830 Act was passed separate treaties were signed with various tribes, in which they had little choice, and by which they were forced to move west. Treaties were signed with the Choctaw, Cherokee and others, and their suffering was so great that their migration, particularly that of the Cherokee, came to be called the Trail of Tears. By 1837, 46,000 had moved west, and many died on the journeys. Every one of the journeys was poorly managed, with insufficient food, shelter and transport. They died of exposure, floods, disease and of other causes. Their lands, covering 25 million acres, were taken over by Whites for their settlements.

There were other acts. The Indian Appropriations Act of 1851 sent Native Americans into reservations, which were too small for their traditional ways of life. By the Dawes Act of 1871, Native Americans lost their sovereignty. It stated that now 'no Indian nation or tribe within the territory of the United States shall be acknowledged as an independent nation, tribe, or power with whom the United States may contract by treaty'. The Dawes Severalty Act of 1887 offered Native Americans the chance to hold small plots and be recognized as American citizens, but this did not benefit them. Their lands, way of life, and bargaining power with the government were lost. Native Americans attempted to fight back, and even won some battles against the American troops, but by 1890, their original settlements were destroyed, and the remaining groups were pushed into reservations.

Two noted events

Led by the Sioux tribe, Native Americans won a battle against American forces under General George Custer at Little Bighorn in 1876. However, in 1890, a massacre of unarmed Native American men, women and children took place at Wounded Knee in South Dakota.

TWELVE YEARS A SLAVE

Twelve Years a Slave is the story of Solomon Northup (b. 1808), a free man who was captured and sold as a slave. After he regained his freedom through the help of his friends, he wrote an account of his years as a slave, which was made into an award-winning film (2013). He was last heard of in 1857, while the Civil War was being fought. No one knows what happened to him after that or when he died.

Northup was rescued and his story became known, but there were many others who were not as lucky. They lived and died as slaves, or were born free and died as slaves.

Among early descriptions of slavery was Harriet Beecher Stowe's (1811–96) powerful novel, *Uncle Tom's Cabin*.

34

South and Central America and Caribbean Islands 1800–1900

In 1800, most of South America was under Spain and Portugal, but during the 19th century the states there gained independence.

INDEPENDENCE MOVEMENTS

The movement for independence was inspired by the French Revolution and the American War of Independence. During the Napoleonic Wars, Charles VI of Spain and his son Ferdinand became hostages of Napoleon. This provided a further reason for the Spanish colonies in South America to try for independence. The struggle for freedom began in part of the La Plata viceroyalty (modern Argentina, Paraguay, Uruguay and Bolivia). In 1810, the Spanish viceroy was deposed in Buenos Ares, and a provisional government established, which was still legally under Spain. Between 1811 and 1813, Paraguay proclaimed independence, both from Spain and the provisional government. Uruguay, which had freed itself from Spain, was taken over by the Portuguese in Brazil, and gained independence in 1828.

Two people who were prominently involved in the liberation of South American states were San Martin and Simón Bolívar. Jose de San Martin (1778–1850) was involved in independence struggles in Chile, Argentina and Peru. Simón Bolivar (1783–1830) helped to bring independence to Venezuela, and founded the Republic of Bolivia. After the wars the independent Spanish states were Gran Colombia, Peru, Chile, and the United Provinces of Rio de la Plata (later Argentina).

San Martin

Simón Bolívar

GRAN COLOMBIA

Among the other countries, Colombia gained independence in 1810, and was then part of a federation known as Gran Colombia. Venezuela declared independence from Spain in 1811, but was not entirely free. In 1819, Simón Bolivar become president of the Republic of Gran Colombia, which included the present states of Venezuela, Quito, Colombia and Panama. In 1829–30 Venezuela and Quito left Gran Colombia. Quito's name was changed to Ecuador, the 'Republic of the Equator'. Colombia and Panama formed the state of Nueva Granada (later Colombia). Panama was under Colombia. In 1846, the US gained rights to cross the Isthmus of Panama. Panama had some amount of self-government, and a

The territory of Gran Colombia in 1830

brief period of independence, but finally became independent in 1903.

MEXICO

Mexico gained independence in 1821. In 1810, a priest named Miguel Hidalgo y Costilla managed to put together 80,000 people in a revolt against the Spanish. He was overpowered and killed in 1811, but the Spanish government was no longer as strong as before. Jose Maria Morelos y Pavon, another priest, led a revolt and declared Mexico's independence in 1814, but a year later, he too was defeated. Vicente Guerrero continued to lead the revolutionary forces. Meanwhile, Agustin de Iturbide, who had led a government army against Guerrero, now signed a treaty with him, which led to independence from Spain. Following independence, Mexico faced many years of instability.

  The Puffin History of the World

BRAZIL

Brazil was under the Portuguese, and the Portuguese king fled there during the Napoleonic Wars in 1808. He returned to Portugal in 1821, but his son remained there. In 1822, Dom Pedro, son of the Portuguese king, proclaimed the independence of Brazil. He became the new emperor, Pedro I. Initially, Brazil had a monarchical system of government, but a republic was proclaimed by the military in 1889. Coffee and rubber were the main crops and supported the economy in the early years of the republic. Over the years, Brazil had a number of both popular and military governments.

GUATEMALA

As we saw in Chapter 21, in Central America, the kingdom of Guatemala, contained the provinces of Guatemala, Chiapas, Nicaragua, El Salvador, Honduras and Costa Rica. Antigua, the capital of the kingdom, was well-developed. When Mexico gained independence in 1821, Guatemala freed itself from Spain and became part of the Mexican empire. In 1823, it asserted independence from Mexico, though Chiapas remained part of Mexico. The other states formed the United Provinces of Central America. Francisco Morazán became the president in 1830. The capital was moved to San Salvador in 1834.

There were attempts at bringing in reforms and economic development, but there were numerous conflicts among the different groups—the Spanish, the Native Americans, Blacks, Mestizos and others. (See Chapter 21 for more on these groups.) Rafael Carrera, a leader from Guatemala, assumed control over Guatemala City in 1838. Morazán resigned in 1840. Guatemala, Nicaragua, El Salvador, Honduras and Costa Rica became independent republics.

SOME OTHER STATES

Belize came under British administration in 1862, when it became a British colony under Jamaica, known as British Honduras. In 1884, it gained independence, but remained under the British crown.

Guyana was under the British (British Guiana). Suriname was under the Netherlands, known as Netherlands Guiana, or Dutch Guiana.

DIFFERENT HISTORIES

Each of these states had its own complex history, but they had some things in common. Many of these new states faced problems. After independence Bolivia experienced numerous coups and countercoups. Several other states went through frequent changes in government.

Brazil, Costa Rica and Chile enjoyed some amount of stability. Chile created a constitution that lasted, apart from a brief interruption, up to 1925. In Venezuela the government of Antonio Guzman Blanco (1870–88) brought in development. Though Argentinian governments faced frequent changes, meat and grain exports helped to increase prosperity.

Another aspect of all the states was the creation of new settlements pushing out the Native Indian groups. These led to conflicts in many of the states. The independent South American countries were also involved in wars and conflicts with one another. Among the main wars were those fought by Paraguay and Chile.

In 1865, Paraguay, under Francisco Solano Lopez (1862–70), wanted to expand its territories and waged war against Argentina, Brazil and Uruguay. This war led to disaster for Paraguay and slowed its economic development for the next 50 years. The government remained unstable for several years after this. During 1879 to 1883, in the War of the Pacific, Chile defeated Peru and Bolivia, and gained some territory.

The Tango, a ballroom dance that developed in Buenos Aires, Argentina, became popular all over the world. By the early 20th century, dancers and musicians from Buenos Aires reached Europe.

CARIBBEAN ISLANDS

The groups of Caribbean islands also desired independence or at least self-government. As we saw in Chapter 22, among the islands, Haiti gained independence from France in 1804.

After struggles against France and Haiti, Santo Domingo became independent as the Dominican Republic in 1844.

A Spanish-American War fought in 1898 led to the independence of Cuba from Spain, though it came under American control. At the same time, the Philippines, Puerto Rico and Guam were given to the United States.

COFFEE IN COSTA RICA

Costa Rica began to grow coffee in the 19th century.

In 1840, the government of Costa Rica passed a law or decree related to coffee.

It said all the labourers building roads should be served a cup of coffee. This would provide them with them extra energy.

Coffee was so popular that it was used in a basic reading text for children in the 1940s. It said: 'Coffee is good for me. I drink coffee every morning. '

35

European Occupation of Australia and New Zealand

After 1800, European occupation of Australia and New Zealand increased.

AUSTRALIA

When Mathew Flinders navigated around Australia from 1801 to 1803, he gave it its name, meaning 'southern'. It was earlier known as Terra Australis or New Holland. Based on Flinders's work, the name 'Australia' gradually began to be used for the whole territory.

Australia's first colony was called New South Wales. Between 1809 and 1821, the governor was Lachlan Macquarie. He constructed churches and other buildings. Sheep and cattle farming began. Macquarie tried to create jobs so that the freed convicts would find work.

Another colony was founded in Victoria in 1803. In 1827, Great Britain claimed the whole area of Australia. The colony of Western Australia was founded in 1829.

Edward Gibbon Wakefield in London had his own ideas about colonization. He believed that plots should be sold to ordinary citizens and land should not be settled by convicts. Based on his ideas, the South Australian Association was founded in 1834. Following this, a South Australian Colony was set up in 1836. In 1850, some powers were transferred to these colonies. In 1856, they gained some self-government.

Soon six colonies were founded. They were connected by telegraph in 1872. And they decided to join together in a federation. A Federal Council was formed in 1895. In 1898, a Constitution Bill prepared the draft for a strong federation.

Finally on 1 January 1901, the Commonwealth of Australia was formed.

Lachlan Macquarie

Aborigines

Despite intentions to treat aborigines, the original inhabitants, as equals, this did not happen in practice, and their population declined. Some Europeans hunted and poisoned aborigines. While a few got employment, most had to retreat into the deserts of inner Australia. Aborigines were not a part of European social life. Schools were established for some aborigine children, but they were not treated well in these. They lost their families, culture, and way of life. Many of these children died. By 1900, there were about 93,000 aborigines in Australia.

Gold

In 1851, gold was discovered in Australia, in New South Wales and Victoria. A 'gold rush' followed, that is, people from Britain, Canada and the USA, as well as those already in Australia, dashed to the gold mine areas. There was a huge spurt in population, from around 4,00,000 in 1850, to 1.2 million in 1860. Gold was exported and led to a rise in prosperity. Cities developed, with new facilities for entertainment and social life. Later, gold was also found in Queensland (1872–82) and Western Australia (1892–93).

Whites only
After some Chinese people reached Australia to search for gold, Australia restricted the entry of non-white people. It developed a policy of admitting only white people.

The explorers
Though parts of Australia were occupied by the early 19th century, its interiors were unknown. Numerous explorers began to cross the land to see what it was like. Among them was Gregory Blaxland in 1813, who went across the Blue Mountains. In 1860, R.O. Burke and W.J. Wills died when returning from an expedition to the Gulf of Carpentaria. John MacDouall Stuart reached the centre of Australia the same year.

Charles Sturt (1795–1869) explored the Murray and Darling rivers as well as other areas. There were many others and through their efforts the vastness of the continent was beginning to be understood.

NEW ZEALAND
In 1800, there were just a few Europeans in New Zealand. The first European child, Thomas King, was born in the Bay of Islands in 1815. European settlements of Kerikeri were founded in 1822 and of Bluff in 1823. In London, Edward Gibbon Wakefield founded a New Zealand Association in 1837, which developed into the New Zealand Company in 1841. This encouraged migration to New Zealand. In 1839, around 2000 British migrated to New Zealand. By 1850, there were more than

22,000. The first constitution was adopted in 1852, and the first legislative assembly was formed in 1854.

The Maoris

When the Europeans first reached there, according to estimates there were about 1,14,000 Maori in New Zealand. In February 1840, the Treaty of Waitangi was drawn up. By this treaty the Maori leaders retained rights to territory as British subjects, but had to give up their sovereignty to the British. In return they were also to receive British protection. At first 45 chiefs signed the treaty, and later another 500. They were in North Island, and the British then claimed sovereignty over North Island. They claimed it over South Island too.

In 1841, New Zealand became a separate British colony. The capital, which was at Russel, was moved to Auckland. Auckland and Wellington were both founded in 1840. In South Island, settlements were founded at Dunedin in 1848, and Christchurch in 1850. In 1861, gold was discovered in Otago, New Zealand, after which there were more immigrants.

The signing of the Treaty of Waitangi, a later painting

Maori numbers had already diminished. Maoris died both from wars and as a result of the diseases that came with the Europeans.

Maori wars

Maoris fought against the British and against one another.

As guns were traded, some Maori groups acquired them and began to attack others. The Moriori of Chatham Islands were dominated by the Ngati Mutunga and Ngati Tama Maori, and almost exterminated.

In 1843, in South Island the Maori chief Ngati Toa tried to prevent the British from occupying more land around Nelson. The Maoris initially had some success. From 1845 to 1846 in North Island there was fighting between the British and the Maoris as well as amongst the Maori groups.

The Waikato War

In North Island, the Maoris lived in their fortified 'pas' and prevented the British from extending their settlements. To form a stronger opposition, the Waikato Maoris decided to elect a king and chose Potatau Te Wherowhero in 1858. Maori tribes then grouped together in an anti-land-selling king movement (Kingitanga). The British wanted to crush this movement and occupy the land for European settlement. A war took place between 1863 and 1864 and after this Maori power was weakened. In 1872 to 1873 there were some attempts to fight the British, but after this the Maoris were too weak to fight against them. (The New Zealand government agreed this war was wrong, and apologized after more than a hundred years, in 1995.)

Women receive the right to vote

In 1893, New Zealand became the first country to give women the right to vote. However, women could not stand for election. In 1894, Australia was the next country to grant women the right.

TASMANIA

The first European settlements reached Tasmania, then known as Van Dieman's Land, in 1803. These consisted of 29 convicts, as well as 10 free settlers and some soldiers. Many more convicts were transported here up to 1853. Self-government was introduced in 1856. The colony became part of Australia in 1901.

The Black War

The Black War was the name given to the conflict that took place between the Europeans and the aborigines in Van Dieman's Land. Different dates are given for this war, and some historians include all the conflicts starting in 1804 as part of this. However, the real war took place from 1828 to 1832. At this time the White settlers were encouraged to capture and kill aborigines. Many were killed and the few survivors were sent to neighbouring islands. By 1835, there were only 150 aborigines left. More died in the islands of diseases.

The last indigenous Tasmanians

Truganini, daughter of a chief, who lived a life full of tragedy, is sometimes considered the last pure–blooded Tasmanian aborigine, but there were others who died at a later date. Truganini was among the last surviving aborigines, who were transported to Flinders Island. Many died of inflenza, and some were moved to Port Philip. Truganini and others became outlaws, and during the attempt to capture them, she was shot in the head. While most of the other outlaws were hanged, she was among those sent back to Flinders Island, and later to Oyster Cove near Hobart. By 1873, she was the only survivor there. Truganini died in 1876, leaving behind a daughter, Louisa, born of a white man.

Fanny Cochrane Smith (1834–1905) was probably absolutely the last indigenous Tasmanian. She was born after the aborigines were moved to Flinders Island. She married an Englishman,

William Smith, and they had 11 children. Fanny is remembered as she made recordings of aboriginal songs (on a wax cylinder, a method used at that time) in 1903. These were the only recordings in Tasmanian language.

Torres Strait Islands
The Torres Strait islanders have connections with Papua New Guinea, and speak a Papuan language. There are about 100 islands. The islanders are different from aboriginal Australians. The islands came under Queensland (Australia) in 1879.

THE PACIFIC ISLANDS
Europeans were crossing the Pacific at this time and taking over the islands. Many of these islands or island groups attained independence or self-government in the 20th century.

HAWAII
King Kamehameha I united all the Hawaiian Islands by 1810 (see Chapter 23) and ruled till his death in 1819. His immediate successor was Kamehameha II who died in 1824 on a visit to England. During the reign of Kamehameha III (ruled 1825–54) a written constitution was introduced, and Kamehameha became a constitutional monarch. A legislature and cabinet formed the government, and the earlier council of chiefs became the House of Nobles. Kamehameha V (ruled 1863–72) was the last ruler of this dynasty. Other kings followed, and Queen Liluokalani became the ruler in 1891, succeeding her brother Kalakaua. Liluokalani aimed to introduce a new constitution that would give more power to the ruler and to the Hawaiian people and Asians. This was not liked by the European and American residents there.

These residents had bought land and planted sugar and pineapples for profit. Labour had been imported from Japan and

China to work on these. After a period of trauma and trouble Hawaii was annexed by the USA in 1898.

Hawaii finally became the 50th state of the USA in 1959.

EXPLORING ANTARCTICA

The continent of Antarctica was still not well known. The Russian expedition under Fabian von Bellinghausen had circled and seen Antarctica in 1820. The British explorer James Ross landed there and explored some parts from 1839 to 1843. In 1895, the Sixth International Geographical Conference was held, and made its exploration the next goal. Reaching the South Pole was the main object. In 1908, an expedition led by Sir Ernest Shackleton came within 180 km of it. In 1911, a Norwegian expedition led by Roald Amundsen reached the Pole on 14 December. Another expedition led by Robert Scott reached there in January 1912.

36

The First World War

'Perpetual peace is a dream and not even a beautiful dream. War is part of God's order.'
Field Marshall von Moltke, 1892.

In 1900, Europe was relatively prosperous. Among the European nations Britain and Germany were highly industrialized. Many nations including Britain, France, Germany, Italy, the Netherlands and Belgium had set up colonies across the world. In other parts of the world, the US in the Americas and Japan in Asia were powerful nations.

A series of wars, ending in a world war between 1914 and 1918, provided a setback to European prosperity and affected the whole world.

THE BACKGROUND
Several events took place between 1900 and June 1914 when the First World War began. Some of them are given below.

Russia and Japan
In 1904 to 1905, a war took place between Russia and Japan. Japan won the war, indicating the extent to which her power had grown. This war caused Russia to feel the need for a protective alliance.

France, Germany and Morocco

France hoped to conquer Morocco, but in 1905 Kaiser Wilhelm, emperor of Germany, offered it protection. A revolution in Morocco in 1911, gave France the opportunity to take over the country. Kaiser Wilhelm sent a gunboat, the *Panther*, to Agadir, a port in Morocco. French and German rivalry increased.

Ottoman problems

In 1908, Austria–Hungary annexed Bosnia from the Ottomans.

From 1911 to 1912, the declining Ottoman empire became involved in a war against Italy. Italy won the war, gaining the three Turkish provinces that formed Libya. Observing the weakness of the Ottomans, some Balkan countries joined together to attack them. The first war took place in 1912 when Bulgaria, Greece, Montenegro and Serbia, known as the Balkan League, attacked the Ottomans. The League won some battles, but the countries involved could not remain united. In 1913, Bulgaria invaded Serbia and Greece. The Ottomans, Romania and Montenegro supported the latter. Bulgaria lost the war and also some of her territory.

Albania, which was part of the Ottoman empire, became independent. These conflicts affected the power structure in Europe. As the dominance of Bulgaria and the Ottomans was reduced, Serbia hoped to make more gains.

Colonial rivalries

In addition there were colonial rivalries across the world, as well as a race to control the seas through better and stronger navies.

Alliances

Another aspect of the war was that two groups of alliances already existed.

The Triple Entente was an alliance of three countries, UK, France and Russia.

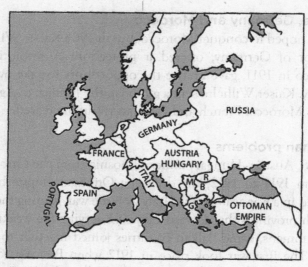

R = ROMANIA
B = BULGARIA
M = MONTENEGRO
G = GREECE
S = SWITZERLAND

Europe in 1914

The Triple Alliance consisted of Germany, Austria-Hungary and Italy.

Later there were some changes and additions to these alliance groups.

The spark that set off the war

None of these factors would have inevitably led to a war. In fact there were two peace conferences held at The Hague in 1899 and 1907. Yet there were so many rivalries among European powers that one event set off a world war. This key event was linked to Serbian nationalism, and Serbia's desire to create the nation of Yugoslavia (southern Slavia) in which Serbs and Croats would join together. Bosnia would be part of this new nation. However, Bosnia, as we saw earlier, had been taken over by Austria-Hungary.

  The Puffin History of the World

In June 1914, the archduke of Austria, Franz Ferdinand, and his wife, Sophie, visited Bosnia. They were shot dead on 28 June by Gavrilo Princep, a member of the Black Hand, a secret Serbian group that wanted a Serbian nation.

The War begins
Austria wanted to act against the killer. Serbia did not cooperate and Austria-Hungary declared war on Serbia on 28 July. Russia began to mobilize her troops to support Serbia. Germany, to support Austria-Hungary, declared war on Russia on 1 August and on France on 3 August.

The Schlieffen Plan
In 1905, Germany had drafted the Schlieffen Plan on the best strategies to use in case of war. Now that war had broken out, Germany tried to put this plan into practice, but it did not work as intended.

Germany's aim was to quickly defeat Belgium and cross through to France. But Belgium was not so easy to conquer, and the siege of Liege in Belgium held up the Germans.

Britain, followed by other powers, joined the war. The First World War had begun.

The Allies and the Central Powers
The Triple Entente group of countries came to be known as the Allies, and the Triple Alliance as the Central Powers. As the war progressed, the alliances changed. Italy declared neutrality in August 1914. In May 1915, Italy joined the Allies. Others who combined forces with the Allies were Romania in August 1916, and the US in April 1917. Japan and Spain also joined them. Russia withdrew from the war in December 1917, because of internal events and problems.

The Central Powers, apart from Germany and Austria-

Hungary, included the Ottomans (joined November 1914), and Bulgaria (joined October 1915). Apart from these main powers, several other countries were involved in the war as 'associated powers' on the side of the Allies. Colonized countries in Africa and Asia were also drawn into the war, as soldiers from some of these fought on behalf of their colonizers. Even those countries not directly involved were touched by the war as the economy of the whole world was affected.

THE NUMEROUS BATTLES

There were battles of all kinds, and long 'fronts' along which the war was fought, in many different areas.

The western front was between Germany and France. The eastern front extended about 1900 km from the Baltic Sea to the Black Sea. This was the Russian front. The southern front was between Italy and Austria-Hungary.

The war was also fought in West Asia. There was an attempt to acquire control of the Dardanelles Strait which was under the Ottomans. There were also conflicts in Africa.

In addition there were clashes at sea and battles in the air.

Many of the battles in the war were indecisive. Some of them lasted for months. The fighting went on and there was no clear result.

The main battles are listed below:

Year	Month	Place	Allies	Central Powers
1914	August	Ardennes, France	France	Germany
	August	Helgioland Bight, Frisian Islands	Britain, naval battle	Germany
	August	Tannenberg, Germany	Russia	Germany

	September–October	Arras, France	France	Germany
1914	September	Marne, France	France and Britain	Germany
1914	October–November	Ypres, Belgium	Britain, France and Belgium	Germany
1915	July	Arras, France	France	Germany
	April–May	Ypres	Britain, France and Belgium, Canada	Germany
1915	April–December	Gallipoli campaign	Britain, France Australia and New Zealand Army Corps	Germany, Ottomans
1916	February–December	Verdun, France	France	Germany
	May–June	Jutland, Denmark (naval battle)	Britain	Germany
	July–November	Somme, France	Britain, France, other allies	Germany
1917	April–May	Arras, France supported by troops of Canada and Australia	Britain	Germany
	July–November	Ypres (Battle of Passchendaele)	Britain	Germany
	October–December	Caporetto, Austria	Italy	Germany, Austria-Hungary
1918	March	Arras, France	Britain	Germany
1918	August–September	Arras, France	Britain with Canadian troops	Germany
	July–August	Marne, France	France	Germany
	September–November	Argonne, France	France, USA	Germany

A German trench occupied by British soldiers. July 1916, *during the Battle of the Somme*

French soldiers advance for a bayonet charge on the western front

PASSCHENDAELE

The war caused great sufferings both for men and animals. There were also tremendous acts of bravery and courage. What is also notable is the empathy for the suffering of the 'enemy' soldiers.

In the passage below, Lt Edwin Vaughan of the 1st/8th Warwickshire (British) regiment describes both the horror of Passchendaele and the fellow feelings of the British for German soldiers who suffered equally. He wrote about a group of Germans who surrendered:

> The prisoners clustered around me, bedraggled and heartbroken, telling me of the terrible time they had been having.... I could not spare a man to take them back, so I put them into shell holes with my men who made a great fuss of them, sharing their scanty rations with them.
>
> From other shell holes from the darkness on all sides came the groans and wails of wounded men; faint, long, sobbing moans of agony and despairing shrieks. It was too horribly obvious that dozens of men with serious wounds must have crawled for safety into new shell holes, and now the water was rising about them and, powerless to move, they were slowly drowning...And we could do nothing to help them.'
>
> (Quoted on p. 390, John Keegan, *The First World War*.)

THE CHRISTMAS TRUCE

In the midst of war, there were some moments of peace. The Christmas Truce of 1914 is one of the remarkable events of the war. It started in some areas on Christmas day, in others on Christmas Eve, or even one week before Christmas, and extended across two-thirds of the British–German front. It was not organized, but spontaneous in every part. Around 1,00,000 British and German soldiers took part.

Separated by barbed wire and trenches, they were close enough to hear the voices of soldiers from the opposing side. A description of one Christmas event, records that lights shone along the German line, and then a beautiful song filled the air, *Stille nacht, heilege nacht* (*Silent night, holy night*). The British soldiers clapped and responded with another Christmas song. This went on for quite some time. Both groups even sang a song together in Latin *Adeste fideles* (*O Come, All Ye Faithful*). Then the two groups of men met, crossed the boundaries, and exchanged small gifts.

Some groups even played football matches.

But still, they had to follow orders, and fight again the next day.

In 1914, there was a short Christmas ceasefire even on the eastern front, between the Austrians and Russians. The French and Germans too shared a truce.

But the officers were against these truces.

There were some short Christmas truces in later years, but these were always cut short by the commanding officers.

Among songs inspired by the Christmas truce of 1914 is *Pipes of Peace* by Paul MacCartney, composed in 1980.

END OF THE WAR

The war ended in victory for the Allies, and the Central Powers suffered a humiliating defeat. The two sides agreed to an

LOSSES IN THE WAR

Civilians killed: 10 million
Armed forces killed: 10 million
Wounded: 21 million
Prisoners and missing people: 8 million.

armistice, that is, to stop fighting on 11 November 1918. A series of peace treaties were signed, emerging from conferences held at Versailles, Saint Germain, Trianon, Neuilly and Sevres.

THE WAR IN LITERATURE AND OTHER MEDIA

The war was described in books, memoirs, diaries and letters. More than 2000 poets wrote poems about the war, which were published. Many more remained unpublished. The war also inspired novels, songs and films. Among the well-known war poets were Siegfried Sassoon (1886–1967), Wilfred Owen (1893–1918) and Rupert Brooke (1887–1915). Sassoon fought in the war and wrote about the horror he experienced. In 1917, he protested against the war in a 'Soldier's Declaration'. He was admitted to hospital soon after where he became friendly with Wilfred Owen, who was also there, suffering from shell shock. Later he wrote a three-volume work, the *Sherston Trilogy*, based on his own life. Wilfred Owen was killed in action during the last days of the war. His poems depicting the horrors of war were mainly published posthumously. Rupert Brooke's poems included the patriotic sonnets *1914 and Other Poems*. He was in the Royal Navy, but died in Greece of blood poisoning.

Here are two lines from Siegfried Sassoon's poem, 'The Dugout', written while he saw his fellow soldier Jowett sleeping, and feared that he would soon die.

'You are too young to fall asleep forever;
And when you sleep you remind me of the dead.'

Among novels, one of the most realistic was *All Quiet on the Western Front*, originally written in German by Erich Maria Remarque, and translated into 28 languages.

EFFECTS OF THE WAR

The war had many short and long-term effects. Its aim was to bring about a lasting peace, but instead the humiliation Germany suffered led to militarism and nationalism and, 21 years later, to another great war. However, the League of Nations—the first world organization for peace—was founded.

The war created economic problems, but there were some positive aspects too. New technology was required, and new inventions such as the radio, car and aeroplane were further developed and became more widespread. The speed of communications and transport increased. New industries developed. The position of women improved as more of them started working outside the home.

The Puffin History of the World

37

Recovering from the War 1918–39

The First World War had ended, but its effects could be seen everywhere. Many people had died, and many more had been wounded. The horrors of war affected everyone, particularly in Europe. Land and buildings had been destroyed. European economies faced crises. Industries declined, as many were related to producing items for the war. Soldiers returning home faced unemployment. Colonies across Asia and Africa were asking for freedom.

Below we look at the main events after the war, in countries across the world.

THE USA

The USA has two main political parties, the Republicans and the Democrats. Woodrow Wilson, a Democrat, was the president of the country during the war years and immediately after. He was disappointed that the Senate, the upper house of the Legislature, accepted neither the Treaties of Versailles nor the

League of Nations. Wilson was succeeded by three Republican presidents: Harding, 1921–23; Calvin Coolidge, 1923–29; and Herbert Hoover, 1929–33.

The US remained prosperous for some time. Though European countries owed it large sums of money that had been borrowed in the war years, the war did not have immediate negative effects on the economy. Industries produced more goods, and wages increased. However, gradually industries began to be taken over by huge trusts and corporations. Profits and wealth became concentrated in the hands of a few.

Prohibition of liquor introduced in 1919 led to the illegal manufacture and sale of alcohol. Gangs fought one another, and gangsters such as Al Capone amassed huge profits. Prohibition was abolished in 1933.

The Great Depression
In 1929, an economic disaster, known as the Great Depression, took place. The Stock Market crashed. Many people faced huge financial losses. They began to withdraw money from banks and those too failed. Industries closed as people had no money to buy their products. Unemployment increased.

The New Deal
Franklin Roosevelt, a Democrat, became the new president in 1933. He introduced new policies to boost the economy. Help was provided to those who had lost everything, the government temporarily took over banks, and laws were passed to provide jobs and to improve working conditions.

These policies improved conditions, but a full recovery took place only after the Second World War started.

Other countries

The Depression affected other countries in Europe. Many were financially dependent on loans from the USA. By 1931, Germany, Britain and Austria were among the countries most affected.

BRITAIN

Britain faced several problems. There was widespread unemployment and industries were declining. Trade unions organized more than 200 strikes between 1919 and 1920, and a general strike took place in 1926. In Ireland there was an agitation for independence. However, Britain managed to deal with these problems. Education was improved, and more social welfare schemes provided. The Labour Party came to power for the first time from January to October 1924, and from 1929 to 1931.

In its numerous colonies, Britain promised that independence or self-government would gradually be granted. Southern Ireland attained dominion status in 1922. The same year Egypt gained some autonomy. Iraq became independent in 1931.

GERMANY

Germany faced a crisis straight after the war. By the Treaty of Versailles, it lost territory in Europe, and its troops and armaments were restricted. Germany also had to accept 'War Guilt', that is, the blame for starting the First World War. The nation had to pay reparations (money) for the damage caused. The huge amount to be paid was fixed in 1921 at 6600 million pounds. The German government and people felt humiliated. By the end of 1918, the Kaiser abdicated. Friedrich Ebert, the leader of the Social Democrat Party, took charge of the government. After an election in 1919, he became the first president of the republic of Germany. After a meeting at Weimar, a new constitution was formed, and the Weimar Republic that lasted till 1933 was born. During this time there were immense problems. In 1923, inflation reached a height. The German currency became totally valueless. The US provided loans through the Dawes Plan of 1924. But the Depression of 1929 led to a disaster. Unemployment increased. In January 1933, Adolf Hitler was appointed as chancellor. As leader of the National Socialist (Nazi) Party, he soon made himself dictator. He began to control all aspects of life in Germany. The government and the people were controlled through a regular police force, as well as the secret police, the Gestapo. Trade unions were banned. Education, all types of communication as well as industrial production were among the many aspects controlled. The theory of a superior 'Aryan' race was put forward. Related to this was the policy of blaming Jews for all the problems Germany faced. The Nuremberg Laws of 1935 declared Jews non-citizens. Their persecution increased in the next few years.

FRANCE

France had won the war, but at great financial cost. In addition, the country had lost 15 per cent of her male population. France remained backward in industrial development and even in agriculture. The economic problems increased after 1929. The Third Republic lasted till 1940, but governments constantly changed.

ITALY

A lot had been promised to Italy for joining the allies, but most of the promises were not fulfilled. The economy and standard of living dropped, and money borrowed from the US had to be paid. Five governments changed between 1919 and 1922. There were strikes in factories, and some feared a communist revolution would take place.

Benito Mussolini formed a fascist party in 1919. In the elections in 1921, the Italian Fascist Party won 35 seats. The fascists were also known as the Blackshirts, because of the shirts they wore. In October 1922, there was a call for a general strike. Around 50,000 Blackshirts marched to Rome. There were others in various towns. The king Victor Emmanuel III did not resist them, but asked Mussolini to take over the government. Mussolini gradually began to rule like a dictator.

Initially, there were some positive aspects to this development. Industry, hydroelectric power, and wheat cultivation increased. There was a plan to build roads, railway stations, new towns and other buildings. An attempt was made to project Italy as a great power. But Italy's progress remained inadequate. It, too, was affected by the Great Depression. In addition there was corruption and inefficiency in the government.

Italy tried to extend its overseas territories and invaded Ethiopia in 1935.

FASCISM

Mussolini said: 'Peace is absurd. Fascism does not believe in it.' Though the fascists had not come to power through violence, they believed in maintaining power through military strength.

Fascism also believed in:

Extreme nationalism, proclaiming one's own nation as the best.

One-party rule. Neither democracy nor communism was tolerated.

Total control by the government over all aspects of people's lives, including education.

Hitler and Mussolini, 1936

SPAIN

In Spain there was a constitutional monarchy. King Alfonso XIII had been ruling from 1885. Alfonso allowed General Primo de Rivera to assume power in 1923. Industries developed and there were new roads, railways and irrigation schemes. But by 1930, the economic crisis reached Spain, and unemployment increased. Primo resigned in 1930 and Alfonso abdicated the next year. A Spanish republic was formed. Problems continued and a civil war took place from 1936 to 1939, between right-wing nationalists and republicans. Italy and Germany sent troops to help the nationalists. After much bloodshed, General Franco set up a fascist government.

GUERNICA

During the civil war the Germans bombed the village of Guernica. The Basque people lived here, and more than 1600 Basque civilians were killed. Pablo Picasso (1881–1973), the great Spanish artist, painted his most famous work *Guernica*, in response to this. *Guernica* is a mural 3.5 m by 7.8 m, depicting the tragedies and suffering of war.

JAPAN

In 1918, Japan was a powerful industrialized country. During the war years Japan had supplied goods both to the Allies and to Asia. But Japan too began to face economic problems, particularly after 1929. China was against the Japanese trade in its territory of Manchuria. To preserve this, the Japanese army invaded and occupied Manchuria. But this had been done without the permission of the Japanese prime minister, Inukai. He protested and was then assassinated by army officers. The army began to dominate Japan. Japan again attacked China in 1937. Hirohito was the emperor of Japan from 1926. He was against these attacks, but felt he did not have the power to stop them.

Turkey

The Ottomans were defeated in the First World War. Muhammad VI was the sultan at this time. By the Treaty of Sevres, signed in 1920, the Ottoman empire had suffered huge territorial losses. However, this treaty never came into effect, because a Turkish national movement led by Mustafa Kemal started. Kemal had participated in the war and led the troops in the defeat of the British at Gallipoli in 1915. He now headed a new government at Ankara. The sultan abdicated and a republic was established in 1923. A new treaty was signed at Lausanne. Mustafa Kemal, later known as Ataturk (father of the Turks), was the first president of the Turkish republic. Kemal created a secular country and began to expand industries and to modernize Turkey.

Europe in 1925

THE LEAGUE OF NATIONS

The League of Nations was founded on 10 January 1920. Its purpose was to maintain peace in the world and solve problems through discussions. Conflicts between Sweden and Finland in 1921, Upper Silesia in the same year, Lithuania in 1923, and Bulgaria and Greece in 1925 were resolved through the League. But the League could not prevent either the invasions that took place in the 1930s, or the Second World War.

ART AND LITERATURE

Art exploded in individualistic styles across the world. Expressionism used different methods to express feelings, rather than to depict reality. Futurism looked at contemporary life and focused on machines, war and danger. Futurist art depicted movement. Dadaism, Fauvism, Cubism and Constructivism were some of the other new trends in art. Dadaism was a style that aimed to shock. It used waste materials or objects

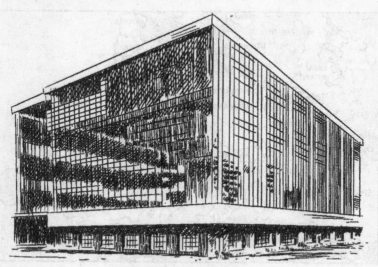

The Bauhaus building, Dessau

not usually thought of as art. Surrealism developed out of Dadaism. It reflected a rejection of Western culture. André Breton (1896–1966) a French poet, is considered the founder of this movement. Fauvism used bright colours in distinctive ways. Cubism included geometric shapes in the depiction of people and objects. Constructivism developed in the USSR and focused on sculptures using wire, metal and glass, and items that had utility. Its principles were used in industrial design.

The Bauhaus architecture and design school was founded in Germany in 1919. This believed in simple and functional styles, which were at the same time attractive and pleasing. It developed into the International Style, using materials like concrete, steel and glass. Art Deco was another innovative form using bright colours, chrome, enamel, polished stone and other materials. It was used in buildings and to make several different objects.

Many of these new trends were reflected in different ways in literature, music and film. The 'stream of consciousness' style also began in literature with Marcel Proust and James Joyce.

MEDIA

Paperbacks were a new trend that made books more accessible. The number of newspapers increased. Radio provided a great change as news and music became available across the world. Telephones provided connectivity. Full-length films were produced, and cinema halls were the new centres of entertainment.

38
Russia
1900–39

In Russia, a revolution established the first communist government in the world in 1917.

TSAR NICHOLAS II

Tsar Nicholas II was in power in Russia from 1894, but he was unable to deal with the problems in Russia. A Russo–Japanese war was fought from 1904 to 1905 and ended with a Japanese victory. A general strike and an attempted revolution followed in 1905. A new Russian constitution came into being in 1906.

The Duma was an elected assembly that existed in Russia between 1906 and 1917. There were four Dumas during this time. Though they had some power, the tsar remained supreme.

Pyotr Stolypin (1862–1911) was the prime minister from 1906 to 1911. He attempted to bring in reforms which would help the peasants. He had some success but was assassinated in 1911.

Meanwhile the Marxist Social Democrat Labour Party was founded. Two revolutionary groups, the Bolsheviks and the Mensheviks developed from it in 1903. Both the parties wanted a revolution, but the methods they intended to use were different.

The Bolsheviks, meaning 'the majority', wanted the involvement of peasants and workers. They were led by Vladimir Ilich Lenin. Another notable leader was Leon Trotsky. The Mensheviks, or 'the minority', believed that the middle classes should be involved in the revolution.

Nicholas II and his wife the Empress Alexandra had become very unpopular. Nicholas had not allowed the Duma to function. It was thought that he had some role in the assassination of Stolypin. In addition, their involvement with Rasputin was not liked at all.

GRIGORI RASPUTIN (1869–1916)

Rasputin was a Russian peasant. He was believed to be very religious and to have had miraculous powers. He helped Tsar Nicholas's son who had haemophilia, and at times seemed to miraculously heal him. Thus he became close to Nicholas's wife Alexandra Feodrovna. He began to influence royal policies in Russia, and therefore was resented by many.

Rasputin

Rasputin tried to stop Russia from joining the First World War, but the tsar did not listen to him. Rasputin continued to be close to the royal couple. Some believed him to be a German spy. He was murdered on 30 December 1916.

A number of books have been written on Rasputin, and films and music have been composed on his life.

From 1912 to 1914, there were strikes and unrest in Russia. Russia then joined the First World War, but this added to its problems. There were defeats and losses of soldiers. Many thousands were killed.

THE REVOLUTION

Two revolutions took place in 1917; the first in March and the second in November. (These are known as the February and October revolutions in Russia, as Russia was still following the Julian calendar). After the March Revolution, Tsar Nicholas abdicated. There were no more tsars; the monarchy had come to an end. A provisional government was formed, first under Prince George Lvov, and then under Alexander Kerensky. Soviets, which were committees elected by workers and soldiers, were in St Petersburg (Petrograd), Moscow, and other cities. Russia continued with the war and suffered more losses.

Lenin had been in exile in Switzerland. The new government allowed him to return to Russia. Led by Lenin and Trotsky, the Bolsheviks seized power on 6 and 7 November. The provisional government was overthrown and a new Soviet government was set up in Petrograd. By the end of November, other cities were under Bolshevik control.

Russia withdrew from the First World War in December. After negotiations with Germany, the Treaty of Brest Litovsk was signed in March 1918. By this Russia lost a huge amount of territory: Poland, Estonia, Latvia and Lithuania, Georgia, Finland, and the Ukraine.

In April 1918, a civil war started between the Bolsheviks and the Mensheviks and others opposed to them. The latter were aided by foreign troops from Europe. Finally by the end of 1920, the Bolsheviks, now known as Communists, won. The Communist Party was now in total control.

THE USSR

On 30 December 1922, the Union of Soviet Socialist Republics (USSR) was formed with four socialist republics: Russian,

Transcaucasian, Ukrainian, and Belorussian. Ukraine had briefly been independent, but communists in the Ukraine joined the USSR. Georgia, Armenia and Azerbaijan were part of the Transcaucasian Republic. The Turkmen and Uzbek Soviet Socialist Republics were added in 1924; the Tadzhik (Tajik) Socialist Republic in 1929; the Kazakh and Kirgiz Socialist Republics in 1936. The same year the Transcaucasian Republic was reorganized into the three republics of Georgia, Armenia and Azerbaijan. More territories were added during the Second World War.

In January 1924, Lenin died after an illness, at the age of 53.

The USSR and the states in Central Asia and East Europe that formed part of it

STALIN

At this time Joseph Djugashvili, who called himself Stalin, meaning 'man of steel' was the Secretary General of the Communist Party in Russia. He was also a member of the Politburo. The Politburo was a seven-person committee that made government decisions. By 1929, Stalin managed to take over total power. He ruled

Stalin

like a dictator until his death in 1953, and did not allow anyone to disagree with him. His opponents were exiled, killed or sent to labour camps in Siberia. On the positive side, Stalin made the USSR a strong nation, expanded industry and introduced collective farms to improve agriculture.

39

The Second World War

The Second World War was fought from 1939 to 1945.

CAUSES

One of the causes of the Second World War was the unfair peace treaties after the First World War (see Chapter 36) and the economic problems that all the countries involved faced. These problems led to the rise of dictators and of militarism.

Germany, in particular, wanted to be a great nation once more. This led many German people to support Hitler in all his policies. Hitler's internal and foreign strategies aimed at reviving German power and creating 'lebensraum' or more living space for Germans. His foreign policies led directly to the war. 'Appeasement' is said to be another cause of the war. This refers to the other European powers 'appeasing' Germany before the war, that is, allowing Germany to take military action that was against the earlier treaties.

Apart from this, the League of Nations that had been formed to maintain peace had not been able to prevent various acts of aggression. Japan invaded Manchuria in 1931. Hitler began conscription in 1935. Conscription, that is, the recruitment into the army without a choice, was banned for Germany by the treaties signed after the First World War. Britain, France and Italy, at first joined together against this. Soon after this, Britain actually signed an agreement with Germany. This Anglo-German Naval Agreement allowed Germany to build submarines. This too was against the treaties. Mussolini from Italy then invaded Ethiopia (Abyssinia) and was not prevented from doing this.

In 1936, Germany then sent troops into the Rhineland. The Rhineland, a region in west Germany, had been occupied by the Allies after the First World War, up to 1930. It was demilitarized by the Versailles treaties, and Germany again broke this agreement by sending troops there. Though the Allies protested, they took no concrete action.

In the same year, Germany then signed an agreement with Italy. This is called the Rome–Berlin Axis. The Anti-Comintern Pact was signed with Japan, against the international communist movement. Italy joined this pact in 1937. During the Spanish Civil War (1936–39), Germany and Italy sent troops and helped Franco to take over power. In 1937, Japan invaded China.

The League and the Allies took no action in all these events.

EVENTS JUST BEFORE THE WAR

In March 1938, there was an Anschluss (union) between Germany and Austria, actually created by an invasion of Austria. More was to follow. The state of Czechoslovakia had been set up by the Versailles treaty. Germany asked Czechoslovakia to hand over the Sudetenland, a border region under Czechoslovakia where a number of Germans lived. Czechoslovakia refused to give up this territory. Talks were held between Britain, France, Germany and Italy, and the Munich Pact was signed in September 1939. Afraid of war, Britain and France agreed that Czechoslovakia should give up this territory, on the condition that Germany should not ask for anything more. An international commission would decide on any further territories. Poland and Hungary too claimed part of Czechoslovakia. Slovakia wanted independence. Hitler persuaded President Hacha of Czechoslovakia to accept his help to keep the territory together. In March 1939, German troops entered Prague, the capital of Czechoslovakia. Czechoslovakia became a German protectorate.

Germany took over the port of Memel from Lithuania, and also demanded Danzig from Poland. Britain and France promised to protect Poland in case of an attack. In May, Italy and Germany signed the Pact of Steel. Italy promised to help Germany in case of war. In August 1939, Germany signed a non-aggression pact with Russia. Following this, on 1 September, Germany invaded Poland. On 3 September, Britain declared war on Germany. Another world war had begun.

THE WAR
Germany, Italy, Japan and the countries that joined them were known as the Axis powers. France, Britain and the countries that joined them were known as the Allies. Altogether, 61 countries participated in the war.

The main phases of the war along with details of some of the major battles are given below:

First phase: September 1939–December 1940
Germany and USSR occupied Poland. After a break of five months, Denmark and Norway were occupied; after this Holland, Belgium and France were attacked and defeated. The Battle of Britain was fought from July–September 1940, and Britain was bombed. Italy declared war in June 1940, and invaded Egypt and Greece.

Poland
In September 1939, Germany began with a blitzkrieg (lightning war) against Poland. The Luftwaffe (German air force) dropped bombs on the railway lines, and defeated the Polish air force. On

the ground German troops used tanks while the Poles responded with cavalry (horses). Polish troops fought with great bravery but it was a tragic battle as their cavalry was no match for the German tanks. France and Britain could not come to their aid in time, and Russia advanced from the east. After a total defeat Poland was divided between Germany and Russia.

Battle of Britain

This air battle took place from 12 August to 30 September 1940. The Germans bombed aerodromes, harbours and weapon factories in Britain. The aim was to destroy the RAF (Royal Air Force of Britain) and then invade the country. The British air force defended well, and numerous German planes were shot down. Britain also bombed Berlin, after which the Germans bombed London. Though there were huge losses on both sides, including deaths of civilians and destruction of property, the British won this battle.

Second phase: 1941 to mid-1942

Hitler invaded the USSR, breaking his pact with them; Japan bombed Pearl Harbour, an American naval base. The Japanese gained control of Indo-China, Malaya, Singapore, Burma, Hong Kong, the Dutch East Indies, the Phillippines, and Guam and Wake Island. The last two were US possessions. The USA then became a late entrant into the war.

Pearl Harbour

The USA had remained neutral during the first stages of the war, though they had helped to finance Britain. On 7 December 1941, Japan bombed Pearl Harbour, the US naval base in Hawaii. Without the USA becoming aware of it, 353 Japanese planes reached Pearl Harbour, and in just two hours bombed and destroyed 350 aircraft and five battleships.

  The Puffin History of the World

Pearl Harbour, the attack on 7 December 1941

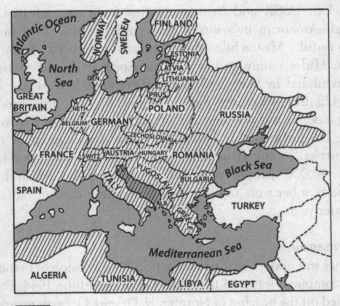

Territory under Germany in late 1942

Third phase: mid-1942 to mid-1943
The Axis powers suffered defeats at Midway Island, in Egypt at El Alamein and Stalingrad in the USSR; air and naval battles continued.

El Alamein
A number of battles were fought in the area of El Alamein in Africa. The last was a huge battle fought in October 1942. In this the German general Rommel leading the Afrika Corps was defeated by the Eighth Army led by General Montgomery of Britain. This victory was a turning point in the war.

Fourth phase: July 1943–August 1945
The Axis powers were defeated by the combined efforts of the US, USSR and Britain. At first Italy was defeated. An Anglo-American invasion of Normandy in June 1944 proved successful. Meanwhile the Russians advanced from the east. Hitler committed suicide in April 1945 and Germany surrendered in May 1945. Japan surrendered in August after the US dropped atomic bombs on the cities of Hiroshima and Nagasaki. It was the first use of nuclear bombs in the world. The US justified this action but it was condemned by most countries. In the Hiroshima and Nagasaki bombings 84,000 and 40,000 people were killed, respectively. Around the same number were injured, and many more died of radiation in later years.

Normandy
France was under German occupation. The invasion of France by the combined forces of the Allies began on 6 June 1944. Forces landed on the beaches of Normandy. Despite German resistance about three million Allied troops landed. France was liberated in August and the Allied troops slowly advanced.

Normandy, Allied soldiers reaching Omaha Beach, 6 June 1944

Hitler's last days

Meanwhile Russia was advancing from the east, and reached Berlin. When defeat seemed sure, Hitler and his close companions moved to underground chambers in Berlin. Hitler married Eva Braun, his long-time partner. He never wanted to be captured, and it is believed that he took poison and died. His body was doused in petrol and set on fire. But some doubted that he had really died and there were many stories that he escaped to some other country. However, most historians believe that he died in Berlin in April 1945.

THE 'FINAL SOLUTION'

Around the world Hitler is remembered for his terrible actions against Jews. He had already placed restrictions on Jews, and during the war years he decided that every single Jew should be killed. This was called the 'final solution'. Jews were rounded up and sent to concentration camps where they lived in terrible conditions. Many were killed in gas chambers. Some escaped or went into hiding.

The entrance to Auschwitz

Auschwitz

Auschwitz was a group of concentration camps in Poland. The first camp was opened in 1940. From 1942 to 1944, Jews were carried by trains to camps, where they were killed in gas chambers. Others died because of the terrible conditions in the

ANNE FRANK

Anne Frank

Anne Frank (Annelies in Dutch) was a young Jewish girl who went into hiding with her family in Amsterdam in the Netherlands. The family lived in some concealed rooms in her father's former office from 1942 to 1944. During this time Anne kept a diary. She and her family were captured in 1944 and Anne died of typhus in the Bergen-Belsen concentration camp, when she was not yet 16. Her father Otto Frank was the only member of the family who survived. After the war her diary was published and is still widely read. It was translated into many languages and also made into a film.

camps. Soviet troops reached the camp on 27 January 1945, and it was only after this that the crimes committed against Jews were confirmed. Over one million prisoners died in Auschwitz. Most were Jews, but thousands of gypsies were also killed. There were other such camps and, according to estimates, six million Jews were killed during the war. This is known as 'the Holocaust'.

LOSSES

There are different estimates of how many died in the Second World War, but altogether it was over 60 million. Military deaths were between 22 and 30 million. In addition, civilian losses are estimated between 40 and 55 million. Another 21 million were displaced, fleeing from enemies, taken as labourers to Germany, or placed in concentration camps.

During and after the war the world changed. We will look at these changes in succeeding chapters.

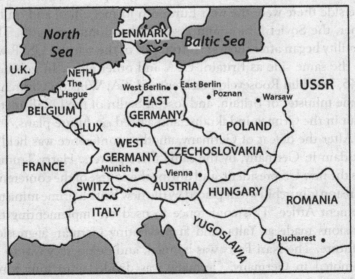

Europe in 1945

40

War and Peace after 1945

After the Second World War ended, most countries in the world wanted peace. Yet almost immediately there were hostile feelings between two groups of countries. On one side there were the west European former allies, and on the other, the Soviet Union and associated communist states. This hostility began after the war. By the end of the war the USSR was on the same side as Britain, USA and other allies. In February 1945, Franklin Roosevelt, president of USA, Winston Churchill, prime minister of Britain, and Joseph Stalin of the USSR met at Yalta in the Crimea in Ukraine and agreed on future plans.

After the defeat of Germany, another conference was held at Potsdam in Germany, by the same three powers. Harry Truman was the new US president, and during the course of the conference Winston Churchill was replaced by the new British prime minister, Clement Attlee. This conference focused on implementing the decisions made at Yalta, and at preventing German aggression in future. The Nazi Party was banned, and democracy was to be promoted in Germany. Germany was divided into four zones under the US, Britain, France and the USSR.

At this conference too, Japan was asked to surrender. Atomic bombs were dropped when the surrender did not take place.

There was unity at the Potsdam Conference, though not as much as at Yalta. Within a year further disagreements started.

Winston Churchill, Harry Truman, and Joseph Stalin at Potsdam in 1945

The USA and Britain felt concerned about the USSR influence extending to east Poland and the Baltic states. In March 1946, Churchill said the USSR was planning on an 'indefinite expansion' of power. He referred to their control as an 'iron curtain' descending across Eastern Europe.

THE COLD WAR

By this time there was hostility between the USSR and communist countries on one side, and USA, Britain, and other democratic countries of Europe, on the other. No war was actually fought, which is why this is called a 'Cold War'. Several events took place during this Cold War. Communism spread to east Europe, North Korea (1948), China (1949), and North Vietnam (1954), leading to more fears that it could spread throughout the world.

The Truman Doctrine and the Marshall Plan

Greece was freed from German control in 1944. The British supported the new monarchy, but communists tried to overthrow it. Britain asked USA for help. President Truman made a statement in March 1947, later called 'The Truman Doctrine'. This affirmed that USA would support people 'resisting subjugation by armed minorities or by outside pressures'.

In June 1947, USA suggested a plan for the reconstruction of Europe, which had been badly affected by the war. It was named after George C. Marshall, the US Secretary of State. This offered financial help for Europe to recover from the war. The Marshall Plan was open to all countries, but Russia did not allow Eastern Europe to join. Stalin believed this would bring countries under the influence of the US, and called it 'dollar imperialism'.

From 1948 to 1952 sixteen countries of Europe received 13,000 million dollars in aid. These countries were Britain (which received the most), France, Italy, Belgium, Luxembourg, Netherlands, Portugal, Austria, Switzerland, Greece, Turkey, Iceland, Norway, Sweden, Denmark and the three zones of Germany not under the USSR. This financial assistance helped these countries to recover from the war. Marshall Aid was distributed by The Organization for European Cooperation (OEEC) that also encouraged trade. The US and Canada joined the organization in 1961, and it was then known as the Organization for Economic Cooperation and Trade (OECD). Later Japan and Australia became members as well.

The Cominform

The Cominform was an organization of communist parties in Europe. It was founded by Stalin in September 1947. The Eastern European states were members. The aim was to develop the countries on the Soviet pattern, and to have trade and cultural interaction mainly within this group of countries. Between 1945 and 1948, Poland, Hungary, Rumania, Bulgaria,

Yugoslavia, Albania and Czechoslovakia became Communist states. Czechoslovakia had a democratically elected government until 1948. In 1949, East Germany joined the Cominform. The Molotov Plan of 1949 provided aid to these countries. An economic council for these countries, the Comecon (Council of Mutual Economic Assistance) was also set up.

The Berlin Blockade

Germany and Berlin had been divided into four zones. In 1948, France, Britain and the US created economic unity for the three sections that were under them. With Marshall Aid, conditions began to improve. A new currency was introduced in these three areas in June. Compared with the zone under the USSR, this area was prosperous. There was a plan to unite them politically into a state of West Germany. The USSR was against this. It started a 'Berlin blockade' and did not let supplies reach Berlin over land. The three countries sent supplies by air for 10 months. They managed to provide food and other supplies for 2.5 million people in Berlin. The blockade was finally lifted in May 1949. This was a defeat for the USSR. It also meant that Germany, as well as Berlin, were divided into two.

NATO

In April 1949, the North Atlantic Treaty Organization (NATO), a defensive pact of 12 countries, was formed. The countries were the US, Canada, Britain, France, Belgium, Holland, Luxembourg, Portugal, Denmark, Ireland, Italy and Norway. However, France withdrew from NATO in 1966.

The Council of Europe

Formed in 1949, the Council of Europe aimed at political unity, but remained an advisory body. Sixteen countries had joined it by 1971.

Germany

In August 1949, the Federal Republic of Germany was formed, known as West Germany. In October of the same year, the zone under the USSR became the Democratic Republic of Germany, also known as East Germany.

The USSR developed atomic weapons by August 1949. Now both the USA and USSR, the two most powerful countries, possessed these weapons. A war between them using these, would have devastated the world.

Korea

A war in Korea from 1950 to 1953 and in Indo-China also formed part of the Cold War. (See chapter 46.)

After Stalin

After Stalin's death in 1953, Nikita Krushchev came to power in the USSR. He stated he wanted 'peaceful coexistence' and tried to improve relations with other countries. His approach had some success. The wars in Korea and Indo-China ended. Russia agreed to withdraw its military base in Finland.

Austria

Austria, too, had been divided into four zones. The situation was similar to that in Germany, with some differences. Unlike Germany, Austria had her own government, though with limited powers. Similar to Germany, the three western zones were more prosperous. In May 1955, the Austrian State Treaty was signed, with the agreement of all concerned powers. By this, all foreign troops were withdrawn and Austria became an independent state retaining the boundaries it had in 1937.

Yugoslavia

Yugoslavia was against being part of the Cominform. Krushchev visited Yugoslavia in 1956 and the Cominform was given up. There was thus more freedom for the Eastern European states.

The Warsaw Pact

However, the Warsaw Pact was founded in 1955 as a counter to NATO. The Warsaw Pact was a defensive agreement which included the USSR and the East European communist states. It was formed after West Germany joined NATO.

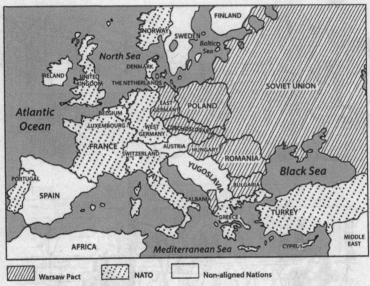

Most of the countries in Europe joined NATO or the Warsaw Pact.

Hungary

In 1956, Hungary withdrew from the Warsaw Pact, and expelled Soviet troops, but this rebellion was crushed.

TENSIONS RISE AGAIN

The USSR and the Western powers had further disputes.

The Berlin Wall

The USSR wanted the western powers to withdraw from West Berlin. Thousands of people had been crossing from the east to the west, as conditions were better there. The Western countries refused and as a result the Berlin Wall was constructed by East Germany in 1961. This high wall, topped with barbed wire, extended along the boundary between East and West Berlin for 28 miles (45 km). It was heavily guarded, and anyone trying to cross over from the East was shot dead.

The Berlin Wall—two views

The Cuban missile crisis

In 1962, the Cuban missile crisis took place. Krushchev made Cuba a base for nuclear missiles. Missiles from here were capable of reaching the USA. The USA thought of invading Cuba, and finally the USSR removed the missiles. This had almost led to a nuclear war, which would have been a terrible disaster for the whole world. After this the two countries set up a 'hot line', a direct telephone link between Moscow and Washington. This was to prevent war by talking, even at the last minute.

Nuclear weapons

In 1963, the USSR, Britain and the USA signed the Nuclear Test Ban Treaty. This was an agreement not to test nuclear weapons above ground. Strategic Arms Limitation Talks (SALT) began in 1969 between the USSR and the USA. More SALT talks were held later.

DÉTENTE

Though more nuclear weapons were made in the 70s and 80s, a period of détente started. Détente refers to 'a relaxation in confrontation', that is, to less hostility. The USA and USSR both wanted to focus on internal development. Relations became friendlier as President Nixon of the USA visited the USSR in 1972 and in 1974. Brezhnev, leader of the USSR, went to the USA in 1973. The Helsinki Agreement was signed in July 1975, which further improved the situation. By this agreement, the USSR, the USA, Canada, and most of the European nations accepted the boundaries created after the Second World War. This provided some stability in the world. In addition, communist nations promised to provide more freedom to their people.

CHINA AND THE USA

China and the USA had also been hostile to each other. The Korean and Vietnam wars had created problems between the two nations. In addition, the USA had not recognized the People's Republic of China. Instead it gave recognition to Nationalist China, that is Taiwan, which was under Chiang Kai-shek. China tried a strategy of 'table tennis diplomacy'. A US table tennis team was invited to China. The team went and, after the visit, China was admitted into the UN. President Nixon, followed by President Ford, visited China. In December 1978, President Carter derecognized Nationalist China, further improving relations.

AFGHANISTAN

In 1979, Babrak Kamal formed a communist government in Afghanistan. The USSR invaded Afghanistan claiming that this was to support the new government, which caused relations with the US to deteriorate once again.

THE UNITED NATIONS ORGANIZATION

The United Nations, an international organization, was founded on 24 October 1945, with the aim of maintaining peace and security in the world, developing friendly relations between nations and encouraging cooperation. It functions through six main bodies, the General Assembly, Security Council, Secretariat, International Court of Justice, Economic and Social Council and Trusteeship Council. The General Assembly has a representative of each country that is a UN member. The Security Council has five permanent members, as well as other elected members. These five members—the US, Britain, Russia, France and China—have the most important role. There are also associated organizations such as the UNDP (United Nations Development Programme) and UNICEF (United Nations International Children's Emergency Fund). UN-sponsored conferences have dealt with many issues such as the environment, population growth and women's rights. Its role in the world was recognized with the Nobel Peace Prize in 2001.

United Nations Headquarters, New York

LITERATURE AND FILM

The Second World War, the Cold War and related themes were described in history and fiction and depicted in films. Numerous spy thrillers were written. Among the most successful writers is John Le Carré (real name David J.M. Cornwell), whose book *The Spy Who Came in from the Cold* (1963), is a classic. He, as well as Ian Fleming (1908–64) who created the character James Bond, wrote a number of books. Len Deighton (b. 1929) is famous for his spy thrillers set in the Cold War. The American writer, Tom Clancy (b. 1947), also focused on this in *The Hunt for Red October* (1984). Graham Greene (1904–91) wrote spy thrillers as well as other books. Others wrote on the problems of Germany and on the Soviet era. George Orwell's *1984* (1949) and *Animal Farm* explored the problems of life in a totalitarian state. Gunter Grass, awarded the Nobel Prize for literature in 1999, wrote both fiction and non-fiction on various themes including German reunification.

41

Europe after 1945

On the whole, the countries in Europe affected by the Second World War recovered well because of the Marshall Plan. As seen in Chapter 40, they joined together in various groups, realizing that it was difficult to defend themselves in isolation. Economic cooperation was also helpful.

SCANDINAVIAN COUNTRIES

The Scandinavian countries of Norway, Sweden and Denmark, are constitutional monarchies. Each has a government headed by a prime minister. These countries are relatively prosperous, with high living standards. The Nordic Council was founded in 1952 to increase cooperation among these three countries, along with Iceland. Finland joined in 1956. The Oresund Bridge, a road and rail bridge linking Denmark and Sweden, was constructed by 2000.

The Faroe Islands, under Denmark, gained self-government in 1948. Greenland, also under Denmark, is an autonomous territory with self-government. It is the world's largest island.

Iceland gained independence in 1944. It had a prosperous economy, but suffered a collapse in the banking structure in 2008, during the world economic crisis.

The Scandinavian countries have a rich culture and have excelled in art, literature and music.

Culture

Norway has produced great writers including Henrik Ibsen (1828–1906) and Knut Hamsun (1859–1952). The latter won the Nobel Prize for literature in 1920. Edward Munch (1863–1944) is a great artist from Norway. In Sweden, Alfred Nobel, a chemist and industrialist, provided funds for the Nobel Prize. Sweden awards five out of the six Nobel prizes while Norway awards the Peace Prize.

PIPPI LONGSTOCKING AND OTHER CHARACTERS

Astrid Lindgren (1907–2002) from Sweden is a very well-known author of children's books. Her most popular character is Pippi Longstocking, a nine-year-old, red-headed, orphan girl. Pippi lives all by herself, along with a horse and a monkey, and has many adventures. Astrid wrote more than 80 books. Among others are stories about Emil, a mischievous boy, who is also a detective!

Danish cinema is recognized as amongst the best in the world. The Dogme movement (dogme is the Danish word for dogma) in the 1990s and early 2000s used handheld cameras in a reaction against big-budget films. There were other rules regarding Dogme films. The main aim was to make films in a natural and traditional way, without special effects. The film should be shot on location, as far as possible in natural light. Props and sets should not be used and the director should not be mentioned. Some of the directors strictly followed these rules while others modified them.

The Danish writer Vilhelm Jensen (1873–1950) won the Nobel Prize for Literature in 1944. Jean Sibelius (1867–1957) of Finland is one of the great classical musicians.

A ROLE IN PEACE

These countries have also had a role in peace negotiations in the world. In 1993, Norway mediated between Israel and the PLO and in 2000, between Sri Lanka and Tamil separatists.

Olaf Palme (1927–86), prime minister of Sweden, made many efforts for world peace but was assassinated in 1986. He was against nuclear weapons and discrimination of any kind. He had also criticized the US involvement in Vietnam.

Martti Ahtisaari

In 2008, Martti Ahtisaari, the Finnish president, was recognized with the Nobel Peace Prize for his role in helping bring harmony, particularly in Kosovo.

BELGIUM

Belgium, Netherlands and Luxembourg joined together in a customs union (Benelux) in 1944 while the governments were still in exile during the war. The union became a reality in 1947. The Benelux Economic Union formed in 1958 (effective from 1960) replaced the earlier customs union. Belgium has a democratic government and a federal structure with three administrative regions. The Netherlands is also known as Holland, which is its largest province. The International Court of Justice is located in this country at The Hague.

SWITZERLAND

Switzerland had remained neutral during the war and was relatively unaffected. Though otherwise a liberal and advanced nation, it was late in giving the vote (1971) and equal rights (1981) to women. Switzerland joined the United Nations in 2002.

Belgium and Switzerland are known for their delicious chocolate.

FRANCE

Though it was on the victorious side, France had great losses during the war. After liberation in 1944, a new constitution was introduced and the Fourth Republic of France was inaugurated. It lasted till 1958. Though industrial production increased, inflation continued and there were weak coalition governments. France lost her territories in Indo-China, and was forced to grant independence to Tunisia and Morocco. There was also a major rebellion in Algeria.

These problems led to the founding of the Fifth Republic with another new constitution in 1958. General de Gaulle was elected as president. De Gaulle formed a strong government. Industry expanded and agriculture improved. Independence was granted to Algeria, which had been a French colony, in 1962. De Gaulle's leadership was appreciated and his popularity increased. However, he began to lose the confidence of the people as inflation rose. There were housing shortages and insufficient schools and hospitals. In addition, De Gaulle's withdrawal from NATO and attempt to make nuclear weapons were disliked. In 1968, there were student strikes spreading across Paris. The students were joined by millions of workers, and it seemed as if a revolution would occur. De Gaulle controlled the situation, but

President De Gaulle

resigned in 1969. The Fifth Republic continued under President Pompidou, followed by Giscard d'Estaing. In 1981, the socialist Francois Mitterand became the president, and was re-elected in 1988. Jacques Chirac was president from 1995 to 2007, followed by Nicholas Sarkozy of the Conservative UMP Party up to 2012. At the time of Chirac's presidency, there were numerous strikes in 2002 to 2003, 2005 and 2007. Francois Hollande of the Socialist Party became the president in 2012.

France is known for experimental literature and cinema and for its great art as well as great food. There have been 12 winners of the Nobel Prize for literature from France. Jean Paul Sartre, philosopher and writer, would have been the thirteenth, but rejected the prize.

GERMANY

The German Federal Republic was formed in West Germany in 1949. Konrad Adenauer of the Christian Democrats Party (CDU) was the chancellor. Under Adenauer, Germany recovered from the war. Industry and general prosperity grew. The Social Democrats (SDU) came to power in 1969, with Willy Brandt (up to 1974) followed by Helmut Schmidt as chancellor. Germany and western Europe were affected by the world recession of 1980.

East Germany became part of the Federal Republic in 1990. There were initial problems of housing shortages, unemployment, and a recession that took place in 1993.

Germany's great writers of the 20th century include Thomas Mann and Herman Hesse. Both wrote a number of books and won Nobel Prizes for literature. Mann's *The Magic Mountain*, and Hesse's *The Glass Bead Game* are considered among the best literature in the world.

ITALY

Italy was defeated in the war in 1943 and then made peace with the Allies. After this, Germany occupied Italy. The Allies pushed the Germans out in 1944. Mussolini tried to escape to Switzerland but was shot dead by Italians on 28 April 1945. The king, Victor Emmanuel, abdicated in 1946. A referendum was held and the people of Italy voted in favour of becoming a republic. A new republic and constitution came into being on 1 January 1948. Italy joined NATO in 1949.

The new republic was faced with corruption, and numerous governments rose and fell. Guilio Andreotti was prime minister from 1972 to 1973, from 1976 to 1979, and from 1989 to 1992, being re-elected several times. The 'mani pulite' (clean hands) movement started after 1992 to remove corruption. It consisted of judicial investigations in which many politicians were accused of corruption and some committed suicide. Four political parties that were in the government declined after this. These were the Christian Democracy, Italian Socialist Party, Italian Socialist Democratic Party and Italian Liberal Party. Silvio Berlusconi, a member of the Forzia Italia, a right-wing party, became prime minister from 1994 to 1996, and from 2001 to 2006, and in 2008, while Ramono Prodi was prime minister from 1996 to 1998, and again from 2006 to 2008. Berlusconi was followed by Mario Monti (2011), Enrico Letta (2013) and Matteo Renzi (2014).

Italy is also known for its organized Mafia. Mafia is a term for a number of powerful criminal groups who have an influence in politics and industry. The Mafia extort money and are involved in illegal trade, but also provide protection to those who pay them. The Italian Mafia spread to the USA. In Italy, the government tried to suppress them from the 1980s.

PORTUGAL

Portugal became a republic in 1910. However, between 1910 and 1926, there were 40 governments. In 1926, General Antonio Carmona became the prime minister after a military coup and was elected president in 1928. His finance minister, Antonio Salazar, who later became prime minister and also held other ministerial posts, controlled Portugal like a dictator from 1932 to 1968. Portugal had a new constitution and a planned economy, but the benefits were mainly for the rich.

Portugal and Spain both remained neutral during the war, though Portugal allowed the allies a base in the Azores. Another military coup took place in 1974. More unstable governments followed, but the situation improved after 1983 with more stable governments and regular elections.

Overseas territories

Portugal lost her territories in India in 1961. In 1974 and 1975, Portugal's African territories gained independence. Finally in 1999, Macao was returned to China. It had been under Portuguese control for 442 years.

SPAIN

General Franco continued to rule Spain till 1975. After the Second World War, Spain was not recognized by the UN and many other nations. However, when the Korean War began in 1950, Franco's dictatorship was seen as a better option than communism. Spain received US aid and was admitted to the UN in 1955. Gradually, the domestic situation improved and Spain's economy flourished after 1961. There were some democratic and liberal reforms.

Spain was officially made a monarchy in 1947 but there was no king until Franco's death. Juan Carlos became king in 1975. In 1976, Adolfo Suarez Gonzales was the new prime minister. Democratic elections were held in 1977, and a new democratic constitution was introduced the following year. Spanish provinces, including the Basque region,gained some autonomy. There were more coup attempts but democracy survived. Jose Zapatero led a socialist government in 2004.

In Spain, the Basque people wanted independence. Franco's government had suppressed them after they claimed independence. The ETA (Euskadi ta Askatana, meaning 'Homeland and Liberty') is a Basque group formed in 1959 that led the independence movement. The ETA made several terrorist attacks. Violence continued despite ceasefires from 1998.

THE UNITED KINGDOM

From 1945 to 1951, there was a Labour government in the UK, with Clement Attlee as the prime minister. Welfare programmes were introduced, and there was the nationalization of the Bank of England as well as of several industries including railways, gas

BRITAIN IN THE 1960s

There was a sense of freedom among the young people, and a turning away from convention. London became the centre of new trends in literature, art, music and fashion.

The pop band from Liverpool, The Beatles, who soon became a worldwide phenomenon, were representative of this trend.

and electricity, coal, and iron and steel. This helped Britain to recover from the war. Several colonies attained independence. A Conservative government followed, and Labour and Conservatives generally alternated in power. Economic problems, including unemployment, continued.

At the time of the Conservative government of Margaret Thatcher, prime minister from 1979 to 1990, the number of unemployed reached 2.8 million. Thatcher was succeeded by another Conservative government under John Major. The Labour Party won a victory in 1997 and Tony Blair became the prime minister. The Labour Party won again in 2001 and in 2005, but lost in 2010. A new government was formed, led by the Conservative prime minister, David Cameron.

THE COMMONWEALTH OF NATIONS

The Commonwealth consists of a group of nations that were once British colonies. Though the term was used earlier, it was legally established by the Statute of Westminster in 1931 as the British Commonwealth. The word British was not used after colonies became independent. The aim of the Commonwealth is to promote friendship, cooperation and democratic functioning among members. Biennial meetings of Commonwealth Heads of Government (CHOGMs) are held. By 2004, there were 53 nations in the Commonwealth.

The Royal Family

In the 20th century, the royal family of Britain had little power, but still occupied a ceremonial role. The rulers were:

George V (ruled 1910–36) changed the family name to Windsor in 1917.

Edward VIII (January–December 1937), abdicated.

George VI (1937–52)

Elizabeth II came to the throne in 1952 and continued as queen in the 21st century. She is also the head of the Commonwealth and of the Church of England.

The British public takes a keen interest in the lives of members of the royal family. Thus, when Princess Diana, the wife of Prince Charles, died in a car crash in 1997, there was an outpouring of emotion. Prince Charles' subsequent marriage to Camilla Parker Bowles did not meet with popular approval but was finally accepted.

Castles and palaces

The royal family has a number of residences including castles and palaces. Among those still used today are Buckingham Palace and Windsor Castle. The origins of Windsor Castle date back to the 11th century, but several modifications and additions were made later. Windsor Castle is used by the queen on weekends. She also stays there for a month in March–April and a week in June. Several weddings and funerals have taken place there. Parts of the castle are open to the public, including St George's Chapel. Queen Mary's Dolls' House is one of the most popular attractions here.

QUEEN MARY'S DOLLS' HOUSE

A dolls' house was completed in 1924 for Queen Mary, wife of King George V. It was the idea of the queen's cousin Princess Marie Louise and was constructed by the architect Sir Edwin Lutyens and other top craftsmen and artists. It was made on a scale of 1: 12, is approximately 1 m tall, and everything in it works. There are miniature bedrooms, carpets, curtains, flush toilets that work, paintings, and even a library for which famous writers specially wrote works which were bound into miniature books. There is a hidden garden too, visible when a

drawer under the building is pulled out. There are thousands of
miniature objects in the house, also electricity and running hot
and cold water, and lifts which work. There is a tiny working
clock. More than 1000 British artists and craftsmen worked on
it. Berry Bros and Rudd (wine and spirits merchants) made
a wine cellar for the doll house, consisting of 1200 miniature
bottles of wine, beer and other drinks.

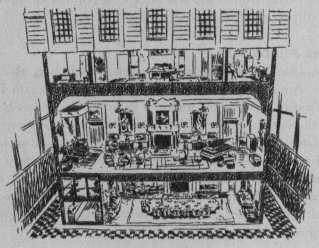

Queen Mary's Dolls' House

IRELAND

As we saw in Chapter 37, southern Ireland gained dominion
status in 1922. This was known as the Irish Free State. Its
independence was recognized in 1931 and a new constitution was
introduced in 1937. It became a sovereign republic in 1949. The
majority in Ireland are Catholics. Northern Ireland remained
with Great Britain and has a Protestant majority.

During 1968 to 1969 there was increasing violence between
the Catholic and Protestant groups in Ireland. The Provisional

IRA was a new group formed in 1969. Its aim was to remove the British from Northern Ireland. There were opposing Protestant groups, including the Ulster Volunteer Force, founded in 1966. Violence continued for several years. Among the worst days was 30 January 1972, known as Bloody Sunday, when 13 Catholics were shot dead by the British. On 21 November 1974, the IRA bombed a pub in Birmingham. Twenty-one people died. Violence continued till the 1990s. In 1997, a ceasefire was declared. More than 3000 people had died over these years. A later arrangement led to the sharing of power between the two groups.

WALES

Education in Wales is mainly in both English and Welsh. Plaid Cymru, the Party of Wales, was established in 1925. Initially it worked to promote the Welsh language but later put forward ideas of nationalism and independence. In 1997, a referendum was held and Wales voted for 'devolution' rather than independence. After elections in 1999, a Welsh Assembly was formed, located at the capital of Cardiff.

SCOTLAND

In 1997, a referendum was also held in Scotland, which voted for the establishment of a Scottish Parliament. This was formed in 1999. In 2011, the Scottish National Party won a majority in the elections. A referendum for Scottish independence was held on 18 September 2014 and the Scots voted against this.

THE EUROPEAN UNION

A need was felt for a European community that would coordinate European affairs.

Jean Monnet put forward the Schumann Plan in 1950. Based on this, the European Coal and Steel community (ECSC) was founded by a treaty in 1951 which came into force in 1952. This was a union for sharing the coal and steel resources of France, Germany, Italy, Belgium, Luxembourg and the Netherlands. These countries founded and joined the European Economic Community in 1957. This led to economic cooperation among these nations. Britain joined in 1973. By 1986, membership had increased to twelve.

The European Atomic Energy Commission was founded in 1957. These three organizations together formed the European Community in 1965 (officially 1967). They became the European Union in 1993. The European Union developed the Euro, a single currency, though not all member countries use it.

Europe in 2010

42
The USSR

After the Second World War, the USSR expanded and also controlled a number of Eastern European countries. Relations with Western Europe and the US improved under the leadership of Nikita Krushchev, following the death of Stalin in 1953.

Krushchev was succeeded by Leonid Brezhnev in 1964. Economic growth slowed, production declined, and the common people faced shortages while high party officials enjoyed luxuries. The KGB and other security forces sent thousands into exile or labour camps. There was inefficiency and corruption, and general dissatisfaction.

Brezhnev died in 1982. He was succeeded by Yuri Andropov, followed by Konstantin Chernenko (1911–85). In 1985, Mikhail Gorbachev became general secretary of the CPSU and the new leader. He brought in new people in the government, including Eduard Shevardnaze as foreign minister and Nikolay Ryzhkov as prime minister. Brezhnev tried to reorganize the Communist Party, reduce corruption and change the power structure, but found it difficult to achieve much.

In April 1986, a nuclear accident took place at the nuclear plant located at Pripyat, a town near Chernobyl in the Ukraine republic of the USSR. This was the worst nuclear accident that had ever taken place. It affected the republics of Ukraine, Belorussia and Russia, and to some extent, East Europe up to Scandinavia. Information regarding this incident reached the government late. This delay in communication was an additional reason for Gorbachev to bring in more changes, symbolized by two terms, 'perestroika' and 'glasnost'. 'Perestroika' meant restructuring and 'glasnost' indicated openness.

In 1987 to 1988, economic reforms were introduced, as part of perestroika. Some amount of privatization was allowed. More reforms were demanded. Gorbachev also started a programme of democratization. He felt the Communist Party was blocking his reforms and changed the constitution to bypass it. There was a new elected Congress of Deputies, which in turn elected a new Supreme Soviet (legislature). Press censorship was removed and new political parties were allowed. Market reforms were started but the economy faced serious problems with inflation and the shortage of products.

International relations improved and several meetings were held with the president of the US. The Strategic Arms Reduction Treaty (START 1) was signed with President Bush in 1991. The USSR also withdrew from Afghanistan in 1988–89.

Gorbachev became president in 1990. He was awarded the Nobel Peace Prize the same year.

The greatest changes took place in Eastern Europe. Communism in these countries had been imposed and protected by the USSR. Gorbachev refused to do so any further.

In and after 1988, the Eastern European countries began to move away from communism. Soviet forces gradually withdrew from East Europe.

Within the Soviet Union, 15 republics held elections in 1990. Most of the republics wanted to be independent, while Gorbachev hoped they would join together voluntarily. In August 1991,

Gorbachev and George H.W. Bush, 1990

there was an attempted coup against him and, though it failed, Gorbachev soon resigned as general secretary of the Communist Party. In December, he resigned as president. Though Gorbachev did not achieve everything he wanted, his policies provided freedom to a number of countries to choose their own path, and ended the Cold War.

By the end of 1991, the USSR had ceased to exist. The republic of Russia took its place in the UN. Russia and some other former republics, joined together in a federation called the Commonwealth of Independent States (CIS).

THE CULTURE OF THE USSR

The USSR provided free education including technical and medical education and excellent facilities for scientific research. It was a leading country in space research and its satellites *Sputnik 1* and *Sputnik 2*, launched in 1957, were the first man-made satellites to orbit the earth. Yuri Gagarin circled the earth in a spaceship in 1961, the first person in space. Its nuclear programme, chemistry and physics research, were also advanced.

Total literacy was a result of its programmes, while when it was founded literacy was barely 30 per cent. The country excelled in sports and games.

It aimed to provide equality to all, but gradually many problems crept in. The party leaders became the new elite, living in luxury, while the ordinary people faced shortages. There was no freedom to express one's views or to criticize the government. Thousands who did so were executed or sent to labour camps in Siberia. Others were sent into exile to the outlying republics. Foreign nationals too were sent to these. Books were written and circulated secretly; this type of literature was termed 'samizdat' and had a wide circulation.

SOLZHENITSYN: A GREAT RUSSIAN WRITER

Aleksandr Solzhenitsyn (1918–2008), who received the Nobel Prize for literature in 1970, spent long years in labour camps. Among his books, *One Day in the Life of Ivan Denisovitch* and *The First Circle* are fictionalized accounts of his life there. *The Gulag Archipelago* is a comprehensive record of the Soviet prison system. *Cancer Ward* and other books and short stories reflect some of the absurdities of life in the USSR, but also record the lives of ordinary people. A more recent work is *Two Hundred Years Together*, the story of Russia's Jewish minority.

Below we look at the former Soviet republics and the countries of Eastern Europe after the decline and break up of the USSR.

EASTERN EUROPE
Poland
In Poland, a trade union called Solidarity was founded in 1980 in Gdansk by shipyard workers. It was led by Lech Walesa, an electrician and trade union leader. Trade unions were not

allowed at this time, but this was formed after a workers strike. Later the same year, in December, Solidarity was suppressed, and martial law declared. The economy was declining. In 1988, the government began talks with the trade union leaders. Elections were held in Poland in June 1989. Solidarity won and a new government was formed with Tadeusz Mazowieki as the prime minister. Lech Walesa received the Nobel Peace Prize in 1983, and was president of the country from 1990 to 1995.

As a post-communist country, Poland brought in many changes to the economy, which initially suffered after 1989, but revived by 1995.

East Germany

In May 1989, a number of East Germans started moving to Hungary. Hungary was introducing reforms. East Germans could enter Hungary without a visa. Erich Honecker in East Germany asked for help from the USSR, but Gorbachev had his own internal problems. In November, the Berlin Wall that had divided East and West Berlin since 1961 was opened. In 1990, East and West Germany were reunited.

Czechoslovakia

In 1989, a peaceful revolution, known as the Velvet or 'Gentle' Revolution, led to elections in Czechoslovakia, and the formation of democratic government in 1990. The writer Vaclav Havel became its first president and was re-elected in 1993 and 1998.

However, in 1993, there was a 'Velvet Divorce'. The Czech Republic and Slovakia separated to form two new nations.

Bulgaria

After the Second World War, Bulgaria became a communist state, with Todor Zhivkov as the main leader from 1954 to 1989.

In 1989, multiparty elections took place and Bulgaria became a democracy. Bulgaria remains a functioning democracy.

Romania

In 1947, Romania became a Communist People's Republic. After a period of extreme repression, Nicolae Ceausescu came to power in 1965 and began to pursue a more liberal and independent policy. Later, he lost popularity as the economy declined and in 1989 was overthrown and executed. After 1989, Romania began political and economic reforms.

Romania has a rich culture and the first half of the 20th century is considered a golden age of literature and the arts.

Moldova

Between the wars, Moldova was part of Romania but came under the Soviet Union in 1940. Moldova became an independent republic in 1991, and joined the CIS. The first democratic elections were held in 1994. Most of Moldova was once a region known as Bessarabia. The majority here are of Romanian origin. However, the USSR combined another region, the Trans-Dneister, previously within Ukraine, and created the Moldovian Soviet Socialist Republic. After the decline of the USSR, this region asserted independence from Moldova in 1990 as Transnistria. Hundreds were killed in the resulting conflict in 1992. Though other states do not recognize it, Transnistria, with its capital of Tiraspol, has its own president, constitution and flag and remains separate, guarded by Russian troops. In 2014, it expressed a wish to join Russia. Another minority region in Moldova, the Turkic-speaking Gagauz, gained autonomy in 1994. Moldova was once known for its wine industry but now has a weak economy. This has led to many attempting to migrate and a high level of human trafficking. In 2001, Vladimir Voronin of the Communist Party was elected president and again in 2005, remaining in power until 2009.

Hungary
Hungary held elections and became a democratic republic in 1989.

OTHER COUNTRIES IN EASTERN EUROPE
Albania
After gaining independence from the Ottomans in 1912, Albania became a republic in 1920, but was subsequently conquered by Italy. As an independent nation again, Albania turned communist. Enver Hoxha, prime minister from 1944 to 1954, continued to lead the country until his death in 1985. The communist hold then loosened, and a non-communist government was formed in 1992. Albania is now a parliamentary democracy. Though it has introduced market reforms, the economy and infrastructure still need improvement.

Cyprus
Cyprus came under several dynasties and empires and finally gained independence from the British in 1960. The main groups in Cyprus are of Turkish and Greek origin and the two had often had conflicts, which revived in 1963. Archbishop Makarios, president from 1960 to 1977, initially on the side of the Greeks, later adopted a more balanced position, but a faction of the Greeks remained extreme. In 1974, Turkish forces occupied part of Cyprus and named the area the Turkish Republic of Northern Cyprus. Turkey still occupies the region, though legally it is under Cyprus.

Greece
During the Second World War, Italy followed by Germany occupied the country and after its liberation, there was a civil

war between communist and non-communist forces. The king was overthrown in 1974, and multiparty elections held. Greece is part of the European Union, but has financial problems.

Yugoslavia (1918–91)

Yugoslavia was a separate nation from 1918 to 1991. The country was initially a monarchy. It had a centralized government, but a new federal form of government was introduced in 1939. The Second World War saw Yugoslavia occupied by the Axis powers. With the king in exile, two main groups struggled to liberate the country. In 1945, the monarchy was abolished and Josip Broz Tito, a communist, who organized a guerrilla movement during the war, became the leader. The country was renamed the Federal People's Republic of Yugoslavia, and contained six republics within it. The different units had some autonomy. Though

The territory of Yugoslavia: 1918–91

communist, Yugoslavia was not totally under the influence of the USSR, and joined the Non-Aligned Movement. Industry and agriculture developed. Tito remained the leader until his death in 1980, but in his last years, the economy began facing problems. After his death, government leadership proved weak, and the different regions began to have strained relations. The country began to disintegrate around 1990.

Serbia, a constituent republic under president Slobodan Milosevic, wanted to dominate the region. In 1991, Croatia, Slovenia and Macedonia asserted independence and in 1992, Bosnia and Herzegovina followed suit. Serbia and Montenegro became the new Federal Republic of Yugoslavia.

Serbia and Montenegro

The Federal Republic of Yugoslavia including Serbia and Montenegro faced serious problems in 1998 as violence erupted in Kosovo, an autonomous region of Serbia. This was finally suppressed.

Serbia and Montenegro formed a looser union in 2003 and remained united till 2006 and then became independent nations, after almost ninety years of some form of unity. However, even during the Milosevic era, Montenegro had its own central bank and separate currency.

Kosovo

Kosovo became independent from Serbia in 2008. This is not accepted by Russia and Serbia, though other countries have recognized it. Kosovo has a mainly Albanian population. It is poorly developed.

Macedonia

Albanians begin an insurgency in Macedonia in 2001, leading to the Ohrid Framework Agreement which provides more rights to minorities.

Bosnia-Herzegovina

The new state of Bosnia-Herzegovina was hit by civil war. Serbs began an attack against Croats and Muslims, aiming to get more territory for themselves. As Croats created their own territory Muslims were left to fight alone, and thousands were killed. In 1994, Bosniaks (Muslims) and Croats agreed to a Bosniak/Croat Federation, while the Dayton Peace Accords put forward a formula for peace. The boundaries of Bosnia-Herzegovina were retained, but within it, the two territories of Bosnia and Herzegovina were created, with Bosnians and Croats, and the Republika Srpska led by Serbs. Initially, a NATO led peacekeeping force was stationed in the country, which in 2004 was replaced by a European Union force. The country is now stable.

Countries of former Yugoslavia after the break up

Croatia

After Croatia declared independence from Yugoslavia in 1991, four years of fighting between Serbs and Croats followed. A small region held by Serbs was returned to Croatia in 1998.

Slovenia

After gaining independence relatively peacefully in 1991, Slovenia has had a stable economy and a functioning democracy.

FORMER SOVIET REPUBLICS

The former Soviet republics or states that gained independence in 1991 in Eastern Europe include Estonia, near the Baltic Sea, Lithuania, Latvia, Belarus and Ukraine.

After independence, Belarus and Ukraine were the first to join the CIS and to establish closer links with Russia.

However, there are new problems in Ukraine with civil war in 2014 in which Russia has some involvement.

Ukraine is the second largest country in Europe after Russia. It has a presidential form of government, and a unicameral legislature.

A SHARED MEMORIAL

On the outskirts of Kiev, capital of Ukraine, is a museum complex founded in the 1980s. Outside is a memorial to the shared sacrifices and victories of the Ukraine and Russia in the Second World War. The memorial monument is a woman, 61 m tall, with a sword in one hand and a shield in the other, which has the emblem of the Soviet Union on it. Eight million Ukrainians died in the war.

Asian republics

The USSR had a number of republics in Asia, which became independent in 1991. The former Central Asian republics are

First president of Turkmenistan, Sapurmurat Niyazov who ruled like a dictator (1990–2006)

now the independent countries of Kazakhstan, Kyrgyzstan, Tajikistan, Turkmenistan and Uzbekistan.

Other USSR republics in Asia which became independent are Armenia, Azerbaijan, and Georgia. South Ossetia and Abkhazia in Georgia have separated and claim independence. Nagorno Karabakh in Azerbaijan, with a mainly Armenian population, has also declared independence.

The Puffin History of the World

43

North America

During the 20th century, both Canada and the US became prosperous countries with high standards of living. However, it was the US which was a major world power.

CANADA

Canada is the second largest country in the world with a huge territory of 9,984, 670 sq km, but its population is only around 34 million. It includes a number of islands mainly in the Arctic Ocean. The islands include Baffin, Victoria, Ellesmere, Banks, Devon, Axel Heiberg and Melville islands.

The government and territories

Canada remained a British dominion in the 20th century. In 1931, the Statute of Westminster provided more autonomy to Canada. The British North American Act of 1949 gave Canada powers to amend its constitution, but these were not total. The British Parliament still maintained some control over amendments. This was finally ended by the Constitution Act of 1982. Canada enjoys full sovereignty, but the British monarch remains the head of the state and is represented by a governor general. The prime minister leads the government, which consists of an elected Parliament with two houses.

A federation

Canada is a federation with ten provinces and three territories. Each has its own symbols and some amount of autonomy. The provinces are: Alberta (joined 1905), British Columbia, Manitoba, New Brunswick, Newfoundland and Labrador (joined 1949), Nova Scotia, Ontario, Prince Edward Island, Quebec and Saskatchewan (1905). The territories are the Northwest Territories, Nunavut, and Yukon Territory.

Nunavut, occupied mainly by Inuits, was separated from the Northwest Territories in 1999. The capital, Iqaluit, is on southern Baffin Island. Inuits have different dialects. In this region, their language is Inuktitut, the majority language in Nunavut, and one of the three official languages there.

Quebec, which is largely French speaking, has put forward demands for independence since the 1950s. However, in 2014, the separatist Parti Quebecois, which was in power in Quebec, lost to the Liberal Party of Quebec, led by a federalist. This provided a setback to possible independence.

During and after the wars

Canada participated in both the world wars.

Canada recovered well after the First World War, but was affected by the Great Depression of 1929. The Conservative Party prime minister Richard Bennet (1930–35) introduced reforms including minimum wages and unemployment benefits, but lost to the Liberal Party in 1935. Mackenzie King of the Liberal Party was the next prime minister.

The Second World War began and almost 1.5 million Canadians participated in it, out of a total population of 12 million. There were over 40,000 deaths. King created a number of welfare schemes and managed to control inflation after the war. He remained prime minister till 1948, and was followed by another Liberal. The economy expanded, and prosperity increased. More immigrants, particularly from Britain, settled in Canada.

After a period of Conservative rule, Pierre Elliot Trudeau of the Liberal Party became prime minister from 1968 to 1979, and again from 1980 to 1984. He allowed more Asians and South and Central Americans into Canada, creating a more multicultural society. English and French were given equal status as official languages.

Canada had been forming closer ties with USA. In 1989, the US–Canada Free Trade Agreement (FTA) was signed.

Under another Conservative government, Canada joined the North America Free Trade agreement (NAFTA), which became effective from 1 January 1994. A new Conservative Party of Canada was formed in 2003 by merging two parties, the Progressive Conservative Party of Canada and the Canadian Alliance. Stephen Harper of this Conservative Party became the prime minister in 2006.

Pierre Elliot Trudeau

Economy

Canada suffered in the 2008 recession, but her banks remained stable.

It has a market economy and well-developed industries. There are numerous mineral resources including zinc, uranium, diamonds, petroleum and natural gas as well as large areas under forests.

Trade is mainly with the USA.

The USA

The USA, consists of 50 states and one district, along with some outlying areas, including Puerto Rico. It has a federal government located at Washington D.C., along with governments in each state. Some powers are shared, but only the Federal Congress makes decisions regarding foreign affairs and defence.

The New Deal and later

The reforms of the New Deal (see Chapter 37) helped the economy, though it did not recover fully. Roosevelt was re-elected three times and remained president till his death in April 1945. Focusing on its internal problems, at first USA did not even join the Second World War. As we saw in Chapter 39, the US participation began in 1941. After the Second World War, the USA played a major role in the Cold War, and in

The States of the USA

McCARTHYISM

The US senator Joseph McCarthy organized the persecution of communists in the US after 1950. He claimed they were a danger to the country. This persecution was named McCarthyism after him.

preventing Communism from spreading in the world. (See Chapter 40.)

Harry Truman, who was the vice president, took over as president when Roosevelt died.

A Democrat, Truman introduced policies known as the Fair Deal. These included old age pensions, a national health scheme and employment programmes. Some of his schemes were not passed by the Congress. At this time the USA was involved in the Korean War. Dwight Eisenhower, a Republican, was the next president from 1953 to 1961. US involvement in the Vietnam War started in 1955.

John F. Kennedy

In 1961, John F. Kennedy became the youngest president at the age of 42.

Apart from dealing with Cold War-related foreign affairs, Kennedy expanded trade with other countries and founded the Peace Corps. This consisted of volunteers who would work in

John F. Kennedy

underdeveloped countries and help to improve conditions. He also introduced reforms that came to be called the New Frontier. These included an expansion of social security and unemployment benefits and a rise in minimum wages.

The New Frontier also proposed full civil rights for African-Americans, which had not yet been granted. The first African-American ambassador

was appointed and a Civil Rights Bill introduced. Unfortunately, Kennedy was shot dead by an assassin on 22 September 1963. His Civil Rights Bill became an Act in 1964.

CIVIL RIGHTS MOVEMENT

Discrimination against African-Americans continued, particularly in the southern states. A Civil Rights Movement started. One of the main leaders was Martin Luther King, who made continuous efforts to end discrimination against blacks. Rosa Parks (1913-2005), an African-American, was another notable leader of the movement. Her refusal on 1 December 1955 to give up her seat in a bus for a white passenger in Montgomery, Alabama, became a symbol of the rights movement. Though not the first such action, it sparked the Montgomery Bus Boycott, led by

Martin Luther King

Martin Luther King, that opposed racial segregation on public transport. The boycott lasted for 385 days. During this time, King's house was bombed and he was arrested, but it ended in success, with a court ruling in December 1956 prohibiting racial segregation in buses. Inspired by Mahatma Gandhi, King continued to use non-violent means to promote his aim of racial equality. Among many others in the movement, was Malcolm X (b.1925; assassinated 1965), an African-American Muslim, who was harsh in his criticism of atrocities by whites. Martin Luther won the Nobel Peace Prize in 1964. Four years later, he was assassinated.

Acts that ended legal discrimination:

Civil rights Act of 1964: banned discrimination in employment and public accommodations

Voting Rights Act of 1965: restored and protected voting rights

Immigration and Nationality Services act of 1965: allowed entry into the US of non-European people

Civil Rights Act of 1968: banned discrimination in the sale or renting of housing

Lyndon Johnson

The Democrat Lyndon B. Johnson became president from 1963 to 1969. He said that he wanted to make the US a 'Great Society', a place where there was no poverty and no discrimination. The Civil Rights Act and other acts for equality were passed and new welfare schemes were introduced. But as the USA became more deeply involved in the Vietnam War, young people turned against this war.

President Nixon and the Watergate Scandal

Richard Nixon, a Republican and president from 1969 to 1974, managed to end US involvement in the Vietnam War. However, he became involved in the Watergate scandal. The Democratic Party had its offices in the Watergate Building in Washington. In 1973, it became known that before the election to his second term in 1972, Nixon's staff had broken into the offices of his opponents in Watergate Building. They had photocopied documents and placed listening devices there. Nixon claimed he did not know about this, but he had to accept responsibility and resign.

US SPACE PROGRAMME

The National Aeronautics and Space Administration (NASA) was founded in 1958. In 1961, Alan Shepherd became the first US astronaut in space. And on 20 July 1969, Neil Armstrong and Edwin Aldrin became the first people to walk on the moon. In 1975, the U.S. Apollo spacecraft and the Soviet Soyuz spacecraft linked together in space.

From Ford to Reagan: 1974–89

Nixon was succeeded by President Gerald Ford (1974–77), Jimmy Carter (1977–81) and Ronald Reagan (1981–89).

At the time of President Ford, there was a world recession and a rise in oil prices because of war in West Asia. The US lost control of South East Asia. There were several world crises including the revolution in Iran in 1979. The USA was involved in a number of international events. In 1983, the USA invaded Grenada and was involved in struggles in the region. In 1978, after a meeting at Camp David, it helped Israel and Egypt to come to an agreement. On 1 January 1979, it established full diplomatic relations with China. And in 1987, the Intermediate Nuclear Force (INF) Treaty was signed with the USSR to eliminate some types of nuclear missiles.

Later presidents

Reagan was succeeded by George H. W. Bush (1989–93), Bill Clinton (1993–2001), George W. Bush (2001–09) and Barack Obama (2009–), a Democrat and the first African-American president of the US.

After 1991, relationships with the USSR and later with Russia, improved. The US continued to be involved in world affairs. In 1991, the US intervened in the Gulf War. In 1993, the North American Free Trade Agreement (NAFTA), to establish free trade between the United States, Canada and Mexico was signed.

Terrorism

From the 1990s, terrorism began to seriously affect the USA. The worst terrorist attack was that on the World Trade Center on 9 September 2001. On this significant day, an American Airlines flight from Boston to Los Angeles was hijacked and plunged into the North Tower of the Trade Center at 8.45 a.m. Another hijacked United Airlines flight hit the South Tower at 9.03 a.m. Another hijacked plane, headed towards Washington, crashed. More than 3000 people were killed in these attacks.

Al Qaeda

The US believed that al-Qaeda, an organization led by Osama bin Laden, was responsible for this atrocity. They began an invasion of Afghanistan, believed to be the base of Osama.

Invasion of Iraq

The US invaded Iraq in 2003. The invasion was caused by reports that Iraq had 'weapons of mass destruction' that it could use against the US and other parts of the world. Though this turned out to be untrue, President Saddam Hussein of Iraq was captured and executed and US troops occupied Iraq.

Economic downturn

Internally, the country faced economic problems that came to a head in 2008 with the failure of important banks and financial institutions. This had repercussions all over the world, despite government attempts to rescue and prop up the banks.

In 2009, President Barack Obama won the Nobel Peace Prize.

Culture

Science, technology, literature, art and cinema (Hollywood) have flourished in the USA since it was formed. Hollywood produces the largest number of films in the world.

ATTITUDES TO NATIVE AMERICANS

While some Native Americans are integrated into life in the USA, others continue to live in reservations. In 1994, the American Indian Religious Freedom Act Amendments provided expanded protection of religious rights and sacred sites for Native Americans.

OCCUPY WALL STREET

A protest movement began in September 2011 with young people occupying Zucotti Park in the Wall Street area of New York. The protest was against economic and social inequality. The theme was that 1 per cent of the population controlled most of the wealth and this inequality should end. It was also against corruption and the influence of large businesses on the functioning of the government. The protesters were pushed out of the area after two months.

This protest movement was part of a worldwide trend of ordinary people protesting against repression and conditions that they considered unfair.

44

Central America and the Caribbean States

The countries of Mexico, South and Central America and the Caribbean islands each had their own unique histories, but at the same time, there were several common aspects. These countries are also known as Latin America.

In 1945, these countries were poorly developed. There were some industries, but industrial growth was insufficient because of a shortage of both capital (money) and of technical knowledge. Because of widespread poverty, items produced often could not be sold within the home country. Exports were necessary for the economy. Many countries depended on the export of just one or two commodities. For instance, Chile mainly exported copper and Bolivia, tin. American companies controlled many of the plantations and industries, and the profits went to them. Many of the countries were under military dictators. These dictators were supported by wealthy landowners. Whenever there was an attempt to bring in reforms, the army and the

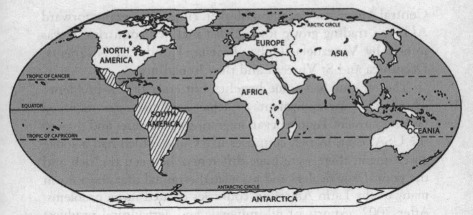

Latin America

landowners tried to prevent it. The USA was involved in the region. Though the USA provided a lot of aid, at the same time they tried to control the politics of the region, and to prevent the setting up of leftist governments.

The Organization of American States was founded in 1948 to increase cooperation. The Latin American Free Trade Association was formed in 1961, but did not have much success.

By the 1980s, most of the countries had huge debts and were facing inflation and financial ruin. Things improved in the 1990s as some debts were cancelled. The countries had to follow IMF policies of globalization and private enterprise. Some countries joined existing free trade associations, while others formed new ones. Mercosur was founded in 1991, with Brazil, Argentina, Uruguay and Paraguay. It had some success but declined after a financial crisis was faced by Brazil and Argentina from 1998 to 2002. The Andean Community consisted of Columbia, Ecuador, Peru and Bolivia. Costa Rica, El Salvador, Nicaragua, Honduras and Guatemala joined the

Central American Common Market. Hugo Chavez put forward ALBA, a trading group for socialist inclined countries. It was joined by Venezuela, Cuba, Bolivia, Honduras, Nicaragua, Dominica and St Vincent and the Grenadines.

The reforms had some benefits, but created new problems. There was unemployment as large agri-businesses replaced peasant farmers. People began migrating to the cities and then to the USA. Even in rich countries like Chile, which had a stable government, there were huge differences between the rich and the poor. Drug dealers and associated criminal organizations in many of the Latin American countries created more problems. After 2002, exports of oil, minerals and agricultural products created prosperity in many countries though the 2008 global economic crisis later affected them.

On the positive side the countries began to modernize. The Latin American countries had been male-dominated, but the position of women now improved. Nicaragua in 1990, Chile in 2006 and Argentina in 2007 had women presidents. In Nicaragua, Violetta Chamorro was president from 1990 to 1997, while Veronica Michelle Bachelet was president of

Chile from 2006 to 2010, and again from 2014. In 2007, Cristina Kirchner became the second woman president of Argentina. She was re-elected in 2011.

Movements for the rights of indigenous peoples began in the 1980s. Most of the countries accepted the principle of equality of all people, but in practice there were problems.

Some more aspects of these countries are given below.

Vicente Fox of Mexico

MEXICO

After independence in 1821 Mexico had a number of unstable governments, followed by a revolution in 1910. After this a new constitution was introduced in 1917. In the 2000 presidential elections, an opposition party won for the first time since 1910, and Vicente Fox of the National Action Party (PAN) became the president, defeating the party in government, the Institutional Revolutionary Party (Spanish: Partido Revolucionario Institucional, PRI). He was succeeded in 2006 by another PAN candidate Felipe Calderon.

After the North American Free Trade Agreement (NAFTA) came into effect in 1994, Mexico's trade with the US and Canada has greatly increased. It also has other free trade agreements with over 40 countries.

CENTRAL AMERICA

Central America is a mountainous region, with active volcanoes and frequent earthquakes. The people in the region today include Native Americans, Spanish, Jamaican and African origin people and mixed groups. (See chapter 21.) Belize has a number of people of African origin. In the countries to the south there are fewer Native Americans and more people of Spanish origin. The region has attempted to coordinate on various issues, and to create organizations for this. The Central American Court of Justice dates back to 1907. The Organization of Central American States was formed in 1951. In 1991, SICA, the System for Central American Integration (Sistema para la Integracion Centroamericana) was inaugurated. There is also a Central American Parliament Bank, and a Common Market (with five countries). Many of the countries in the region faced several coups followed by military dictatorships. The US–Central America Free Trade Agreement (CAFTA) formed in the 21st century, includes Guatemala, El Salvador, Honduras, Nicaragua and the Dominican Republic.

Belize was earlier known as British Honduras. It gained autonomy in 1964 and became fully independent in 1981 (it adopted its new name in 1973). Having been under Britain, Belize's official language is English. All the other countries in Central America have a mixed Spanish and indigenous culture, along with African elements.

Costa Rica is one of the few countries in this region that is a stable state. It is more prosperous than its neighbours. Coffee remains a major crop, but there are also industries including electronics A new constitution was introduced in 1949. Women and people of African descent got the right to vote. The armed forces were abolished and replaced by a civil guard.

Civil war and unstable governments often affected Guatemala, El Salvador and Honduras. In the 21st century, drug trafficking and drug related violence has increased in these countries. Thousands, including children on their own, try to enter the USA illegally, hoping for protection and a better life.

Nicaragua had a corrupt government and administration. In 1979, a leftist group, the Sandinista Liberation Front (founded in 1961), overthrew the Somoza dynasty that had ruled as dictators from 1937. The Sandinistas were led by Daniel Ortega Saavedra, who was the president from 1984 to 1990, and again in 2006.

Panama: After an agreement with the US, the Panama Canal was built between 1904 and 1914, remaining under US control until it was transferred to Panama in 1999–2000. Manuel Noriega was the military dictator from 1983 to 1989. He was initially supported and later deposed by the USA. This is just one instance of USA's interference in the region.

Panama's economy benefits from the revenue earned from the Canal.

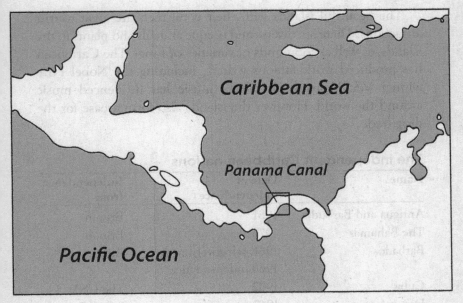

The Panama Canal

CARIBBEAN ISLANDS

The hundreds of islands consist of 27 island groups. There are 13 independent states. Each island group has its own history. Cuba, the largest nation, is the only communist state. The other large countries are Haiti and the Dominican Republic. These two gained independence in the 19th century. Gradually, many other islands became independent in the 20th century, though some remain under various countries. From 1958 to 1962, ten British territories formed the West Indies Federation. These later became independent, but are often still referred to as the West Indies. The Caribbean islands have various regional organizations, some with states of South and Central America. Among these organizations are the Caribbean Community (Caricom) and the Association of Caribbean States (ACS).

The beautiful islands with their coral reefs are great tourist attractions. There are diverse and unique animals and plants in the islands, as well as thousands of varieties of fungi. The Caribbean has produced world-famous writers, including the Nobel Prize winner V.S. Naipaul. Caribbean music has influenced music around the world. However the islands also form a base for the drug trade.

The independent Caribbean nations

Name	Date of independence	Independence from
Antigua and Barbuda	1981	Britain
The Bahamas	1973	Britain
Barbados	1961, self-government; 1966 independence	Britain
Cuba	1902	The USA
Dominica, Commonwealth of	1967, internal autonomy; 1978 independence	Britain
Dominican republic	1821, 1844, 1865	France, Haiti, Spain
Grenada	1974	Britain
Jamaica	1962	Britain
Haiti		
St Lucia	1979	Britain
St Vincent and the Grenadines	1979	Britain
St Kitts and Nevis	1983	Britain
Trinidad and Tobago	1962	Britain

Below we compare the histories of the two largest nations, Cuba and Haiti. It is not possible here to look at the history of each island nation.

Cuba

After Cuba was taken over by the USA in 1898, the country became an independent republic in 1902. However, the USA provided financial aid and American companies controlled the economy. The economy was mainly dependent on sugar exports to the USA. There was a wide division between rich and poor, and considerable poverty. In 1952, Fulgencio Batista gained power. He was supported by the army and ruled as a dictator. Fidel Castro, a young lawyer, began a movement to overthrow Batista and bring in reforms. Many supported Castro, and with the help of Che Guevara from Argentina, Batista was overthrown on 1 January 1959.

Helped by the American CIA, supporters of Batista invaded Cuba and landed at the Bay of Pigs in 1961. Castro managed to defeat them. He then became a communist and Cuba too became a communist state. The Cuban Missile crisis followed in 1962. (See Chapter 40.)

Cuba became increasingly friendly with the USSR, while the US and Latin American states looked on the communist government with suspicion.

When Castro took over, Cuba was extremely backward. In the first ten years under Castro there was great progress in agriculture, industry, and the reduction of corruption. In 1980, there was an economic crisis as both the sugar and tobacco crops failed. In 1994, a rise in oil prices contributed to a new economic crisis, and many people emigrated to the USA.

Fidel Castro and Che Guevara

Cuba's relations with other countries gradually improved. Among the many interactions with other nations, a meeting of the Non-Aligned Movement was hosted in 1979. The Pope visited in 1998, and the Ibero–American summit was held in Cuba in 1999. A G-77 summit was held in Havana in 2000. Gradually the USA too relaxed its stand and began food exports to Cuba.

Castro was prime minister from 1959 to 1976, and president from 1976 to 2008. As his health was failing, his brother Raul became the president in 2008. Many criticized Castro, but he also inspired leaders such as Nelson Mandela and Ahmad Ben Bella.

CHE GUEVARA

Ernesto 'Che' Guevara was a Marxist Revolutionary from Argentina. He participated in the Cuban Revolution, and was part of the Cuban government till 1965. He wrote a book on methods of guerrilla warfare, in which he was an expert, and hoped to spread revolution across South America. However, he was killed in Bolivia in 1967. Che is a legendary figure for revolutionaries all over the world.

Haiti

Haiti has had a turbulent history even after independence. The USA frequently intervened in its affairs and the country was under USA occupation from 1915 to 1934. Political instability continued. In 1957, Francois Duvalier, known as 'Papa Doc' a black nationalist, became the president. He was notorious for the Tonton Macoutes, a special armed force that he used to get rid of his political rivals. He became president for life, and ensured the succession of his son, who became president when Francois died in 1971. The nineteen-year-old Jean Claude Duvalier, or 'Baby Doc', remained president till 1986, despite political and social unrest and growing poverty. He then escaped from the country, which was faced with further instability. During the rule of both father and son, thousands of people were killed.

Finally Jean-Bertrand Aristide, became president in 1991 and, though removed by a coup, was restored to power by the USA in 1994. After elections, Rene Preval, an associate of Aristide, became president in 1996. Though there were attempts at reforms, the poor economic situation led to strikes and violent protests. Teachers, doctors and transport workers were among those involved in protests. Aristide was back in power in 2000, but further chaos led to his overthrow in 2004. There was increasing violence, and troops from the USA, Canada and France rushed there to try and bring order. With a UN stabilization force present, elections were held again, but violence, drug trafficking, and great poverty still continue. A French-speaking minority control the wealth, while Creole speakers live in poverty.

Over the years Haiti has faced many floods, storms and hurricanes, as well as a major earthquake in 2010.

45

South America

There are 12 countries in South America. Portuguese is the official language in Brazil, English in Guyana, and Dutch in Suriname. In the remaining countries, Spanish is the official language. In Paraguay, Guarani, a Native American language is another official language. Other Native American languages are also spoken in these countries.

South American countries have joined together in a number of unions, including the Union of South American Nations (UNASUR), founded in 2008.

BRAZIL

After independence Brazil had a monarchical system of government, but it was proclaimed a republic by the military in 1889. After this, there were both elected and military governments. In 1985, elections were held after a period of 21 years, after which there has been civilian rule. Brazil faced an economic crisis, with inflation going from 300 per cent in 1985, to 1500 per cent in 1991. Subsequently, it was brought under control, through new economic measures.

Brazil today is the leading economic and political power in the region, with well-developed agricultural, mining, manufacturing, and service sectors and a presence in world markets. It is the world's leading producer of coffee. However, within the country income distribution is unequal and crime remains a major problem.

Brazil forms part of BRICS an economic group of Brazil, Russia, India, China and South Africa.

ARGENTINA

After the Second World War, Juan Peron became the leader of the country. He was removed in 1955, re-elected in 1973, and died in 1974. The military had an influence on the intervening subsequent governments, and took over direct control in 1976. Civil rule was restored in 1983. Argentina suffered from several economic crises in the 20th century, including in 2001 to 2002, which led to a political crisis. An economic recovery soon began, but this was followed by inflation, leading to new problems.

VENEZUELA

After attaining independence, Venezuela had several different governments. Hugo Chavez became the president in 1999, and introduced '21st Century Socialism'. His socialist policies included centralization and the nationalization of industries. Minimum wages were increased. The country has rich resources of petroleum, natural gas, iron ore, gold, bauxite, diamonds and other minerals, as well as hydropower. Oil is an important part of the economy.

Hugo Chavez

COLOMBIA

Colombia's present constitution dates to 1991 and has been amended several times. Colombia has a number of political parties, as well as revolutionary groups. Among the latter is the Revolutionary Armed Forces of Colombia (FARC). Colombia still faces problems of inequality, and unemployment. It is also infamous for its drug trade and related problems.

GUYANA AND SURINAME

Guyana is part of the Caricom (Caribbean Community) economic group and a member of the Commonwealth. Though still facing poverty, the economy is growing.

Suriname had been under the Dutch from the 17th century. With the abolition of slavery in 1863, workers were imported from India and Java. Limited self-government was granted in 1954, while full independence was gained in 1975.

In 1980, the civilian government was overthrown by a military coup, and a socialist republic was declared. A democratic election took place in 1987, but the government was again overthrown in 1990. However the following year, an elected coalition government came to power. For the first few years after independence, Suriname received substantial Dutch aid. Later the mining industry, particularly alumina, gold and oil dominated the economy. Both countries have tropical rainforests and diverse flora and fauna.

CHILE

Chile is a long, narrow country, located along the Pacific coast with the Andes Mountains to the east. It also controls a number of islands, including Easter Island. It has rich mineral resources, particularly copper, as well as nitrates, iron ore, limestone, coal, manganese, oil and natural gas, silver and gold. There are some dense rainforests, as well as a desert region in the north.

Salvador Allende became the elected president in 1970.

Allende introduced socialist policies and nationalized industries.

In 1973, he was killed by General Pinochet, who took over power as a dictator. Finally, in 1989, elections were held and Patricio Aylwin Azócar became the president. Economic reforms were introduced, and Chile became a stable, democratic nation, with a market-oriented economy. However, there are wide gaps between the rich and poor.

Salvador Allende

ECUADOR

Civil wars and revolutions followed independence. A new constitution led to civilian governments from 1979, but political instability continued. By 2008, Ecuador's twentieth constitution was inaugurated. Ecuador has good mineral resources, forests, and wildlife.

Ecuador also controls the Archipielago de Colon (Galapagos Islands), a protected region. These islands were visited by Charles Darwin and the unique life-forms there provided him with some of his ideas on evolution.

PERU

Peru too has had instability, dictatorships, and guerilla warfare by revolutionary groups. President Alberto Fujimori, of Japanese origin,was elected in 1990, 1995 and in 2000. Initially he brought in some stability and improved relations with the neighbours. Protests against him forced his resignation in 2000. Alejandro Toledo became the first president of Native American origin in 2001. The economy began to improve after 2004. However revolutionary groups, including the Maoist Sendero Luminoso (Shining Path), were still active.

BOLIVIA

After independence Bolivia faced numerous coups and unstable governments. After 1982, conditions have improved with the establishment of democratic civilian rule, though problems of poverty, social unrest, and an illegal drug trade continued.

Bolivia's economy was largely dependent on tin exports, but the collapse of this market led to an economic crisis in the early 1980s. A series of reforms were instituted from 1985 that helped to boost the economy and reduce poverty. The election of Evo Morales in 2005, who became president in 2006, turned the country towards socialism. A new constitution was inaugurated in 2008 that also guaranteed rights to indigenous peoples. There were several fiscal reforms and the economy began to improve. Morales was re-elected in 2009 and in 2014, reflecting the success of his policies.

PARAGUAY

Military coups and instability dominated the second half of the 20th century and extended into the twenty-first.

Paraguay has a market economy consisting mainly of microenterprises and agricultural activity. It is the sixth largest soy producer in the world.

URUGUAY

As in the neighbouring countries, there was political instability in Uruguay. Revolutionary activities of the leftist Tupamaro group, led to military rule from 1973 to 1985. In 2004, Tabare Vazquez of the leftist Frente Amplio Coalition won the elections, followed in 2009 by José Mujica, a former Tupamaro leader.

Uruguay is known for its advanced education and social welfare systems.Uruguayan culture today largely reflects that of western Europe with some indigenous influence.

CULTURE

The whole region of Latin America has a rich and varied culture in literature, art, music and cinema. Among the great writers are Jorge Luis Borges (1899–1986) of Argentina, Jorge Amado (1912–2001), Jose Lins de Rego (1901–57) and Erico Lopes Verissimo (1905–75) of Brazil, Miguel Angel Asturias of Guatemala, who won the 1967 Nobel Prize for literature, and Octavio Paz (1914–98) of Mexico, who won the Nobel Prize in 1990. Two great poets of Chile who have won Nobel Prizes for Literature, are Gabriela Mistral and Pablo Neruda. Gabriel Garcia Marquez of Colombia and Maria Vargas Llosa of Peru have also won Nobel prizes for literature.

From Ecuador Jorge Carrera Andrade (1903–78), a poet and diplomat, is considered one of the best Spanish-language poets of the 20th century.

The countries of South America

46

China, Japan, Mongolia and Korea

Before and after the Second World War, these countries had somewhat different histories, as described below.

CHINA

A Chinese republic, first established in 1912, was re-established in 1916 under Sun Yat-Sen and the Kuomintang (KMT), a nationalist party. However, the period from 1916 to 1928 is known as the Warlord Era. Former generals took control of individual provinces, which were almost independent. These fought against one another. In 1917, the Kuomintang formed a government at Canton and tried to maintain unity. The Chinese Communist Party (CCP) was founded in 1921 and cooperated with the Kuomintang. Sun Yat-Sen died in 1925 and was succeeded by General Chiang Kai-shek. At this time, the USSR was helping the KMT and many communists were part of the KMT. Chiang began the Northern March in 1926 to take over areas held by the warlords. Helped by the communists, the Northern March was successful, but by April 1927, Chiang expelled all communists from his party. Chiang also started a campaign to kill as many communists as possible. The CCP was led by Mao Zedong. In 1931, Mao became the chairman of the Central Executive Committee of the CCP. He and the communists retreated to the mountains between Hunan and Kiangsi, where they focused on creating a strong army. But soon, even here, they were surrounded by the KMT armies.

The Long March
In October 1934, about 1,00,000 communists managed to break through the KMT forces. Looking for a safer place, they began a march that covered 9656 km in 368 days. They crossed 18 mountain ranges, 24 rivers and 12 provinces. They followed strict rules of conduct. They made friends with and helped the ordinary people that they met. They managed to occupy 62 cities, but thousands of communists died during the march. Only 20,000 reached the Shensi province where they founded a new base in Yenan. The communists continued to gain popularity, while the KMT were condemned as they were corrupt and inefficient. By 1937, the communists had five bases. By 1945, this rose to 19. Around 100 million people lived in the territories under their control. And by October 1949, the communists led by Mao Zedong finally defeated the KMT and formed the Communist People's Republic of China.

The new republic
The new republic faced many problems. The Japanese invasion and the civil war had ruined the country. As a communist nation, China was influenced by Russia's planning process, but soon embarked on her own path. A new constitution was drawn up. There was an elected National People's Congress, for which all people over the age of 18 could vote. This in turn elected the State Council and the chairman of the republic. Mao was the first chairman. He was assisted in his government and reforms

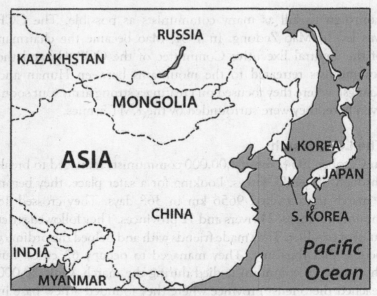

China and neighbouring countries

by Zhou Enlai. To increase agricultural productivity cooperative farms were set up by redistributing land from large owners to peasant groups comprising 100–300 families. In 1953, a Five-Year Plan began, focusing on the development of heavy industry.

The Great Leap Forward

In 1958, there was an emphasis on new economic policies, adapted to specifically Chinese conditions, known as the Great Leap Forward. Communes were created with up to 75,000 people each, divided into brigades and work teams. Communes included collective farms and small factories.

The Cultural Revolution

In 1966, the Cultural Revolution began. This aimed to bring about a total change in China. Tradition and ancient culture were condemned. Thousands of books, manuscripts and ancient art objects were destroyed. Intellectuals and the elite were attacked. Higher educational institutions were closed. Schools and factories, too, were shut down. The Red Guards, mostly young students, were involved in the movement. The aim of the movement was to focus on development for the common people, and to revive enthusiasm for the revolution. However, both education and industry suffered at this time.

Mao

Red Guards

MAO SUITS

Created by Sun Yat-sen, and known in Chinese as Zhongshan zhuang, the Mao suit is a two-piece outfit of jacket and trousers. During the Cultural Revolution it was worn by most workers to create a sense of equality. After Mao's death, its use was gradually reduced.

After Mao

After the death of Mao in 1976, Deng Xiaoping became the leader. A new policy of gradually introducing market reforms in the economy began. In a marked change, Deng Xiaoping put forward a slogan—'To get rich is glorious'. Poverty declined. Religion had been banned, but after a new constitution in 1978, religion could be practised again. By the year 2000, China was a major power, with one of the fastest growing economies in the world. Its growth continues up to the present.

> ### MAO'S THOUGHTS—THE LITTLE RED BOOK
>
> Selections from Mao's speeches and writings were put together in a book with a bright red cover. In the West this came to be called 'The Little Red Book'. It was extremely influential in many parts of the world, and led to the growth of Maoism as a branch of Marxism.

Taiwan

Meanwhile, Chiang Kai-shek and the Kuomintang had moved to Taiwan. Initially, their government was recognized in the UN as China. However, the People's Republic of China took its place in 1971 and gradually gained recognition across the world. Taiwan, which calls itself the 'Republic of China', still maintains its independence, though the People's Republic of China considers Taiwan its 23rd province. China has 22 other provinces, five autonomous regions where there are mainly ethnic minorities and four special municipalities. In addition, Hong Kong SAR and Macao SAR became separate administrative regions in 1997 and 1999 respectively.

Tibet

China claims sovereignty over Tibet. However, Tibetans led by the Dalai Lama reject this. The Dalai Lama took refuge in India in 1959. Many Tibetan refugees live in India, with the freedom to practise their own religion. The Tibetans have a government in exile in Dharamsala, India. China claimed that Mongol control made Tibet a part of China from the 13th century onwards. However, from 2008 China has changed its earlier views, and said instead that Tibet had been a part of China 'since human activity began'.

The 14th Dalai Lama

MONGOLIA

In 1650, the Mongol khan of Urga (present Ulaanbaatar) was given the title of 'Living Buddha'. The Living Buddha and the secular aristocracy jointly ruled the country, which was under the Qing dynasty of China. Mongolia declared independence from China in 1911. In 1921, the Mongolian People's Revolutionary Party established a Provisional People's Government. After the last Living Buddha died in 1924, the Mongolian People's Republic was established. This was under the influence of the USSR.

After the decline of the USSR and the withdrawal of Soviet assistance around 1990, Mongolia introduced a new constitution in 1992. A unicameral legislature known as the Great Hural replaced the earlier bodies, and the head of state is an elected president. The country faced economic problems but soon began economic reforms. The Mongolian government encourages theatre, art and music. Though Buddhism was suppressed from 1924 to 1991, more than 100 monasteries have since opened, though even today a number of people remain non-religious.

KOREA

During the Second World War, Korea had been occupied by the Japanese. In 1945, it was divided into two by the US and USSR for military reasons. The aim was to unite the two after removing all Japanese forces, but because of the hostility between the US and USSR, this did not happen. In 1948, South Korea became the Republic of Korea with an elected government and its capital at Seoul. North Korea, under Russian influence, was called the Democratic Republic of Korea. Its capital was at Pyongyang, and it had a communist government. The USA and USSR then withdrew from the region.

North Korea invaded South Korea in June 1950 in an attempt to unify the region. However, the North said it was the South that was the invader. The USA felt that North Korea's aggression was backed by the USSR and was another attempt to extend its control. The USA and 15 other countries, including Britain, Canada, Australia and New Zealand, sent troops to support South Korea. These troops had UN backing, but Russia was not involved in the decision. The troops defeated North Korea and reached the border of China. China now joined in with 3,00,000 troops, pushing the UN forces back to South Korea. It was believed that General Douglas MacArthur of the USA was in favour of using nuclear weapons against China. MacArthur later denied this, but the use of nuclear weapons was authorized by the military chiefs, though they were not used. A negotiated peace seemed possible when the Chinese army suffered losses in 1951. After peace talks, the original border was maintained. Both Koreas suffered as at least four million people were killed.

JAPAN

By the time the Second World War took place, Japan had become a great power. Japan had already invaded China in 1937. During the war, Japanese armies crossed through and conquered most of South East Asia. The Malay Peninsula, the Philippines, the Netherland East Indies (Indonesia), Burma (now Myanmar) and some far away Pacific islands were among the conquests. These conquests were brought together in the Greater East Asia Co-prosperity Sphere. However, Japan did face defeats in the latter part of the war, including naval defeats.

Japan was devastated and destroyed by the atomic bombs dropped in August 1945. Then it was occupied by American and other allied troops till 1952. The country was not allowed to have an army. A new constitution was forced on it in 1947. According to the new constitution, the emperor became a symbolic head, while Japan had an elected Parliament. The prime minister is the head of the government. The constitution also stated that Japan had renounced war forever. There were reforms in the central and provincial administration and in the police force. Land was distributed to tenant farmers.

At first the USA did not try to help Japan's economy. But as the Cold War developed, the USA thought of making Japan a strong ally. Japan had a series of stable governments. Japanese industry grew and Japanese products were much in demand. Though USA influence was resented by many in Japan, it became a prosperous country. While retaining some of its traditions, Japan was modernized.

Economy and industries

Japan's economy had good growth rates from the 1960s to the 80s. From the 1990s there was a decline, with a revival after 2005. Japan was affected by the global crisis of 2008.

Japanese products are popular throughout the world. Its car and consumer electronics industries have had great successes. It is also known for its biomedical research and manufacture of robots. Japan has also developed environment-friendly technology such as hybrid electric vehicles.

Culture

Japanese culture includes indigenous elements with outside influences. In religion, both Shintoism and various types of Buddhism remain popular. Many follow both Shinto and Buddhist practices. Traditional crafts such as ikebana, origami and ukiyo-e are still practised as well as the tea ceremony and traditional dance and theatre, though all these have new elements. Manga, a Japanese comic-book form, is also popular in other parts of the world. Music is traditional, Western and fusion. Modern popular Japanese music, influenced by Western music styles, is known as J-pop. Most Japanese wear Western clothes, with the traditional kimono worn only on special occasions. Japanese films have reached great heights. The film directors Akira Kurosawa and Masaki Kobayashi are renowned all over the world. Among writers, Yasunari Kawabata (1899–1972) and Kenzaburō Ōe (b. 1935) have won Nobel prizes for literature in 1968 and 1994 respectively.

NATURAL DISASTERS

Japan has suffered several earthquakes over the centuries. These are often followed by tsunamis. Among the many earthquakes after 1900, two stand out: the 1923 Great Kanto earthquake, in which over 1,00,000 people died, and the earthquake of 2011.

On 11 March 2011, after a major earthquake, there was a 15 m tsunami. This disabled the power and cooling at three Fukushima Daiichi nuclear reactors. One hundred thousand people had to be evacuated to avoid radiation. The earthquake, which was 130 km offshore from the city of Sendai, had a magnitude of 9 on the Richter scale. The whole country shifted by a few metres to the east. The coastline dropped half a metre. The tsunami that followed flooded 560 sq km and killed 19,000 people. One million buildings were destroyed. The earthquake did not affect the nuclear reactors but the tsunami did. There were hundreds of aftershocks and more earthquakes in April. In the last century there have been eight tsunamis in the region.

Japan tsunami: vehicles washed away in a coastal area of north-eastern Japan

Japan is a member of several international and Asian organizations. It is the only Asian country in the G8, is also a member of ASEAN and APEC and participates in the East Asia Summit.

47

South Asia and Afghanistan

INDIA, PAKISTAN AND BANGLADESH

India, Pakistan and Bangladesh were together known as India up to 1947. India was a British colony. Indian troops were used by Britain in both the First and the Second World Wars.

India's struggle for independence started in the 19th century. Finally, after the Labour government in Britain agreed to India's demand, independence was granted in 1947. But instead of one country, two nations were created—India and Pakistan. Pakistan was to consist of areas that were mainly occupied by Muslims. Though both new nations hoped for peace, independence was accompanied by extreme violence. Around one million people were killed, and 10 million migrated across the western borders, leaving all their possessions behind, in an attempt to reach safety. In addition, the army, police and the entire administrative machinery had to be divided, and this, too, was a complicated problem.

India

In January 1950, India was declared a republic. The country is divided into 29 states and seven union territories, and powers are shared between the central government and the states, though only the central government is responsible for defence, war and peace, foreign policy and some other matters. The central government consists of two houses of Parliament and is headed by a prime minister. The president is the ceremonial head of state. Despite many problems, India has remained a democracy, holding regular elections. It is actually the largest democracy in the world.

Mahatma Gandhi (1869–1948), who led India's freedom movement based on the principles of truth and non-violence, was India's greatest political and spiritual leader. He was assassinated in 1948 by a fanatical Hindu. A great moral force, Gandhi had the ability to bring peace through his presence. Political movements in various parts of the world, including those of Martin Luther King and Nelson Mandela, have been inspired by him.

Mahatma Gandhi

India's first prime minister was Jawaharlal Nehru (1889–1964), who had participated in the freedom movement and was deeply influenced by Mahatma Gandhi. Led by him, the government started a programme of planned development. Nehru was also a leader of the Non-Aligned Movement.

India has had several conflicts with Pakistan, mostly over the northern state of Kashmir. A separatist movement in Kashmir, accompanied by terrorist activities, has intensified since 1989.

India has also faced border problems with China, leading to a war in 1962. One reason for the conflict was India's providing shelter to the Dalai Lama, the leader of Tibet, in 1959. Over

1,00,000 refugees from Tibet gradually reached India. The Tibetan government in exile is located in India.

Apart from external conflicts, India also faces internal armed aggression. Internal conflicts include Maoist movements and other rebellions.

After Independence, India has worked towards resolving its many problems, particularly that of under-development. Economic reforms, introduced after 1990, have improved the economy, but widespread poverty still exists.

Culture

According to the constitution, India is a secular state. Hinduism is the main religion practised, but there are eight others, as well as numerous local cults and beliefs. There are 22 recognized languages, and English is also widely used. Rabindranath Tagore was the first Asian to win the Nobel Prize for literature in 1913. India produces films in all languages, but its Hindi film industry, popularly known as Bollywood, is the second largest in the world.

Pakistan and Bangladesh

Pakistan was created in two parts, East and West, separated by 1600 km of Indian territory. West Pakistan faced riots at the time of Independence. Governments were unstable with numerous coups and dictatorships.

Pakistan lost its territory of East Pakistan in 1971, which became the independent nation of Bangladesh. Pakistan also has several terrorist groups and faces bomb attacks as well as inroads of the Taliban. It currently has an elected government. Despite all this, Pakistan has a rich culture and its writers in English, such as Nadeem Aslam and Daniyal Muinuddin, have gained international fame.

Shaikh Mujibur Rahman became the prime minister of independent Bangladesh in 1972 and president in 1975 but was assassinated later the same year. Following this, Bangladesh faced a series of coups and military regimes but later a democratic government was revived.

SRI LANKA

Sri Lanka, earlier named Ceylon, gained independence from Britain in 1948. Its name was changed to Sri Lanka in 1972. In 1959, Srimavo Bandarnaike became the first woman prime minister in the world after the assassination of her husband, Solomon Bandarnaike.

Srimavo Bandarnaike

The Liberation of Tamil Tigers Eelam (LTTE) was formed in 1976 by Tamils of Indian origin. These were descendants of Tamil labourers sent to the island by the British. The LTTE wanted a separate state and a civil war began. In 2009, the Sri Lanka government gained control of the areas occupied by the LTTE and eliminated their top leaders.

NEPAL AND BHUTAN

These two landlocked mountainous countries to the north have close relationships with India. Hinduism predominates in Nepal and Buddhism in Bhutan.

THE MALDIVES

The Maldives, an island nation in the Indian Ocean, was a British colony that gained independence in 1965.

SAARC

In 1985, the South Asian Association for Regional Cooperation (SAARC) was formed with the seven South Asian countries mentioned above. Afghanistan joined it in 2007.

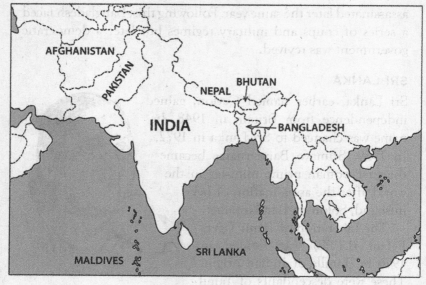

SAARC countries

NON-ALIGNED MOVEMENT (NAM)

The Non-Aligned Movement formally began in a conference at Belgrade in 1961, and intially had 25 members. India, Yugoslavia, Egypt, Guinea and Indonesia were among its founder members. The main aim of NAM was to have friendly relations and cooperation amongest themselves without joining in the Cold War. After the end of the Cold War, NAM focused on economic and other types of cooperation. By 2003, NAM membership had risen to 116 countries.

AFGHANISTAN

Afghanistan, though never directly a part of the USSR, was occupied by Soviet troops from 1979 to 1989. After Soviet withdrawal, there was a civil war in Afghanistan. The Taliban, a fundamentalist Islamic group, began to grow in power. Between 1995 and 1997, the Taliban gained control in Afghanistan.

After the bombing of the World Trade Centre in the United States in September 2001 (see Chapter 43), the USA asked the Taliban to surrender Osama bin Laden to them. When this did not happen, the USA and UK invaded Afghanistan and were later joined by troops of other countries. The Taliban continued guerrilla warfare against the occupying forces and the Afghanistan government. In 2011, Osama bin Laden was killed by forces of the USA in north-west Pakistan. The US aims to withdraw most of its troops from Afghanistan by the end of 2014 but attacks by the Taliban continue.

48

West Asia

PALESTINE AND ISRAEL

Palestine is an ancient region in West Asia with boundaries that varied over time. It was once the homeland of the Hebrews, and also the region where Christianity arose. Islam, too, has holy sites in the region.

Long ago, the Hebrews or Jews lost their original homeland and were scattered in different countries. Jews were persecuted in many European nations and began to look for a new homeland. Meanwhile, Palestine with a mainly Arab population was under the Ottoman Turks. As the Ottoman Turks declined, Arabs in Palestine and neighbouring areas began a revolt against them in 1916. The British, particularly Colonel T. E. Lawrence, known as 'Lawrence of Arabia', helped the Arabs in their revolt. The British promised that Arabs would be allowed to set up independent states after the First World War was over. At the same time, Britain and France agreed to divide the territories between them. Promises to the Arabs were not kept, and Iraq, Transjordan and Palestine thus came under a British mandate in 1922, and Syria and Lebanon under France. (A mandate was a region to be 'looked after' and made ready for self-government.)

Iraq soon gained self-government, followed by full independence in 1932. Transjordan became independent in 1946. But Palestine was a complicated problem. By the Balfour Declaration of 1917, Britain had said that it would support a homeland for Jews in Palestine. Later, to pacify the Arabs, Britain clarified that it did not mean the whole of Palestine would be for Jews. There would be plenty of place for Arabs. Britain hoped the two groups would live together. Many Jews migrated to the region and settled there. Problems began between Jews and Arabs. Meanwhile the Second World War took place. The persecution of Jews during the war added to their desire to find a homeland.

In November 1947, the UN suggested a division of Palestine. In 1948, the British gave up their mandate and left the region.

Israel

In May 1948, David Ben–Gurion, a Jewish leader, declared that a Jewish land known as Israel was now an independent state in the Palestine region. Troops from Egypt, Syria, Iraq, Lebanon and Jordan attacked Israel, but Israel survived and even expanded its territories. One million Palestinian Arabs left the region. More wars took place in 1956, 1967 and 1973, and conflicts continue till today.

David Ben-Gurion became the first prime minister of Israel. By a law passed in 1950, all Jews were entitled to migrate to Israel. More Jews settled in the region. Israel received economic and military aid from the US, and built up a strong army.

For internal development, the kibbutz or commune was

David Ben-Gurion

established, where people lived and worked together. Children were cared for together in a separate children's area. The kibbutz system still exists, but has changed in many ways. Agriculture and industry developed in Israel, and the economy became prosperous though there were periods of high inflation. Israel continues to have an Arab population of around 20 per cent.

SAYED KASHUA (b. 1975)

Sayed Kashua is an Israeli Arab and a well-known author. He writes in Hebrew, runs a TV show and has published three novels, all of which have been translated into English. Born and brought up in Israel, Kashua finally left the country during the Israel-Palestine conflict in July 2014. He said that he was no longer accepted in a country he considered his own. Among his books are *Dancing Arabs* and *Let It Be Morning*, both based on the lives of Arabs in Israel.

Palestine

Arabs living in Palestine could not accept the existence of Israel. In 1964, the Palestinian Liberation Organization (PLO) was founded, bringing together various Palestinian groups including Al Fatah, Al Saiqa and the Popular Front for the Liberation of Palestine. Many professionals, workers and students also joined it. Initially, the PLO aimed to replace Israel with a secular Palestinian state. Palestine made a declaration of independence in 1988. In the same year, the PLO gave up terrorism as a way of achieving its aims. Hamas, a militant Palestinian group was also formed at this time.

In 1994, the Palestinians began self-rule in the Gaza strip and in Jericho on the West Bank.

This followed a historic peace treaty signed between Israel and the PLO in 1993. The Palestine National Authority (PNA)

was formed to administer these territories. The PNA looked after civil matters, while Israel retained control over foreign affairs and some aspects of security. Together with the PLO, the PNA negotiated for further withdrawals from Palestinian territory by Israel. Yasser Arafat, the PLO leader, was president of PNA until his death in 2004.

Yasser Arafat

In 2006, Hamas won the elections to the Legislative Council of the PNA.

Several conflicts have taken place between Hamas and Israel, including from 2008 to 2009 and in 2014.

Over 130 nations have recognized Palestine as an independent nation, though Israel has not granted it recognition. In November 2012, the UN General Assembly gave Palestine the status of a 'non-member observer state'.

IRAN

Iran did not participate in the First World War, though there were battles on Iranian territory for its oil resources. In 1923, Reza Khan, a military commander, took over the government. Ahmad Shah, the last ruler of the Qajar dynasty, was removed. In 1925, Reza Khan became the ruler of Iran and was known as Reza Shah Pahlavi. He modernized the country and provided more rights to women. During the Second World War, the Allies occupied parts of Iran to protect the oilfields from the Axis powers. Reza Shah abdicated, and was succeeded by his son, Muhammad Reza Shah Pahlavi, in 1941. In 1963, a series of social and economic reforms known collectively as the White Revolution was introduced. Iran's prosperity and standard of living rose.

However, there was growing opposition to the Shah's reign in the 1970s. The Shah suppressed all protests. Religious groups were against the modernization and westernization of Iran, while students and intellectuals were against the Shah's secret police, Savak, and his autocratic government. In 1979, an Islamic leader, Ayatollah Ruhollah Khomeini gained control over Iran, which was then declared a republic. Since then Iran has gone through different phases, including a war with Iraq and several general elections. The fifth president, Muhammad Khatami (from 1997 to 2005), introduced liberal reforms, and proposed a 'Dialogue among Civilizations', a theme that was adopted by the UN. Even after his presidency, Khatami promoted discussions on religion and reform and is popular among liberal youth. Hasan Rouhani, another moderate leader, became the president in 2013.

Iran's economy is largely based on oil.

IRAQ

Iraq has major oil resources, a key factor in its modern history. Its Kurdish minority is another aspect and has often created problems in the country. Iraq came under British influence during the Second World War. In 1943, it declared war on the Axis powers. A constitutional monarchy was established in 1953 under King Faisal II and elections were held. However, many were opposed to Iraq's USA connections. In 1958, a republic was proclaimed and in 1963 the secular Baath Party came to power. In 1979, Saddam Hussein of the Baath Party became the president. Saddam Hussein improved the administration and introduced social and economic reforms. However, he followed an aggressive foreign policy.

A war with Iran was fought from 1980 to 1988. Iraq invaded Kuwait in 1990 to 1991, but was defeated by a US-led coalition. In 2003, the US and the UK invaded Iraq, believing that it had dangerous weapons and was a threat to peace. Saddam Hussein was removed from power and later executed in 2006. Resistance to occupying forces led to continuous warfare from 2003. With continuous battles and unrest, the economy of Iraq was severely affected. In 2005, a transitional government was elected. A new government was formed led by Nouri al-Maliki in 2006. The US and other occupying forces withdrew by the end of 2011. A new crisis began

Nouri al-Maliki

during 2013 to 2014 with a war launched by ISIS. Nouri al-Maliki resigned in August 2014.

ISIS, the Islamic State in Iraq and the Levant, also known as IS or ISIL, is a militant Islamic group formed in 2013, which began taking over cities and regions in Syria and Iraq. In 2014, it captured a number of areas, including the Kurdish territory in Iraq, where it massacred and enslaved the Yazidis, a minority group. ISIS aims to lead a global Islamic movement, but has not gained much support from other Islamic groups.

JORDAN, LEBANON AND SYRIA

Jordon, Lebanon and Syria also have a role in West Asian politics and have been involved in conflicts with Israel. Syria and Lebanon were under a French mandate. France granted independence to Syria in 1941, but continued to occupy the country till 1946. Similarly, France granted Lebanon independence in 1926, but remained in occupation till 1946.

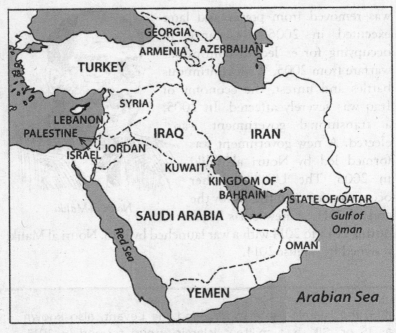

West Asia

THE ARABIAN PENINSULA

Bahrain, Kuwait, Oman, Qatar, Saudi Arabia, United Arab Emirates (UAE) and Yemen are states located on the Arabian Peninsula in south-west Asia, at the junction of Africa and Asia. Along with other states they are part of the Arab League. The Syrian desert to the north of the peninsula includes north-east Jordan, south-east Syria and western Iraq.

Bahrain gained independence from Britain in 1971. Kuwait's foreign policy and defence were controlled by Britain from 1899 to 1961.

The states of the UAE consist of seven emirates, among which are Abu Dhabi, Dubai and Sharjah. These seven were known as the Trucial States of the Persian Gulf as their defence was controlled by Britain through a truce. They gained full control over their states in 1971.

North Yemen gained independence from the Ottomans in 1918, while South Yemen, earlier known as Aden, was under Britain and became independent in 1967. North and South Yemen were finally united in 1990. In Saudi Arabia, the Al Saud dynasty gained importance in the 18th century and gradually occupied most of the peninsula.

Six Arab states joined together in 1981 in the Gulf Cooperation Council. These were Bahrain, Saudi Arabia, the Sultanate of Oman, Kuwait, Qatar and the United Arab Emirates. All six nations have certain features in common. Located in the Persian Gulf, they are hereditary monarchies. Bahrain and Kuwait have elected legislatures and Oman has an elected advisory council. In the UAE a Federal National council is an advisory body, with members elected by a nominated electoral group. With substantial oil and gas reserves, these states have high per capita incomes. Up to the 1930s, the pearl industry and pearl diving was the main economic activity but it declined because of the rise of the cultured pearl industry, particularly in Japan. In all six states, a similar dialect of Arabic is spoken. Most of the peninsula, except for Yemen, is unsuited to agriculture. Grain, coffee and fruits are cultivated on narrow coastal plains and oases, while camel, goats and sheep are widespread. The oil industry rules the six states. Saudi, UAE, Kuwait and Qatar are among the top ten oil and gas exporters in the world.

Construction, financial services and technical institutions have grown around the oil industry. In rural areas there are traditional handicrafts including carpet weaving. Music styles, food and clothes are also similar in these countries. The UAE and Saudi are the wealthiest countries in the region. There are many residents in the region who are non-nationals. This reaches

89 per cent in UAE and 20 per cent in Saudi. There are mainly Sunni Muslims in the area, though there are also Shia minorities, particularly in Yemen, Kuwait and Bahrain. Oman has Muslims of the Ibadi sect.

THE ARAB SPRING

The Arab Spring refers to a series of protests beginning in December 2010 in the Arab world that spread across a number of countries. The Arab Spring affected Tunisia, Libya, Egypt and Yemen, where rulers were removed from power; Bahrain and Syria, where there was civil war; as well as Iraq, Jordan, Kuwait, Morocco, Israel, Sudan, where there were protests. Some protests also took place in Oman and Saudi Arabia, Palestine, and in Africa, in Mauritania, Djibouti, Western Sahara, Uganda and Burkina Faso.

49
South East Asia after 1945

Most of South East Asia had been colonized by Western countries and later occupied by Japan during the Second World War. After the war, these countries gained independence.

MYANMAR

Myanmar (known as Burma till 1989) became part of the British Indian empire, gaining independence in 1948.

U Nu, who, along with U Aung San, had led the nation to freedom, was the main leader from the time of independence to 1962, when his government was overthrown by General Ne Win. Ne Win was deposed in 1988. In the succeeding elections held in 1990, the National League for Democracy (NLD) won but the military refused to hand over power to them.

Aung San Suu Ki

To retain power, the ruling military suppressed the NLD. The NLD leader Aung San Suu Ki, the daughter of U Aung San, was placed under house arrest from 1989 to 1995, 2000 to 2002, and 2003

Aung San Suu ki

to 2010. After her release, she became a member of Parliament through by-elections held in 2012. She has won several awards for her peaceful struggle for democracy, including the Nobel Peace Prize in 1991.

A new approach
U Thein Sein, prime minister from 2007 to 2011, became the president of Myanmar in 2011. He is known for his liberal approach.

Myanmar has a Buddhist culture. Most of the minority Rohingya Muslims have not been granted citizenship and face persecution. Rohingyas are treated as illegal residents and do not have the right to own land, or other rights granted to citizens.

THAILAND
In the 19th century, Thailand lost some territories to France and came under British influence. It was never occupied by a European power. Between 1936 and 1937, the country renegotiated all foreign treaties and became free from foreign influences. During the Second World War Thailand allied with Japan but after the war became a USA ally.

King Bhumibol Adulyej, Rama IX, became the king in 1946. The king only has an advisory role, as Thailand is a constitutional monarchy, and the main power is with the prime minister. From 2005, Thailand has seen many protests and changes in government. In May 2014, the government came under military control.

Culture
Thai culture is a mix of different influences, including Chinese, Myanmarese, Indian and Khmer. Buddhism is the main religion.

LAOS

Laos gained independence from France in 1949, but remained within the French Union.

After independence, the communist Pathet Lao was in conflict with right-wing groups and came to power in 1975, supported by Vietnam. From 1986, more liberal economic policies were introduced. Laos culture is linked with Buddhism and there are numerous Buddhist temples in the country.

The Ho Chi Minh Trail

During the Vietnam War, supplies reached Vietnam along a route through Laos known as the Ho Chi Minh Trail. This route was bombed by the US. (See below for more on this war.)

CAMBODIA

Norodom Sihanouk was the king of Cambodia from 1941 to 1955. However, Cambodia was still under France, and gained independence only in 1953. Sihanouk continued to play a major role in Cambodia. In 1955, he abdicated and placed his father on the throne. Sihanouk instead became prime minister, and in 1960 the head of state. Communist forces known as the Khmer Rouge started a rebellion in 1968 that led to a civil war. Sihanouk was deposed in 1970 by General Lol Nol, who was pro-USA. Meanwhile North Vietnam had set up bases in Cambodia. Sihanouk went to China, and joined with the communist Khmer Rouge.

Pol Pot

Led by Pol Pot, the capital, Phnom Penh, was captured in April 1975 by the Khmer Rouge. Sihanouk again became the head of state but resigned as he had no power and numerous atrocities were committed by the Khmer Rouge. (Cambodia at this time was renamed Kampuchea, and later Democratic Kampuchea.) As prime minister, Pol Pot sought to establish a utopia, a state without money or private property, but in reality unleashed a reign of terror leading to around 1.7 million deaths. Cambodians are believed to have died from execution, starvation, and other difficulties.

In December 1978, Vietnam invaded Cambodia and evicted the Khmer Rouge from the cities. The Vietnamese occupation of Cambodia continued for ten years and was marked by civil war. Conditions improved after 1991.

Norodom Sihanouk becomes king again

A constitutional monarchy was re-established in 1993 with Norodom Sihanouk once again becoming the king. Sihanouk tried to maintain peace between different groups in the government. His son, Norodom Sihamoni, succeeded him as king in 2004. From 2004 to 2008, the economy grew and expanded.

Cambodian culture has Indian and French influences, combined with local traditions.

VIETNAM

France conquered Vietnam by 1883 and it became a part of French Indo-China in 1887. During the Second World War, Indo-China was occupied by the Japanese.

Ho Chih Minh

Ho Chi Minh

Ho Chih Minh (1890–1969), a communist, organized a struggle for independence, forming the League for Vietnamese Independence (Vietminh). In 1945, after the Second World War, Vietnam asserted its independence. The French resisted and an armed struggle began. In 1954, the French forces suffered a major defeat at Dien Bien Phu. However, the USA did not want an independent communist country coming into existence and became involved in the region. According to the agreements under the Geneva Accords of 1954, Vietnam was divided into the Communist North and non-Communist South. In South Vietnam, a civil war started. The communist Vietcong, who had the support of North Vietnam, fought to overthrow the South Vietnamese government. The aim was to unite the country. The United States involvement in supporting South Vietnam lasted for several years. The USA sent troops and used bombs and chemical weapons, killing thousands. The youth, and many others in America turned against this war. Finally USA forces withdrew in 1973.

Unity

In 1975, North Vietnam took over South Vietnam and united the country in 1976. The Vietnamese government is dominated by a single party, the Communist Party of Vietnam or CPV. From 1986, Vietnam introduced economic reforms and has liberalized the economy. The country's exports to the United States increased by 900 per cent from 2001 to 2007. Vietnamese culture includes both Chinese and French influences.

THE PHILIPPINES

The Philippines was granted self-government by the United States in 1935 as a preparation for total independence. Japan occupied the country during the Second World War. After the war it became independent in 1946. It is divided into 80 provinces and 120 chartered cities. The Philippines has faced several coups and separatist movements.

MALAYSIA

The Federation of Malaysia includes 13 states with 11 on the southern half of the Malay Peninsula and two on the island of

Borneo, apart from territories under the federal government. The head of state is elected by the nine hereditary rulers of the Malay state and holds the post for five years.

In 1948, the British territories on the Malay Peninsula joined together to form the Federation of Malaya. It gained independence in 1957 with Tunku Abdul Rahman as the first prime minister. Singapore and the East Malaysian states of Sabah and Sarawak on Borneo joined the federation in 1963, which was then known as Malaysia. The new federation faced several troubles. Singapore left the federation in 1965. There were also ethnic problems and disputes with Indonesia. Despite continuing problems, Prime Minister Mahathir bin Muhammad (1981–2003) succeeded in improving and diversifying the economy. Malaysia's ethnic diversity is reflected in its culture, which has diverse religious festivals, cuisines, dance, music and theatre.

INDONESIA

The Republic of Indonesia consists of a large number of islands of which 6000 are inhabited. Java, Sumatra and Sulawesi are the main islands. Parts of New Guinea and Borneo are included in Indonesia.

Indonesia was under the Netherlands before the Second World War. During this war, the islands came under Japan and with Japan's defeat in 1945, Indonesia declared its independence. This was recognized by the Netherlands only in 1949. Sukarno was the first president of Indonesia from 1945 to 1968 and was replaced by General Suharto. Indonesia faced a number of problems including a wave of killings from 1965 to 1966 of communists and others. Over 5,00,000 are believed to have been killed at this time. These killings took place after an attempted coup, which was blamed on the Indonesian Communist Party, though the evidence regarding their involvement in this is not clear. There are also separatist movements in the country.

In 2004, an earthquake and tsunami off the coast of Sumatra left 2,00,000 dead in Indonesia.

President Sukarno

The country has a mixed economy, with increasing industrialization, exploitation of oil and natural gas and a large service sector. Indonesian culture is a mix of early Hindu and Buddhist influences, Islamic and Arabic, South East Asian, Polynesian, Dutch and Chinese cultures.

BRUNEI

Brunei is located on the island of Borneo. In the late 19th century, Brunei came under Britain but the sultan remained the nominal head. It gained independence in 1984 but had already introduced a written constitution in 1979. Brunei's economy is based on oil and natural gas. Its GDP is among the highest in Asia, and the hereditary sultan, who heads the government, is one of the wealthiest people in the world.

TIMOR

The island of Timor is also located in South East Asia.

In the 19th century, it was divided between the Dutch and the Portuguese. Dutch Timor became part of Indonesia in 1950. Portuguese or East Timor gained independence in 1975, but was conquered by Indonesia in 1975 to 1976.

After a long struggle, East Timor attained independence in 2002 and is known as Timor-Leste.

SINGAPORE

Singapore was under the British, but gained self-government in 1959. It joined the Malaysian Federation in 1963. Two years later it left the federation. It is a tiny, prosperous and independent state, headed by a directly elected president. The state includes one main island and 59 islets.

The Puffin History of the World

50

Africa:
Independent States

In the 20th century, the slave trade had ended but Europeans still continued to exploit Africa in various ways. They ruled through European officers and by nominating and supporting local rulers. While stating that they were 'civilizing' Africa, Europeans on the whole did not try to develop or improve the areas they governed. Land was taken over by Europeans and exploited by governments and merchant companies. Numerous Africans were killed during the years of colonization. As Lothar von Trotha, a German lieutenant-general wrote, 'I wipe out rebellious tribes with streams of blood and streams of money.' Von Trotha commanded German forces in East and West Africa from 1894 to 1905, and was known for his ruthless massacres of Africans.

After the First World War, German territories in Africa were taken over by Britain and France as mandates. After 1920, conditions varied in different parts of Africa. In South Africa Europeans had taken possession of most of the land, establishing farms. In West Africa, particularly in the mandated areas, conditions were better.

Missionaries began to establish some schools but as traditional societies changed, many Africans could only find work as semi-skilled labour. However, some Africans went to the Europe and the USA to study and returned to lead national movements. Islamic leaders also began movements against the Europeans as their rights and traditions had been removed.

The Second World War added to the problems in Africa. Mines and plantations were set up and exploited for meeting the needs of war. Peasants in rural areas could not grow food and moved to towns where they lived in poor conditions. Nationalism began to reach a height in Africa. Africans wanted rights for Africans and an end to white rule and discrimination.

Countries in Africa rapidly gained independence after the Second World War. Though the European powers tried, they were unable to hold on to their territories any longer. Only in South Africa did independence take long to arrive.

A list of the states and their dates of independence are given below.

COUNTRIES AND THEIR DATES OF INDEPENDENCE

Country	Year of independence	Gained independence from
Algeria	1962	France
Angola	1975	Portugal
Benin (earlier Dahomey)	1960	France
Botswana	1966	Britain
Burkina Faso	1960	France
Burundi (earlier Urundi)	1962	Belgium
Cameroon	1960, 1961	France, Britain

The Puffin History of the World

Cape Verde	1975	Portugal
Central African Republic	1960	France
Chad	1960	France
Comoros Islands	Autonomy, 1961; three islands joined to form an independent nation in 1974.	France
Congo, Democratic Republic of (earlier Belgian Congo); named Zaire from 1971 to 1997	1960	Belgium
Congo, Republic of (Brazzaville)	1960	France
Cote d'Ivoire	1960	France
Djibouti (earlier French territory of Afars and Issas)	1977	France
Egypt	1952	Britain
Equatorial Guinea	1968	Spain
Eritrea	1993	Ethiopia (earlier under Britain)
Ethiopia	1941	Under Italy 1936–41, otherwise free from colonial rule
Gabon	1960	France
Gambia, The	1965	Britain
Ghana (earlier Gold Coast)	1957	Britain
Guinea	1958	France
Guinea-Bissau	1974	Portugal
Kenya	1963	Britain

Lesotho (earlier Basutoland)	1966	Britain
Liberia (earlier Monrovia)	1847	The US established as a state for freed slaves in 1922
Libya	1951	Britain and France (earlier under Italy)
Madagascar	1975	France
Malawi (earlier Nyasaland)	1964	Britain
Mali	1960	France
Mauritania	1960	France
Mauritius	1968	Britain
Morocco	1956	Spain and France
Mozambique	1975	Portugal
Namibia	1990	South Africa
Niger	1960	France
Nigeria	1960	Britain
Rwanda	1962	Belgium
Saharawi or Saharan Arab Democratic Republic	Independence declared and recognized by more than 70 nations by 1982	Morocco
San Tope and Princepe	1975	Portugal
Senegal	1960	France
Seychelles	1976	Britain
Sierra Leone	1961	Britain
Somalia	1960 (former British Somaliland separates in 1991)	Britain and Italy
South Africa	1931	Britain
South Sudan	2011	Sudan
Sudan	1956	Britain and Egypt
Swaziland	1968	Britain

Tanzania	1961 Tanganyika 1963 Zanzibar (join together as Tanzania in 1964)	Britain
Togo	1960	France
Tunisia	1956	France
Uganda	1962	Britain
Zambia (earlier North Rhodesia)	1964	Britain
Zimbabwe (earlier South Rhodesia)	1980	From white-minority government that became independent from Britain in 1965

As these new countries gained independence, they faced a number of problems. They had to accept boundaries that were not based on communities or historical relationships. New systems of government had to be created and different groups of people had to be united.

Below we look at some aspects of the history of the independent nations of Africa. Each country began with great hopes for the future. There were some remarkable early leaders. However, by around 1965 there was a realization that bringing about a transformation was not easy. To try to solve their problems African leaders began to meet and form organizations and groups. They stayed away from the politics of the Cold War. Some joined the Non-Aligned Movement and associated with other former colonies in Asia. Many countries tried to find new forms of government. Some turned to socialism and others struggled under military dictatorships. Civil wars became common. By the 1980s, several countries were troubled with internal disturbances and economic difficulties.

But there were positive aspects too. Some states remained stable and maintained functioning democracies. Discoveries of oil in many nations helped to boost their economies. Unique wildlife and extensive national parks brought in tourists from all over the world. There were new trends in literature, music, cinema, art and sports. African intellectuals and historians began to understand and analyse their own pasts. Many of the problems the new countries faced were the result of long colonial rule, oppression and exploitation. Now at least Africa was for Africans, and each country gradually worked at resolving its problems.

It is not possible to look at the history of each of the independent countries, but below we look at some of the countries along with general trends.

NORTH AFRICA

Egypt occupies north-east Africa and the Sinai Peninsula and controls the Suez Canal. Known for its great ancient civilization, Egypt remains one of the most important African nations because of its strategic position.

Egypt gained independence from Britain in 1922, but was fully independent only from 1952, after removing all British influence. A new republic was formed in 1953.

Anwar al Sadat

Gamal Abdul Nasser was the president from 1956 to 1970. Nasser nationalized the Suez Canal and worked for the unity of Arab nations. He was a leader of the Non-Aligned Movement and a respected figure in the world. Nasser also promoted Arab unity. Egypt faced several wars including the 1967 war with Israel, during which Israel occupied the Sinai Peninsula. After Nasser's death, the vice president, Anwar al

Sadaat became the president. After the Yom Kippur War with Israel in 1973, Sadaat signed a peace agreement in 1979, which angered other Arab nations. He was assassinated in 1981. Hosni Mubarak became the next president and remained in power up to 2011, being re-elected several times. Meanwhile, militant Islam was growing in Egypt. In February 2011, Mubarak gave up the presidency after a series of anti-government protests. He was later arrested. The thousands of people gathering at Tahrir Square in Cairo became the symbol of similar protests in other parts of the world.

After Mubarak, the government came under the Supreme Council of the Armed Forces. Mohammad Morsi of the Muslim Brotherhood became the president in June 2012. When he began to rule like a dictator, a new series of protests started and Morsi was removed in a military coup. Abdel Fattah el-Sisi, the former head of the armed forces, was elected as the next president in May 2014.

Algeria's independence was achieved after a long and fierce struggle led by the FLN (Front de Liberation Nationale). Ahmad Ben Bella was the first president in 1962, but was replaced by Houari Boumediene in 1965. It became a socialist state in 1976. The Islamic Salvation Front began protests against the government in 1991 and a civil war followed. Abdelaziz Bouteflika was elected president in 1999, and re-elected twice. He brought a measure of stability to the country.

Libya used to be a constitutional monarchy but in 1969 the king, Idris I, was overthrown and a republic established, led by Muammar Al Gaddafi. Relations with the United States were poor but Muammar Gaddafi remained in

Muammar al Gaddafi

power until the street protests that formed part of the 'Arab Spring' of 2011. After several battles, the anti-Gaddafi forces captured power, and Gaddafi was killed. Libya had fresh violence and struggles in 2014.

Both Algeria and Libya have rich oil reserves.

Tunisia became a republic in 1957. In 1987, Zine El Abidine Ben Ali became the president of Tunisia, and was re-elected several times. He remained in power till 2011 when street demonstrations and protests led to his resignation. This has been called the Jasmine Revolution. Later, a new constituent assembly was elected.

SAHARAWI REPUBLIC

The region of western Sahara, previously under Spain, was occupied by Morocco and Mauritania after the departure of Spain in 1976. The Polisario Front, fighting for independence, declared a government in exile, based in Algeria. Mauritania withdrew from the region in 1979, when the whole area was occupied by Morocco. The region is known as the Saharawi (or Saharan) Arab Democratic Republic. It has been recognized by a number of states, though not by the UN. It is also part of the African Union.

In 1989, the states of Morocco, Algeria, Tunisia, Libya and Mauritania came together in the Arab Maghreb Union, aiming towards economic integration.

The Puffin History of the World

51
Africa: Other Independent States

EAST AFRICA

Among the countries of East Africa, **Sudan** has good mineral resources including petroleum, natural gas, gold and silver. However, following independence it had unstable governments and civil wars. Conflicts in the western region of Darfur have also led to deaths of 2,00,000–4,00,000 people. In addition there were conflicts between North and South Sudan, which led to more than two million dead and over four million displaced people. Finally South Sudan became independent in 2011. A civil war started in 2013.

Ethiopia was almost free from colonial rule except from 1936 to 1941.

Haile Selassie was emperor of Ethiopia from 1930 to 1936 and again from 1942 to 1974, when he was removed from power by a military coup. Selassie had provided a new constitution and introduced land reforms,

Haile Selassi

but corruption within the government and prolonged drought in the country led to his overthrow. Ethiopia then came under the Derg, a Marxist group. Derg or Dergue, meaning a council or committee, is the short form for the council that ruled Ethiopia from 1975 to 1987. From 1984 to 1985, a famine occurred in the country leaving more than a million dead.

Somalia too has experienced a number of civil wars. Somaliland and Puntland are two regions within it that have asserted their independence. Local conflicts contributed to the rise of pirates in Somalia who often capture ships to acquire wealth. Recent anti-piracy measures have led to a decline in their activity.

THE RASTAFARIANS

The Rastafarians are a group of religious and political sects that originated in Jamaica in the 1930s. In the 1950s, Rastafarianism spread to North America and Europe and to some of the indigenous groups of Australia and New Zealand. The name comes from Ras Tafari, the original name of the emperor Haile Selassie. He was the symbol of black liberation, as he was the only African king who had managed to resist European powers. The aim of the Rastafarians was originally to resist the colonization by whites. Later numerous different sects developed.

Kenya is one of the relatively stable states in the region.

Jomo Kenyatta, a leader in the struggle for independence, was the first prime minister and then the president of Kenya, and provided it with a good administrative foundation. In 1961, Julius Nyerere became the first president after independence in **Tanganyika**, and attempted to bring in development. A teacher and educationist, Nyerere is known as 'the father of the nation'. His ideas still inspire the culture of **Tanzania**.

472   The Puffin History of the World

Tanzania is the largest producer of sisal and cloves (from Zanzibar) in the world. Diamonds, gold, natural gas and salt are among other minerals exploited.

In **Uganda,** Milton Obote was the first prime minister. In 1966, under a republican constitution he became the president. The army commander Idi Amin seized power in 1971 and ruled as a dictator till 1978. Between 1,00,000 and 3,00,000 Ugandans are believed to have been killed during Idi Amin's presidency. Conditions began to improve in 1986, when Yoweri Mueveni took over the government, but Uganda still faces several problems. The 'Arab Spring' protests of 2011 to 2012 also spread to Uganda.

Burundi and **Rwanda** were involved in civil wars. In 1994, thousands of Tutsis, an ethnic group, were killed in Rwanda. In 2005, there was a peaceful general election in Burundi after a new constitution was introduced.

These countries started joining together in regional organizations. In 2001, Tanzania, Uganda and Kenya set up a regional parliament and a court of justice. In 2005, they joined together in a customs union. In 2009, Rwanda and Burundi joined the East African Community Customs Union.

In 2004, the Kenyan ecologist Wangari Maathai won, the Nobel Peace Prize for her contribution to sustainable development, democracy and peace.

WEST AND WEST-CENTRAL AFRICA

Among these countries **Cape Verde** and **Senegal** have been relatively stable democracies. Senegal's first president from 1960 to 1981, Leopold Sedar Senghor, was a poet and philosopher. Coups and civil wars have taken place in most of the other countries. **Sierra Leone** faced a civil war from 1991 to 2002 that resulted in thousands of deaths and the displacement of over two million people.

In **Ghana**, Kwama Nkrumah was the first prime minister and later the president. He was removed after a coup in 1966. More coups followed but there was some stability after 2000.

Nigeria has a number of different ethnic groups, including the Yoruba, Igbo, Hausa and Fulani. Military rule was common after 1966, as well as conflicts between different groups. Between 1967 and 1970 the Igbo created a separate republic, Biafra, but this led to a civil war. More than one million Biafrans died. Ethnic conflicts continued even after that.

Oil finds in Nigeria have improved the economy.

CENTRAL AFRICA

In this region, **Cameroon** and **Gabon** are relatively peaceful. A number of these nations have rich resources of oil.

After independence in 1960, the **Central African Republic (CAR)** had an unstable government and went through numerous coups. From 1976 to 1979, it was known as the Central African Empire, under the autocratic rule of Jean Bedel Bokassa, who called himself the emperor, and held power from 1965.

Patrice Lumumba was a tragic figure of the **Democratic Republic of Congo**. He became the prime minister after independence from Belgium in 1960. Almost immediately, Katanga province, which had good mineral resources, tried to set up a separate state. Katanga was helped by Belgian troops, and Lumumba was arrested and later executed. Later sources suggest that both Belgium and the United States wanted him killed. In fact in 2002 the Belgian government apologized for the 'moral responsibility' it had for his death. Lumumba is regarded as a national hero and martyr, both in the Congo and in several other parts of the world.

SOUTHERN AFRICA

The region of southern Africa includes the countries of Angola, Botswana, Lesotho, Malawi, Mozambique, Namibia, South Africa, Swaziland, Zambia and Zimbabwe. To the east, in the Indian Ocean, are the islands of Comoros and Madagascar. Further east are Mauritius, Reunion islands and Seychelles.

After the Anglo-Boer War of 1899 to 1902, the British were the main power in southern Africa, except in Angola and Mozambique under Portuguese control. In 1910, the Union of South Africa was formed as a dominion under Britain. To the north were Northern Rhodesia, Southern Rhodesia, and Nyasaland, also under British rule. Though South Africa wanted to incorporate the three landlocked British territories of Basutoland (Lesotho) Bechuanaland (Botswana) and Swaziland, it was not able to, but they remained dependent on South Africa for trade and labour. However, South Africa conquered the colony of South West Africa (now Namibia) from the Germans during the First World War.

In general, white settlers were determined to retain political and economic control in the region, despite conflicting interests among different white groups. The 20th century saw the rise of new classes, including an African middle class and working class. Traditional African royalty and aristocracy also had a role in projecting demands and grievances. Nevertheless, white settlers managed to retain their dominance and apartheid affected all levels of life.

After the Second World War there were pressures to decolonize southern Africa. Those under direct British rule achieved independence relatively peacefully. These became Lesotho, Botswana, Swaziland, Zambia and Malawi. Southern Rhodesia declared independence from Britain and came to be known as Rhodesia after 1965. The white minority government here was led by Ian Smith. A long struggle was launched by Africans under the leadership of Robert Mugabe and Joshua Nkomo.

Finally Rhodesia attained independence as Zimbabwe in 1980. After another long struggle Namibia gained independence from South Africa in 1990.

In South Africa there was a struggle for equality. After 1948, a strict policy of apartheid was followed. Apartheid literally means 'separateness'. Apartheid meant blacks and whites were separated, both politically and socially. They could not live in the same areas. There was white dominance. The Bantu Self-government Act of 1951 attempted to move blacks into separate 'homelands'. In 1961, South Africa became a republic, but apartheid continued. Though there was some reform of these policies in the 1980s, blacks were still discriminated against.

MANNENBERG: A SONG OF FREEDOM

In 1974, a composition of Abdullah Ibrahim (earlier known as Dollar Brand), entitled *Mannenberg*, was released in an album in Cape Town. It became an instant success. *Mannenberg* combined South African musical forms with American jazz-rock fusion. In the 1980s, the song became the anthem of the struggle against apartheid. It was sung and played at anti-apartheid rallies across South Africa.

Nelson Mandela

Nelson Mandela of the African National Congress was the leader of the movement that sought to end discrimination. He was in prison for 27 years. Finally he was freed in 1990 after Frederik Willem de Klerk became the president. The first elections in which blacks were allowed to vote were held in 1994. Nelson Mandela became president

Nelson Mandela

from 1994 to 1999. He and Klerk jointly won the Nobel Peace Prize in 1993.

> Angola and Mozambique attained independence from Portugal after considerable struggle. Marxist governments followed.

The South African region has rich mineral deposits, including diamonds, platinum, gold and uranium.

AFRICAN UNION

Within Africa there are a number of organizations aiming for both political and economic unity and cooperation. The African Union, previously the Organization of African Unity, was founded in 1963, and now has 54 members, including almost all the states of Africa. There are several other regional organizations.

CULTURE

After independence, culture in African countries has flourished. The continent has more than 2000 languages. Africans also write in English, French and other European languages. Literature from Africa reflects the problems, conflicts, dreams and desires of people of the new nations.

From Egypt Naguib Mahfouz (1911–2006), who wrote in Arabic, won the Nobel Prize for literature in 1988. Nawal El Saadawi (b. 1931) and Alifa Rifaat (1930–96) are among well-known women writers of Egypt. Algeria has a rich literature in both Arabic and French. Shaaban Robert (1902–62), a Tanzanian poet and author, wrote in Swahili. Nigeria has produced many good writers. Chinua Achebe (b. 1930) of Nigeria writes in English. Of his many books, his African trilogy, *Things fall Apart*, *No Longer at Ease* and *Arrow of God*, deals with Igbo society and conflicts with Western ideas. Wole Soyinka (b. 1934) won the Nobel Prize for literature in 1986. He writes plays, poetry and novels. He was also involved in Nigerian politics, and has translated novels from Yoruba. Chimamanda Ngoza Adichie (b. 1977) has written the brilliant novel *Half of a Yellow Sun*, depicting the war in Biafra. It has also been made into a movie. These are just a few of the many talented writers in contemporary Africa.

Numerous films, too, are produced across Africa. Egypt produces over a hundred films every year. Tunisia is known for different kinds of films and has been hosting the Carthage Film Festival from 1966. Ousmane Sembene (1923–2007) from Senegal, a film-maker, poet and novelist, is considered the father of Black African Cinema.

Burkina Faso hosts the Panafrican Film and Television Festival of Ougadougou (FESPACO) every two years, considered the most important film festival in Africa.

Africa has innumerable different kinds of music. There is fusion music, pop, rock, jazz, and other types. Traditional African music with new forms is still popular.

THE MBIRA

The mbira is a popular melodic instrument used in traditional and other music. Many different versions of the mbira exist, with various local names. The smallest in the Kalahari has six notes, while those in Zimbabwe use up to 33 notes. The mbira has metal strips or 'tongues' that are depressed and released to sound the notes.

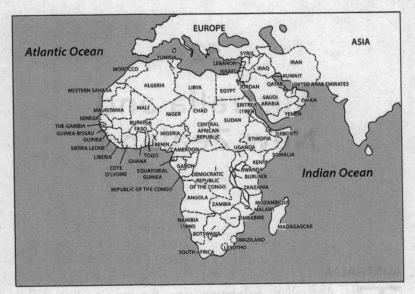

Africa: Independent nations

52

Australia and New Zealand

AUSTRALIA

The Australian federation was formed in 1901. The federation now consists of six states and two territories. The states are: New South Wales, Queensland, South Australia, Victoria, Tasmania and Western Australia. The territories consist of the Australian Capital Territory, and Northern Territory (created from South Australia in 1911). Indigenous Australians form about 32 per cent of the population of the Northern Territories.

Australia also has some islands including Lord Howe (politically part of New South Wales) and Macquarie islands (politically part of Tasmania), and several others.

In 1911, Canberra became the capital of Australia.

Though Australia had been united in 1901, a sense of unity emerged gradually.

An Australian identity began to be formed during the First World War, when 3,30,000 Australians joined the war. Out of these, 60,000 died. The Australian and New Zealand Army corps (ANZAC) fought together at Gallipoli in 1915 and suffered great losses. In memory of this, Anzac Day, 25 April every year, is a national holiday in both Australia and New Zealand.

Australian industries increased during the war, but were affected by the Great Depression.

Australia participated in the Second World War on the side of Britain. Heavy industries developed during the war, and after.

Australia's head of state is the British monarch, represented by a governor-general, while the head of government is the prime minister. There is a bicameral legislature. The main political parties are the Australian Labour Party, the Liberal Party, the National Party of Australia and the Australian Democratic Party.

After the Second World War Australia became a member of the United Nations, and signed a pact of mutual assistance with USA and New Zealand (ANZUS).

The population of the country gradually increased, initially with more immigration from Europe. New universities and educational institutions were established.

Illustration from a poster commemorating Anzac Day

Robert Menzies of the Liberal Party, prime minister from 1949 to 1966, brought in many changes. Australia had been only for whites, but now Asians were allowed to come to Australia to study, and gradually were permitted to settle there. The 'whites only' policy was given up, though it was officially removed only in 1973.

Papua New Guinea, which was under Australian control, gained independence in 1979.

The Australia Act of 1986 ended British influence on legislation in Australia.

In 1999, a referendum was held on making Australia a republic, but the vote was in favour of retaining the British monarch as the head.

By the 21st century Australia was a part of several world and regional organizations. The country was industrially advanced and had achieved a high standard of living.

Rights and reforms for indigenous people

The indigenous people (aborigines) were gradually granted more rights. In 1967, they received the right to vote and full citizenship. In 1976, the Aboriginal Land Rights Act was passed in the Northern Territories.

However, there were some setbacks. In 1971, in the Gove Land Rights Case, Justice Blackburn passed a ruling that before British occupation, Australia was terra nullis (unoccupied land), and hence there were no native land titles possible. This judgement was finally overturned in the Mabo Case in 1992, in which the High Court of Australia said that the concept of terra nullis was invalid. In 1993, the Native Title Act was passed to grant land rights to aborigines in Australia.

In 1999, the Australian Parliament passed a motion of 'reconciliation' with aborigines. National Reconciliation Week was held in 2000 and as part of this 2,50,000 people participated in the People's Walk for Reconciliation across Sydney Harbour Bridge in May.

In 2008, the prime minister, Kevin Rudd finally apologized to the 'Stolen Generations'. This was a term for the children taken away from their parents from 1910 to 1970 and placed in white families or orphanages. Such displacement had a devastating effect on the children.

Culture

A unique Australian culture gradually developed. There are numerous art galleries, centres for performing arts, libraries and museums. Art, literature and music have two broad themes, those of the indigenous population, and of the later settlers.

Patrick White (1912–90) is one of the best-known Australian authors. He was the first Australian to win the Nobel Prize for literature in 1973. *Riders in the Chariot* and *The Eye of the Storm* are among his most famous books. Aboriginal oral literature

CHILDREN'S BOOKS

Children's books are numerous in Australia, including picture books and multicultural books. One of the earliest entertaining novels for children is called *Seven Little Australians* (1894), written by Ellen Turner. Norman Lindsay's *The Magic Pudding* (1918), May Gibbs's *Snugglepot and Cuddlepie* (1918) and Dorothy Wall's *Blinky Bill* (1933) about a koala bear are among early books that are still favourites.

Later books have numerous different themes. Oodegeroo Noonuccai also wrote children's books, including *Stradbroke Dreamtime* (1972), and others from an indigenous viewpoint.

was very ancient, but began to be written down and recorded. David Unaipon (1872–1967) is among aboriginal authors, who wrote the *Legendary Tales of the Aborigines*. Oodegeroo Noonuccai (1920–93) is considered the first modern aborigine poet. Her book of poems, *We Are Going*, was published in 1964.

Among the many musicians, John Antill (1904–86) was a well-known composer whose ballet *Corroboree* is considered a landmark in Australian music. In 1962, the National Australian Ballet Company was founded in Melbourne. In 1958, the Australian Commonwealth Film Unit was established.

George Russel Drysdale (1912–81) was a noted Australian painter and photographer.

Peter Singer is an Australian philosopher known throughout the world.

Errol Flynn (1909–59) from Tasmania became a famous Hollywood actor.

> Australia has a number of unique plants, birds and animals. Among the animals are marsupials, which include the koala and the kangaroo.

NEW ZEALAND

New Zealand is a parliamentary democracy. The British monarch is the head of state, represented in New Zealand by a governor general, while the prime minister heads the government. The legislature is unicameral. New Zealand does not have a written constitution.

In 1907, New Zealand officially became a dominion of Britain.

Between 1891 and 1912, liberal governments, supported by Labour parties, were in power. They introduced land reforms and social welfare systems. Like Australia, New Zealand also participated in the First World War and was inspired by a sense of nationalism, though it lost 18,000 men. In 1935, after the world war and the Great Depression, the Labour Party came to power, nationalizing some industries and organizing a welfare state. New Zealand also joined in the Second World War.

Following the world wars, New Zealand had faced increased demands from Maoris for more rights and the return of their land. Finally in 1995 there was an agreement in New Zealand to pay compensation and return land illegally seized in the 1860s to the Maoris.

Privatization began in the 1990s leading to improvement in the economy.

Culture

New Zealand has libraries, museums and orchestras. Maori culture is based on oral tradition and song, but Maori writers are now part of mainstream literature. Keri Hulme, a Maori, won the Booker prize and the Pegasus Prize for Maori literature in 1985 for her novel, *The Bone People* (1983). Janet Frame (1924–2004) is one of the greatest writers of New Zealand.

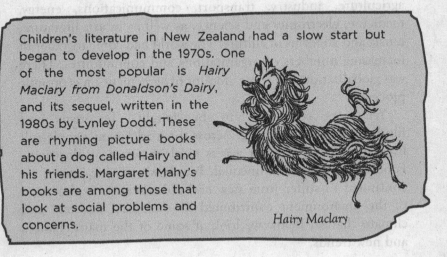

Children's literature in New Zealand had a slow start but began to develop in the 1970s. One of the most popular is *Hairy Maclary from Donaldson's Dairy*, and its sequel, written in the 1980s by Lynley Dodd. These are rhyming picture books about a dog called Hairy and his friends. Margaret Mahy's books are among those that look at social problems and concerns.

Hairy Maclary

53
The Past and the Future

In the year 2014 there were commemorations and memories of the First World War that had taken place one hundred years ago.

Much had changed in these hundred years.

There were developments in every sphere of life, including agriculture, industry, transport, communications, energy, medicine, electronics and science, as well as in art, literature, music and all forms of culture. The world had come together in increasing numbers of organizations and communities. There was globalization and some amount of agreement on economic processes.

Yet wars continued to be fought. Terrorism and fundamentalism was rising. Across the world many people still lived in poverty, without access to clean water or electricity. Food distribution was unequal. People were living longer, yet continued to suffer from new and old diseases. Exploitation of the environment contributed to ecological disasters and climate change. Below we look at some of the main changes and new trends.

Fundamentalism is a term that indicates a return to the basic or fundamental aspects of religion. It actually leads to very rigid views and rules of life. Fundamentalists are against new ways of thinking, modernization and reform. Islamic fundamentalists are against education for women. There are fundamentalists in other religions too.

AGRICULTURE AND FOOD

In agriculture, there was initially more intensive use of machinery along with chemical fertilizers. Genetically modified (GM) crops, and many other innovations increased productivity. There are also new techniques in animal husbandry. At the same time there is a move to return to a more natural world, with organic farming and natural conditions for farm animals. In food there is a trend towards fad diets such as the paleo diet, as well as a move towards vegetarianism and veganism.

PRODUCTION AND THE WORKFORCE

In production, the Ford system (Fordism) first introduced by Henry Ford (1863–1947), an American industrialist, had led to the breakup of the manufacturing process into small units. This system, followed for a long time, and used in different areas of manufacturing, considerably increased productivity, but began changing with a demand for variations. A new creativity was required, and more people became involved in industrial design.

In factories, the workers became more aware of their rights, leading to conflicts with the employers or owners. Service industries increased, employing over half of the working population in industrialized countries. Some companies have introduced flexible timings, as well as learning and entertainment opportunities.

With increased connectivity and videoconferencing, working from home has become possible in various sectors.

ELECTRONICS

Innovations and inventions in the electronic industry made new types of goods available to consumers. There were continuous improvements in televisions, and other household items such as washing machines. In communications, the Internet, computers, laptops, tablets and smartphones change and improve every day. Email, instant messaging, apps of all kinds and videoconferencing are used by millions. The phenomenal growth can be seen in some examples. In 1970, there were about 50,000 computers in the world. These were rather slow and clumsy compared with those of today. By 2005, numbers had risen to over one billion personal computers in the world. As for television, from a slow start, by 2010, there were more than 1.6 billion television sets in use across the world.

Some key dates

Development of the microchip: 1958

The microchip has revolutionized computers, phones and other items as huge amounts of data can be stored on a tiny chip.

World Wide Web: opened for public use in 1991

Internet use in 1993: 14 million people

Internet use in 2005: over one billion

Internet use in 2010: over 2 billion

Internet use in 2014: 3 billion (estimated)

(Source: International Telecommunication Union)

First cellular phone: 1978

According to estimates, by the end of 2014, there will be 7.3 billion cell phones in the world, more than the world population.

Computerization has affected many sectors of the economy

such as booking rail and air tickets, banking transactions and online shopping.

PLASTICS AND CHEMICALS
Major technical innovations have taken place in the field of plastics and man-made fibres.

The chemical industry, along with medical research, has brought in a new range of pharmaceutical products.

GENETIC ENGINEERING
In the 1990s, there were the first successes in genetic engineering. In molecular biology, Francis Crick and James Watson's discovery of the double-helix structure of DNA in 1953 transformed the science of genetics. After several attempts, the first animal, the sheep Dolly, was cloned in 1996. In 2000, the first draft mapping of the entire human genome was completed. In genetics, a human geneology project has begun to trace the descent of human beings.

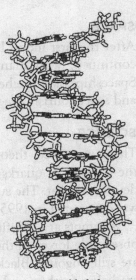

Double helix

TRANSPORT
There have been revolutionary changes in transport. In the 1950s, propeller aircraft flew at speeds of 300–400 mph; by 1976, supersonic aircraft had speeds of more than 1450 mph, though average commercial aircraft speeds are lower.

Transport networks have extended across high mountains and through tunnels made under the sea, such as those connecting Japanese islands or the channel tunnel linking Britain with the continent.

ENERGY

Energy sources include nuclear power, natural gas and geothermic energy, as well as coal, oil and hydro power. Renewable energy includes solar and wind power, the use of biogas, and energy created from a variety of materials including garbage. Total world energy consumption is steadily rising. In 1990 total energy use in terawatt-hours was 1,02,569, which in 2008 had risen to 1,43,851.

SPACE

After the first moon landing in 1969, the exploration of space continued, with manned spaceships and surveys of planets. Spaceships have reached and explored Mars. Private space flights and space tourism are taking place with increasing frequency.

SCIENCE

There were new theories of the structure of the atom, with the concept of quarks being put forward in 1963, and further developed later. The subatomic particle known as the top quark was discovered in 1995.

Attempts at a 'unified field theory' that would explain all the observable forces in the universe, including the force of gravity, are still ongoing. Black holes, exploding stars and dark matter are being further explored. Research in science continues and new studies by astrophysicists confirmed the age of the universe as 13.7 billion years.

GLOBALIZATION

Globalization is a reality today. It includes increased connectivity and ecological, cultural and economic interdependence across the world. The reduction in forests, wildlife, and mineral and other resources, along with air and water pollution affect all countries. The migration of people, as well as connectivity through new media provide knowledge about people, places and events in different parts of the world. The global economy forms a major part of globalization. The World Bank, the International Monetary fund and the World Trade Organization are among the most important international economic organizations. Foreign exchange and capital markets are linked in the world. There are also huge companies and corporations that operate in many countries. Even in 1929, a financial crisis in one country (the Depression of the USA) affected other parts of the world. The latest financial crisis took place in 2008.

2008—THE WORLD FINANCIAL CRISIS

This financial crisis began in USA and spread across the world. It was the third such crisis since the Second World War, and the worst since 1929–30. In the USA, the Stock Market, investment banking industry, insurance sector, mortgage lenders and some commercial banks suffered. The crisis began in the housing market, when mortgage holders were unable to pay back their loans.

Britain, France, Germany, Switzerland, the Benelux countries were among those affected. Banks were supported by government funds, or managed to raise money elsewhere. Greece, Hungary, Latvia and Iceland faced more serious problems. In Asia, Japan and China were among the countries affected. Across the world there was a fall in production and increasing unemployment. The situation stabilized by the middle of 2009, though some negative effects continued. Books were written, and films produced based on this crisis. The documentary *Inside Job* received an Academy Award in 2010.

International organizations are a part of globalization. Apart from the United Nations and world economic organizations there are several others that we have already mentioned, such as the European Union (see Chapter 41) and various regional organizations. G8, a group of eight economically advanced countries, and G77, a group of developing countries, are among the other important organizations.

SOCIAL MEDIA

Social media is a huge part of globalization. There are innumerable websites where people can share their ideas, photographs and videos: YouTube for uploading videos, Flickr for photographs, blogs for writing about anything under the sun, Facebook for finding friends and meeting people, and Twitter, a microblogging site are among the most popular. By 2008, Facebook had 100 million users, and by July 2014 the number reached 1.32 billion. Twitter has 271 million active monthly users. There are also instant messaging sites and apps (applications) such as Whatsapp. Virtual worlds and online games are another part of social media. A popular virtual world is Second Life, where users can create and live an imaginary life. Second Life has approximately one million users in 2014.

Second Life: a virtual state fair

The use of social media has also led to new types of currency. Among the most popular is Bitcoin, an online currency created through software. Bitcoins can be bought and traded. In August 2014, over 13 million bitcoins existed.

MUSIC

Music is also globalized. Among the most popular forms of music are Hip-hop, Urban Pop and R&B (Rhythm and Blues) also known as Contemporary Urban, along with Rock, Pop and Ethnic music, particularly Reggae. Though each country has its own unique forms, these trends have affected music worldwide. Electronic instruments and sounds are often used today in music composition.

POPULATION GROWTH AND CLIMATE CHANGE

Estimates are that by 2030 world population will reach 10 billion, five times that of 1950. This would lead to a further drain on the world's resources, including minerals, energy and food and water sources. Climate change and global warming are also affecting the world.

HUMAN RIGHTS

A world concern is to extend human rights to people everywhere. Human rights are usually granted by the state, but vary in different areas. Generally they include the rights to certain freedoms and to the rule of law. Equality, non-discrimination based on religion, colour, country of origin, or gender are some of the rights. The rights of children, of mentally and physically challenged, and of gays are guaranteed in some countries. Civil rights such as freedom of speech generally exist within democracies. The right to health care and care in old age are rights available primarily in developed countries. Torture is a moral issue that confronts the world. Whether its practice can ever be justified or rationalized, legally or otherwise, is an issue that is being debated.

OTHER RIGHTS AND CONCERNS

The future of democracy, and of the right of countries to decide on their internal issues without interference from other countries are among other concerns. Proponents for animal rights are also growing across the world. In his book *Animal Liberation* (1975), the Australian philosopher Peter Singer (b. 1946) says that the issue is related to human growth and ethics. He states that human domination of animals is indefensible.

Peter Singer

THE FUTURE

What does the future hold? No one really knows. In August 2014, as we end this survey of the world's history, wars were taking place in Syria, Libya, Iraq, the Ukraine and Israel-Palestine. There were several other local conflicts too. The world is affected by dwindling resources, ecological and other disasters, and climate change. Terrorism is growing and large states have broken up into smaller ones.

At the same time many organizations and people continue to work for peace and for a better world. New inventions continue to be made in medicine, technology and other fields; astronomers reach far beyond the earth and there are new discoveries regarding outer space. The quest for knowledge never ceases.

 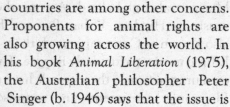 The Puffin History of the World

Index

European Union (European
  Community), 389-90, 398, 400
evolution, theory of, 244, 427

Facebook, 492
fairy tales and children's literature,
  Europe (1800-914), 247-48
famine in Ireland, 261, 264
Fantasy and Invention, 245
Farghana, 91, 102, 104
Faroe Islands, 35, 378
Farraday, William, 241
Farrukhsiyar, 108
fascism, 349
Fasilidas (Basilides), king of Ethiopia
  (ruled 1632-67), 168
Fath Ali Shah, 283
Fenian Brotherhood, 264
Ferdinand I (1558-64), 26
Ferdinand II (1619-37), 26, 28, 29
Ferdinand III (1637-57), 26
Ferdinand V of Castile, 29, 206
Ferdinand of Aragon, 38
Ferdinand, Franz and Sophie, 337
Ferdinand, Joseph of Bavaria, 31
Ferdinand of Saxe Coburg-Botha, 277
Ferdinand of Spain, 320
Fernandes, Duarte, 151
feudalism in Europe, 13-14, 141
Fez kingdom, 171
Figueroa, Garcilaso, 210
Fiji and Tonga, 227-28
financial crisis (2008), 412, 491
Finland, 352, 372, 378; came under
  Russia, 36-37, 268
First Nations (indigenous people), 188
Fitche, Johann Gottleib, 48
Flickr, 492
Flinders, Mathew, 326
Florida, 195, 315

Flynn, Errol (1909-59), 484
Fon State (Dahomey), 175, 176
food: Australia, New Zealand and
  adjacent islands, 222, 226;
  Caribbean Islands, 217; Europe,
  49; Japan, 142, 143; North
  America, 189, 191, 200; South
  East Asia, 160; West Central Asia
  and Russia, 99-100
foot binding, 135-36
Ford, Gerald (1974-77), 410, 411
Ford, Henry (1863-1947), 487
foreign policy: France, 64; Great
  Britain, 261-62; India, 441; Iraq,
  450; Kuwait, 452; Nepal, 281;
  Russia, 272
Fort Orange, 196
Fothergill, William, 241
Fountain of Four Rivers, The, 55
Fox, Vicente, 417
Frame, Janet, 485
France, French (1500-1799), 14, 32,
  60-72, 179; abolished slavery, 216;
  British, war (Seven Years' War),
  32-33, 73, 197-98; bloackade
  of Britain, 231; coalition wars
  against, 72, 230, 268; colonization
  and exploitation of Africa, 186,
  463; Europe against, 230-31;
  received Flanders, 41; invasion on
  India, 106, 108, 109; invaders and
  settlers in North America, 194,
  195, 197; invaded Prussia, 231;
  railways, 239; Revolution (1789),
  33, 46, 47, 49, 68-72, 88, 98,
  216, 229, 233, 234; Spain, war,
  29; Thirty Years' War, 29, 30, 64,
  65; invasion on Trinidad, 218;
  invades United Provinces, 41; war
  of three Henrys, 62-63

(CDU), 382; East and West Germany reunited, 395; and France, war, 64, 65, 337, 338; Federal Republic (West Germany), 382–83; politics and national movement, 21; Nuremburg Laws, 348; railways, 239; religious peace, 28; revolutionary movements, 251; and Russia, non-aggression pact, 361; Social Democrats (SDU), 382; in thirty years war, 29, 30; unification of, 254; Weimar Republic, 347; and First World War, 336, 337, 341, 347–48; and Second World War, 359–60, 361, 362, 364

Gesner, Konrad (1516–1565), *Historiae Animalium*, 9–10

Gettysberg, Battle of (1863), 317

Geysir, 37

Ghaghara, Battle of, 102

Ghana, 474

Ghent, Treaty of, 315

Gia Long, emperor of Vietnam, 298

Gibraltar, 32

Giffard, Henri, 243

Girey, 90

Girodet-Trioson, Anne-Louis (1767–1824), 236

Girondins, 71, 72

Gitkan, 189

Gladstone, William, 257, 264

globalization, 415, 486, 490–91, 492, 493

Glorious Revolution (Bloodless Revolution), 84, 88

Godunov, Boris, 94

Gogh, Vincent van (1853–90), 246

Gogol, 273

gold and silver, 4, 19, 99; Africa, 171, 174, 176, 178, 182, 185, 307, 471, 473; in Australia and New Zealand, 223, 327–28, 329; Caribbean Islands, 213, 215, 216; Japan, 143, 146; South and Central America, 200, 206, 207, 209, 211, 425, 425, 477

Gondar, 168

Gong, Prince, 289

Gonja kingdom, 170, 305

Gonzales, Adolfo Suarez, 385

Gorbachev, Mikhail, 391, 392–93, 395

Gordon, Charles, 304

Gordon, George. *See* Byron, Lord

Gothic architecture, 38

Gourges, Dominique de, 195

government, trends in Europe (1500–1800), 11–12

Goya, Francisco (1746–1828), 245

Grand Alliance, 31

Grant, James Augustus, 309

gravity, theory of, 57

Great Britain. *See* United Kingdom

Great Depression (1929), 346–47, 348, 349, 404, 406, 481, 485, 491

Great Game (Russia and Britain struggle over Afghanistan), 281–82

Great Leap Forward, 432

Great Northern War (1700–21), 96, 97

Great Sun, 192

Greece, 116, 119, 369, 397–98, 491; independence, 250–51, 268; and First World War, 335

Greenland, 35, 378

Gregorian calendar, 33–34

Gregory, Pope, 34

Grenada, 165, 212

Grenadines, 212, 416

Hidatsa, 189
Hikayat Aceh, 164
Hinduism, 3, 442
Hindus, 280, 441
Hirohito, Japanese emperor, 350
Hispaniola, 207, 214, 215-16, 217
Hitler, Adolf, 348, 359, 361, 362, 364-65
Ho Chih Minh (1890-1969), 457, 458
Ho clan, 156
Hobbes, Thomas, *Leviathan*, 47
Hoegbadja, 176
Hohenheim, Theophrastus Bombastus von (Paracelsus) (1493-1541), *Opus Paramirium*, 59
Hokkaido, 147
Hokusai, Katsushika (1760-1849), 144; *Thirty-six Views of Mt Fuji*, 144-45
Holland. *See* Netherlands
Hollande, Francois, 382
Holocaust, 367
Home Rule movement, 264
Homruz, 152
Honduras, 203, 206, 208, 214, 323, 415-16, 417, 418
Honecker, Erich, 395
Hong Kong, 362; was given to British, 287; Hong Kong SAR, 434
Hong Taiji (Abahai), 128
Hong Xiuquan, 288-89
Hoover, Herbert, 346
Hope Diamond, 67-68
Hornbooks, 51
House of Windsor (Saxe Coburg-Botha), 257, 277
housing, North America, 189, 191, 193
Howard, Catherine, 75

Hoxha, Enver, 397
Hsinbyumashin, Queen of Burma, 295-96
Huascar, 207
Huayna Capac, Inca emperor, 207
Hubertsburg, Treaty of (1763), 33
Hudson Bay, 196, 197, 311
Hudson Bay Company, 311, 312
Huguenot settlement, 195
Hulme, Keri, 485
human geneology project, 487
human rights, 493
human trafficking, 396
Humayun, 102-3
Hume, David (1711-76), 47
Hungary, 32, 42-43, 112, 116, 360, 373, 395, 397, 491
hunting and fishing, North America, 189, 190, 191
Huron people, 195, 197
Husain Ali, Mirza (Bahaullah) (1817-91), 167, 284-85
Hussain I (ruled 1694-1722), 122
Hussein, Saddam, 412, 450-51
Huyghens, Christian (1625-95), 58
Hyder Ali, 109
Hyderabad, 105, 108

Ibadi sect, 126, 454
Ibero-American summit, 422
Ibn Batuta (1325-55), 2
Ibrahim al Sahrif, 167
Ibrahim Pasha, 303
Ibrahim, Abdullah, 476
Ibsen, Henrik (1828-1906), 379
Iceland, 35, 37, 173, 370; gained independence (1944), 378
Idris Alooma (rules c 1580 or 1570-1617, 1571-1603), 173
Idris I, 469

Igbo, 474, 477

Ihara Saikaku (1643–93), 145

Ikebana and the tea ceremony, Japan, 147

Imam Ahmad of Adal, 168

Imperial Diet, 25

impressionism, 246

Incas, 14, 202, 203, 206, 207–8, 210. *See also* Central America

independence movements in South America, 320–21

India (1500–1800), 1, 3, 32, 102–10, 165, 180, 185; and Seven Years war, 33; Vasco da Gama reached, 4

India (1800–1914), British rule, 262, 278–82, 440; drain of wealth, 279; First War of Independence (1857), 279–81; reform movements, 279

India: World War II and after, 426, 440–41; China, war (1962), 441; Pakistan conflict over Kashmir, 441

Indian Ocean, 475

individualism, 48

Indo-China, 362, 372, 381, 458

Indonesia, 22, 161–65, 300–1, 460–61

Industrial Revolution, industrialization, 286; Europe, 186, 237–41; Great Britain, 237, 238, 239, 240, 241, 258–59; USSR/Russia, 272, 399

Ingria, 97

Inkerman, 269

inoculation, technique, 244

insurgency in Macedonia, 399

international communist movement, 360

International Court of Justice, 380

International Geographical Conference, Sixth (1895), 333

International Monetary Fund (IMF), 415, 491; policies, 415

international relations, 392

International trade network, 133

Internet, 488

Interregnum (1740–42), 26

Intuits, 188

Iran, 266, 283–84, 449–50; Revolution, 411; Russia, war (1804–1813), 268, 283; different sects and new religions, 284

Iraq, 121, 276, 450–51, 452, 454, 494; under British mandate, 446; became independent, 347, 447; Iran war, 450; United States invasion, 412, 450

Ireland, 81–82, 84, 88–89, 173, 194, 371; dominion status, 347, 388; Provisional IRA, 388–89; revolutionary movements, 251, 264, 388–89; Scotland and Wales, 264; Ulster Volunteer Force, 389

Iroquois, 189, 190, 197

Isabella of Castile, 38, 214

Isfahan, 122, 123–24

Ishida Mitsunari, 141

Islam, 3, 106, 112, 116–17, 158, 161, 167; Fulani groups, 178, 474; Ibadi sect, 125; Shias, 126;–Isna Ashari sect, 120, 126;–Ismaili Shia sect, 284;–and Sunnis, divide, 126, 453; Islamic kingdoms, 178; Tijammiya sect, 305; Zaidi Shia group, 126

Islamic law, 112, 117, 305

Islamic Salvation Front, 469

Islamic State in Iraq and Syria (ISIS), 451

Islas Filipinas (Philippine Islands), 159

Ismail I, ruler of Azerbaijan and Iran, 120, 121

Muinuddin, Daniyal, 442
Mujica, José, 428
Munch, Edward (1863–1944), 379
Munich Pact, 360
Munro, Alice, (b. 1931), 406
Munster, Treaty of, 41
Murad Bey (d. 1631), 166
Murad Bey II, 167
Murad III (ruled 1574–1595), 114
Muscovy. See Russia
music and dance, 493; Africa, 478; Australia, 483; China (1500–1800), 131–32; Europe (1500–1800), 56;–Europe (1800–1914), 244–46; in Great Britain, 77; Russia, 273
Muslim Brotherhood, 469
Muslims (Mudejars), 38, 280, 304, 400, 440
Mussolini, Benito, 19, 348–49, 360, 383
Mutapa empire, 182
Mutsohito, Japanese emperor, 148, 293 (spl Mutsuhito)
Mutunga, Ngati, 330
Myanmar (Burma), 149–51, 152, 153, 154, 295–96, 362, 455–56; kingdom of Bagan, 149; British control, 281; Rohinya Muslims, 456
Mysore, 105, 108, 109; three wars (1772–1818) against
Marathas consolidated British territory, 109

Nadir Shah, 103, 122–23, 282
Nagasaki, 141, 142, 144
Nagaya, Maria, 93
Naipaul, V.S., 420
Najd, 125

Nakota, 189
Namibia, 475
Nanak, Guru, 106
Nanjing, 289; Treaty of (1842), 287
Napier, John, 58
Naples, kingdom, 12, 230, 231, 253
Napoleon III, 254
Napoleon Bonaparte. See Bonaparte, Napoleon
Nasiruddin, Shah of Iran, 283, 284
Nasmyth, James, 239
Nasser, Gamal Abdul, 468
Natal, 307, 308
Natalya, 96
Natchez Bluffs, 192–93
National Action Party (PAN), 417
National Aeronautics and Space Administration (NASA), 410
National Australian Ballet Company, 484
National Literary Society, Dublin, 264
National People's Congress, 431
nationalism, Africa, 474
Native Americans, 188–90, 198–200, 209, 211, 323; converted to Christianity, 200; and European settlers, marriages, 199; women, 199
natural disasters, 8; China, 135; Japan, 438
Navarino Bay, 268
Navigation Acts, 312
navigational techniques, 3–4
Ndomgo, 179
Ne Win, General, 455
Necker, Jacques, 70
Negro slaves, 216
Nehru, Jawaharlal (1889–1964), 441
Nelson, Horatio, 230
Neo-Confucian principles, 133, 147

North Sea, 8
Northern Atlantic Ocean, 225
Northern March, 430
Northup, Solomon (b. 1808), *Twelve Years a Slave*, 319
Norway, 35, 37, 361, 370, 371, 378
Nostradamus (Michel de Nostredame) (1503-1566), 52
notation system North America, 189
Nova Scotia, 32, 197, 311, 312
Novgorod, 92, 93, 193
Nuclear Test Ban Treaty, 375
nuclear weapons, 375, 393
Numidia, kingdom of, 171
Nurgaci, invaded China, (1621), 127-28
nursery rhymes, 263-64
nutmeg, 164-65
Nuyts, Peter, 223
Nyame, 176
Nyaungyan dynasty, 150
Nyerere, Julius, 472
Nystadt, Peace of (1721), 36, 97 (check spl vari Nystad)
Nzinga, 179

Oba Esigie (ruled 1504-1550), 172
Obama, Barack (2009-), 411, 412
Obote, Milton, 483
Oda Nobunaga (1534-1582), 139-40
Ohrid Framework Agreement, 399
Ojibwa, 190, 197
Oman, 125, 181, 452-54
Omdurman, Battle of, 304
Opera, 56
Opium Wars, 286-87
Opoku Ware (ruled 1720-1750), 176
Orange Free State and Transvaal, 307, 308

Orbus Pictus (Jan Amos Komensky/ Comenius), 50-51
Ordos-Suiyan, 137
Oresund Bridge, 378
Organization for Economic Cooperation and Trade (OECD), 370
Organization for European Cooperation (OEEC), 370
Organization of African Unity (OAU), 470, 477
Organization of American States, 415
Organization of Central American States, 417
original sin, 48
Oromo, 168-69
Osaka, 141, 143
Osei Tutu (ruled 1690-1712), 175-76
Osman, 111
Ossian receiving the ghosts of Napoleon's generals, 235
Ottoman Empire, Ottomans, 91, 95, 96, 111-19, 121, 126, 167, 173, 185, 229, 230, 250, 252, 302-3, 397, 446; decline, 116, 266-77, 335; defeat at Lepanto, 113; defeated Safavids, 111; fratricide, 117; invaded Cyprus, 113; and Italy, war, 335; control over North Africa, 166; occupied coastal regions, 168; and Portuguese, conflict over Muscat, 125; Russian invasion, 269-70; ships, 114; Turks, 120; and World War I, 335, 338
Overijssel, 40
overseas territories, 384
Overture, 235
Owen, Wilfred (1893-1918), 343
Oyo kingdom, 174-75, 306
Ozette, 193

Pacific Islands, 332
Pacific Ocean, 5, 205, 206, 225, 226, 227
Pagarayung kingdom, 164
Pahlavi, Muhammad Reza Shah, 449
Paine, Thomas (1737-1809), Age of Reason, 48; Rights of Man, 47
Pajang sultanate, 162
Pakistan, 440, 442-43. See also Bangladesh
Palatiniate, 65
Palau Islands, 228
Palestine, 116, 454, 494; and Israel, 446-47; Palestinian Liberation Organization (PLO), 448-49; Palestine National Authority (PNA), 448-49; Popular Front for the Liberation of Palestine, 448
Palladio, Andrea (1518-80), Quattro Libri della Architectura, 54
Palme, Olaf (1927-86), 380
Pamirs, 129
Panama, 205, 206, 207, 214, 418; independence, 321-22
Pandey, Mangal, 280
Panipat, Battle of (1526), 102
Papal states, 253
Papua New Guinea, 332, 482
Paracelsus. See Hohenheim, Theophrastus Bombastus von
Paraguay, 320, 324, 415, 424, 428
Paris, Peace of (1763), 33, 197, 311; (1783), 215, 314
Paris, Treaty of (1856), 269; (1898), 298
Park, Mungo (1771-1806), 186-87
Parks, Rosa (1913-2005), 409
Parnell, Charles Stewart, 264
Parr, Catherine, 75
Pascal, Blaise (1623-1662), 46
Pasquale Paoli, 229

Passchendaele, 341
Pasteur, Louis (1882-1895), 244
pasteurization, 244
Paul I (ruled 1796-1801), 98, 267
Pavon, Jose maria Morelos y, 322
Paxton, Joseph, 258
Pearse, Richard, 243
Pederson, Vilhelm (1820-59), 248
Pedro I (Dom Pedro), emperor of Brazil, 322-23
Pemba, 180
Penang, 161; under British, 299
Penn, William, 196
Pennsylvania, 196, 314
Penobscot, 189
Pepys, Samuel (1633-1703), 86
Pequot tribe, 198
Perak sultanate, 161
Perdis, 161
Peri, Jacopo (1561-1633), 56
Peron, Juan, 425
Persian empires, 1
Persian Gulf, 284, 452
Peru, 203, 212, 228, 321, 324, 415, 427-28; Spanish control, 207, 208
Pestalozzi, 51
Peter I (Pyotr Alexeyvich) (1682-1725), 95, 96-97, 99; Russia after (1725-1762), 97-98
Peter III, 98
Philip II (ruled 1556-98) of Spain, 28, 38, 75, 159
Philip IV of Spain, 65
Philip V of Spain, 31, 38
Philip of Anjou, 31
Philippe II of Orleans, 68
Philippines, 5, 32, 158-60, 163, 210, 325, 362, 437, 459; under Spain, 298; was granted to United States,

298-99; volcanic eruptions and earthquakes, 158

Phnom Penh (Phnom Duan Penh), 154, 155, 457

Phu Xuan, 156, 157

Picasso, Pablo (1881-1973), 350

Picket, Conrad (alias Celtis) (1459-1509), 53

Piedmont-Sardinia, 252; declared war on Austria, 253

Pilgrim Fathers, 195

Pinochet, General, 427

Pippi Longstocking and other characters, 379

pirates and slaves in Africa, 173-74, 219; Somalia, 472

Pius V, Pope, 113

Pizarro, Francisco, 207-8

plantation crops: Cuba, 218; Jamaica, 218; Sri Lanka, 281; Ulster, 88

plants, animals and birds, 8-9

Plassey, Battle of (1757), 107, 109

plastics and chemicals, 489

Plato, 48

Poivre, Pierre, 165

Pol Pot, 457

Poland, 32, 43, 50, 94, 98, 360; divided among Austria, Russia and Prussia, 271; and Lithuania united, 43; railways, 239; integrated into Russia, 270; Russia, war (1654-1667), 95; a trade union called Solidarity, 394-95; and World War II, 361-62, 365-67, 370

Polder, 39

Polish-Lithuanian Commonwealth, 43

political instability, Uruguay, 428-29

political reforms in Europe (1500-1800), 12

polygny in North America, 190, 199, 200

Polynesians, 2, 189

Pompeii, 193

Pompidou, George, 382

Pope, Alexander (1688-1744), 58

population: Australia, 481; Europe (1500-1800), 10; growth and climate change, 493; South America, 202

Portugal, 4, 42, 143, 155, 230, 231, 308, 370, 371, 384, 477; decline, 170; economic reforms, 12; military coup, 384; natural disasters, 8; Napoleon attacked, 231; trade with Gulf of Guinea, 4

Portuguese explorers, settlers and invaders, invasions, 143, 164, 168; Africa, 178, 179, 180-81, 182-84, 185, 186; Australia and New Zealand, 227, 228; Benin, 172; Brazil, 208, 321; India, 103, 106, 107, 109, 384; Indonesia, 163; Japan, 142; Macao, 384; Malaysia, 161, 163; Morocco, 169;—driven out from, 170; Muscat, 125; South and Central America, 202, 204, 208, 211; South East Asia, 461; Sri Lanka, 281; Vietnam, 156

postage stamp, 261

Potatau Te Wherowhero, Maori king, 330

Potato: in Europe (1500-1800), 14-15; in Russia, 99, 273

Potlaches, 190

pottery in North America, 189

poverty, 486

Prague, Peace of (1635), 29

Prasat Thong, king, 153

Pressburg, Treaty of, 230

the Tsars, 92, 95; women, 19; and
World War I, 335, 337, 338; and
World War II, 364
Russian State Bank, 272
Russianization, 272
Rwanda-Burundi, 181
Ryswick, Peace of (1697), 66, 216 (spl
variation Ryswyk)
Ryzhkov, Nikolay, 391

al-Saadat, Anwar, 468–69
El-Saadawi, Nawal (b. 1931), 477
Saadi dynasty, 169
Saavedra, Daniel Ortega, 418
Saavedra, Miguel de Cervantes
(1547–1616), Don Quixote, 53
Safavids of Iran, 90, 91, 111, 114, 115,
120–23
Safi al-din, Shaikh, 120
Sagauli, Treaty of, 281
Saharawi Republic, 470
al-Said dynasty, 125, 181
Saifawa dynasty, 172–73
Saigon (Ho Chi Minh city), 298
Sakhalin, 271
Salazaar, Antonio, 384
Salim I (ruled 1512–1520), 111
Salim II (ruled 1566–1574), 113, 117
Salim III (ruled 1789–1807), 274
Salish, 189
Salvation Army, 260
Samarkand, 91, 104
Samoa islands, 228
Samundera Pasai sultanate, 163
Samurai, 148
San Stefano, Treaty of, 271
Sandinista Liberation Front, 418
Sandwich islands, 225
Sani al Mulk, 284
Sanlúcar de Barrameda, 5

Santa Domingo, 205
Santi, Raffaello, 44
Sarawak, British protectorate, 300
Sardinia, 38, 43, 269; war against
France, 71
Sarimanok Garuda, 160
Sarket Islam, 300
Sarkozy, Nicholas, 382
Sarsa Dengel, king of Ethiopia, 168
Sartre, Jean Paul, 382
Sasanian dynasties, 284
Sassoon, Siegfried (1886–1967), 343
Saturn Devouring his Sons, 245
al-Saud dynasty, 453
Saudi Arabia, 116, 452, 453, 454
Savage, Abijah, 219
Savoy, 31
Saxe-Coburg-Gotha. See House of
Windsor
Saxony, 32, 66
Sayyid Ali Muhammad (1819–50),
284–85
Scandinavian countries, 35–36, 378–80
Schelling, 48
Schlieffen Plan, 337
Schmalkalden, 28
Schmidt, Helmut, 382
schools in Great Britain, 259–60. See
also education
Schreiner, Olive, The Story of an
African Farm, 310
Schubert, Franz (1797–1828), 246
Schuman, Robert (1810–56), 246
Schumann Plan, 389
science and mathematics, 490; in
Europe (1500–1800), 57–59;–
(1800–1914), 244
Scotland, 81–82, 84, 87–88, 260, 264;
religion, 87; Scottish National
Party, 389

Silesia, 32, 42

Sinan, Koca Mimar (1490–1588), 117

Singapore, 165, 299, 362, 460, 462

Singer, Peter (b. 1946), 484; *Animal Liberation*, 494

Singkil, 160

Sioux tribe, 189, 319

Siraj-ud-daulah, Nawab of Bengal, 109

Sisavang Vong (Vatthana), king of Louangphrabang, 297–98

Sisi, Abdel Fattah el-, 469

slavery, slave trade, 172, 184–86, 232, 308; abolition, 317, 426; Africa, 200, 209, 211, 218–19, 309–10; Dahomey, 176; was abolished in France, 216; banned in Great Britain, 260; Madagascar, 178; abolished in United States, 316, 317

Slovenia, 399, 401

smallpox epidemic; in Australia, 224

Smith, Adam (1723–90), *The Wealth of Nations*, 248

Smith, Fanny Cochrane (1834–1905), 331

Smith, Ian, 475

Smith, William, 331

Smolensk, 95

social media, 492

socialism, 249, 428

society in North America, 190

Society of Jesus, 23

Sokoto Caliphate, 305

Solomon, King of Ethiopia, 168

Solor Islands, 161

Solzhenitsyn, Aleksandr (1918–2008), 394

Somalia, 167, 472

Somoza dynasty, 418

Sonderbund, 255

Songhe empire, 305

Sophia (granddaughter of James I), 85

Sophia (sister of Ivan V), 95–96

Sotho kingdom, 306

Soto, Hernando de, 211

Souligna Vongsa, King of Laos (ruled 1637–1694), 154

South Africa, 310, 425, 463, 464, 475, 476; conflicts, 306–7, 308

South America and Central America (1500–1800), 1, 5, 14, 202–11, 216; the first Europeans, 204–5

South America: (1800–1900), 320–23;—independence movements, 320–21; World War II after, 414, 424–29

South Asia and Afghanistan, 440–45

South Asian Association for Regional Cooperation (SAARC), 443

South Carolina railway, 239

South East Asia: 1500–1800, 2, 3, 133; Myanmar, Thailand, Laos, Cambodia, Vietnam, 1500–1800, 149–57; Philippines, Malaysia, Indonesia, Brunei, Papua New Guinea, 158–65; after 1800, 295–301; after 1945, 411, 455–62

Southern Africa, 475–77; apartheid, 475–76

sovereign state, 11

Soviet Union, 267; former Republics, 401

Soyinka, Wole (b. 1934), 478

space, 490

Spain, Spanish, 6, 38, 83, 113, 155, 159, 169, 197, 205, 213, 215, 216, 228, 231, 298, 308, 314, 315, 384–85, 470; agriculture, 14; American War (1898), 298, 325; Armada, 41; the Basque people,

385; Castille and Aragon, 38; economic reforms, 12; end of military supremacy, 30; explorers, 227; feudalism, 14; France, wars, 77; invasion on Japan, 142; missionaries converted Native Americans to Christianity, 209; Napoleon attacked, 231; railways, 239; and Seven Years war, 33; succession war (1701–1713), 31–32, 41, 66; trade with Portugal, 4; South America, colonization of/ invasions on, 202, 204, 205–6, 320–22, 325; settlers in North America, 194; trade with Gulf of Guinea, 4; and United States, 385; and World War I, 337;—after, 350

Spanish Inquisition, 38–39; Netherlands (present Belgium) and Sicily, 32, 38, 39, 41, 65; territories in Americas, 39

Speke, John Hanning, 308

Spenser, Edmund (1552–1599), 77

Spice Islands, 5, 164

spinning and weaving, Europe (1800–914), 238–39

Spinoza, Baruch (1632–1677), *Ethica Ordine Geometrico Demonstrata*, 46

Spotswood, Alexander, governor of Virginia, 220

Sputnik 1 and 2, 393

Spyri, Johanna (1827–1901), 248

Sri Lanka, 151, 152, 281, 443

St Kitts and Nevis, 212

St Lucia, 212

St Petersburg, 97, 98, 99

St Vincent, 212, 416

Stalin (Joseph Djugashvili), 249, 357, 368, 370, 372, 391

Stambuloff, Stefan, 277

Stanislaus II Augustus, 43

Stanislaus Leszczynski, 36, 43

Stanley, Henry Morton, 309

steam, use in Europe (1800–1914); steam engines, 239;

steam hammer, 239; steamships, 240, 295

Steen, Jan, 56

Stendhal, 234

Stephenson, George, 239

Stolypin, Pyotr (1862–1911), 354

Stowe, Harriet Beecher (1811–96), *Uncle Tom's Cabin*, 319

Strategic Arms Limitation Talks (SALT), 375

Strategic Arms Reduction Treaty (START I), 392

Stravinsky, 273

Stuart, John MacDouall, 328

Stuarts in exile, 78, 85

Sturgeon, William, 242

Sturt, Charles (1795–1869), 328 (check spl)

Stuyvesant, Peter, 196

subsidiary alliance, 278

Sudan, 167, 172, 177, 302, 303–4, 454, 471; British rule, 304; civil war, 471; Ethiopia, war, 304

Sudetenland, 360

Suez Canal, 303, 468

Sufi literature, 164

sugar plantations in Cuba, 218

Suharto, General, 460

Suika, 147

Sukarno, 460

Sulaiman I (ruled 1520–1566), 112, 113, 117

Sulaiman Mosque, Istanbul, 117

Sulawesi, 460

Russia, 269, 270; Sealed Knot, 82 settlers in North America, 194, 195, 196-99; expansion in South and West Asia, 278-85; Test Acts (1673 and 1678), 84; raids on Trinidad, 218-19; Toleration Act (1689), 85; Triennial Act (1694), 85; women, 19

United Kingdom (UK) (British, Great Britain, England): (1800-1914), 250, 256, 303, 309, 327; and American war of Independence, 312-13; Anti-Corn Law League, Manchester, 261; claim over Australia, 326; won a battle at Brandywine Creek, Pennsylvania, 314; Catholic Emancipation Act, 260; British colonies, expansion, 280; Corn Laws, 261; culture, 262-63; economy, 258; Factory Act (1874), 259; foreign policy, 261-62; Great Exhibition, 258; in India, 106, 107-8, 109-10; and Ireland, 256-65; control over Myanmar, 296; new laws for children, 258-59; the Parliament, 257; Reform Bill of 1832, 257; Reform Acts of 1867 and 1884, 257; revolutionary movements, 251; schools, 259-60; Ten Hour Act (1847), 259; and Thailand treaty, 297; United States, war (1812-1815), 315; and World War I, 335, 337, 341, 347; defeat at Yorktown, Virginia, 314

United Kingdom (UK) (British, Great Britain, England): and World War II, 360-62, 364, 368, 371, 375, 384; and after, 468, 491; British North American Act

(1949), 403 castles and palaces; United Kingdom, 387; and West Asia, 446

United Kingdom (UK) 1960s, 385; Royal Family, 386-87

United Nations (UN) (League of Nations), 344, 346, 352, 359, 384-5, 393, 423, 434, 436, 447, 449, 470, 481, 491

United Provinces, 11, 30, 31, 40-41, 232, 323

United States of America (USA), 196, 287, 291, 327, 392, 406-13; American Indian Religious Freedom Act, 412; American Union of States, 317; Britain war (1812-1815), 315; Central America Free Trade Agreement (CAFTA), 417; civil rights movement, 408-9; Civil Rights Act (1964), 408, 409, 410; Civil War (1861-65), 316-17, 319; Confederation States of America, 317; Dawes Act (1871), 318; Dawes Severalty Act (1887), 318; financial crisis (2008), 491; formation of, 312-19; Homestead Act 91862), 315-16; Indian Appropriation Act (1851), 318; Indian Removal Act (1830), 317; Peace Corps, 408; other additions to territory, 315; railways, 239; Space programme, 410; Stamp Act (1765), 312-13; USSR Intermediate Nuclear Force (INF) Treaty, 411; and Vietnam, 380, 408, 410; World Trade Centre, bombings (9/11), 411, 445; and World War I, 337, 345-46; and World War II, 368, 369, 370, 406

312, 315, 320; Nine Years War (1594–1603), 88; Thirty Years war (1618–1648), 28–30, 64, 65; over trade and commerce, 16; between Portuguese, Johor and Aceh, 161; of three Henrys, 62–63; in West Central Asia and Russia, Great Northern War (1700–1721), 96, 97

Warsaw Pact, 373

Washington, George, 314, 318

Wat Chaiwatthanaram, 153

Waterloo, Battle of, 42

Watson, James, 109, 487

Watt, James, 239

Weatherford, Jack, 200

Wedgewood, Cicely Veronica, 30

Weene, King of Kongo, 179

Wellesley under British, 299

Wellesley, Lord, 278

Wells, H.G., 262

Welsh, 194; national movement, 265

Wenxiang, 289

West Asia, 173, 180, 446–54; The Safavids and other dynasties, 120–26; and World War I, 338

West and West-Central Africa, 463, 473–74

West Central Asia and Russia, 90–101

West Indies, 165

Westinghouse, George (1846–1914), 242

Westphalia, 230, 231; Peace of (1648), 30, 42

Wheatstone, Charles, 241

White Lotus Rebellion (1796–1804), 288

White Revolution, 449

White, Patrick (1912–90), 483

Whitehead, Gustav, 243

Wiigwaasabak scrolls, 190

Wilkins, John, 43

William I, King of Netherlands, 255

William II, German Emperor (Kaiser Wilhelm II), 254–55, 335, 347

William III of Orange, 40–41, 84–85

William IV, 41, 256

William of Rubrick (1220–1293), 2

William Pitt the Younger, 89

William, King of Prussia, 254

Williams, William, of Pantycelyn (1717–1791), 89

Wills, W.J., 328

Wilson, Woodrow, 345–46

Windsor Castle, 387

wireless telegraphy (radio), 242

Wladislaw, 94

Wolfe, James, 197

women, 416; in Europe (1500–1800), 19–20; education, 49; inheritance rights, 20

Worcester, Battle of, 81

Wordsworth, William, 245

workhouses, 260

working hours, 240–41

World Bank, 491

world economic crisis, 378

World Trade Organization (WTO), 491

World War I, 300, 334–44, 359, 360, 404, 446, 449, 463, 475, 480, 484, 486; effects, 344; end of, 342–43; in literature and other media, 343; losses, 342; recovering from (1918–39), 345–53

World War II, 299, 301, 346, 352, 355, 357, 359–67, 378, 395, 397, 398, 404, 406, 425, 430, 436, 447, 449, 458–59, 460, 464, 475, 481, 485; causes, 359–60; events just before the war, 360–61; first phase (September 1939–